BARRON'S

SAT *

SUBJECT TEST
LITERATURE

5TH EDITION

Christina Myers-Shaffer, M.Ed.
Former Department Chair
Georgetown Independent School District
Georgetown, Texas

Independent Consultant and Educational Writer

BARRON'S

All inquiries should be addressed to:
Barron's Educational Series, Inc.
250 Wireless Boulevard
Hauppauge, New York 11788
www.barronseduc.com

ISBN (book only): 978-0-7641-4615-2
ISBN (book & CD-ROM Pkg): 978-1-4380-7080-3

Library of Congress Catalog Card No. 2011010827

Library of Congress Cataloging-in-Publication Data
Myers-Shaffer, Christina.
    SAT subject test in literature / Christina Myers-Shaffer. — 5th ed.
      p. cm.
    Includes index.
    ISBN 978-0-7641-4615-2
    ISBN 978-1-4380-7080-3
    1. Literature—Examinations—Study guides. 2. SAT (Educational test)—
Study guides. I. Title.
    PN62.M94 2011
    807.6—dc22   2011010827

Printed in the United States of America

9 8 7 6 5 4 3 2 1

Acknowledgments

The author gratefully acknowledges the following copyright holders for permission to reprint material used in this publication:

Page 95: From "Pied Beauty" from *Poems of Gerard Manley Hopkins* by Gerard Manley Hopkins. Reprinted with permission of Oxford University Press.

Page 112: From "Barn Burning," *Collected Stories of William Faulkner* © 1939 by William Faulkner. Reprinted by permission of Random House, Inc.

Page 184: Excerpt from *The Great Code* © 1982, 1981 by Northrop Frye. Reprinted with permission of Harcourt Brace & Company.

Page 309: "An Encounter with Honey Bees" by Lillian E. Myers © 1999 by Lillian E. Myers. Reprinted by permission of Lillian E. Myers. All rights reserved.

"Bell-tones" (page 75), "Pity the Poor Raccoon" (page 96), "Know Yourself" (page 96), "Alphabet Soup" (page 103), "Stressed and Unstressed" (page 77), "Is It Euphemism or Euphony?" (page 174), and "That Sound" (page 138) by Lillian E. Myers © 1996 by Lillian E. Myers. Reprinted by permission of Lillian E. Myers. All rights reserved.

"Runaways" (on CD-ROM) by Lillian E. Myers © 1999 by Lillian E. Myers. Reprinted by permission of Lillian E. Myers. All rights reserved.

Every effort has been made to trace the copyright holders and we apologize in advance for any unintentional omissions. We would be pleased to insert the appropriate acknowledgment in any subsequent edition of this publication.

Contents

PART II. STRENGTHEN YOUR READING COMPREHENSION SKILLS   53

The following chapters target the terms, concepts, and skills you need to get
a higher score on the SAT STL.

Chapter 5.
What Literary Terms Do I Need to Know?   55

An Index: Have some fun and put checkmarks by all the terms you recognize.
You probably are better off than you think!

Chapter 6.
What Literary Elements Will Be on the Test?   59

We help you learn about each of the following literary elements by introducing
and explaining Term Alerts and literary concepts and by providing example
questions and instruction to help you improve your skills.

The Seven Literary Elements	Page
Meaning	60
Form	74
(Narrative) Voice	109
Tone	126
Character	145
Use of Language	168
Meaning(s) in Context	202

Chapter 7.
How Are These Elements Tested?   233

The five selections in this chapter, with their practice questions, correct answers,
and explanations strengthen your skills by illustrating how the elements work
together in poems and passages.

Chapter 8.
How Am I Doing Now?   247

Diagnostic Test Two will point out specific areas for improvement.

The SAT STL involves more than knowing terms and having comprehension skills. It's a timed test.

Chapter 9.
How Do I Get Through the Test in Just One Hour? 277

You need to set a pace and learn to focus, so we give you seven full-length practice tests in Part III. As always, correct answers and explanations follow each test. Be sure to use the strategies for pacing and focusing that you will learn in Chapter 1 to make the most of this practice.

How Difficult is the SAT STL?

Depending on your individual skills and reading experience, the version of the real SAT STL you will be taking may seem easy—or difficult. Obviously, practice can help; but who has time to practice "easy" tests? For a higher score, you need to prepare just in case the test is outside what is now your "easy" range. We want to make your practice time count toward improving your skills and to help you face even the hardest questions. Therefore, we have included in the practice tests, not just the easy, but also the more difficult types of questions you may face on test day. Our goal is for you to be so well prepared that the real SAT STL you take will seem easy!

Be Encouraged!

The SAT STL is a challenging test, but preparing for it can lead to a higher test score, improve your reading performance in other subjects, and *even be fun*. Relax and enjoy yourself!

> If you want to succeed on the SAT STL,
> **START HERE.**

ABOUT THIS BOOK . . .

How do I get a higher score on the SAT Subject Test Literature (SAT STL)?

To get a higher score on the SAT STL, you need to (1) learn test-taking strategies, (2) strengthen your reading comprehension skills, and (3) practice.

Are you tired of taking tests? We understand, and we're on your side. But we also know it's important for you to get the best score you can.

Don't be tempted to take shortcuts. Sure, you can memorize a list of literary definitions and concepts, take a few practice tests, and maybe get by. The problem is that the SAT STL isn't a memorization test; it's a SKILLS TEST. Do you have the skill to recognize when a writer is using allusion and how that use affects meaning and tone? Can you tell the difference between the voice of the writer and that of the speaker? You may know a sonnet when you see one, but do you have the skill to use its rhyme scheme to help you unlock its meaning?

We can help.

Of course, we give you test-taking strategies, definitions, and concepts that may appear on the test. Then we zone in on your skills. Our no-nonsense guide illustrates the kinds of questions you might face by providing example poems and passages with tips, questions, answers, and explanations that are tied to specific literary terms and concepts. We really want to help you achieve the highest score you can on the SAT STL.

PART I
LEARN TEST-TAKING STRATEGIES

What Is My First Step?

CHAPTER 1

The College Board, headquartered in Princeton, New Jersey, administers the SAT Program. The two main categories of tests that make up the SAT Program are the SAT and the SAT Subject Tests. The results of these tests are used by educational counselors, student-placement personnel, and scholarship committees, among others, to assist students in their post-secondary academic careers.

SAT REASONING TEST

As its name implies, the SAT measures your mathematical and verbal reasoning abilities. The results of the SAT provide a comparative measure of your preparation and abilities to those of other students. Your score is used in conjunction with your high school grades, activities, class rank, and other factors (depending on the requirements of the particular institution) to provide you and a wide range of academic professionals with a picture of how you have done, an idea of how you are doing, and most significantly a basis for projection of how you are likely to do in a post-secondary setting.

SAT SUBJECT TESTS

The Subject Tests that you need to take will be determined by the requirements of the post-secondary institution to which you are planning to apply and what subject areas are likely to be significant to your personal academic plan. Your academic counselor should be able to assist you in these areas. As with the SAT, the SAT Subject Tests are used in conjunction with many other factors for admission (both to post-secondary institutions and to programs within those schools), for predicting future performance, for placing you within programs, and for guiding you in your academic choices.

Your first step should be to consult with your academic counselor and teachers about how enrolling in the SAT Program fits your personal educational goals.

THE COLLEGE BOARD

You can request the SAT *Paper Registration Guide* by writing to

College Board SAT Program
P.O. Box 025505
Miami, FL 33102

or you can ask questions and register online at http://www.collegeboard.com.

What Can I Expect on the SAT STL?

CHAPTER 2

The SAT Subject Test in Literature is one of the Subject Tests (Achievement Tests) administered by the College Board.

THE LITERATURE TEST FORMAT

TIME LIMIT
60 MINUTES

As with most of the SAT Subject Tests, the Literature Subject Test is entirely multiple-choice. You will have about one hour to take the test.

Here are some of the key features concerning the structure and content of the Literature Subject Test.

The Literature Test:

• Attempts to measure your skills in reading literature.

• Contains from six to eight reading selections.

• Asks about 60 multiple-choice questions based on those reading selections.

• Requires extended verbal abilities, particularly in reading comprehension and figurative language.

• Contains selections from English and American prose, poetry, and drama written during the Renaissance through the twentieth and (as time progresses) the twenty-first centuries. Some selections other than English or American but written in English might be included.

• Asks from four to twelve questions per selection.

• Asks questions about meaning, form, narrative voice, tone, character, use of language, and meaning(s) in context.

• Requires a knowledge of basic literary terminology.

• Includes selections that are complete short works or excerpts from longer works.

 TIP

ON THE SAT LITERATURE TEST . . . GRAMMAR RULES!
But (you say) this test is on literature, not grammar. Well, yes and no. Sometimes understanding what you read depends on understanding the grammar used. Consequently, you might be asked on the test to identify the main subject or verb in a complex sentence, for example. Also, you may need to be able to recognize subordination, coordination, parts of speech, verb tenses, and so forth, to understand what the writer means or what the question is asking. No doubt about it, you need to review parts of speech and sentence structures because when it comes to literature, grammar rules!

The individual selections might be, for example, taken from nineteenth-century American prose, sixteenth-century English drama, twentieth-century poetry written in English by a South African, and so forth. The percentage distributions shown in the following graphs, however, represent averages and may—or may not—be reflected in any given test. (The slanted lines represent variable numbers. For example, a test may contain 40 to 50 percent selections from English literature.)

The Literature Test does *not*

- Include test questions about literary periods, authors' biographies, or literary criticism

- Require preknowledge of selections on the test

- Require you to study a specified reading list

After each selection on the Literature Test, you will find the year the work was first published. Knowing the date of publication can help you better understand the context of the work.

The Selections on the Literature Test

SOURCE:	0–20 30 40–50 60 70 80 90 100 %
English	||||||||||///////////
American	||||||||||///////////
Other	////////

CENTURY:	0 10 20 30 40 50 60 70 80 90 100 %
16th–17th	||||||||||||
18th–19th	||||||||||||
20th–21st	||||||||||||||||

GENRE:	0–20 30 40–50 60 70 80 90 100 %
Prose	||||||||||///////////
Poetry	||||||||||///////////
Drama	////////

How Can I Improve My Test Score?

When you take a test that measures your reading comprehension and analysis skills, you need to use logic, context, and common sense. The following review and strategies are based on these three ideas.

SHORT-TERM STRATEGIES

The SAT Subject Test in Literature consists of about 60 multiple-choice questions, with five answer choices (A through E) for each question. The question stem might be worded in two ways:

- As a question, such as "What is the meaning of 'establishment' as it is used in line 2?"
- As an incomplete sentence, such as "The vehicle of the metaphor in line 3 is"

1. How to Deal with Test Questions

- REGULAR MULTIPLE-CHOICE QUESTIONS

  What is the speaker's attitude? (Question stem)

  (A) Angry   (A through E answer choices)
  (B) Raucous
  (C) Profane
  (D) Morbid
  (E) Defensive

The regular multiple-choice question is similar to a series of five true-false questions, because you are examining each answer choice to see if it is true or false. Usually, the true answer choice is the correct one. Caution: **In these questions, you may encounter more than one answer choice that is to some degree true or correct, in which case you would select the answer choice that is best.**

Watch Out

• NOT, LEAST, OR EXCEPT QUESTIONS

All the following appear in lines 1–4 EXCEPT

(A) personification
(B) simile
(C) metaphor
(D) paradox
(E) apostrophe

Which of the following is the LEAST accurate description of the dog in line 12?

(A) Fierce
(B) Friendly
(C) Fiendish
(D) Fiery
(E) Furious

Which of the following uses of language does NOT appear in lines 1–4?

(A) Personification
(B) Simile
(C) Metaphor
(D) Paradox
(E) Apostrophe

Some test questions might contain the words EXCEPT, LEAST, or NOT. In these questions, you are looking for the response that does not apply to the situation or that is inappropriate to the question stem—just the opposite of a regular multiple-choice question.

• ROMAN NUMERAL QUESTIONS

In this passage, the rose is

   I. an emblem
  II. a vehicle for metaphor
 III. an allegorical representation

(A) I only
(B) II only
(C) I and III only
(D) II and III only
(E) I, II, and III

In these questions, you will be given several words, phrases, or clauses that are labeled with Roman numerals. The answer choices allow you to select either individual ideas or combinations of ideas as possible correct answer choices.

The practice tests in this book will provide you with opportunities to work with each of these three different types of multiple-choice questions.

STRATEGY

Short-Term Tips and Strategies

Read through all the answer choices—do not stop when you reach the "correct" answer. Reason: Answer Choice B, for example, may indeed be "correct"; however, in multiple-choice questions you may be looking for the answer that is most accurate among more than one "correct" answer. You may later find that Answer Choice E is a better answer than B!

- After you read through all the answer choices, eliminate those that are clearly not the correct answer choice. Keep your mind focused by crossing off the incorrect answer choices in your test booklet.

- Compare the answer choices that remain, taking close note of key words in the question stem, including requirements such as "What is the effect..." or "as used in the selection."

- If you cannot decide on a final answer, continue with the next question, then return if time allows.

- Circle (in your test booklet only) the numbers of any questions you skip. These circles will save time when you return to them.

- Each time you skip a question, you should check your answer sheet to be sure you haven't lost your place.

- If pressed for time, eliminate all you can, then guess.

- Keep your answer sheet clean of any extra marks. Be sure to darken the bubbles completely and neatly.

- Keep in mind that

  1. You get one point for each correct answer.
  2. You lose one-fourth of one point for each wrong answer.

---

2. How to Deal with Literary Terms and Concepts

The College Board expects you to know basic terms that relate to interpreting literature. They do not require you to memorize what they call "highly specialized terms," in other words, advanced terms. The problem is that not everyone agrees on which literary terms are "basic." For example, some literature test instructors include "anthropomorphism" on their basic lists; but others consider the term too advanced.

There are some terms, however, that you really should know, terms that either have appeared on previous tests or may reasonably be tested on the SAT Subject Test. In the pages that follow, **Term Alerts** will point out these important literary terms, give you definitions, examples, and opportunities to practice dealing with the terms in SAT-type questions. Additionally, you will find a literary term and concept index on page 55 to help you locate any specific terms you want to review.

If I really don't know an answer, should I guess?

You can base your decision on these scoring rules:
1. You get one point for each correct answer.
2. You lose one-fourth of one point for each wrong answer.
3. Omitted questions and questions for which you mark more than one answer choice are not counted.

◎ **STRATEGY**

Do not just memorize the definitions of the literary terms. The Literature Subject Test is a skills test. Yes, you should be able to define a "metaphor"; but on the test, you need to have the skill to recognize a metaphor when it appears in a selection and identify what comparisons are being made. Do use the examples and practice questions in Chapter 6 to help you refine this skill.

You may see unfamiliar or advanced terms used as incorrect answer choices on the test. For example, in past tests, the College Board included "apostrophe" (a term some teachers consider beyond "basic") as an incorrect answer choice. If you encounter an unfamiliar term among the answer choices, do not panic. You may find that the correct answer is a term you know. If not, you can use your knowledge of the basic terms to help you eliminate all the clearly incorrect answers to reduce the possibilities. To give you experience, the tests in this book include some less familiar terms as answer choices.

Beyond basic definitions (such as that a simile is a comparison using "like" or "as"), you need to be able to recognize when the concepts behind the literary terms are being used and the effects their uses create.

For example, you should be able to recognize that "The woman felt like a small child whose pet dog was missing" contains a simile that in context might make the woman seem in a state of panic, hurt, and fear with perhaps implied elements of emotional immaturity. A resulting test question might ask the following:

> In the line, "The woman felt like a small child whose pet dog was missing," comparing the woman to a child who lost her pet has the effect of
>
> (A) condemning her anger
> (B) making the woman seem unstable
> (C) limiting her options for response
> (D) emphasizing a sense of worry
> (E) reinforcing a sense of disillusionment

If the woman has just lost something of great value to her, the answer might be D (losing a pet can cause worry); however, you cannot be sure without the context. What if the paragraph from which this sentence is taken is describing in detail the woman having hallucinations of friends who had left her life thirty years earlier? A woman feeling "like a small child whose pet dog was missing" in these circumstances would perhaps make her seem more "unstable" (B).

3. How to Deal with Vocabulary in the Question Stems and Answer Choices

The importance of enlarging your vocabulary before you take the test cannot be overstated.

Perhaps the most direct and effective way to increase your vocabulary is to adopt a sense of language awareness when you read. Just memorizing words and meanings may have little lasting value. On the other hand, as you are reading works of literature, class assignments, magazine articles, or even the daily newspaper, make note of new words as they are used in context. By associating the words with how they are used, you can increase your vocabulary in a meaningful way. Begin looking for opportunities to use these words in your own class work and personal writings.

Even if you have a large vocabulary, you might encounter words in the answer choices on the SAT Literature Test that you cannot define. If you do not understand a word, be calm. Examine the question stem, the context of the selection, and all the other answers; or you might reduce the possible choices down to make an educated guess.

Do not allow an unfamiliar literary term or vocabulary word to upset you and cause you to break your concentration or pacing during the test. **Expect to see some words you do not recognize and plan ahead how to deal with them.** Whether you reduce the number of possible answers and then take a guess or just skip the question, you want to keep moving forward to those questions you can answer correctly. The exercises and tests in this book occasionally include answer choices that some call "over-the-top" vocabulary. Use these to learn how to deal with unfamiliar vocabulary and terms.

Students have made incorrect answer choices on questions they might have otherwise answered correctly because they did not understand the meaning of a word used in the question stem or answer choices.

4. How to Deal with Vocabulary in the Selections

About sixty percent of the selections on the SAT Subject Test in Literature are taken from works written before 1900. How can you, as a modern reader, learn to understand the meanings of words and how they are used in a poem written, for example, in 1780?

First, the literary elements or perspectives are universal and can apply to any literature, regardless of time and place. Master them and you will be on your way to understanding what you are reading.

Second, like spotting clues in an Agatha Christie mystery, **using context skills is a strategy that can help you bridge the gap between the past and the present**. To provide you with opportunities to develop context skills, this study guide emphasizes pre-1900 literature. You should not let nonstandardized spellings, obsolete words, regional diction, or culturally based expressions confuse you. Use context.

TERM ALERT   You should know this term: **context**

Definition: Context refers to the information that comes before or after a given word, phrase, sentence, or paragraph and helps the reader understand the exact or intended meaning. Generally, the reader studies the context to find clues to meaning.

Sometimes the writer will provide you with clues to meaning. The following examples illustrate some of the more direct types of context clues.

Context Clue	Example
1. definition	Some older churches contain feretories, shrines used to house relics of saints.
2. example	There are some members of the lily family that we eat every day, for example, garlic.
3. restatement	"She won't need your help anymore, Wally. In other words, get out and don't come back."
4. comparison	An oriel is like a large bay window with attitude.
5. contrast	Unlike the silk flowers in the hall, origami is made with paper.
6. synonym	He sent in troops to quash, or subdue, the rioting crowd.
7. detail	Frontogenesis occurred over central Texas last night. Cold air from the north collided with warm Gulf air to produce thunderstorms.

How do you determine the meaning, however, when the writer does not give you any direct clues? You can look for prefixes and suffixes and examine the root or base of the word. Another way is to look at the part of speech. What function does the mystery word serve in the sentence?

One of the most valuable strategies you can use for determining meaning from context, in general, is making inferences.

TERM ALERT   You should know this term: **inference**

Definition: To make an inference from context is to draw a conclusion or make an assumption based on the evidence within the text. For example, what can you infer from this sentence?

> **Rosemarie threw aside the freshly picked daffodils as she ran to rescue her child from the oncoming eighteen-wheeler.**

We can infer that it is springtime (when daffodils bloom) and that Rosemarie and the child are along a highway.

Inference is especially helpful when a word has multiple meanings:

> **Elizabeth loved spinning wool from her own sheep. Many evenings would find her with her *distaff* in one hand and her spindle in the other.**

We can infer that the distaff is a piece of equipment used to spin wool and that Elizabeth probably lives on a farm.

> **The genetic disorder once again appeared in the *distaff* side of the family. None of the men showed any symptoms.**

We can assume that the women are showing the symptoms.

> **He would do only what he considered "men's work." *Distaff* was totally out of the question for his weekend's activities.**

We can infer that he will not do what he considers "women's work."

Example

These lines come from *Wuthering Heights* by Emily Brontë (1847):

> But his [Earnshaw's] self-love would endure no further torment—
> I heard, and not altogether disapprovingly, a manual check given to her saucy
> tongue—The little wretch [Catherine] had done her utmost to hurt her
> *Line* cousin's sensitive though uncultivated feelings, and a physical argument was
> *(5)* the only mode he had of balancing the account, and repaying its effects on
> the inflicter.

TIP

Pay close attention to the main verb in line 2 and the descriptive adjective with "argument" in line 4.

The "manual check" probably was

(A) Catherine suddenly becoming silent
(B) Earnshaw scolding Catherine
(C) Catherine abruptly holding her tongue
(D) Catherine holding her hand over her mouth
(E) Earnshaw slapping Catherine

Explanation: What evidence is in this selection? Catherine and Earnshaw (cousins) are fighting. She hurt his feelings. The "manual check" has made the argument physical (line 4). The narrator "heard" the "manual check," which was applied to Catherine's "saucy tongue" (mouth). The only conclusion that can be drawn from this evidence is that he slapped her.

Correct Answer: **E**

Example

Read the following poem, "Early Affection" by George Moses Horton (1865).

> I lov'd thee from the earliest dawn,
>   When first I saw thy beauty's ray,
> And will, until life's eve comes on,
> *Line*   And beauty's blossom fades away;
> *(5)*   And when all things go well with thee,
>   With smiles and tears remember me.
>
> I'll love thee when thy morn is past,
>   And wheedling gallantry is o'er,
> When youth is lost in ages blast,
> *(10)*   And beauty can ascend no more,
>   And when life's journey ends with thee,
>   O, then look back and think of me.

The meaning of "wheedling gallantry" (line 8) can be seen in the paraphrase

(A) flattering attention
(B) brave action
(C) coaxing boldness
(D) amorous intrigue
(E) polite attention

Explanation: By definition, "gallantry" can mean any of the answer choices, but "wheedling" can mean "flattering" (A) or "coaxing" (C). Again, turn to context: Lines 9–10 establish lost beauty that would no longer attract flattering attention.

Correct Answer: **A**

Begin using context clues as you respond to the practice questions throughout this book. You will learn more about context in Literary Element Number 7, Meanings of Words, Phrases, and Lines in Context (Meanings in Context).

LONG-TERM STRATEGIES

1. Focus

Learning to focus your attention when taking the test prevents you from reading the test selections mechanically, only to find when you begin to answer the questions, you do not understand or remember what you just read. Here are some strategies to help you focus:

- Begin each selection with a three-step approach:

  Step One. Skim the question stems. Why? If you know the subjects of the questions, your reading will have more purpose.

  But do not skim the answer choices. Why not? It would take too much time and, because they contain incorrect answer choices, they can be confusing as you read the selection.

  Step Two. Read the selection, spotting as many answers as you can, placing checkmarks beside them as you go.

  Step Three. Read the question stems and answer choices, returning to the selection as necessary to make your answer selections.

- Feel free to underline, circle, or checkmark words and phrases, sentences, or lines in the selections. Use whatever marks help you concentrate and pace your work. Put a slash mark (/) in poems where one sentence ends and another begins to help clarify the meaning.
- Caution: Remember time is important. Do not linger too long making notes.
- Do you need total silence to concentrate or do you thrive on chaos? If the "I can hear a pin drop" quiet of a strict testing situation unnerves you, take your practice tests in quiet surroundings so you can experiment with ways to concentrate. Perhaps, conversely, you are easily distracted and focus better in total silence. We know that in the real world there is noise. Do not become so dependent on quiet, perfect conditions that you fall apart when things happen.
- To focus your attention, learn to talk to yourself internally as you read. Develop a mental relationship with what you read.
- Take note of mechanical elements in the selection, such as words in italics, dates, sparse dialogue, and so forth. Sometimes focusing on these elements can help you concentrate and return quickly to details in a selection.

- **Speed Counts! There is a sixty minute time limit.** Obviously, you need to think clearly to think quickly; therefore, you may need to spend a little longer starting your focus techniques on the first selection. Once you have begun, try to establish a pacing or rhythm so that you answer all the questions you feel sure about before returning to those questions that you left unanswered.

Familiarity speeds your thinking. Take as many of the seven practice tests in the back of this book as you can before the day of the test.

2. My Own Words (MOW)

MOWing a selection (putting it into My Own Words) helps establish the subject, identify the main idea, and discern the speaker's purpose. Each of these ideas could be the subject of a test question. You can MOW an entire selection, a single stanza or paragraph, or even an individual sentence or line. MOWing is a two-step procedure: First, you paraphrase the ideas of a line or sentence, putting them into your own words. Second, you summarize or condense the facts or ideas as concisely as possible. A summary is short. A statement of the theme is a type of summary.

Example

Read the following poem written by Walt Whitman (ca. 1817).

A Noiseless Patient Spider

A noiseless patient spider,
I marked where on a little promontory it stood isolated,
Marked how to explore the vacant vast surrounding,

Line It launched forth filament, filament, filament, out of itself,
(5) Ever unreeling them, ever tirelessly speeding them.
And you O my soul where you stand,
Surrounded, detached, in measureless oceans of space,
Ceaselessly musing, venturing, throwing, seeking the
spheres to connect them,
(10) Till the bridge you will need be formed, till the ductile anchor hold,
Till the gossamer thread you fling catch somewhere, O my soul.

TIP

Notice that the speaker is talking to his own soul in line 6—a clue to the meaning of the poem.

What is the subject of this poem?

(A) A spider
(B) Space
(C) The work ethic
(D) Anchoring of the soul
(E) Building bridges

Explanation: At first glance, the subject is a spider—on a literal level. But is a spider *really* the poet's subject, or is a spider the means he uses to approach another, more abstract subject?

Try using summary and paraphrase to discover the answer.

Paraphrase (put into your own words) lines 1–2: _____

_____

Paraphrase line 3: _____

_____

Paraphrase lines 4–5: _____

_____

Write one sentence that *summarizes* lines 1–5:_____

_____

Paraphrase lines 6–7: _____

_____

Paraphrase line 8: _____

_____

Paraphrase lines 9–10: _____

_____

Write a sentence that *summarizes* lines 6–10: _____

_____

Compare your response with this one:

> Lines 1–2: The speaker saw a spider standing alone on a promontory.
> Line 3: The spider checked out its surroundings.
> Lines 4–5: It spun a web.
> Summary of lines 1–5: The speaker watched a spider spin a web.
> Lines 6–7: The speaker's soul is standing detached in space.
> Line 8: His soul is checking out his surroundings.
> Lines 9–10: His soul is seeking to become attached to something.
> Summary of lines 6–10: The speaker's soul, like the spider, is detached and is seeking to be attached.

Now, based on the paraphrase and summary, what is the subject? It can be expressed many ways: anchoring of the soul, isolation, the soul.

This theme is a product of a metaphor (an implied comparison). In the first stanza, the speaker describes how a spider is isolated in space, spinning a web. In the second stanza, he describes how the soul is isolated in space, attempting to fling "the gossamer thread"—to become attached (like a spider spinning its web).

The theme is that the soul, like a spider, is isolated and detached, trying to make connections with its surroundings.

Correct Answer: **D**

3. Break It Down (BID)

When you BID (Break It Down), you examine the specific elements at work in the selection *and* in the question. You can BID any genre and any question. Two of the most effective uses of this strategy follow.

- How to BID a poem:

When you first glance at a poem on the test, you should immediately notice

1. how many lines are in the poem,
2. the rhyme scheme, and
3. the rhythm.

Why are these three elements important? The number of lines, rhyme scheme, and rhythm of a poem help determine its form. The following chart summarizes major forms you should know for the test.

Form	No. of Lines	Rhyme Scheme	Regular Meter
Sonnet	14	Varies	Iambic pentameter
Blank verse	Varies	None	Iambic pentameter
Free verse	Varies	None	None
Couplets	2 lines (rhyme); total lines of poem vary	*aabbcc*, etc.	Varies
Heroic couplets	2 lines (rhyme); total lines of poem vary	*aabbcc*, etc.	Iambic pentameter

On the test, you may have to identify whether a given poem is a sonnet, blank verse, free verse, or written in couplets or heroic couplets. **If you can spot these forms quickly, you will save valuable time.**

- How to BID relationship questions:

Sometimes test questions will focus on relationships, such as patterns, change, contrasts, similarities, multiple themes, progressions, and structural parallelisms.

If you become sensitive to relationships when you first encounter a selection, often you can save time and think more clearly as you progress through the questions.

Example

Do you see the relationship central to "Man-Woman" (ca. 1855) by Lydia H. Sigourney?

> *Man's home is everywhere.* On ocean's flood,
>   Where the strong ship with storm-defying tether
>   Doth link in stormy brotherhood

Line   Earth's utmost zones together,

(5)   Where'er the red gold glows, the spice-trees wave,
>   Where the rich diamond ripens, mid the flame
>   Of vertic suns that ope the stranger's grave,
>   He with bronzed cheek and daring step doth rove;
>   He with short pang and slight

(10)   Doth turn him from the checkered light
>   Of the fair moon through his own forests dancing,
>   Where music, joy, and love
>   Were his young hours entrancing;
>   And where ambition's thunder-claim

(15)   Points out his lot,
>   Or fitful wealth allures to roam,
>   There doth he make his home,
>   Repining not.

> *It is not thus with Woman.* The far halls

(20)   Though ruinous and lone,
>   Where first her pleased ear drank a nursing mother's tone;
>   The home with humble walls,
>   Where breathed a parent's prayer around her bed;
>   The valley where, with playmates true,

(25)   She culled the strawberry, bright with dew;
>   The bower where Love her timid footsteps led;
>   The hearthstone where her children grew;
>   The damp soil where she cast
>   The flower-seeds of her hope, and saw them bide the blast,—

(30)   Affection with unfading tint recalls,
>   Lingering round the ivied walls;
>   Where every rose hath in its cup a bee,
>   Making fresh honey of remembered things,
>   Each rose without a thorn, each bee bereft of stings.

You can physically see a balanced relationship: line 1 and line 19. You know without reading another word that this poem is about contrast: man contrasted to woman. Subject? Their views of home. Of course, you should be able to state their respective views.

Which of the following pairs does NOT express the central contrast of this poem?

(A) "music, joy, and love" (line 12); "a parent's prayer" (line 23)
(B) "He with short pang and slight" (line 9); "affection with unfading tint recalls" (line 30)
(C) "Earth's utmost zones" (line 4); "The home with humble walls" (line 22)
(D) "daring step" (line 8); "timid footsteps" (line 26)
(E) "allures to roam" (line 16); "Lingering round the ivied walls" (line 31)

Which of the following works best reflects the theme of this poem?

(A) *The Wizard of Oz*—a girl learns the value of home
(B) *Gone With the Wind*—a woman is determined to restore her home
(C) *Women: The Misunderstood Majority*—an examination of myths about women
(D) *The Husband's Message and The Wife's Lament*—two Old English poems calling for reunion with a missing spouse
(E) *Men Are from Mars, Women Are from Venus*—an exploration of gender-based differences

Another element to focus on in a literary work is the possibility of progression or change. Questions can ask about changes in many things, such as character or viewpoints of speakers; or they can center on a lack of change.

In Sigourney's poem, man leaves his home, "Repining not." Look at the description of woman. Do you see any progressions?

Which of the following best describes the woman's progression in the poem?

(A) Nurse → wife → parent → widow
(B) Childhood home → marital home → nursing home
(C) Infant → child → wife → mother
(D) Infant → child → field laborer
(E) Ruin → humility → love → memories

Correct Answers: **A, E, C**

4. Test Taker to Test Maker (TT→TM)

In this study strategy, your mind shifts from test taker to test maker; and you view literature with new understanding. The idea is simple: As you read literary selections to prepare for the test, ask yourself what questions you would ask if you were the test writer. Learning to recognize how questions can be asked gives you more control over the test because you can sometimes anticipate what questions to expect. It can be fun to say after a test, "I *knew* they would ask that question, and I was ready!"

Here are two samples to get you started.

Example 1

Epitaph in Bookish Style

The Body
of
Benjamin Franklin
Line   Printer
(5)   (Like the cover of an old book
Its contents torn out
And stript of its lettering and gilding)
Lies here, food for worms.
But the work shall not be lost.
(10)   For it will (as he believed) appear once more
In a new and more elegant edition
Revised and corrected
by
The Author.

1. Define the form: An epitaph is a short poem intended for a tombstone.
2. Identify the subject: Ben Franklin's dead body
3. Who is speaking? Probably Franklin

Now, paraphrase:

Lines 1–4 and line 8: _____

_____

Lines 5–7: _____

_____

Lines 9–14: _____

_____

Next, turn this analysis into a question over voice. We will give you the answer choices; you provide the question.

Question: _____

(A) fearful
(B) unacceptable
(C) mournful
(D) optimistic
(E) ominous

Correct Answer: **D**

(Possible question: What is the speaker's attitude toward death?)

This poem gives you another opportunity to look at the contrast question. Think about the contrast of the two ideas at work here: Franklin's dead body eaten by worms versus life in a new body "more elegant" and "Revised and corrected."

This time you provide the correct answer and one incorrect answer.

The central contrast in this poem is reflected in all the following EXCEPT

(A) old, new
(B) _____, _____
(C) contents torn out, appear once more
(D) _____, _____
(E) stript, Revised

Correct Answer: **B**

For your incorrect answer, you should look for words that represent the contrast. For your correct answer, look for words that do not represent the contrast, such as "old book," "the work."

A Question for Thought and Discussion

Why did Franklin write his epitaph in the shape of a tree?

Example 2

Here is a selection from Poe's "A Descent into the Maelström":

> "It could not have been more than two minutes afterwards until we suddenly felt the waves subside, and were enveloped in foam. The boat made a sharp half turn to larboard, and then shot off in its new direction like a
> *Line* thunderbolt. At the same moment the roaring noise of the water was com-
> (5) pletely drowned in a kind of shrill shriek—such a sound as you might imagine given out by the water-pipes of many thousand steam-vessels, letting off their steam all together. We were now in the belt of surf that always surrounds the whirl; and I thought, of course, that another moment would plunge us into the abyss—down which we could only see indistinctly on
> (10) account of the amazing velocity with which we were borne along. The boat did not seem to sink into the water at all, but to skim like an airbubble upon the surface of the surge. Her starboard side was next the whirl, and on the larboard arose the world of ocean we had left. It stood like a huge writhing wall between us and the horizon.

1. First, what figurative language does Poe use? Seek and find four similes. (Circle them in the paragraph.)
2. Also, look at this sentence:

> At the same moment the roaring noise of the water was completely drowned in a kind of shrill shriek—

In the context of the paragraph, there are four different figures of speech used in this sentence. What are they?

a. _____
b. _____
c. _____
d. _____

Answers and Explanations:

1. Similes: Like a thunderbolt; a sound as…water-pipes of many thousand steam-vessels; like an air-whirl; like a huge writhing wall.

2. The sentence contains a fascinating blend of images. On the surface, each word has a meaning that seems literal. Roaring is a loud noise; noises can be drowned or muffled by other noises. However, in the context of a very figure-laden description of a whirlpool with an "abyss" and a "huge writhing wall" of water, this line takes on powerfully figurative meaning.

For the sound of water to be "drowned" becomes contradictory (paradoxical); that it would be overpowered by yet more water is ironic. The noise is roaring, metaphorically comparing it to a wild beast capable of "writhing." This image, combined with the sound being drowned and the new sound being a "shrill shriek" (like a person might make), makes this sentence intensify the sense of fear and danger. Figures of speech used: irony, paradox, personification, metaphor.

Of course, you could ask an identification question: "like a thunderbolt" is… (B) a simile. Or you could ask about what the similes mean in the sentence:

The figurative language used in the first two similes are meant to describe

(A) direction
(B) visual impact
(C) direction and sound
(D) the water and steam vessels
(E) speed and sound

Correct Answer: **E**

Instead, move to the next level and write a question about the effects of the similes used.

Select one of the four similes and list two to three *effects* created by it. For example, the simile "like a huge writhing wall" makes the water seem beastlike.

Finally, write your question. You can give one correct effect and two or three incorrect or some other combination. You can even list all correctly identified effects.

The simile, "_____," has which of the following effects?

I. _____
II. _____
III. _____
IV. _____

(A) I only
(B) II only
(C) III only
(D) _____
    (a combination, such as I and III only)
(E) I, II, III, (and IV, if needed)

What is your correct answer?

As you read selections in this book, continue thinking like a test writer by asking yourself "What would make good questions over this selection?"

MENTAL STRATEGIES

1. How to Prepare Yourself When You Study

Begin with a positive attitude toward reading and understanding literature. Realize that the critical reading and thinking skills you develop in preparing for this test can help you in other subjects and areas in life. This study is worth the effort.

Because critical reading is a skill, it requires practice over time. Pace yourself and set goals. Practice on a regular basis is probably the most effective way to prepare your mind to think critically for the test. Another way to increase your skills is to take challenging literature classes.

Take good care of yourself; eat correctly, and exercise your body as well as your mind. Concentrate totally when you are studying, but get adequate rest and relaxation at intervals, as well. Add variety to your test preparation. Sometimes study alone. At other times you might want to join friends or a study group to discuss the literary element chapters or quiz each other over terms and definitions. Do what works the best for you.

2. How to Prepare Yourself for the Day of the Test

Prepare for the test day by planning comfortable clothes, assembling any materials you need (including several #2 pencils with good erasers), getting a good night's sleep, and eating a proper diet.

Be sure to confirm the day, time, and location of the test and allow yourself time the night before to review terms and concepts.

During the test, listen to all verbal directions and read all written instructions carefully. Pace yourself. Do not struggle over any one question. Move on; then return to unanswered questions after answering all those with certain answers.

Finally, be quiet, calm, and relaxed. After you have prepared your mind to think critically, the test becomes just another opportunity to use your critical reading skills and test-taking strategies.

At this point, you should understand the structure of the test and be ready to refresh your memory and skills. Now it is time to see where your strengths and weaknesses are with Diagnostic Test One.

Where Do My Reading Comprehension Skills Stand Now?

CHAPTER 4

The purpose of Diagnostic Test One is to

1. introduce you to the format and structure of the test
2. acquaint you with the types of questions that may be asked
3. illustrate and explain the content of questions that are based on interpretive thinking skills
4. help you identify your strengths—and your weaknesses—in critical reading and the seven major literary elements

Diagnostic Test One is not intended to be an easy test. You need to know what you need to know. Do not be concerned about any questions that you miss; the answers are explained after the test, and the concepts behind the questions are explained later in the book.

To take this test, remove the answer sheet (see page 27) to record your answers. Allow yourself one hour (using a timer or clock to time yourself).

Be sure to read all directions carefully.

Remember: You may *not* use other papers, books, or reference materials of any kind.

After you complete the test, use the Answer Key (see page 41) to check your answers and to determine your raw score. Then use the Analysis: Diagnostic Test One (see page 43) to help you evaluate your answer choices.

Answer Sheet

DIAGNOSTIC TEST ONE

1 Ⓐ Ⓑ Ⓒ Ⓓ Ⓔ	16 Ⓐ Ⓑ Ⓒ Ⓓ Ⓔ	31 Ⓐ Ⓑ Ⓒ Ⓓ Ⓔ	46 Ⓐ Ⓑ Ⓒ Ⓓ Ⓔ
2 Ⓐ Ⓑ Ⓒ Ⓓ Ⓔ	17 Ⓐ Ⓑ Ⓒ Ⓓ Ⓔ	32 Ⓐ Ⓑ Ⓒ Ⓓ Ⓔ	47 Ⓐ Ⓑ Ⓒ Ⓓ Ⓔ
3 Ⓐ Ⓑ Ⓒ Ⓓ Ⓔ	18 Ⓐ Ⓑ Ⓒ Ⓓ Ⓔ	33 Ⓐ Ⓑ Ⓒ Ⓓ Ⓔ	48 Ⓐ Ⓑ Ⓒ Ⓓ Ⓔ
4 Ⓐ Ⓑ Ⓒ Ⓓ Ⓔ	19 Ⓐ Ⓑ Ⓒ Ⓓ Ⓔ	34 Ⓐ Ⓑ Ⓒ Ⓓ Ⓔ	49 Ⓐ Ⓑ Ⓒ Ⓓ Ⓔ
5 Ⓐ Ⓑ Ⓒ Ⓓ Ⓔ	20 Ⓐ Ⓑ Ⓒ Ⓓ Ⓔ	35 Ⓐ Ⓑ Ⓒ Ⓓ Ⓔ	50 Ⓐ Ⓑ Ⓒ Ⓓ Ⓔ
6 Ⓐ Ⓑ Ⓒ Ⓓ Ⓔ	21 Ⓐ Ⓑ Ⓒ Ⓓ Ⓔ	36 Ⓐ Ⓑ Ⓒ Ⓓ Ⓔ	51 Ⓐ Ⓑ Ⓒ Ⓓ Ⓔ
7 Ⓐ Ⓑ Ⓒ Ⓓ Ⓔ	22 Ⓐ Ⓑ Ⓒ Ⓓ Ⓔ	37 Ⓐ Ⓑ Ⓒ Ⓓ Ⓔ	52 Ⓐ Ⓑ Ⓒ Ⓓ Ⓔ
8 Ⓐ Ⓑ Ⓒ Ⓓ Ⓔ	23 Ⓐ Ⓑ Ⓒ Ⓓ Ⓔ	38 Ⓐ Ⓑ Ⓒ Ⓓ Ⓔ	53 Ⓐ Ⓑ Ⓒ Ⓓ Ⓔ
9 Ⓐ Ⓑ Ⓒ Ⓓ Ⓔ	24 Ⓐ Ⓑ Ⓒ Ⓓ Ⓔ	39 Ⓐ Ⓑ Ⓒ Ⓓ Ⓔ	54 Ⓐ Ⓑ Ⓒ Ⓓ Ⓔ
10 Ⓐ Ⓑ Ⓒ Ⓓ Ⓔ	25 Ⓐ Ⓑ Ⓒ Ⓓ Ⓔ	40 Ⓐ Ⓑ Ⓒ Ⓓ Ⓔ	55 Ⓐ Ⓑ Ⓒ Ⓓ Ⓔ
11 Ⓐ Ⓑ Ⓒ Ⓓ Ⓔ	26 Ⓐ Ⓑ Ⓒ Ⓓ Ⓔ	41 Ⓐ Ⓑ Ⓒ Ⓓ Ⓔ	56 Ⓐ Ⓑ Ⓒ Ⓓ Ⓔ
12 Ⓐ Ⓑ Ⓒ Ⓓ Ⓔ	27 Ⓐ Ⓑ Ⓒ Ⓓ Ⓔ	42 Ⓐ Ⓑ Ⓒ Ⓓ Ⓔ	57 Ⓐ Ⓑ Ⓒ Ⓓ Ⓔ
13 Ⓐ Ⓑ Ⓒ Ⓓ Ⓔ	28 Ⓐ Ⓑ Ⓒ Ⓓ Ⓔ	43 Ⓐ Ⓑ Ⓒ Ⓓ Ⓔ	58 Ⓐ Ⓑ Ⓒ Ⓓ Ⓔ
14 Ⓐ Ⓑ Ⓒ Ⓓ Ⓔ	29 Ⓐ Ⓑ Ⓒ Ⓓ Ⓔ	44 Ⓐ Ⓑ Ⓒ Ⓓ Ⓔ	59 Ⓐ Ⓑ Ⓒ Ⓓ Ⓔ
15 Ⓐ Ⓑ Ⓒ Ⓓ Ⓔ	30 Ⓐ Ⓑ Ⓒ Ⓓ Ⓔ	45 Ⓐ Ⓑ Ⓒ Ⓓ Ⓔ	60 Ⓐ Ⓑ Ⓒ Ⓓ Ⓔ

Diagnostic Test One

Directions: The following questions test your understanding of several literary selections. Read each passage or poem and the questions that follow it. Select the best answer choice for each question by blackening the matching oval on your answer sheet. **Special attention should be given to questions containing the following words: EXCEPT, LEAST, NOT.**

Questions 1–10 are based on the following passage.

All eyes were now turned on the country lad, standing at the door, in his worn three-cornered hat, grey coat, leather
Line breeches, and blue yarn stockings, leaning
(5) on an oaken cudgel, and bearing a wallet on his back.

Robin replied to the courteous innkeeper, with such an assumption of confidence as befitted the Major's relative.
(10) "My honest friend," he said, "I shall make it a point to patronize your house on some occasion, when"—here he could not help lowering his voice—"when I may have more than a parchment threepence
(15) in my pocket. My present business," continued he, speaking with lofty confidence, "is merely to inquire my way to the dwelling of my kinsman, Major Molineux."

(20) There was a sudden and general movement in the room, which Robin interpreted as expressing the eagerness of each individual to become his guide. But the innkeeper turned his eyes to a written
(25) paper on the wall, which he read, or seemed to read, with occasional recurrences to the young man's figure.

"What have we here?" said he, breaking his speech into little dry fragments. " 'Left
(30) the house of the subscriber, bounden servant, Hezekiah Mudge,—had on, when he went away, grey coat, leather breeches, master's third-best hat. One pound currency reward to whosoever shall lodge
(35) him in any jail of the province.' Better trudge, boy, better trudge!"

Robin had begun to draw his hand towards the lighter end of the oak cudgel, but a strange hostility in every counte-
(40) nance induced him to relinquish his purpose of breaking the courteous innkeeper's head. As he turned to leave the room, he encountered a sneering glance from the bold-featured personage
(45) whom he had before noticed; and no sooner was he beyond the door, than he heard a general laugh, in which the innkeeper's voice might be distinguished, like the dropping of small stones into a
(50) kettle.

(1851)

1. The "wallet" that Robin bears on his back in line 5 probably refers to his

(A) money bag
(B) pocketbook
(C) knapsack
(D) billfold
(E) jacket decal

2. Of the literary devices listed below, which is used in lines 47–50 to describe the innkeeper's voice?

   (A) Metaphor
   (B) Personification
   (C) Paradox
   (D) Simile
   (E) Apostrophe

3. That the innkeeper "seemed to read" the paper (line 26) implies that

   (A) he is illiterate
   (B) he is fabricating the paper's contents
   (C) he has the notice memorized
   (D) he feels reticent about reading it aloud
   (E) he is eager to warn the boy of danger

4. How does contrast of Robin's appearance to his attitude contribute to the tone of this selection?

   (A) It uses direct threat to create a hostile tone.
   (B) It incorporates humility to create an impertinent tone.
   (C) It includes paradox to create an aggressive tone.
   (D) It emphasizes hyperbole to create a retaliatory tone.
   (E) It uses situational irony to create a comic tone.

5. The tone of "My honest friend" (line 10) in the context in which it is said sounds

   (A) conciliatory
   (B) condescending
   (C) impatient
   (D) polite
   (E) kind

6. Robin "could not help lowering his voice" (lines 12 and 13) probably because he

   (A) wants the innkeeper to realize his honest intentions
   (B) does not want to appear too affluent
   (C) is ashamed of his lack of money
   (D) feels intimidated by the others in the room
   (E) fears the others would rob him

7. The sarcastic tone in lines 41–42 is the result of

   (A) paradox
   (B) hyperbole
   (C) verbal irony
   (D) alliteration
   (E) symbolism

8. The description of the innkeeper's speech in line 29 is

   (A) an allusion
   (B) a simile
   (C) a recurrent theme
   (D) personification
   (E) a metaphor

9. The innkeeper's use of the word "trudge" in line 36 is intended as

   (A) harsh reality for a threatening effect
   (B) verbal irony for a comic effect
   (C) situational irony for a tragic effect
   (D) overstatement of the boy's condition
   (E) a parody of the traveling genre

10. In the context of the selection, how can "cudgel" (lines 5 and 38) be defined?

   I. A walking stick
   II. A weapon
   III. A type of cane

   (A) I only
   (B) II only
   (C) III only
   (D) I and II only
   (E) I, II, and III

Questions 11–19 are based on the following poem.

Proof to No Purpose

You see this gentle stream, that glides,
Shoved on, by quick-succeeding tides:
Try if this sober stream you can
Line   Follow to th' wilder ocean,
(5)   And see, if there it keeps unspent
In that congesting element.
Next, from that world of waters, then
By pores and caverns back again

Induct that inadultrate same
(10) Stream to the spring from whence it came.
This with a wonder when ye do,
An easy, and else easier too:
Then may ye recollect the grains
Of my particular remains,
(15) After a thousand lusters hurled,
By ruffling winds, about the world.

(1648)

11. The central denotative theme of the poem addresses the subject of

    (A) water cycles
    (B) how oceans are formed
    (C) seasons and weather of the world
    (D) life cycles
    (E) the instabilities of life

12. As seen in lines 3 and 5, the speaker's attitude toward the silent auditor seems to be somewhat

    (A) mocking
    (B) challenging
    (C) loving
    (D) deferential
    (E) churlish

13. Within the context of this poem, the speaker's "remains" in line 14 can be seen as his

    I. work left to be done
    II. remnant of material possessions
    III. dead body
    IV. surviving writings

    (A) I only
    (B) II only
    (C) II, III, and IV only
    (D) II and III only
    (E) III and IV only

14. As the word is used in line 14, "particular" describes the speaker's "remains" as all the following EXCEPT

    (A) apart from others
    (B) personal
    (C) special rather than general
    (D) precise
    (E) considered separately

15. What is the outcome of the speaker's use of the phrase "unspent / In that congesting element" (lines 5–6)?

    (A) The use influences the reader to regard the stream as lost forever in the ocean.
    (B) The use creates a sense of nature's economy.
    (C) The use establishes an alliterative pattern with line 7.
    (D) The use contradicts the return of the stream to its source in line 10.
    (E) The use makes the stream seem like an exhausted person in an overcrowded situation.

16. Figuratively, the stream represents

    (A) part of the water cycle
    (B) the source for the ocean
    (C) people in a state of innocence
    (D) literary works
    (E) the natural elements of life

17. Of the literary devices listed below, which is used in line 3?

    (A) Parody
    (B) Allusion
    (C) Personification
    (D) Apostrophe
    (E) Assonance

18. The octosyllabic construction of the poem (eight syllables per line) contributes to its

    (A) sense of conformity
    (B) hypnotic effect
    (C) cyclical tone
    (D) tone of urgency
    (E) regulated imagery

19. In the poem's title, "to No Purpose" means

    (A) irrelevant
    (B) unresolved
    (C) without design
    (D) untalented
    (E) misdirected

<u>Questions 20–26</u> are based on the following passage.

> SETTING: *Morning-room in Algernon's flat in Half-Moon Street.*
> *The room is luxuriously and artistically furnished.*

LADY BRACKNELL   It really makes no matter, Algernon. I had some crumpets with Lady Harbury, who seems to me to be living entirely for pleasure now.

Line
(5) ALGERNON   I hear her hair turned quite gold from grief.

LADY BRACKNELL   It certainly has changed its color. From what cause I, of course, cannot say.

(10)   ALGERNON *crosses and hands tea.*

Thank you. I've quite a treat for you tonight, Algernon. I am going to send you down with Mary Farquhar. She is such a nice woman, and so attentive to
(15) her husband. It's delightful to watch them.

ALGERNON   I am afraid, Aunt Augusta, I shall have to give up the pleasure of dining with you tonight after all.

(20) LADY BRACKNELL [*frowning*] I hope not, Algernon. It would put my table completely out. Your uncle would have to dine upstairs. Fortunately he is accustomed to that.

(25) ALGERNON   It is a great bore, and, I need hardly say, a terrible disappointment to me, but the fact is I have just had a telegram to say that my poor friend Bunbury is very ill again. [*Exchanges*
(30) *glances with Jack*] They seem to think I should be with him.

LADY BRACKNELL   It is very strange. This Mr. Bunbury seems to suffer from curiously bad health.

(35) ALGERNON   Yes; poor Bunbury is a dreadful invalid.

LADY BRACKNELL   Well, I must say, Algernon, that I think it is high time that Mr. Bunbury made up his mind whether
(40) he was going to live or to die. This shilly-shallying with the question is absurd. Nor do I in any way approve of the modern sympathy with invalids. I consider it morbid. Illness of any kind is hardly a thing to
(45) be encouraged in others. Health is the primary duty of life. I am always telling that to your poor uncle, but he never seems to take much notice…as far as any improvement in his ailments goes. I should be
(50) much obliged if you would ask Mr. Bunbury, from me, to be kind enough not to have a relapse on Saturday, for I rely on you to arrange my music for me. It is my last reception, and one wants something
(55) that will encourage conversation, particularly at the end of the season when everyone has practically said whatever they had to say, which, in most cases, was probably not much.

(1895)

20. Lady Bracknell's attitude can be seen as

(A) anxious
(B) opinionated
(C) sympathetic
(D) encouraging
(E) resentful

21. Lady Bracknell's air of authoritative condescension is ironic because

I. she knows it is "at the end of the season" and everyone has had his or her say, which is not much (lines 56–58)
II. Algernon, as well as Algernon's uncle, do not seem to respect or obey her orders
III. she is unable to determine the cause of Lady Harbury's change in hair color

(A) I only
(B) II only
(C) III only
(D) I and II only
(E) I, II, and III

22. What does the stage direction [*Exchanges glances with Jack*] in lines 29–30 tell you about Algernon's character?

    (A) He is far more worried about Bunbury than he wants his aunt to know.
    (B) He is not really worried about Bunbury but still feels it is his duty to go.
    (C) He is sincere about not wanting to miss dining with his aunt.
    (D) He may not be telling the truth about Bunbury.
    (E) He does not want to appear ungrateful to his aunt.

23. Based on the speaker's tone, how should Algernon's use of verbal irony in lines 5–6 be regarded?

    (A) A mean-spirited hatred
    (B) A childish rambling
    (C) A witty repartee
    (D) A titillating discourse
    (E) A ludicrous burlesque

24. Lady Bracknell's comments throughout the passage reveal her to be

    (A) pious
    (B) obsequious
    (C) indecisive
    (D) sympathetic
    (E) pompous

25. The stage direction [*Exchanges glances with Jack*] in lines 29–30 indicates that Jack might be Algernon's

    (A) confidant
    (B) villain
    (C) protagonist
    (D) antagonist
    (E) *vers libre*

26. The expressions "shilly-shallying" (lines 40–41), "modern sympathy" (lines 42–43), and "primary duty" (lines 45–46) produce which of these effects?

    (A) They strengthen Lady Bracknell's argument, making it obvious that in a contest of wills she would win.
    (B) They underscore Lady Bracknell's opinion that good health is the decided result of attitude.
    (C) They suggest that to be ill is to lack sympathy for others.
    (D) They provide a contrast to Algernon's obvious deep concern for his ill friend.
    (E) They imply motivation on Lady Bracknell's part to help people overcome their illnesses.

Questions 27–35 are based on the following poem.

My friend, the things that do attain
The happy life be these, I find:
The riches left, not got with pain;
The fruitful ground; the quiet mind;

Line
(5) The equal friend; no grudge, no strife;
No charge of rule, nor governance;
Without disease, the healthy life;
The household of continuance;

The mean diet, no dainty fare;
(10) Wisdom joined with simpleness;
The night dischargéd of all care,
Where wine the wit may not oppress:

The faithful wife, without debate;
Such sleeps as may beguile the night;
(15) Content thyself with thine estate,
Neither wish death, nor fear his might.

(1547)

27. The central theme of the poem is the

    (A) resplendent nature of a happy life
    (B) finding a happy life in "the mean estate"
    (C) self-denial necessary to pursue a happy life
    (D) contrast of a sumptuous life against a meager existence
    (E) beguiling nature of "the rich estate"

28. How does the personification of death affect the meaning in line 16?

    (A) The inevitability of death is emphasized.
    (B) The ultimate end of both friend and speaker are revealed.
    (C) Death becomes the friend of the poet.
    (D) Pain (line 3), disease (line 7), and wine (line 12) all play into death's hands.
    (E) Death, as someone not to be feared, is less threatening than an abstract concept.

29. Which of the following statements summarizes the relationship of lines 1–2 to the rest of the poem?

    (A) They establish the rhyme pattern.
    (B) They set a pattern of contrasts.
    (C) They introduce the topic.
    (D) They reveal an attitude of covetousness.
    (E) They reinforce a sense of tension.

30. Another way of saying "The household of continuance" (line 8) is

    (A) an unbroken home
    (B) family wealth
    (C) genetically based good health
    (D) a large inheritance
    (E) a family estate

31. In the poem's context, "pain" (line 3) can be thought of as all the following EXCEPT

    (A) physical hurt
    (B) punishment
    (C) mental anguish
    (D) expiation
    (E) penalty

32. "Wisdom joined with simpleness" (line 10) is a(n)

    (A) metaphor for a simple life
    (B) metrical accent within the stanza
    (C) paradox to emphasize that a simple life is wise
    (D) hyperbole to emphasize the great value of simplicity
    (E) ironic point of departure within the theme

33. The attitude of "I" (line 2) to "My friend" (line 1) can be seen as

    (A) conciliatory
    (B) impatient
    (C) didactic
    (D) critical
    (E) impersonal

34. The word "beguile," as it is used in line 14, conveys which of the following ideas?

    I. Pass the time pleasingly
    II. Relieve weariness in
    III. Deceive or cheat

    (A) I only
    (B) II only
    (C) III only
    (D) I and II only
    (E) I, II, and III

35. Line 6 refers to

    (A) the peace that comes from not charging items, thus reducing debt
    (B) not engaging in attacks and warlike behavior
    (C) avoiding political activities
    (D) not taking on the responsibilities of being in control or in a position of authority
    (E) resistance to rules and forms of government

<u>Questions 36–44</u> are based on the following passage.

Mrs. Stuart, having just returned from Italy, affected the artistic, and the new applicant found her with a Roman scarf
Line about her head, a rosary like a string of
(5) small cannon balls at her side, and azure draperies which became her as well as they did the sea-green furniture of her marine boudoir, where unwary walkers tripped over coral and shells, grew sea-
(10) sick looking at pictures of tempestuous billows engulfing every sort of craft, from a man-of-war to a hencoop with a ghostly young lady clinging to it with one hand, and had their appetites effectually taken
(15) away by a choice collection of water-bugs and snakes in a glass globe, that looked like a jar of mixed pickles in a state of agitation.

Madame was intent on a water-color
(20) copy of Turner's "Rain, Wind, and Hail," that pleasing work which was sold upside-down and no one found it out. Motioning Christie to a seat she finished some delicate sloppy process before speaking. In
(25) that little pause Christie examined her, and the impression then received was afterward confirmed.

Mrs. Stuart possessed some beauty and chose to think herself a queen of society.
(30) She assumed majestic manners in public

and could not entirely divest herself of them in private, which often produced comic effects. Zenobia troubled about fish-sauce, or Aspasia indignant at the
(35) price of eggs will give some idea of this lady when she condescended to the cares of housekeeping.

Presently she looked up and inspected the girl as if a new servant were no more
(40) than a new bonnet, a necessary article to be ordered home for examination. Christie presented her recommendation, made her modest little speech, and awaited her doom.

(45) Mrs. Stuart read, listened, and then demanded with queenly brevity:

"Your name?"

"Christie Devon."

"Too long; I should prefer to call you
(50) Jane as I am accustomed to the name."

"As you please, ma'am."

"Your age?"

"Twenty-one."

"You are an American?"

(55) "Yes, ma'am."

Mrs. Stuart gazed into space a moment, then delivered the following address with impressive solemnity.

"I wish a capable, intelligent, honest,
(60) neat, well-conducted person who knows her place and keeps it. The work is light, as there are but two in the family. I am very particular and so is Mr. Stuart. I pay two dollars and a half, allow one after-
(65) noon out, one service on Sunday, and no followers. My table-girl must understand her duties thoroughly, be extremely neat, and always wear white aprons."

"I think I can suit you, ma'am, when I
(70) have learned the ways of the house,"
meekly replied Christie.

(1873)

36. The primary effect of the curtness of the
dialogue in lines 47–55 is

(A) confusion over who said what
(B) stream-of-consciousness narration
(C) an omniscient point of view
(D) an overbearing tone
(E) a melodramatic style

37. That Mrs. Stuart "gazed into space" in line
56 implies that

(A) she has a memory problem
(B) what follows is a memorized speech
given often
(C) she is searching for just the right
words
(D) Christie has impressed her deeply
(E) what follows is an expression of her
true feelings

38. The first paragraph includes all the following except

(A) personification
(B) simile
(C) mixed sensory imagery
(D) hyperbole
(E) verbal irony

39. That Christie formed an early impression of
Mrs. Stuart that was "afterward confirmed"
(line 27) implies that Christie's modest (line
43) and meek (line 71) demeanor may be

(A) a sincere gesture
(B) a frank appraisal
(C) not efficacious
(D) an affectation
(E) an unfeigned response

40. The tone of lines 49–50 can be considered

(A) patronizing
(B) accusatory
(C) sycophant
(D) passive
(E) responsive

41. The underlying potential conflict presented
in this selection is based on

(A) nationality
(B) age
(C) taste
(D) education
(E) class distinction

42. The narrator's attitude toward Mrs. Stuart,
Christie, and their encounter seems to be

(A) deeply bitter
(B) mostly bewildered
(C) lachrymal
(D) regretful
(E) somewhat amused

43. The tone of the first and second paragraphs
is

(A) mocking, comic, and censorious
(B) comic, sporting, and encouraging
(C) foreboding, resentful, and challenging
(D) solemn, respectful, and comforting
(E) provocative, energetic, and engaging

44. Mrs. Stuart's attitude toward herself can best
be described as

(A) perceptive
(B) self-delusional
(C) superficial
(D) psychotic
(E) self-deprecatory

Questions 45–54 are based on the following
poem.

That time of year thou mayst in me behold
When yellow leaves, or none, or few, do
    hang
Upon those boughs which shake against
    the cold,
Bare ruined choirs, where late the sweet
Line   birds sang.
(5) In me thou see'st the twilight of such day
As after sunset fadeth in the west;
Which by and by black night doth take away,
Death's second self, that seals up all in rest.
In me thou see'st the glowing of such fire,
(10) That on the ashes of his youth doth lie,

As the deathbed whereon it must expire,
Consumed with that which it was nour-
   ished by.
This thou perceiv'st, which makes thy love
   more strong,
To love that well which thou must leave ere
   long.

(1609)

45. Lines 5, 9, and 13 contain changes in

   (A) internal rhyme
   (B) voice
   (C) end rhyme scheme
   (D) rhythm
   (E) scansion

46. The progression of "ruined" (line 4) to
   "fadeth" (line 6) to "expire" (line 11) can be
   seen as

   (A) a resistance to death
   (B) a progression of life to death
   (C) love transcending death
   (D) the instability of life
   (E) fear of death

47. The poem's subject is

   (A) dead trees
   (B) sunsets
   (C) dying fires
   (D) making love grow stronger
   (E) approaching death

48. In lines 1–4, the speaker compares the coming of winter to

   (A) a winter landscape
   (B) a leafless tree
   (C) a time when birds leave
   (D) his own period of old age
   (E) his inability to engage in youthful
      activity

49. In lines 5–8, the speaker uses twilight as a

   (A) symbol of depression
   (B) metaphor for approaching death
   (C) personification of death
   (D) representation of his state of mind
   (E) transitional device

50. Of the following literary identifications,
   which best describes the ashes as they are
   used in lines 9–12?

   I. A metaphor for life that is spent
   II. The termination of the sunset
   III. A symbol of youth

   (A) I only
   (B) II only
   (C) III only
   (D) I and II only
   (E) I, II, and III

51. What is the speaker's tone in lines 1–4?

   (A) Arrogant
   (B) Ironic
   (C) Shocked
   (D) Lonely
   (E) Encouraged

52. What is the effect of the progression from
   "yellow leaves" to "none" to "few" in line 2?

   (A) It emphasizes the lateness of the
      season.
   (B) It shows that the speaker's vision is not
      clear.
   (C) It represents unfulfilled dreams.
   (D) It implies human uncertainties about
      life and death.
   (E) It contrasts the "ruined choirs" in
      line 4.

53. Lines 13–14 relate to the rest of the poem
   in which of the following ways?

   (A) They summarize the point that when
      death is near, love should intensify.
   (B) They intensify the sadness of the
      autumn, sunset, and dying fires.
   (C) They reinforce the sense of struggle
      for life.
   (D) They introduce love as an answer for
      old age and death.
   (E) They serve to change both subject and
      attitude.

54. How does the personification of sleep in line 8 affect the meaning?

    (A) Sleep becomes a friend offering rest and solace.
    (B) The comparison to a sunset is intensified.
    (C) The speaker reinforces his struggle for life.
    (D) Sleep is made more threatening as a reflection or shadow of death.
    (E) Sleep resists death and makes night less threatening.

Questions 55–60 are based on the following passage.

    The unity of government which constitutes you one people is also now dear to you. It is justly so, for it is a main pillar in
Line the edifice of your real independence, the
(5) support of your tranquility at home, your peace abroad, of your safety, of your prosperity, of that very liberty which you so highly prize.

    But as it is easy to foresee that from dif-
(10) ferent causes and from different quarters much pains will be taken, many artifices employed, to weaken in your minds the conviction of this truth, as this is the point in your political fortress against
(15) which the batteries of internal and external enemies will be most constantly and actively (though often covertly and insidiously) directed, it is of infinite moment that you should properly estimate the
(20) immense value of your national union to your collective and individual happiness....

    The name of American, which belongs to you in your national capacity, must
(25) always exalt the just pride of patriotism more than any appellation derived from local discriminations. With slight shades of difference, you have the same religion, manners, habits, and political principles.

(30) You have in a common cause fought and triumphed together. The independence and liberty you possess are the work of joint councils and joint efforts, of common dangers, sufferings, and successes.

                    (1796)

55. "The unity of government which constitutes you one people is also now dear to you. It is justly so, for it is a main pillar in the edifice of your real independence, the support of your tranquility at home" (lines 1–5). Of the following statements concerning Washington's comment, all are correct EXCEPT which statement?

    (A) They are aphoristic.
    (B) They state a conclusion.
    (C) They serve to establish the tone.
    (D) They establish distance between speaker and subject.
    (E) They contain metaphorical language.

56. In this selection, the speaker's tone can be considered

    (A) paternal and patriotic
    (B) patronizing and discouraging
    (C) intensely ironic
    (D) enthusiastically optimistic
    (E) disappointed

57. The "truth" described in lines 12–13 probably is that

    (A) tranquility, peace, and safety are highly prized
    (B) some people may try to undermine truth
    (C) happiness is of immense value
    (D) various interest groups try to weaken government unity
    (E) independence depends upon unity of government

58. Of the statements that follow, which is the best description of the relationship between the first paragraph and the second?

(A) The second paragraph simply reiter-ates the main point of the first paragraph.

(B) The second paragraph creates a sense of emotional tension.

(C) Both paragraphs serve to support a change in public policy.

(D) The point of the first paragraph ren-ders moot the main idea of the second paragraph.

(E) The second paragraph introduces an optimistic tone.

59. What organizational pattern does the speaker use to persuade his audience?

(A) Classification

(B) Process analysis

(C) Conclusion-premise relationship

(D) Spondaic stress

(E) Metrical scan

60. What is the literary function of the phrase "political fortress" in line 14?

(A) Metaphor for a system of beliefs under attack

(B) Reference to independence

(C) Hyperbole for truth

(D) Literary allusion to governmental systems

(E) Affective fallacy

Answer Key: Diagnostic Test One

Step 1. Score Your Test

- Use the following table to score your test.
- *Compare* your answers with the correct answers in the table:
- ✓ Place a check in the "Right" column for those questions you answered correctly.
- ✓ Place a check in the "Wrong" column for those questions you answered incorrectly.
- If you omitted answering a question, leave both columns blank.

Step 2. Analyze Your Test Results

- *Read* the portions of the "Analysis: Diagnostic Test One" (analysis follows the scoring table) that apply first to those questions you missed.
- *Scan* the rest of the analysis for those questions you answered correctly. This analysis provides the correct answer, identifies the literary element tested by each question, and briefly discusses the answer choice(s).

Step 3. Learn from Your Test Results

- *Circle* the question number on the Answer Key Table for each of the questions you answered incorrectly. Which literary elements were these questions testing?

    Obviously, many of the questions are actually testing more than one literary element. Consequently, these identifications serve only as a guide to pinpoint "problem" areas.
- *Review* the seven literary elements.

For Further Help in Literary Elements	See Page:
1. MEANING	60
2. FORM	74
3. NARRATIVE VOICE	109
4. TONE	126
5. CHARACTER	145
6. USE OF LANGUAGE	168
7. MEANING(S) IN CONTEXT	202

ANSWER KEY: DIAGNOSTIC TEST ONE

SCORING			LITERARY ELEMENT TESTED						
RIGHT	WRONG	ANSWER	1	2	3	4	5	6	7
		1. C							*
		2. D						*	
		3. B							*
		4. E				*			
		5. B				*			
		6. C					*		
		7. C						*	
		8. E						*	
		9. B						*	
		10. E							*
		11. D	*						
		12. B			*				
		13. C						*	
		14. D							*
		15. E						*	
		16. D						*	
		17. C						*	
		18. C				*			
		19. A							*
		20. B			*				
		21. B						*	
		22. D					*		
		23. C				*			
		24. E					*		
		25. A					*		
		26. B							*
		27. B	*						
		28. E						*	
		29. C		*					
		30. A							*

Diagnostic Test One

SCORING			LITERARY ELEMENT TESTED						
RIGHT	WRONG	ANSWER	1	2	3	4	5	6	7
		31. D							*
		32. C						*	
		33. C			*				
		34. D							*
		35. D							*
		36. D				*			
		37. B			*				
		38. A						*	
		39. D			*				
		40. A				*			
		41. E	*						
		42. E		*					
		43. A				*			
		44. B			*				
		45. C		*					
		46. B		*					
		47. E	*						
		48. D						*	
		49. B						*	
		50. A						*	
		51. D				*			
		52. D							*
		53. A		*					
		54. D						*	
		55. D						*	
		56. A				*			
		57. E							*
		58. B		*					
		59. C		*					
		60. A						*	

TO OBTAIN YOUR RAW SCORE:

_____ divided by 4 = _____

Total wrong   Score W

_____ minus _____ = _____

Total right   Score W   Score R

Round Score R to the nearest whole number for the raw score.

TIP

Take as many of the full-length tests (beginning on page 281) as you can to refine your pacing.

What Does a Diagnostic Test Score Mean?

On an actual SAT STL, your raw score will be converted to a scaled score. On a diagnostic test, however, your overall score is not as important as highlighting specific strengths and weaknesses. You can look at scores when you take the practice tests.

In addition to noting which questions were difficult and which ones were easy, how did you do on time? Were you able to complete the test in 60 minutes? If not, be sure to review the focus strategies on page 14.

Analysis: Diagnostic Test One

NOTE: Many of the questions in Diagnostic Test One test your skills in more than one literary element, and each answer analysis might be viewed from multiple perspectives. Consequently, this analysis should be used as only a part of your study program.

1. **(C)** Element 7 (meanings in context) If you are unaware that a knapsack used to carry food and clothing was sometimes called a "wallet," you can still find the correct answer by eliminating obviously incorrect answers. The description of Robin's clothing indicates a time before the use of jacket decals. Pocketbook refers to a handbag or purse. Billfolds are generally carried in concealed locations. Even an inexperienced traveler would know not to sling a money bag across his back.

2. **(D)** Element 6 (use of language) "… like the dropping of small stones into a kettle" is a comparison using "like," a simile.

3. **(B)** Element 7 (meanings in context) If the notice really described the boy, would these men deliberately allow "One pound currency" to walk out of the room? Their laughter once the "country lad" who put on airs leaves the room supports the idea that the innkeeper made up the description as a joke.

4. **(E)** Element 4 (tone) The irony of Robin's situation is so amusing that the men enjoy a joke at his expense.

5. **(B)** Element 4 (tone) What in other contexts might be a form of polite address sounds patronizing or condescending when said with "an assumption of confidence" (lines 8–9).

6. **(C)** Element 5 (character) Clues to Robin's attitudes are found in his "assumption of confidence" (lines 8–9), his "speaking with lofty confidence" (line 16), his expectation of one day doing business there (lines 11–12), and his supposition that his position will influence the others to guide him. He feels important and would probably be ashamed to reveal his lack of money.

7. **(C)** Element 6 (use of language) The "courteous" innkeeper has just threatened the boy with possible arrest and insulted his sense of superiority. From Robin's perspective, he is no longer "courteous."

8. **(E)** Element 6 (use of language) His speech is being described as "little dry fragments," in an implied comparison of something heard to something seen, tasted, or felt. Some would view this metaphor as an example of synaesthesia (a mixture of sensory images).

9. **(B)** Element 6 (use of language) To trudge is to walk in a weary manner. The innkeeper is threatening the boy with possible arrest as a runaway servant, a situation calling for rapid flight, not slow walking.

10. **(E)** Element 1 (meanings in context) Usually, a cudgel refers only to a rather short weapon. Context shows that this cudgel, however, is long enough to lean upon and, consequently, could be and probably was used as a walking stick or cane.

11. **(D)** Element 1 (meaning) Although you might be tempted to select answer A because the first thirteen lines do, indeed, contain an eloquent (but incomplete) description of the earth's water cycle, this answer is inadequate because the question stem asks about the *central* theme—the one that is the structural support for the entire poem. Seasonal aspects and weather of the world are mentioned, but the central theme is reflected in the last four lines that reveal that lines 1–12 are being used with the cycles of life—answer D.

12. **(B)** Element 3 (narrative voice) The poem evidences the speaker as one who is trying to make a point. First, he uses the water cycle analogy to establish what would seem to be a rather straightforward metaphor. Notice, however, the tone in which he addresses the silent auditor, particularly in lines 3 and 5: "Try if…you can…And see…." Couple this tone with the forceful use of "Then" in line 13 when he says "<u>Then</u> may ye recollect the grains / Of my particular remains" [emphasis added] and you will discover a speaker whose attitude is challenging (B). What do you think has caused this attitude?

13. **(C)** Element 6 (use of language) Obviously, the "remains" of the speaker can be seen as his dead body (III), the "grains" of which he challenges the silent auditor to "recollect." Also, an argument might be made that upon the speaker's death, his remnant of material possessions (II) would be left to be recollected (brought together); however, on a highly figurative level, the "remains" can be seen as the speaker's surviving writings (IV) that are "particular" (personal) and that the silent auditor would "recollect" (recall or remember) after "a thousand lusters" (fame or renown) "hurled by ruffling winds" (disturbing or rippling air that bears trends or information).

14. **(D)** Element 7 (meanings in context) Answers A through E are all definitions of "particular"; consequently, context is essential to determining which meaning is not applicable to this situation. A major clue is in the description of the stream that flows into and becomes part of the ocean but then returns to the springs from which it originated. Likewise, the speaker suggests that the silent auditor "recollect" (implying a gathering again) his "particular remains"—those that are separated from those mixed in the "world of waters" (line 7) or "about the world" (line 16). This association of ideas supports selection of definitions that reflect this sense of individualism: apart from others (A), personal (B), special rather than general (C), and considered separately (E). Precise (D) does not conform to the established association.

15. **(E)** Element 6 (use of language) The word "spent" means to be exhausted or without energy. To be "unspent," then, would mean to have energy. The speaker contends that the silent auditor should "see, if there it [the stream] keeps unspent"—remains full of energy—"in that congesting [overcrowded] element" of the ocean. This subtle personification renders the stream to seem like an exhausted person in an overcrowded situation (E).

16. **(D)** Element 6 (use of language) On a literal level, the stream flows as a source for the ocean. On a figurative level, the root of its meaning can be found in the last four lines of the poem in which the speaker establishes two levels of meaning: (1) based on the life cycle of the human body and (2) based on his personal literary works ("particular remains") and their recollection. Using this second level as a basis, the stream can be seen as literary works (perhaps the personal works of the speaker) that gently flow into the "wilder ocean" (line 4) of the world's body of literary conventions and criticisms where it (line 5) becomes exhausted "In that congesting [overcrowded] element" (line 6). Eventually, it returns to the "spring from whence it came" (inspiration?—line 10).

17. **(C)** Element 6 (use of language) Personification is giving human attributes to nonhumans: "sober stream." Also, the repeated initial consonant(s) is an example of alliteration.

18. **(C)** Element 4 (tone) The speaker uses several literary devices (including alliteration, assonance, regular rhythm and rhyme, diction, and octosyllabic con-

struction) to project the smooth, cyclical tones that extend to support the imagery of the poem's figurative meaning—answer C.

19. **(A)** Element 7 (meanings in context) The phrase "to the purpose" means something is relevant or pertinent (such as: Is that remark to the purpose?). Consequently, "to no purpose" would be something that is irrelevant. What do you think is the significance of the title to the poem's literal and to its figurative meanings?

20. **(B)** Element 3 (narrative voice) Lady Bracknell has very distinct opinions (B). Notice her opinions about Lady Harbury, about Algernon's reason not to dine with her, about Mr. Bunbury's illness, and about her reception guests.

21. **(B)** Element 6 (use of language) Irony, in this case, involves the difference between the way Lady Bracknell views herself and the way she is viewed by those around her. She obviously has an air of authority (note that she does not hesitate even to order people to be healthy) and a sense of condescension (note her air of superiority over her reception guests). But do those around her respect her opinions or orders? Algernon refuses her invitation to dine and his uncle does not heed her advice.

22. **(D)** Element 5 (character) In determining motivation and character, context is extremely important. How sincere is Algernon about his "sick" friend? Clues can be found in Lady Bracknell's comments that Bunbury's illness is "very strange" (line 32), that he suffers from "*curiously* bad health" (line 34—emphasis added), and that he brushes with death frequently (lines 39–41)… perhaps Algernon is not telling the truth.

23. **(C)** Element 4 (tone) In answering this question, the first step is to determine what is ironic in Algernon's statement. Verbal irony occurs when the speaker's meaning is different from what he or she says, usually revealing the speaker's attitude or opinion on the subject. One can assume that Lady Harbury has been through a traumatic event (causing her grief or what would normally be expected to cause her grief). In such circumstances, a person's hair generally does not turn gold from grief. Also, note that Lady Bracknell points out that Lady Harbury "seems to me to be living entirely for pleasure now," so Algernon is aware that Lady Harbury is not really grieving at all. His comment that "her hair has turned quite gold from grief" really means that grief had nothing to do with her hair turning gold. Although his comment, when coupled with that of Lady Bracknell, is suggestive that Lady Harbury is acting in a way unbecoming a person in grief, his observation is by no means titillating (exciting) or burlesque (an amusing imitation of a literary work). Does anything in his dialogue indicate that he hates her (A)? Does he ramble on about it? No, he simply makes this witty reply (C), then drops the subject.

24. **(E)** Element 5 (character) A pompous character is one who is self-important (an exaggerated sense of her own importance). This trait can be seen in Lady

Bracknell's attempts to control others: She tells Algernon "I am going to send you down with Mary Farquhar" (lines 12–13). She is willing to make her husband dine upstairs to balance her table. She even commands sick people to control their illnesses for her convenience and to facilitate her dinner party plans.

25. **(A)** Element 5 (character) A confidant (A) is someone in a play who acts to establish the character of someone else by being a sounding board, by reacting with the other character, or by some other means revealing the personality of the more dominant or main character. In this case, when Jack exchanges glances, he gives the reader/viewer clues into Algernon's personality and motives.

26. **(B)** Element 7 (meanings in context) Nothing in the selection supports the idea that Lady Bracknell's strong will prevails over that of others—except perhaps over Algernon's uncle at dinner. Neither is "deep concern" on the part of Algernon established. Although Lady Bracknell may be motivated to help Algernon's uncle be healthy, these strongly connotative words do reveal that Lady Bracknell believes people should not encourage illness in others by expressing sympathy, but rather invalids should make health a duty and simply decide to be well (B). Lack of sympathy on the part of ill people is not discussed.

27. **(B)** Element 1 (meaning) The structure of this poem helps to define its central idea: first, the writer sets forth his topic—these are the "things" that make a happy life. He then lists those things, all of which are found in a simple, humble lifestyle, or in other words, "the mean estate" (B).

28. **(E)** Element 6 (use of language) Personification is the attributing of human qualities to inanimate objects or abstract ideas. The unknown and abstract can be very frightening; however, by encouraging the reader to think of death in human terms is to make it less fearful, less threatening. Be aware, though, that context is *very* important in recognizing the effects of personification or of any literary use of language. The context of this poem allows the personification of death to render death less threatening, but the context of another work might mean that such personification would turn death into a monster.

29. **(C)** Element 2 (form) In this particular poem, the complete rhyme scheme or pattern cannot be determined from just the first two lines—the rhyme pattern of the entire poem needs to be examined. Neither covetousness (D) nor contrast (B) are revealed here, and tension also is not an element (E). The first two lines do, however, introduce the topic (C).

30. **(A)** Element 7 (meanings in context) The central idea of the poem is that a simple, humble life can be very happy; therefore, wealth (B), an inheritance (D), and an estate (E) are in antithesis to the speaker's main point. Although no inherited diseases or illnesses would make for a happy situation, a household (home, family, and the affairs of the home) of continuance (an unbroken succession) would be a home not broken (by anger or separation).

31. **(D)** Element 7 (meanings in context) (A), (B), (C), and (E) can all be associated with pain; but expiation (D) is a condition of having made reparation or amends for wrongdoing and, as such, could be considered a *release from pain* of guilt.

32. **(C)** Element 6 (use of language) Being "simple" is often viewed as the opposite of being "wise." Here the concepts of simpleness and wisdom are used in a paradox to point out that simpleness (from the perspective of simplicity in living) can, in fact, be quite wise.

33. **(C)** Element 3 (narrative voice) A conciliatory attitude (A) has connotations of winning over or placating, implying that some division has taken place. Yet there is no indication in this poem of any separation between the two people in thought, emotion, or action having taken place, except the difference of opinion concerning lifestyles *implied* by the poet's sense of need to write this poem expounding the benefits of a simple lifestyle. Neither does the speaker seem impatient (B) or impersonal (E). Although he may be somewhat critical (again, by implication) of the high stress life of wealth, his attitude mostly is didactic (C) as he wants to instruct his friend—to teach him about the pursuit of happiness.

34. **(D)** Element 7 (meanings in context) In a "night discharged of all care" (line 11) the time would be passed pleasingly (I) and would relieve weariness (II), but would not deceive or cheat (III).

35. **(D)** Element 7 (meanings in context) A "charge" is a responsibility or duty when in a position of "rule" or in a position of governance (control and the exercise of authority). A simple life, then, would mean avoiding the "headaches at the top"—positions of responsibility.

36. **(D)** Element 4 (tone) As the mistress of the house, the "queenly" Mrs. Stuart sets the tone of the interview. She "demanded" answers with what the narrator calls "queenly brevity."

37. **(B)** Element 3 (narrative voice) The narrator emphasizes Mrs. Stuart's casual attitude toward the interview (lines 38–41) and presents the process as if it has become a ritual for her.

38. **(A)** Element 6 (use of language) The paragraph contains similes ("like a string," "like a jar"), mixed sensory imagery ("a jar of mixed pickles in a state of agitation"), hyperbole ("every sort of craft"), and verbal irony (a "choice" collection of snakes—in a bedroom!). It does not, however, contain personification (human characteristics given to an inanimate object, animal, or abstract idea).

39. **(D)** Element 3 (narrative voice) Christie is bold enough to "examine" her new employer, perceptive enough to form correct impressions even after a brief

examination, and intelligent enough to make a "modest little speech" before she "awaited her doom." Christie is giving answers in the demeanor she believes Mrs. Stuart is seeking.

40. **(A)** Element 4 (tone) A person's name is an integral part of her individuality. Not to be viewed as an individual person in this circumstance is demeaning and patronizing.

41. **(E)** Element 1 (meaning) Although Christie's age and nationality are mentioned and Mrs. Stuart's lack of taste is evident, the wide gap between servant and mistress is emphasized by Mrs. Stuart's insulting words and attitude.

42. **(E)** Element 3 (narrative voice) The narrator describes Mrs. Stuart as "comic," Christie as someone awaiting "her doom," and she details their encounter in a comic tone.

43. **(A)** Element 4 (tone) The narrator mocks the taste of her marine boudoir, silently laughs at reactions of "unwary walkers," and censors her "affected" sense of art.

44. **(B)** Element 3 (narrative voice) The narrator does not describe Mrs. Stuart as a society leader, but that she "think[s] herself a queen of society" who "assumed majestic manners in public and could not entirely divest herself of them in private."

45. **(C)** Element 2 (form) This 14-line, iambic pentameter poem's end rhyme scheme is in the tradition of the English (sometimes called Shakespearean) sonnet. Consequently, the end rhyme pattern changes in lines 5, 9, and 13:

line	1	behold	a
line	2	hang	b
line	3	cold	a
line	4	sang	b
line	5	day	c
line	6	west	d
line	7	away	c
line	8	rest	d
line	9	fire	e
line	10	lie	f
line	11	expire	e
line	12	by	f
line	13	strong	g
line	14	long	g

46. **(B)** Element 2 (form) This poem is a sequence of three metaphors comparing old age and approaching death to a season of the year (when things are still there but "ruined"), to the end of a day (a briefer period, when light "fadeth"),

and to the dying down of a fire (that can be extinguished in a brief moment, when the life of the fire "expire[s]").

47. **(E)** Element 1 (meaning) This poem is primarily about old age and death. Trees, sunsets, and fires are used as vehicles within the poem.

48. **(D)** Element 6 (use of language) We are to "behold" "in me" (the speaker) "That time of year." How can a time of year be seen in a person? This poem is built upon a conventional metaphor that has been used many times in literature and in the popular culture:

> spring = birth and youth
> summer = prime of life
> fall = retirement and "golden years"
> winter = old age and death

Forms of this metaphor can be found in poetry, in music, and even in expressions such as "a May-December romance."

49. **(B)** Element 6 (use of language) The metaphor here is an implied comparison: the speaker's approaching death is like the twilight after sunset—a time just before death comes in line 8. Sunrise and sunset representing life and death is another conventional metaphor commonly found in literature.

50. **(A)** Element 6 (use of language) The reader sees in the speaker the "fire" (line 9) that lies on the "ashes of his youth" (line 10); consequently, if the fire is his life, the ashes are what remains of the life that is spent or gone.

51. **(D)** Element 4 (tone) The leaves of summer have yellowed, fallen, and no doubt blown away (line 2) and the birds with their sweet songs are gone (line 4), leaving the tree (representing the speaker) alone—shaking against the cold (line 3).

52. **(D)** Element 7 (meanings in context) The speaker wants the reader to "behold" (line 1) in him the "time of year" (line 1)—obviously the late fall of life. But in this request, he must also look at himself. At first he sees how late in the season it is (the trees have "yellow leaves"). Then he observes "or none," suggesting an emotional sense of loss. Yet he adds "or few" leaves "do hang." Why? Is he not yet ready to face completely "bare" limbs (line 4)? This suggests human uncertainties about life and death on the part of the speaker.

53. **(A)** Element 2 (form) This final couplet makes the point of the poem—the summary concept that when someone is old and dying, like a tree in winter (lines 1–4), the sun about to set (lines 5–8), and a fire going out (lines 9–12), this condition should "make thy love more strong" (line 13).

54. **(D)** Element 6 (use of language) The personification (the giving of human qualities) to sleep "that seals up all in rest" (line 8) makes sleep more threatening as "Death's second self" (line 8).

55. **(D)** Element 6 (use of language) Washington makes an implied comparison (a metaphor) in these lines, likening unity of government to a support pillar and likening real independence to an edifice or large building. In so doing, he states a conclusion: Real independence requires unity of government (B). He states a principle (unity of government is a main support of real independence) in a concise, somewhat aphoristic manner (A). The rather impassioned, definitely persuasive tone (C) is established in part by the use of "dear" and "It is justly so." These lines do not, however, establish distance between speaker and subject (D). On the contrary, use of the word "also" implies that unity of government was "dear" to the speaker some time ago.

56. **(A)** Element 4 (tone) The speaker's fatherly (paternal) concern for the well-being of his fellow-Americans can be seen in the second paragraph where he expresses concern that you "should properly estimate the immense value of your national union to your collective and individual happiness…." The patriotic tone is throughout, particularly in the third paragraph in which he directly addresses "the just pride of patriotism."

57. **(E)** Element 7 (meanings in context) The "truth" that "different causes" will try "to weaken in your minds" is that "unity of government… is a main pillar in the edifice of your real independence"—independence depends upon unity of government (E).

58. **(B)** Element 2 (form) The first paragraph makes the reader emotionally care about government unity by associating it with such connotatively charged words as "peace…safety…prosperity." Then the second paragraph poses a threat to "that very liberty which you so highly prize," a threat of artifices (tricks), a threat of minds weakened to "truth," a threat of "batteries of internal and external enemies…." Making the reader care, then posing a threat creates a sense of emotional tension.

59. **(C)** Element 2 (form) Of the four forms or types of composition (narration, description, exposition, and argumentation), this portion of Washington's speech is mostly argumentative; his purpose is to convince his listeners of the truth of his proposition. Writers can include the elements of several methods of organization in argumentation; however, argumentation generally has at its core the examination of a possible relationship between a conclusion and a premise (evidence from which the conclusion can be drawn.) One conclusion-premise relationship in this passage is:

Conclusion: "The unity of government…is dear to you."
Premise: [because it makes possible] "your real independence…your tranquility at home, your peace abroad…."

Do you see any other conclusions and premises?

60. **(A)** Element 6 (use of language) The speaker uses a military metaphor (an implied comparison) to describe the threats against the "truth" of governmen-

tal unity. He describes their systems of beliefs as a "political fortress" and the tricks and attempts on the part of the "internal and external enemies" to destroy those beliefs as "batteries" (tactical military weapons).

Selections Used in Diagnostic Test One

Questions

1–10: *My Kinsman, Major Molineux* by Nathaniel Hawthorne

11–19: "Proof to No Purpose" by Robert Herrick

20–26: *The Importance of Being Earnest* by Oscar Wilde

27–35: "My Friend, the Things That Do Attain" by Henry Howard, Earl of Surrey

36–44: *Work: A Study of Experience* by Louisa May Alcott

45–54: "That Time of Year" by William Shakespeare

55–60: "Farewell Address" by George Washington

PART II

STRENGTHEN YOUR READING COMPREHENSION SKILLS

CHAPTER 5

What Literary Terms Do I Need to Know?

CHAPTER 6

What Literary Elements Will Be on the Test?

The Seven Literary Elements

Meaning

Form

(Narrative) Voice

Tone

Character

Use of Language

Meaning(s) in Context

CHAPTER 7

How Are These Elements Tested?

CHAPTER 8

How Am I Doing Now?

Diagnostic Test Two

What Literary Terms Do I Need to Know?

If you are short on time, glance over the Index of Terms and Concepts and go directly to those that are unfamiliar or that you would like to review. If you have time, however, be smart and review each chapter sequentially. Even though you may know how to define the terms and concepts, you may be surprised how much reviewing these chapters will help your performance on the test.

TERM ALERT   LEVEL ONE: THE ESSENTIALS

You really need to know the following terms and concepts for the test. Begin with these.

Alliteration 126	Heroic couplet 17, 79	Personification 169
Allusion 169	Hyperbole 169, 170	Plot 77
Antagonist 145	Iambic pentameter 77	Protagonist 145
Blank verse 17, 79	Inference 12	Rhyme 79
Character(ization) 145	Irony 170	Rhythm 77
Context 11	Metaphor 169	Simile 168
Couplet 17, 79	Narrative 77	Sonnet 17, 79
Diction 170	Onomatopoeia 126	Theme 60
Free verse 17, 79	Paradox 169	Tone 126

TERM WATCH **LEVEL TWO: BE ON THE SAFE SIDE**

This list consists of terms and concepts that some SAT Literature Test–prep educators think might appear on the test. Others, however, do not include them on their "most likely" list. Which of the terms and concepts in Group Two will the SAT Literature Test that you take include? Only time will tell. You may already know most of them; but to be on the safe side, glance over this list for any that are unfamiliar.

Allegory 172	Exciting force 84	Point of view 109, 110
Anachronism 172	Exposition 80, 84	Resolution 84
Analogy 172	Fable 80	Rhetorical question 171
Anastrophe 208	Falling action 80, 84	Rising action 80, 84
Anecdote 60	Farce 80	Rhyme scheme 80
Anthropomorphism 170	Figure of speech 170	Satire 80, 110
Antihero(ine) 145	Figurative language 168, 170	Setting 79, 127
Antithesis 172	First-person view 110	Soliloquy 85
Apostrophe 172	Foil 145	Sprung rhythm 80
Aside 85	Genre 79	Stanza 83
Assonance 127	Introduction 84	Style 127
Ballad 84	Metonymy 170	Surrealism 84
Climax 80, 84	Monologue 85	Symbol 62, 171
Comedy 80	Ode 83	Synecdoche 171
Complication 80, 84	Oxymoron 172	Syntax 202
Concrete poetry 84	Parable 80	Theater (absurd) 84
Conclusion 84	Parody 85	Tragedy 80
Consonance 128	Parallelism 202	Tragic hero(ine) 145
Crisis 84	Pastoral 127	Turning point 84
Dénouement 80, 84	Pathos 145	Voice 109
Elegy 83	Perspective 109	Third-person view 109, 110

TERM REVIEW **LEVEL THREE: OTHER TERMS AND CONCEPTS**

This list represents just a few of the many terms and concepts that you have learned over the years and probably take for granted. Don't. Instead, remember that the questions will test your skills in identifying and understanding how the terms and concepts are used in literary selections. A review of any that seem vague or unfamiliar can get your mind thinking in the right literary direction.

Aphorism 203	Interior monologue 109
Argumentative purpose 60	Legend 88
Atmosphere 129	Literal meaning 61, 168
Cliché 204	Maxims 209
Climate 145	Mood 128
Confidant(e) 146	Myth 88
Conflict 80, 84	Narrative purpose 60
Connotation 203	Organizing principles (list) 87
Denotation 203	Pathos 145
Descriptive purpose 60	Persona 110
Dialect 209	Persuasive purpose 60
Dramatic monologue 85	Poetic diction 209
Empathy 145	Poetic license 96
Epigram 80, 85	Poetic syntax 208
Epithet 172	Pun 173
Euphemism 173	Realism 85
Euphony 130	Romance 85
Expository purpose 60	Sarcasm 170
Expressive purpose 60	Sequence patterns (list) 86
Feeling 129	Stereotype character 147
Flashback 146	Stream of consciousness 109
Folktale 88	Superhero(ine) 146
Foreshadowing 146	Tale 86
Hero(ine) 145	Tall tale 86
Idiom 204	Thesis 61
Image(ry) 168	Topic 60
Implication 204	Understatement (meiosis) 169, 170
Informative purpose 60	Villain(ess) 145

What Literary Elements Will Be on the Test?

CHAPTER 6

The purpose of the Literature Test is for you to show how well you can analyze and interpret selections taken from works of literature. The questions are based on various literary elements. These include: Meaning; Form; (Narrative) Voice; Tone; Character; Use of Language; and Meanings of Sentences, Lines, Phrases, and Words in Context, hereinafter called Meaning(s) in Context.

Each of the literary elements can be identified individually; however, they also join together to unify the writing and produce a blend that is unique to that particular work.

Example

To illustrate how the elements share concepts and functions, read these lines taken from John Donne's "The Legacy."

> When last I died, and dear, I die
> As often as from thee I go,
> Though it be but an hour ago
> —And Lovers' hours be full eternity—
>
> (ca. 1600)

Lines 1–4 are structured as elements

(A) in antithesis
(B) that overstate the case
(C) that understate the case
(D) of a narrative poem
(E) of a riddle

Explanation: These lines contain an exaggeration or hyperbole (a *Use of Language*). The speaker claims to die every time he leaves his lover. The hyperbole introduces his theme, a combination of *Meaning* and *Form*. Is the speaker (*Character*) sincere (*Voice* and *Tone*)? Only context might show.

Correct Answer: **B**

LITERARY ELEMENT NUMBER ONE: MEANING

In any given literary selection, what is the writer's purpose? What is the speaker's point? Can you take the words at face value? The answers to these and similar questions are at the heart of a work's meaning.

What terms do I need to know that relate to meaning?

To refresh your memory, review these terms:

TERM ALERT | **1. Theme**

Definition: The *theme* summarizes or asserts to the reader some main point, doctrine, or generalization about life, love, religion, the condition of the world, and so forth. Occasionally, the writer will directly state the theme, but more often it is implied.

In some prose fiction, the theme can be seen as the "message" or "moral of the story." *Aesop's Fables* are noted for the concise nature of their theme statements.

TERM WATCH | **2. Anecdote**

Definition: An anecdote is a brief narrative centered on an event or incident.

TERM REVIEW | **3. Descriptive or expressive purpose**

Definition: In description, the prose writer, poet, or dramatist attempts to "paint a picture with words." Description can be factual (describing, for example, the color and dimensions of an object) or impressionistic (such as expressing what love feels like).

TERM REVIEW | **4. Expository or informative purpose**

Definition: Exposition explains or tells how to do something. Most instructional textbooks are written with an expository purpose. The expository or informative writer includes ideas and facts about the focus subject.

TERM REVIEW | **5. Narrative purpose**

Definition: A narrator tells a story. The story may focus on an incident or brief episode (as in an **anecdote**), chronicle a hero's adventurous relationship to the history of a nation (as in an epic poem), or follow the history of a family's generations (as in a saga). An important element of narration is time—events unfolding through time.

TERM REVIEW | **6. Argumentative and/or persuasive purpose**

Definition: A writer or speaker uses argumentation to convince readers or hearers of the truth (or falsehood) of a proposition. The purpose of persuasive writing, however, is to convince the reader or hearer that some action must be taken. Expository, informative, and argumentative writing focuses on the subject; persuasion focuses on the reader or listener, as well.

TERM REVIEW | **7. Topic**

Definition: The topic is the subject of a work, usually expressed as a word or short phrase. Examples include war, love, business, and children. Some very popular topics are survival, children raised by animals, UFO invasions and abductions, lost pets, the end of the world, and good versus evil.

8. Thesis

Definition: The theme, the central idea of the work, is also called the **thesis** in non-fiction prose. The thesis refers to the writer's position on the subject. The thesis may be directly stated or may be implied; it might lead off the first paragraph of the selection or the author might "build" his or her main points to a concluding thesis.

What else do I need to know about meaning?

1. The Writer's Purpose

You should be able to identify why the work was written. Is the author's purpose to (1) describe something or express an emotion, (2) explain how to do something or how something works, or to inform the reader, (3) tell a story or chain of events, (4) argue a point or persuade the reader to do something?

Although a literary selection may be identified as having predominantly one purpose, writers often use elements of the other three types to aid in the development of the main purpose. For instance, description is frequently used in narration; describing details about oppressive heat, black water, and clinging leeches helps the narrator tell his or her story of convicts escaping a swamp-bound prison camp. An expository writer, aiming to "tell the facts," can narrate an anecdote (an episode or event) to help the reader better understand the information; and political writers often incorporate illustrative narration in their persuasive speeches.

2. The Effects of a Work

Determining the meaning of a work also involves looking at its *effect*. The emotional impact, the impression the work leaves on the reader, is part of its effect. Skillful writers will plan a certain effect (perhaps feelings of anger, aversion, joyful laughter). Sometimes an effect happens unintentionally, without the writer's deliberate plan or even conscious knowledge. A test question might ask what effect a word, phrase, line, situation, or the entire work has on the reader or on a character within the work.

3. Levels of Meaning

Another way to determine the meaning of a literary selection is to look for different levels of meaning.

The **literal** meaning is based on taking the work at its "face value"—without examining any figurative levels.

At the **allegorical** level, particularly in narrative works, each object, person, place, and event represents something else, with the characters of the narrative personifying abstract qualities. An entire work may be allegorical (as, for example, in *Pilgrim's Progress* in which the man named Christian meets Mr. Worldly Wiseman—a story in which people and places represent the qualities after which they are named) or a literary selection may incorporate a few allegorical elements.

Symbolic words and phrases have dual meanings, the literal or face value meaning and a representative meaning. The symbol stands for something else but in a less structured way than an allegory. "Old Glory, Mother, and apple pie" are symbols of down-home American patriotism.

At the **figurative** level, the writer strives for a meaning other than or beyond the standard or literal meanings of the words by using figurative language. Examples include simile (a comparison using "like" or "as"—lips as red as a rose) and metaphor (an implied comparison—rose-red lips).

4. The Parts Versus the Work as a Whole

In a testing situation, you may be asked to determine the meaning of an entire selection or of just a portion of that selection. You may be asked to identify how the meaning of each part contributes to the whole, or how it contrasts that meaning.

5. The Subject and Main Idea

The meaning of a work also includes the statement of its topic, theme, or thesis.

6. Conflict

At the center of meaning in a narrative or drama is conflict. Conflict (the good guys versus the bad guys, the obstacles to overcome, the love of winning, and so forth) will naturally affect meaning. Meaning often results from how the characters deal with conflict.

How could questions over meaning be worded?

The following selections and their questions illustrate some of the ways meaning might be tested.

> **Example 1**

Descriptive/Expressive Purpose

These four lines from a poem by Percy Bysshe Shelley (1819) are very emotionally expressive. First, identify the speaker's expressive purpose. In other words, what types of emotions is he describing? Then you can spot the one he is NOT describing.

> From thy nest every rafter
> Will rot, and thine eagle home
> Leave thee naked to laughter,
> When leaves fall and cold winds come.

The speaker's description of the silent auditor's future is NOT

(A) extreme
(B) pessimistic
(C) contemptuous
(D) dangerous
(E) optimistic

Explanation: A *silent auditor* or listener is addressed by the speaker, but does not respond to the speaker. In this poem, the silent auditor is being compared to a young eagle whose nest falls from rotted rafters, leaving him or her naked and subject to the contemptuous disgrace of laughter and the dangers of cold.

Correct Answer: **E**

Example 2

Informative Purpose

Although somewhat narrative, notice the textbook style of this more modern selection.

> In a brilliant move to unify the kingdoms against the Danes, King Alfred consolidated the people on the basis of their "Englishness," with the English language at the heart of their new awareness of national identity. In a sense,
> *Line* King Alfred used the English language to establish and at the same time save
> *(5)* a nation. Once the people were united against the Danes, Alfred moved boldly ahead. He replaced Latin with English, had English chronicles written to give the people a sense of history, established a standardized English writing system, and earned for himself the title of "founder of English prose" by writing (in A.D. 887) the first example of completed English prose
> *(10)* (*Handbook*).

(1996)

The speaker's main purpose in the selection is to

(A) inform readers about how Alfred used English language politically
(B) make Alfred the Great famous
(C) give Alfred the Great the credit due him
(D) inform readers about English prose
(E) explain how *Handbook* came to be the first English prose

Explanation: In looking for a main purpose, examine the selection as a whole. What is it all about? Alfred used the English language to save England from the Danes. Answers B, C, and E are true, but too narrow to be the main purpose. Answer D is too general.

Correct Answer: **A**

Example 3

Anecdote

This passage is taken from Anne Royall's account of her visit to "Peal's Museum" in 1826.

> The first object of my inquiry was the mammoth skeleton, but I was greatly disappointed in its appearance.... I beheld it without surprise or emotion.... I could not forbear smiling at a gentleman who, like myself, had
> *Line* formed extravagant notions of the mammoth. He stooped under the rail in
> (5) order to examine it minutely, and scraping a part of the skeleton with his pen-knife, swore "it was nothing but wood," saying to his friend, that he was cheated out of his money; they both retired displeased.

TIP

To answer this question, you must know the word "anecdote" <u>and</u> recognize <u>why</u> Royall uses an anecdote.

The anecdote within the passage is used mainly

(A) in antithesis
(B) as hyperbole
(C) to contrast the speaker's view
(D) as a revelation of the characters of people
(E) to reinforce the speaker's point

Explanation: Although the anecdote (a little story, in this case used within a larger account) provides some descriptive detail and reveals how people can react in a situation, the speaker identifies herself with the gentleman ("who, like myself"). The result is a reinforcement of her point. She is not alone in her opinion.

Correct Answer: **E**

Example 4

Persuasive Purpose

Clearly, the portion of Abbey Kelly Foster's speech (1851) that follows is meant to persuade her listeners. The question, however, requires you to identify what she wants her listeners to do.

> My friends, I feel that in throwing out this idea, I have done what was left for me to do. But I did not rise to make a speech—my life has been my speech. For fourteen years I have advocated this cause by my daily life.
> *Line* Bloody feet, sisters, have worn smooth the path by which you have come up
> (5) hither. You will not need to speak when you speak by your everyday life. Oh, how truly does Webster say, action, action is eloquence! Let us, then, when we go home, go not to complain, but to work. Do not go home to complain of the men, but go and make greater exertions than ever to discharge your everyday duties.

The speaker's central call to action can be summarized as which of the following?

(A) Put your money where your mouth is.
(B) The early bird catches the worm.
(C) A stitch in time saves nine.
(D) A picture is worth a thousand words.
(E) Don't just talk the talk, but walk the walk.

Explanation: "Do not go home to complain …, but go and make greater exertions…." This speech aims to convince, to persuade the hearers to action.

Correct Answer: **E**

Example 5

Emotional Impact Affecting Meaning

How do you feel about a fly drinking from your cup? The effect of the first four lines of "The Fly" by William Oldys (ca. 1750) may make you want to stop reading, but eventually he makes a serious point.

> Busy, curious, thirsty fly,
> Gently drink, and drink as I;
> Freely welcome to my cup,
Line   Could'st thou sip, and sip it up;
(5)   Make the most of life you may,
> Life is short and wears away.
> Just alike, both mine and thine,
> Hasten quick to their decline;
> Thine's a summer, mine's no more,
(10)   Though repeated to threescore;
> Threescore summers when they're gone,
> Will appear as short as one.

The focus of this poem is

(A) the speaker's fondness for a fly
(B) a fly drinking from the speaker's cup
(C) the fly's impending death
(D) the relative brevity of life
(E) the speaker's impending death

Explanation: Each of the above five answer choices correctly addresses some level of meaning in this poem. The best description of the poem's focus, however, is the answer choice that summarizes the speaker's intent or main point. Why does the speaker fondly welcome the fly to drink from his cup (A and B)? Because the fly's life is short (C). Why does the speaker care that the fly's life is short? Because the speaker's life also seems short (E). What is the <u>effect</u> (emotional impact) of this comparison on the poem's meaning? It establishes, in relation to the life cycle, a similarity between the speaker and the fly: that whether life lasts a summer or threescore summers, life is relatively short.

Correct Answer: **D**

Example 6

Levels of Meaning

In Alfred, Lord Tennyson's "Dark House" (ca. 1885), what is the speaker doing?

> Dark house, by which once more I stand
> Here in the long unlovely street,
> Doors, where my heart was used to beat
> So quickly, waiting for a hand,
>
> *Line*
> (5) A hand that can be clasped no more—
> Behold me, for I cannot sleep,
> And like a guilty thing I creep
> At earliest morning to the door.
>
> He is not here; but far away
> (10) The noise of life begins again,
> And ghastly thro' the drizzling rain
> On the bald street breaks the blank day.

The condition of the speaker is that he

(A) has been evicted
(B) has insomnia
(C) is insane
(D) is dreaming
(E) is unemployed

As used in this poem, the "dark house" represents

(A) nightmares
(B) ghosts
(C) abandonment and loneliness
(D) grief and death
(E) urban decay

The description in line 7 implies

(A) the speaker is subhuman
(B) avoidance of the law
(C) secrecy and shame
(D) the house is haunted
(E) a need for confession

TIP

When test questions deal with levels of meaning, always begin by identifying the literal meaning.

Explanation: The speaker literally cannot sleep in line 6. The house is a "dark house" because the speaker can no longer clasp the hand of the one who lived there (lines 4–5), making the place a symbol of the speaker's grief over the probable death of his friend. Line 7 compares the speaker to "a guilty thing" that creeps, a very emotional comparison that implies a sense of secrecy and shame. As readers, we cannot help but wonder why he feels this way. Does he feel somehow responsible for the person's death? Does he feel guilty because he is alive and his friend is not? Perhaps he is ashamed to show such emotion openly? Had they argued and not had opportunity to restore fellowship?

Correct Answers: **B, D, C**

Example 7

Parts → Whole

Reexamine Shakespeare's sonnet that you worked with in Diagnostic Test I. Notice that the silent auditor of this poem, the person being addressed by the speaker, appears to be the object of his love.

> That time of year thou mayst in me behold
> When yellow leaves, or none, or few, do hang
> Upon those boughs which shake against the cold,
> Bare ruined choirs, where late the sweet birds sang.
> In me thou see'st the twilight of such day
> As after sunset fadeth in the west;
> Which by and by black night doth take away,
> Death's second self, that seals up all in rest.
> In me thou see'st the glowing of such fire,
> That on the ashes of his youth doth lie,
> As the deathbed whereon it must expire,
> Consumed with that which it was nourished by.
> This thou perceiv'st, which makes thy love more strong,
> To love that well which thou must leave ere long.

Line appears at line 4; *(5)* at line 5; *(10)* at line 10.

In lines 1–4, the speaker's purpose is to

(A) confess he is growing older
(B) predict the weather
(C) hint at health problems
(D) protest the coming cold
(E) describe a fall scene

In lines 5–8, the speaker makes death seem

(A) frightening
(B) longed for
(C) beautiful
(D) fading
(E) inevitable

In lines 9–12, the speaker deals with

(A) the fiery passions of youth
(B) youth and eventually life being gone
(C) the fires of love being extinguished
(D) deathbed arrangements
(E) burning wood

The silent auditor's love is "more strong" (line 13) because

(A) the speaker must leave in the fall
(B) the silent auditor has sleeping sickness
(C) the speaker has suffered burns
(D) the speaker is dying
(E) the silent auditor is trapped with an aging lover

Explanation: The speaker compares growing old and dying to the approach of winter (lines 1–4), the end of a day (lines 5–9), and a dying fire (lines 9–12). However, each comparison reveals a slightly different side to his meaning. First, he confesses that he is growing older (line 1). Next, he says that death is inevitable (line 8). Finally, the speaker deals with the fact that he is no longer young—his youth is burned up ashes. Taken all together, three parts of the poem tell us that the speaker is dying. The speaker's point? Love me now while you can (the final couplet).

Correct Answers: A, E, B, D

Example 8

Main Subject and Theme

The question following these lines taken from Frances Willard's speech in 1876 seems simple, but it requires you to identify the <u>main</u> subject when more than one subject is possible.

> . . . . He told us of the news that day that had brought about Neal Dow, and the great fight for prohibition down in Maine, and then he said: "I wonder if poor, rum-cursed Wisconsin will ever get a law like
> *Line* that!" And mother rocked awhile in silence, in the dear old chair I love,
> *(5)* and then she gently said: "Yes, Josiah, there'll be such a law all over the land some day, when women vote."
>
> My father had never heard her say as much before. He was a great conservative; so he looked tremendously astonished, and replied in his keen, sarcastic voice: "And pray, how will you arrange it so that women shall
> *(10)* vote?" Mother's chair went to and fro a little faster for a minute, and then, looking not into his face, but into the flickering flame of the grate, she slowly answered: "Well, I say to you, as the Apostle Paul said to his jailor: 'You have put us into prison, we being Romans, and you must come and take us out.'"

(15)   That was a seed-thought in a girl's brain and heart. Years passed on, in which nothing more was said upon the dangerous theme. My brother grew to manhood, and soon after he was twenty-one years old he went. with Father to vote.

What is the main subject of this passage?

(A) Parenthood
(B) Growing up
(C) Prohibition
(D) Interpersonal relationships
(E) Women's suffrage

Explanation: Both Prohibition and women's suffrage are subjects here, but which one is the *main* subject? Paragraph 1: Prohibition laws will come when women vote. Paragraph 2: A confrontation occurs over women voting. Paragraph 3: A young girl watches men go off to vote.

Correct Answer: **E**

What is "the dangerous theme" in the last paragraph?

(A) Voters must enact Prohibition laws in Wisconsin.
(B) Mother should become involved in the Prohibition movement.
(C) Mother should arrange for women's suffrage.
(D) Father must vote for Prohibition laws in Wisconsin.
(E) Men must give women the right to vote.

Explanation: First, establish why the theme is dangerous. The danger is revealed in the mother's response to her husband's question about how she would "arrange it so that women shall vote." Her answer is an allusion to Paul, the Apostle, who questioned his jailors' right to incarcerate him, a Roman citizen. The context makes the reference clear. They violated his innate rights by putting him in jail just as, in the context of the mother's opinion, men had violated women's innate right to vote. The jailors must grant Paul's freedom from jail; men must grant women their freedom to vote.

Correct Answer: **E**

Example 9

Main Point

This passage is taken from Samuel Johnson's *The Rambler*, No. 4 (1750).

I remember a remark made by Scaliger upon Pontanus, that all his writings are filled with the same images; and that if you take from him his lilies and his roses, his satyrs and his dryads, he will have nothing left that can be *Line* called poetry. In like manner almost all the fictions of the last age will van- *(5)* ish, if you deprive them of a hermit and a wood, a battle and a shipwreck.

The speaker's main point is that

(A) the writings of Scaliger are critical
(B) the errors of Pontanus include overuse of certain images
(C) fictions of the last age are difficult to understand
(D) past writers have overused conventional characters and images
(E) poetry and fiction depend on conventional characters and images

Explanation: Conventional characters and images, such as those mentioned in the selection, are those that recur in various literary forms. Even if you do not know what a satyr or dryad might be, you can tell his point from "lilies and his roses." The overuse of them can make the character or image become expected and stereotypical. Although answers A and B are in the passage, these statements are too narrow for the theme statement. The speaker generalizes to say that past writers (represented by Pontanus and those of the "last age") filled their poetry and fictions with conventional characters (represented by hermits) and images (represented by lilies and roses).

Correct Answer: **D**

Example 10

Conflict

You should immediately see the conflict between Hardcastle and his wife in Oliver Goldsmith's *She Stoops to Conquer* (1773). This conflict forms the basis of the main idea of the selection.

Act I

Scene.—*A Chamber in an old-fashioned House*

Enter Mrs. Hardcastle *and* Mr. Hardcastle.

Mrs. Hardcastle. I vow, Mr. Hardcastle, you're very particular. Is there a creature in the whole country, but ourselves, that does not take a trip to town now and then, to rub off the rust a little? . . .

Line *Hardcastle.* Ay, and bring back vanity and affectation to last them the whole
(5) year. I wonder why London cannot keep its own fools at home. In my time, the follies of the town crept slowly among us, but now they travel faster than a stage-coach. . . .

Mrs. Hardcastle. Ay, *your* times were fine times, indeed; you have been telling us of *them* for many a long year. Here we live in an old rumbling mansion,
(10) that looks for all the world like an inn, but that we never see company. Our best visitors are old Mrs. Oddfish, the curate's wife, and little Cripplegate, the lame dancing-master: And all our entertainment your old stories of Prince Eugene and the Duke of Marlborough. I hate such old-fashioned trumpery.

(15) *Hardcastle.* And I love it. I love every thing that's old: old friends, old times, old manners, old books, old wine; and, I believe, Dorothy [*taking her hand*], you'll own I have been pretty fond of an old wife.

The main idea of the discussion between Hardcastle and his wife is

(A) visiting neighbors
(B) vanity
(C) resistance to change
(D) gossip with neighbors
(E) growing older

Explanation: What are they talking about? She hates things that are "old-fashioned" and wants "to rub off the rust a little," to remove the old and expose a fresh, new surface. He resists such change; he loves the old: a conflict.

Correct Answer: **C**

Test Taker → Test Maker

If you were writing SAT Literature tests, what questions about meaning would you ask? Here is an opportunity for you to approach meaning from the test writer's point of view.

Read the following selection from *The Prairie Traveler*, published in 1859 and described as "A Hand-book for Overland Expeditions." The writer, Captain Randolph B. Marcy, offers survival strategies to his nineteenth-century readers who want "to make the overland journey to the Pacific."

The main object at which I have aimed in the following pages has been to explain and illustrate, as clearly and succinctly as possible, the best methods of performing the duties devolving upon the prairie traveler, so as to meet
Line their contingencies under all circumstances,...
(5)   STORMS.
In Western Texas, during the autumn and winter months, storms arise very suddenly, and, when accompanied by a north wind, are very severe upon men and animals; indeed, they are sometimes so terrific as to make it necessary for travelers to hasten to the nearest sheltered place to save the lives of their ani-
(10) mals. When these storms come from the north, they are called "northers;" and as, during the winter season, the temperature often undergoes a sudden change of many degrees at the time the storm sets in, the perspiration is checked, and the system receives an instantaneous shock, against which it requires great vital energy to bear up. Men and animals are not, in this mild climate, prepared for these capricious meteoric revolutions, and they not
(15) unfrequently perish under their effects.
While passing near the head waters of the Colorado in October, 1849, I left one of my camps at an early hour in the morning under a mild and soft atmosphere, with a gentle breeze from the south, but had marched only a short distance when the wind suddenly whipped around into the north,
(20) bringing with it a furious chilling rain, and in a short time the road became so soft and heavy as to make the labor of pulling the wagons over it very exhausting upon the mules, and they came into camp in a profuse sweat, with the rain pouring down in torrents upon them.
They were turned out of harness into the most sheltered place that could
(25) be found; but, instead of eating, as was their custom, they turned their heads from the wind, and remained in that position, chilled and trembling, without making the least effort to move. The rain continued with unabated fury during the entire day and night, and on the following morning thirty-five out of one hundred and ten mules had perished, while those remaining could hardly
(30) be said to have had a spark of vitality left....
The mistake I made was in driving the mules after the "norther" commenced. Had I gone immediately into camp, before they became heated and wearied, they would probably have eaten the grass, and this, I have no doubt, would have saved them; but as it was, their blood became heated from over-
(35) work, and the sudden chill brought on a reaction which proved fatal. If an

animal will eat his forage plentifully, there is but little danger of his perishing with cold. This I assert with much confidence, as I once, when traveling with about 1500 horses and mules, encountered the most terrific snow-storm that has been known within the memory of the oldest mountaineers. It com-
(40) menced on the last day of April and continued....

A great place to begin is to identify the writer's purpose(s). Put checkmarks before any of the following purposes that apply. There may be more than one.

_____descriptive   _____narrative

_____expressive   _____argumentative

_____expository/informative   _____persuasive

Discussion

How many did you check? He tells us what a "norther" is and how to deal with one (expository/informative purpose). He uses traces of descriptive language ("capricious meteoric revolutions"). He uses anecdotal narrative (pointing out his own mistakes) to illustrate what he is describing and to convince readers that he is telling them accurate information (argumentative purpose).

This selection is a gold mine for questions over multiple purposes. What incorrect answer choices would you list for this question stem? We'll give you the first one to get started. Be sure to write a correct answer (E).

What is the writer's main purpose?

(A) To describe a norther*

(B) _____

(C) _____

(D) _____

(E) _____

> ⊚ **STRATEGY**
>
> The best strategy to find the writer's main purpose or idea among many possible purposes or ideas is to determine the context.

How did you word your correct answer choice (E)? The context of this selection is an experienced prairie traveler (the writer) instructing less experienced travelers. In this context, the writer uses a mixture of informative, descriptive, and narrative writing **to persuade travelers to go immediately into camp when a norther approaches.** You could state your correct answer directly, or you could be less specific: **To warn and instruct travelers about northers.** Sometimes an answer might be worded as if it is the "moral" of the story: **To persuade readers to do as he says and not what he did when in a norther.**

MEANING IN CONCLUSION

Actually, meaning does not conclude at this point. Meaning provides the foundation for the other six literary elements. Consequently, you will be seeing a lot more about meaning in the chapters that follow.

*Incorrect because this answer is too narrow to be the main purpose in this context.

LITERARY ELEMENT NUMBER TWO: FORM

The College Board has specified that the SAT Subject Test in Literature will include selections from three major forms: **prose**, **poetry**, and **drama**. Under these three "umbrella" genres you will find many other genres. The SAT STL consists of about 40 to 50 percent poetry, 40 to 50 percent prose, and 0 to 20 percent drama.

• Prose

Prose is expression (whether written or spoken) that does not have a regular rhythmic pattern. Prose does have rhythm (called **prose rhythm**), but its rhythm lacks any sustained regularity.

Example

Read these lines taken from Edgar Allan Poe's "The Man in the Crowd."

> As I endeavored, during the brief minute of my original survey, to form
> some analysis of the meaning conveyed, there arose confusedly and paradox-
> ically within my mind, the ideas of vast mental power, of acution, of penu-
> *Line* riousness, of avarice, of coolness, of malice, of blood-thirstiness, of triumph,
> *(5)* of merriment, of excessive terror, of intense—of extreme despair. I felt
> singularly aroused, startled, fascinated.

(ca. 1845)

How does the narrator create a prose rhythm that mirrors his thoughts?

(A) Paradoxical diction
(B) Stream-of-consciousness analogies
(C) Parallel syntax
(D) Use of abstract over concrete diction
(E) Poetic diction

Explanation: Notice the rhythm of his building mental confusion. He has "ideas of vast mental power, of caution, of...of...of...of...of...of...of...of intense—of extreme despair."

Correct Answer: **C**

• Poetry

Poetry is expression that is written in verse, often with some form of regular rhythm. The basis of poetic expression is a heightened sense of perception or consciousness.

A poem can look like prose, and prose can contain poetic elements.

Example

Bell-Tones

Bells have been ringing and marking time in my life. Bells to come for and bells to go by. Bells to ring and bells to hear. Easy bell-tones turn to clattering bells ringing, finally becoming muted into many soft death knells.

Line
(5) I started with Tinker Bell, then listened to school bells between playing in fields of bluebells. Happy bells ringing; proms, parties, and dancing, playing happily and listening to the ringing of sleigh bells. Church bells comforting and confirming and wedding bells promising our love Always; such joy, bluebonnets and baby bonnets, with happy baby bells on baby booties.

Dinner bells called me; laundry bells startled me; cake timers beckoned
(10) me; liberty bells stirred me; jingle bells amused me until all the bells jangled and wrangled metallic as door bells and telephone bells ringing in pairs demanded me.

Then bells rang for help…time to get up, time to sleep, time to eat, time to leave, time to escape danger, time to come and time to go. Bells marked
(15) the hours and the times of my life. Now the beautiful bluebells in fields are calling me once again, mute bells singing soft notes as Church bells sound in blissful bell-tones, while we are waiting for the joyful ringing rapture of the Resurrection.

by L. E. Myers
(1996)

All the following can be said about this poem EXCEPT

(A) it contains personification
(B) the sound of the poem reflects its meaning
(C) ringing bells are symbolic of life's major events
(D) it consists of traditional stanzas
(E) it contains repetition of initial consonants

Explanation: In this question, you are looking for the one answer choice that is false. The poem does contain personification ("bluebells … calling me"). Also, the meaning is reflected and intensified by elements of rhythm (sound) throughout the work, such as the back-and-forth bell-like movement in "time to sleep, time to eat, time to leave…." The ringing bells represent (are symbolic of) major events from birth (baby booties) to death ("soft death knells"). The initial consonant *b* is repeated throughout, with *r* and *p* also repeated in places. Such a sound device is called alliteration. The stanzas, however, look more like prose paragraphs than the traditional stanzas of a poem.

Correct Answer: **D**

Obviously, a clear-cut distinction between prose and poetry is difficult to establish; you need to be constantly alert to the poet's use of prose techniques and the prose writer's borrowing of poetic devices.

• Drama

Drama is a story intended to be acted out on a stage.

Obviously, elements of drama can be found in prose fiction and in narrative poetry. The dramatist can also, however, incorporate elements of prose and poetry within the development of the drama. Take the use of poetic forms in drama as an example. In Elizabethan drama, Marlowe's lower-class characters speak in prose, but the "Good and Bad Angels" speak in blank verse. Of William Shakespeare's plays, a large number are written in blank verse. Shakespeare used poetic elements throughout his dramas to create moods, to project character, to develop plot, and even to signal the mechanical elements of the play.

Example

A striking example is in Shakespeare's *The Tragedy of Julius Caesar* (ca. 1600).

> Act V Scene V
>
> MARCUS BRUTUS. Hence! I will follow.
>   [*Exeunt* CLITUS, DARDANIUS, *and* VOLUMNIUS.]
>   I prithee, Strato, stay thou by the lord:
>   Thou art a fellow of a good respect;
>   Thy life hath had some smatch of honour in it:
>   Hold, then, my sword, and turn away thy face,
>   While I do run upon it. Wilt thou, Strato?
>
> STRATO. Give me your hand first: fare you well, my lord.
>
> MARCUS BRUTUS.
>   Farewell, good Strato.—Caesar, now be still:
>   I kill'd not thee with half so good a will.
>   [*He runs on his sword, and dies.*]

The last words of Marcus Brutus before his suicide are structurally dramatized through the use of

(A) heroic couplet
(B) archaic words
(C) direct address
(D) melodrama
(E) name-dropping

Explanation: Shakespeare ingeniously uses couplets to cue entrances and to close scenes. In this case, he rhymes "still" with "will" to further the dramatic effect of the moment when the struggle between Caesar and Marcus Brutus ends. The two rhyming lines are written in iambic pentameter, making them an example of heroic couplet.

Correct Answer: **A**

Here is the point: Do not make assumptions. **Just because a selection is prose does not mean it cannot contain poetic and dramatic elements.** Dialogue in a drama can be written in poetic form, and poetry, too, can borrow from prose and drama.

What is form?

Meaning might be called the "what?" (as in "What is the writer trying to say?") in a literary selection, and form can be called the "how?" ("How does he or she say it?"). Form includes many different patterns of development or methods of organization that can be used for self-expression, providing information, persuasion, and entertainment.

What terms do I need to know that relate to a work's form?

You should know these terms:

1. Plot and narrative

Definition: A narrative is an account of actions and events. A plot is a summary of the action of the story, including the words and deeds of the characters.

But what precipitates this action? Why does the reader care about the words and deeds of the characters? Conflict. The motivating, driving force that involves both characters and (if written well) involves the readers in the narrative is **conflict**. Conflict makes readers care. Conflict means opposition: person versus person, person versus group, person versus environment, person versus nature, or person versus self. The plot, then, with conflict as its driving force, provides unity for the work.

2. Rhythm

Definition: Rhythm in poetry is a variation of stressed and unstressed sounds that has some type of regular pattern, with grouping of the sounds into units.

3. Iambic pentameter

Definition: Iambic pentameter is a very popular rhythm in English and American poetry. It consists of five units (meters) of unstressed, then stressed syllables in one line of poetry. How can you tell if a poem is written in iambic pentameter?

When you **scan** or read a line of poetry for its rhythm, you first identify which kind of **foot** is being used. A foot is the unit formed by a strong stress or accent (/) and the weak stress(es) or unaccented syllable(s) that accompany it (X).

Iambic foot is illustrated by L. E. Myers in the first stanza of her work called "Stressed and Unstressed":

Iambic foot (X /) unstressed, stressed

X / X / X / X /
Iambic is a line of verse,

    X / X / X /
    That first is weak, then strong.

X / X / X / X /
If this light rhyme you do rehearse,

    X / X / X /
    You're sure to do no wrong.

(1996)

TERM ALERT

TERM ALERT

TERM ALERT

After determining the type of foot, you need to identify the **meter**. Meter refers to how many feet are *in each line.*

Traditionally: one foot   = monometer
two feet   = dimeter
three feet   = trimeter
four feet   = tetrameter
five feet   **= pentameter**
six feet   = hexameter
seven feet   = heptameter
eight feet   = octameter

Iambic pentameter, then, consists of five units, each consisting of a weak or unstressed syllable, followed by a strong stress in a line of poetry.

These lines, taken from Shakespeare's "Sonnet 18," illustrate iambic pentameter:

X /   X /   X /   X /   X /
Shall I / compare / thee to / a sum / mer's day?

X /   X /   X /   X /   X /
Thou art / more love / ly and / more tem / perate:

X   /   X /   X /   X /   X /
Rough winds / do shake / the dar / ling buds / of May,

X   /   X   /   X /   X /   X /
And sum / mer's lease / hath all / too short / a date:

PRACTICE

Of the following pairs of lines, select the sets written entirely in iambic pentameter.

    I. Whoso walks in solitude
       And inhabiteth the wood
   II. Now that the winter's gone, the earth hath lost
      Her snow-white robes, and now no more the frost
  III. And hide in cooling trees, a voice will run
     From hedge to hedge about the new-mown mead
  IV. I feel a newer life in every gale;
     The winds that fan the flowers
   V. Ah! sun-flower! weary of time,
     Who countest the steps of the Sun

(A) I and II
(B) II and III
(C) III and IV
(D) IV and V
(E) III, IV, and V

Explanation: Although questions about rhythm on the actual test will be aimed at a specific poem, the question above gives you an opportunity to practice identifying iambic pentameter lines. Both lines in I lack five beats; II and III are iambic pentameter; in IV the first line is iambic pentameter, but the second has only three beats. (Sometimes the poet will change rhythms or alternate rhythms within a poem.) In V, the rhythm is not iambic (X/) in either line.

Correct Answer: **B**

4. Rhyme

TERM ALERT

Definition: Rhyme is when two or more words have a sound in common or echo one another.

The degree to which words rhyme is affected, of course, by pronunciation. You should be aware that pronunciations have changed in time, pronunciations differ nationally between American English and British English, and pronunciations differ regionally. Essentially, the argument is summarized by "Did you pick a 'tomato' (long *a*) or 'tomawto' from your garden?" and "Is your mother's sister your 'aunt' (pronounced as *ant*) or your 'awnt'"? Differences can be subtle, as in *quinine* (American *kwi-nin* with long *i* in both syllables, British *kwin-en* with short *i* in the first syllable and long *e* in the last) or striking, as in *clerk* (American pronunciation usually rhyming with *work*, British pronunciation usually rhyming with *lark*), used by John Donne in "And though fowl now be scarce, yet there are clerks, / The sky not falling, think we may have larks."

5. Free verse

TERM ALERT

Definition: Free verse is just that—free of a regular meter. Free verse often (but not always) is characterized by short, irregular lines and no rhyme pattern. Free verse depends on the effective and intense use of pauses, words selected not only for meaning but for how that meaning is intensified by their position in the poem.

6. Blank verse

TERM ALERT

Definition: Blank verse is written in iambic pentameter, but with no rhyme pattern. It is the major verse form used by Shakespeare in his plays.

7. Couplet and **heroic couplet**

TERM ALERT

Definition: A couplet consists of two grouped lines that rhyme. Heroic couplets are written in iambic pentameter.

8. Sonnet

TERM ALERT

Definition: A sonnet is a 14-line poem written in iambic pentameter. You should be able to identify a given poem as a sonnet.

9. Genre

TERM WATCH

Definition: Genre is the product of a work's sequence pattern, organization of thought, subject, and/or structure (parts).

10. Setting

TERM WATCH

Definition: The setting is the time and place of the story, as well as the socioeconomic background of the characters.

TERM WATCH ## 11. Plot structure

Definition: In its simplest, most predictable form, a narrative plot looks like this:

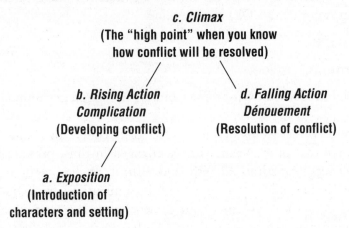

Some genres have very predictable plotlines and are sometimes called formula plots. They consist of variations on the same plotline story after story.

TERM WATCH ## 12. Effects that result from plot

Tragedy. In a tragic narrative, humans do not and cannot overcome inevitable failure; although they may demonstrate grace and courage along the way.

Comedy. A comic effect is produced when the plot leads the characters into amusing situations, ridiculous complications, and a happy ending.

Satire. A narrative is satiric when it makes a subject look ridiculous. The subjects being derided can range from an individual to society. When a satire is in the extreme, it is called a **farce**.

TERM WATCH ## 13. Fable

Definition: The ***fable*** centers on a moral. The moral is often expressed in an ***epigram*** put forth by the writer or one of the characters at the end. Examples include the famous fables of Aesop.

TERM WATCH ## 14. Parable

Definition: The ***parable*** teaches a lesson by using very tightly structured allegory. As pointed out by Professors William Harmon and the late C. Hugh Holman of the University of North Carolina at Chapel Hill in *A Handbook to Literature* (Macmillan Publishing Company, 1992), the most famous parables are those of Jesus Christ. (Examples include the "Prodigal Son," the "Parable of the Sowers," and the "Parable of the Workers.")

TERM WATCH ## 15. Sprung rhythm

Definition: Gerard Manley Hopkins coined the term "sprung rhythm." He liked it because it produces a rhythm that sounds like natural speech rhythms. There are complex rules for the stresses of poems written in sprung rhythm. Simply stated, each foot begins with a stressed syllable, and the numbers of syllables in a foot varies from one foot to the next.

16. Rhyme scheme

Definition: The *rhyme scheme* is the pattern of the end rhyme of each line.

To illustrate determining the rhyme scheme of a poem examine, line by line, Robert Browning's "Meeting at Night" (ca. 1880):

Line 1: **The gray sea and the long black land;**
The line ends with the word "*land*" and is assigned the letter **a**.

Line 2: **And the yellow half-moon large and low;**
Because "*low*" does not rhyme with "*land*," it is given the letter **b**.

Line 3: **And the startled little waves that leap**
"*Leap*" does not rhyme with "*low*" or "*land*," so it is given the letter **c**.

Line 4: **In fiery ringlets from their sleep,**
"*Sleep*" and "*leap*" do rhyme; therefore, "*leap*" is given the letter **c**, also.

Line 5: **As I gain the cove with pushing prow,**
Line 5 picks up the rhyme of line 2 ("*prow*" and "*low*"—eye-rhyme) and is consequently labeled **b**.

Line 6: **And quench its speed i' the slushy sand.**
This last line of the first stanza ends with *sand,* rhyming with line 1. This line is given the letter **a**.

The rhyme scheme, then, of the first stanza is **a b c c b a**.

Now look at the second stanza. What is the rhyme scheme?

> Then a mile of warm sea-scented beach;
> Three fields to cross till a farm appears;
> A tap at the pane, the quick sharp scratch
> And blue spurt of a lighted match,
> And a voice less loud, through its joys and fears,
> Than the two hearts beating each to each!

The rhyme scheme of the last stanza is **d e f f e d**.

What are some of the possible effects of the rhyme scheme of "Meeting at Night"? Emphasis…unity of thought…perhaps using the rhyme scheme to contribute to the tone. Subliminally, the cyclical nature of the rhyme scheme may give the reader a sense of movement and expectation—an expectation that is fulfilled—that is emotionally satisfying in the first stanza when the speaker comes ashore and the last stanza when he is reunited with the one waiting for him. This sense of movement, expectation, and fulfillment that results from the rhythm, rhyme, and meaning of the poem can form the basis for a test question.

Example

In this poem, the relationship of lines 1–4 to lines 5–6 and of lines 7–10 to lines 11–12 reflect the speaker's progression from

(A) danger to safety
(B) understanding to fear
(C) resistance to acceptance
(D) challenge to attainment
(E) communication to noncommunication

Explanation: Notice in lines 1–4 that the speaker is in a challenging situation: at sea surrounded by "startled little waves that leap in fiery ringlets"; however, he "gain[s] the cove" and makes it ashore in lines 5–6. This progression from challenge to attainment is mirrored in the second stanza as he is challenged to cross the beach and fields and to gain the attention of the one lighting the match in lines 7–10, then attains reunion in lines 11–12.

Correct Answer: **D**

Pronunciations change over time. You may encounter **eye rhyme** (visual rhyme) in which words look like they should rhyme (and at one time perhaps they did) but do not, such as *horse, worse* or *move, love*. Another type of rhyme is **imperfect rhyme** (also called partial, slant, or half rhyme) that is only a close alignment: *afternoon, broom*.

How do you determine the rhyme scheme in a poem on the test when the pronunciations of one or more of the end-line words are unfamiliar to you because of changes in pronunciation over time or when the rhyme is imperfect? Here is a stanza from Shakespeare's "The Phoenix and the Turtle":

> Let the priest in surplice white
> That defunctive music can,
> Be the death-divining swan,
> Lest the requiem lack his right.

"White," "can," "swan," and "right"—what seems to be an *abca* rhyme scheme: When you look at the next two stanzas, however, the rhyme scheme appears to be somewhat different. (Because the rhyme schemes of individual stanzas are being compared, each stanza will begin with "a" for the first line.)

TIP

You can use context to find the rhyme scheme.

And thou treble-dated crow,	a
That thy sable gender makest	b
With the breath thou givest and takest,	b
'Mongst our mourners shalt thou go.	a

Here the anthem doth commence:	a
Love and constancy is dead;	b
Phoenix and the turtle fled	b
In a mutual flame from hence.	a

Based on the context of the rhyme scheme of the other stanzas, the poet intends "can" and "swan" to rhyme for an **abba** pattern.

Once you have identified a poem as a sonnet (14 lines in iambic pentameter), the end rhyme scheme *sometimes* can be a clue to meaning and structure. English sonnets can be identified by an *abab cdcd efef gg* rhyme scheme. The structure is a vehicle for a step-by-step progression of ideas that is either summarized or reversed by the final couplet. If, on the other hand, the sonnet's rhyme scheme divides it into two parts, often with an *abbaabba cdecde* rhyme scheme, then the sonnet is **Italian (sometimes called Petrarchan)**. In an Italian sonnet, you can anticipate that the first eight lines will contain either a statement or a question that will be answered, explored, or somehow addressed in the last six lines. Also, you might look for the two sections to provide a contrast of ideas.

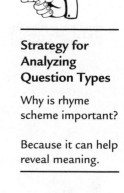

Strategy for Analyzing Question Types

Why is rhyme scheme important?

Because it can help reveal meaning.

English Sonnet		Italian Sonnet	
a		a	
b		b	
a		b	
b		a	makes a
		a	statement or
c		b	asks a question
d	progression	b	
c	of ideas	a	
d			
		(sometimes	
		contrasts	
		ideas)	
e		c	
f		d	
e		e	explores
f		c	concept or
		d	answers
g	summary or	e	question
g	reversal		

Not all sonnets are in this form; however, identification of the rhyme scheme can provide clues to help you answer questions about the poem's meaning and structure. Question 46 and its analysis in Diagnostic Test One exemplify finding the progression of ideas leading to the summary or reversal in an English sonnet.

17. Stanza

TERM WATCH

Definition: A stanza consists of lines that are grouped together in a poem because of the rhythm, rhyme scheme, and/or meaning.

18. Elegy

TERM WATCH

Definition: An elegy is a lament over the death of someone or the loss of something.

19. Ode

TERM WATCH

Definition: An ode is a complex, serious, long lyric poem. Odes are very unified with just one theme handled in an extremely dignified manner. The purpose of many odes is to eulogize someone or something.

TERM WATCH **20. Ballad**

Definition: Ballads are narrative songs that may be sung or simply recited. The subjects are usually courage or love. They sometimes contain repetition of words or phrases for effect (a refrain), and consist of four-line stanzas in an *abcb defe* rhyme scheme. Generally, a ballad is in iambic foot (with alternating lines of tetrameter and trimeter).

TERM WATCH **21. Concrete poetry**

Definition: Concrete poems are highly graphic, modern poems that are also graphic art.

TERM WATCH **22. Dramatic structure**

Definition: Usually, plays include the following:

- **Exposition or introduction**
  During the opening of the play, the setting is established and the audience meets the main characters.

- **Conflict or exciting force**
  The **conflict** is the point at which you recognize a threat to something and/or to someone. Obstacles are placed in the way of the protagonist (the main character). Called the **exciting force**, these obstacles set into motion the rising action in the play. Being able to identify the exciting force in the structure of a drama is very important because it gives the characters motivation for their words and deeds and it gives the audience motivation to care.

- **Rising action or complication**
  Once the exciting force has set the action in motion, the struggle builds dramatic tension toward a confrontation. This stage in the dramatic structure consists of a series of emotional highs and lows, with each high gaining intensity. The conflict becomes more complicated.

- **Climax, crisis, or turning point**
  Then it happens—the inevitable moment of confrontation. This is the point of **climax**—the turning point in the plot—the point at which there is a reversal from rising action to falling action.

- **Falling action**
  Briefer than rising action, the falling action may still have some suspenseful moments. For the most part, however, it gives the reader or audience a sense of completion, with the various unsettled issues at work within the plot reaching some state of resolution.

- **Resolution, dénouement, or conclusion**
  The hero has won or lost; issues are resolved; order is restored.

TERM WATCH **23. Theater of the Absurd** and **surrealism**.

Definition: Most likely, any play selections on the Literature Test will have recognizable elements of plot. You need to realize, however, that plays written in the Theater of the Absurd from (1950s and 1960s) do not. These dramas consist of images of confused people in a strange (in terms of understanding) world. A pattern emerges but not plot. They often contain elements of surrealism (dream images and imaginary expressions).

24. Monologue

TERM WATCH

Definition: When an actor delivers a speech in the presence of other characters who listen, but do not speak.

25. The aside

TERM WATCH

Definition: When an actor speaks directly to the audience; however, the rest of the actors on stage supposedly cannot hear him or her.

26. Soliloquy

TERM WATCH

Definition: When an actor delivers a speech when he or she is alone, expressing thoughts.

27. Parody

TERM WATCH

Definition: A parody is a comic or satiric imitation of a more serious work. It generally ridicules a work, an author, or a style.

28. Romance

TERM REVIEW

Definition: A romantic narrative (called a *prose romance*) has clear distinctions between the "good guys and the bad guys," an adventurous plot, and events that occasionally demand that the reader believe the otherwise unbelievable.

29. Realism

TERM REVIEW

Definition: A realistic narrative is in contrast to the romance. It tries to mirror real life, not present life as the reader thinks or wishes it could be. In realism, the leading characters are not necessarily beautiful or handsome, rich or talented. The plot revolves around events that people face every day in a real world.

30. Dramatic monologue

TERM REVIEW

Definition: A persona (someone who is not the poet) unintentionally reveals his or her character by expressing a poem in dramatic circumstances. There may or may not be a silent auditor or listener (the person to whom the monologue is being addressed).

31. Epigram

TERM REVIEW

Definition: Epigrams are short poems that are characteristically witty with a twist in the thought at the end. An epigram, however, can also be defined as simply a clever saying used for a variety of purposes, including to eulogize, to compliment, or to satirize.

This anonymous Latin epigram sums up the point:

> Three things must epigrams, like bees, have all,
> A sting, and honey, and a body small.

What else do I need to know about form?

1. Sequence Patterns

As you identify and study the form of a literary selection, give attention to *sequence* or *order* of presentation. Here is a review of the most common ways writers sequence their work:

- Chronological sequence—tells what happened according to time
- Climactic order—arranged from the least important to the most important
- Deductive order—arrangement based on deductive reasoning (from the general to the specific)
- Inductive order—arrangement based on inductive reasoning (from the specific to the general)
- Problem-solving sequence—presents a problem, then suggests or explains the solution
- Spatial sequence—describes a location
- Topical order—presents ideas by topics
- Mixed order—arrangement that is a blend of patterns

TIP

Sequence patterns and organizing principles are used by poets, as well as prose writers.

2. Organizing Principles

Once the overall sequence pattern is established, the writer generally must organize his or her thoughts within that pattern. The chart on page 87 provides you with a review of the basic organizing principles most commonly used in literature.

3. Prose Nonfiction

Generally, the main nonfiction genres include **essay** (formal, academic, and informal), **biography, autobiography** (including diaries, journals, letters, memoirs, and confessions), and **informational text** (including instructional works).

4. Prose Fiction

Fiction is an imaginary literary narrative that can come in any form—prose, poetry, or drama. In prose fiction, you are probably familiar with many of the genres that are based on the subject of the work, such as western, detective (crime stories or murder mysteries), utopian (about a perfect world), science fiction, and gothic, to name a few.

Shorter narratives often rely on their subjects for genre identification:

- The *tale* centers on an outcome. As a result of this focus, the tale may not be as tightly structured as some of the other short narrative genres. Look to O'Henry for some example tales.
- The *tall tale* centers on the exaggerated feats of (generally) American heroes. Examples include such characters as Paul Bunyan and Davy Crockett (but some tall tales have been written in other countries).

Organizing Principles

Basic Organization Principle:	Definition:	Example:
Analogy	Comparisons using the known to explain or clarify the unknown	Fried frog legs (the unknown) taste a lot like fried chicken (the known).
Cause and Effect (Causal Analysis)	Establishing a relation between outcomes and the reasons behind them	She fired him (effect) because he drank on the job (cause).
Comparison/Contrast	Pointing out similarities and differences of subjects	His management style is bold, like Kennedy's (comparison), but less organized (contrast).
Definition	Clarifying by using synonyms or by pointing out uniqueness within a general class	Mucilage, liquid glue (synonym), was used to hold the inlaid pieces of the mosaic—a picture (general class) that's made of inlaid pieces (unique feature).
Description	Using words to convey sensory impressions or abstract concepts	The temperature was −32°F (objective description), with a frigid wind blowing blankets of snow over the ice (subjective description).
Analysis and Classification (Division)	Dividing a subject into parts (analysis) or grouping information by class	The elements of Earth's crust are mostly oxygen and silicon (analysis). Gold, silver, and copper, which are all found in the ground, have been known to man for many years (classification).
Example	Using illustrations to clarify, explain, or prove a point	A case in point is this column of this summary.
Induction	Reasoning that arrives at a general principle or draws a conclusion from the facts or examples	He was late for supper, late for our wedding, and even a late delivery when he was born (examples)—that man is habitually late (conclusion)!
Deduction	Reasoning that uses a syllogism (two premises and a conclusion)	Premise I: When it rains more than 5 inches, the river floods. Premise 2: It has rained 6 inches. Conclusion: The river is overflowing its banks.
Narration	Telling what happened or is happening in chronological order (recounting events or telling a story)	I walked to the refrigerator, opened the door, pulled out the turkey, and spilled an open carton of milk.
Process (Analysis)	Explaining how something happened or happens (works)—sometimes instructional in purpose	First, cream the sugar and butter. Next, add eggs and milk; then blend in the sugar, flour, and baking powder. Finally, pour into the cake pan and bake at 350° for 50 minutes.

- The *folktale* is a narrative that originally was transmitted orally. Elements of the folktale are commonly found in tall tales and fables.
- The *legend* relates the life of a hero whose life is of legendary proportions.
- The *myth* once was believed to be true but is now accepted as fiction. These stories are generally of anonymous origin and include supernatural elements.

5. Poetry

The rhythm, rhyme, rhyme scheme, and physical appearance of a poem affect its meaning and tone. These elements can be the basis of test questions.

Poems are sometimes identified by mode, the prevailing method by which the writer treats the subject. Two of the more common modes are **narrative** (telling a story) and **lyric** (expressing feelings or ideas in a meter and rhyme that could be sung).

You will find variations within modes. For example, narrative poems can be taken to "epic proportions"—literally. An epic poem is a long poem written in the narrative mode with a legendary main character, heroic figures, an adventurous plot, and an expansive setting.

6. Drama

Of course, the structure of a drama (its introduction, conflict, rising action, climax, falling action, and conclusion) can be filled with possible test questions. Don't overlook, however, two widely used effects that also might be tested:

- **Foreshadowing**—Hints at the future that can build anticipation and tension
- **Flashbacks**—Descriptions or enactments of past events for the purpose of clarifying the situation, usually as it relates to the conflict

7. Validity and Logical Fallacies

Be alert to the validity of the reasoning of a writer or speaker. Some things that are written are not valid; some things that are written are not true. You need to be able to distinguish the following:

- Valid arguments (logical conclusions based on true premises) from logical fallacies (errors in reasoning caused by false premises or illogical consequences)
- Whether the invalidity of the faulty thinking is intentional or unintentional
- Whether the valid or invalid argument is the voice of the speaker or the voice of the writer and whether they agree

When you are asked a question about the meaning in a selection, you need to watch for any logical fallacies (errors in reasoning) that can affect the meaning.

HERE IS THE POINT: Be sure you carefully consider whether any given point or idea is based on fact or opinion. Are the facts being misused? Is the opinion valid?

How could questions about form be worded?

The following selections and their questions illustrate some of the ways form might be tested.

Example 1

Sequence and Organization

Susanna Moodie wrote the following selection.

As the sun rose above the horizon, all these matter-of-fact circumstances were gradually forgotten and merged in the surpassing grandeur of the scene that rose majestically before me. The previous day had been dark and stormy, and a heavy fog had concealed the mountain chain, which forms the stupendous background to this sublime view, entirely from our sight. As the clouds rolled away from their grey, bald brows, and cast into denser shadow the vast forest belt that girdled them round, they loomed out like mighty giants—Titans of the earth, in all their rugged and awful beauty—a thrill of wonder and delight pervaded my mind. The spectacle floated dimly on my sight—my eyes were blinded with tears—blinded by the excess of beauty. I turned to the right and to the left. I looked up and down the glorious river; never had I beheld so many striking objects blended into one mighty whole! Nature had lavished all her noblest features in producing that enchanting scene.

Line (5)

(10)

Structurally, this passage is

(A) climactic and deductive
(B) climactic and spatial
(C) spatial and topical
(D) spatial and inductive
(E) chronological and spatial

Explanation: The speaker describes scenes (spatially) as she sees them (chronologically).

Correct Answer: **E**

Example 2

Organizing Principles

Here is a selection taken from Thackeray's *Vanity Fair* (1848):

> What is there in a pair of pink cheeks and blue eyes forsooth? These dear Moralists ask, and hint wisely that the gifts of genius, the accomplishments of the mind, … and so forth, are far more valuable endowments for a
> *Line* female, than those fugitive charms which a few years will inevitably tarnish.
> *(5)* It is quite edifying to hear women speculate upon the worthlessness and the duration of beauty.
>
> But though virtue is a much finer thing, and those hapless creatures who suffer the misfortune of good looks ought to be continually put in mind of the fate which awaits them….

The organizational pattern used by the narrator to make his main point is best described as

(A) cause and effect
(B) definition
(C) process analysis
(D) analysis and classification
(E) comparison and contrast

Explanation: Do you see the organizational clue? The comparative degree: "more valuable," "much finer."

Correct Answer: **E**

Strategy for Analyzing Question Types

Be sure you understand the organizing principles described in the chart on page 87 to answer this question.

Example 3

Sequences and Organization

Read the following poem, "Early Affection" by George Moses Horton (1865).

> I lov'd thee from the earliest dawn,
>   When first I saw thy beauty's ray,
> And will, until life's eve comes on,
> *Line*   And beauty's blossom fades away;
> *(5)* And when all things go well with thee,
> With smiles and tears remember me.
>
> I'll love thee when thy morn is past,
>   And wheedling gallantry is o'er,
> When youth is lost in ages blast,
> *(10)*   And beauty can ascend no more,
> And when life's journey ends with thee,
> O, then look back and think of me.

I'll love thee with a smile or frown,
  'Mid sorrow's gloom or pleasure's light,
(15)   And when the chain of life runs down,
  Pursue thy last eternal flight,
When thou hast spread thy wing to flee,
Still, still, a moment wait for me.

I'll love thee for those sparkling eyes,
(20)   To which my fondness was betray'd,
Bearing the tincture of the skies,
  To glow when other beauties fade,
And when they sink too low to see,
Reflect an azure beam on me.

The structural theme of this poem can best be described as

(A) chronological sequence
(B) climactic order
(C) narrative description
(D) definitive analysis
(E) causal analysis

Explanation: Although the dawn, morning, and sunset imagery hints at chronological sequence, each stanza repeats the same structural pattern: "I lov'd thee/I'll love thee," followed by the poet expounding upon the extent of his love (cause), concluding with a statement of the desired effect.

Correct Answer: **E**

Example 4

Prose Nonfiction

The selections on the test are generally short. As a result, the nonfiction genres could be tested indirectly, focusing on their characteristics, especially as they relate to the writer's purpose.

Lord Chesterfield wrote these lines in 1739:

     If you would particularly gain the affection and friendship of particular people, whether men or women, endeavor to find out their predominant excellency, if they have one, and their prevailing weakness, which everybody
Line has; and do justice to the one, and something more than justice to the other.
(5)   Men have various objects in which they may excel or at least would be thought to excel; and, though they love to hear justice done to them, where they know that they excel, yet they are most and best flattered upon those points where they wish to excel, and yet are doubtful whether they do or not. As for example: Cardinal Richelieu, who was …

The speaker probably intends the text to be

(A) instructional
(B) biographical
(C) confessional
(D) a formal essay
(E) a humorous essay

Explanation: Beyond just giving information, the speaker instructs, using directives and an example. An interesting note: Lord Chesterfield wrote these words in a letter to his son, making the work *both* informational (instructional) and autobiographical (a letter). He wants to teach his son, so he writes him a letter.

Correct Answer: **A**

Example 5

Narrative and Plot

The following series of questions over Poe's "The Man of the Crowd" (1840) illustrates how test writers sometimes sequence the questions to help you analyze the selection.

This selection comes from Poe's "The Man of the Crowd."

With my brow to the glass, I was thus occupied in scrutinizing the mob, when suddenly there came into view a countenance (that of a decrepit old man, some sixty-five or seventy years of age,)—a countenance which at once *Line* arrested and absorbed my whole attention, on account of the absolute idio- *(5)* syncrasy of its expression. Any thing even remotely resembling that expression I had never seen before. I well remember that my first thought, upon beholding it, was that Retszch, had he viewed it, would have greatly preferred it to his own pictural incarnations of the fiend. As I endeavored, during the brief minute of my original survey, to form some analysis of the *(10)* meaning conveyed, there arose confusedly and paradoxically within my mind, the ideas of vast mental power, of caution, of penuriousness, of avarice, of coolness, of malice, of blood-thirstiness, of triumph, of merriment, of excessive terror, of intense—of extreme despair. I felt singularly aroused, startled, fascinated. "How wild a history," I said to myself, "is writ- *(15)* ten within that bosom!" Then came a craving desire to keep the man in view—to know more of him. Hurriedly putting on an overcoat, and seizing my hat and cane, I made my way into the street, and pushed through the crowd in the direction which I had seen him take; for he had already disappeared. With some little difficulty I at length came within sight of him, *(20)* approached, and followed him closely, yet cautiously, so as not to attract his attention.

(1840)

Where is the speaker when he first sees the man?

(A) In the street
(B) In a crowd of people
(C) Walking from building to building
(D) Inside a building looking out
(E) On a subway train

As presented, this portion of the narrative is best described as

(A) the exposition
(B) the exposition and rising action
(C) the rising action and climax
(D) the climax and falling action
(E) the falling action and dénouement

The speaker's actions can be summarized as

(A) preempting the man's authority
(B) following the man
(C) violating the man's privacy
(D) harassing the man
(E) stalking the man

Explanation: His "brow to the glass" (line 1) shows that he is looking out the window. He then makes his way "into the street" (setting). Although the privacy issue is a tempting answer, actually the speaker is stalking the man by *covertly* following him (plot). Finally, this paragraph as it is presented (out of context) is a description of exposition (the man and his circumstance introduced) and the rising action (the speaker follows him amid increasing inner turmoil).

Correct Answers: **D, B, E**

This selection contains elements that are best described as

(A) tragic and realistic
(B) comic and romantic
(C) satiric and tragic
(D) romantic and realistic
(E) realistic and satiric

Explanation: The plot has adventurous elements but no clear distinction between the "good guys and the bad guys." Who is the hero? The man is compared to Retszch's representations of a fiend. The speaker is an obsessed stalker, such as one might hear about on the evening news. Is failure inevitable? Perhaps not, but the elements are in place for a tragic ending.

Correct Answer: **A**

This selection can be described as all the following EXCEPT

(A) suspenseful
(B) psychological
(C) utopian
(D) tragic
(E) realistic

Explanation: Notice that the speaker not only tells us that he follows the man, but also tells us in detail his thinking when he sees and follows him. By the end of the paragraph, the reader is asking, "What happens next?" in anticipation of what follows. This description is not, however, of a perfect (utopian) world.

Correct Answer: **C**

Example 6

Rhythm and Meaning

You should be able to recognize when the rhythm and changes in the rhythm affect the meaning of a poem.
Here is Tennyson's "Break, Break, Break."

TIP

Rhythm and changes in rhythm are clues to the poem's meaning.

> Break, break, break,
>   On thy cold gray stones, O Sea!
> And I would that my tongue could utter
>   The thoughts that arise in me.
>
> *Line*
> *(5)*   O well for the fisherman's boy,
>   That he shouts with his sister at play!
> O well for the sailor lad,
>   That he sings in his boat on the bay!
>
> And the stately ships go on
> *(10)*   To their haven under the hill;
> But O for the touch of a vanished hand,
>   And the sound of a voice that is still!
>
> Break, break, break,
>   At the foot of thy crags, O Sea!
> *(15)*   But the tender grace of a day that is dead
>   Will never come back to me.

(ca. 1880)

The contrast in rhythm of the first line of the last stanza to the rhythm of the second stanza serves to

(A) accentuate the harshness of the speaker's mood about his position in life
(B) change the poem's emphasis from the speaker to the sea
(C) weaken the speaker's argument
(D) heighten the impact of the sea's danger
(E) reinforce that the sea represents normal life

Explanation: "Break, break, break" makes a strong spondaic foot that sounds harsh and reflects the speaker's feelings of "a day that is dead." In contrast, the second stanza trips along like the children playing.

Correct Answer: **A**

Example 7

Sprung Rhythm

Pied Beauty

Glory be to God for dappled things—
For skies of couple-color as a brindled cow;
For rose-moles all in stipple upon trout that swim;
Line Fresh-firecoal chestnut-falls; finches' wings;
(5) Landscape plotted and pieced—fold, fallow, and plow;
And all trades, their gear and tackle and trim.
All things counter, original, spare, strange;
Whatever is fickle, freckled (who knows how?)
With swift, slow; sweet, sour; adazzle, dim;
(10) He fathers-forth whose beauty is past change:
Praise him.

by Gerard Manley Hopkins
(ca. 1880)

The rhythm of this poem emphasizes

(A) a fiery nature
(B) natural landscapes
(C) propriety
(D) percussion
(E) irregularity

Explanation: Line 1 establishes the subject: dappled (variegated, spotted) things, things that are irregular. The rest of the poem expounds upon this subject. Likewise, the sprung rhythm is irregular.

Correct Answer: **E**

Example 8

Rhyme

Pity the Poor Raccoon

Pity the poor raccoon.
He could run fast 'cause he stayed slim and trim;
But one day right at noon he heard a loon's tune
Line   That bedazzled and mystified him.
(5)   "What's that sound?" he bemused, for he felt quite amused
'Til a hound heard the sound when Raccoon left the ground.
He was trapped! He was cornered! But he wasn't forlornered.
The hound saw a flash and his teeth he did gnash
For the prey he had treed just turned tail and fleed.

by L. E. Myers
(1996)

TIP

Rhyme can
affect meaning
and tone.

The rhymes used contribute to the poem's

(A) defensive tone
(B) comic tone
(C) serious tone
(D) austere tone
(E) sentimental tone

Explanation: Notice the pairing of "cornered" with "forlornered" and of "treed" with "fleed." The poem's subject and rhymes combine to produce a comic tone. These are **forced rhymes** "invented" by the poet. Forced rhymes are examples of **poetic license**—when a poet departs from the usual use of rhyme, diction, syntax, and other such conventions.

Correct Answer: B

Example 9

Free Verse

Of course, you might be asked to identify free verse when you see it; however, you should also be able to identify how this form can affect meaning.

Notice the use of free verse in "Know Yourself" by L. E. Myers (1996):

There is a
truth
with us
Line   and in us.
(5)   Is this the truth?

There is a
lie
with us,
but not in us.
(10)   Is this the truth?

The meaning of this poem is based on

(A) a pun
(B) repetition
(C) a contrast
(D) sentence structure
(E) its brevity

Explanation: Notice the physical isolation of "truth" in the first stanza and "lie" in the second, placing an emphasis on their contrast of meanings.

Correct Answer: **C**

Example 10

Blank Verse

Here is an excerpt from William Wordsworth's rather lengthy "Lines Composed a Few Miles above Tintern Abbey on Revisiting the Banks of the Wye During A Tour, July 13, 1798."

> Five years have passed; five summers, with the length
> Of five long winters! and again I hear
> These waters, rolling from their mountain-springs
> *Line* With a soft inland murmur, Once again
> *(5)* Do I behold these steep and lofty cliffs,
> That on a wild secluded scene impress
> Thoughts of more deep seclusion; and connect
> The landscape with the quiet of the sky.

Strategy for Analyzing Question Types

The form of this poem (blank verse) contributes to its meaning.

The lack of rhyme in this poem emphasizes

(A) movement
(B) false impressions
(C) quietness
(D) grand thinking
(E) seclusion

Explanation: Notice the iambic pentameter rhythm and lack of punctuation at the ends of the lines. As a result, the reader is pulled from one line to the next, like time passes and water rolls. If the lines had been written with an identifiable rhyme scheme, the emphasis on movement would have been diminished.

Correct Answer: **A**

Example 11

Dramatic Monologue

Notice some of the literary elements at work in this small excerpt from Tennyson's "Ulysses." Written in the first person, the speaker is Odysseus (Ulysses), a Greek hero of the Trojan War and the king of Ithaca.

It little profits that an idle king,
By this still hearth, among these barren crags,
Matched with an agéd wife, I mete and dole
Line Unequal laws unto a savage race,
(5) That hoard, and sleep, and feed, and know not me.
I cannot rest from travel; I will drink
Life to the lees. All times I have enjoyed
Greatly, have suffered greatly, both with those
That loved me, and alone; on shore, and when
(10) Through scudding drifts the rainy Hyades
Vexed the dim sea. I am become a name;
For always roaming with a hungry heart
Much have I seen and known—cities of men
And manners, climates, councils, governments
(15) Myself not least, but honored of them all—
And drunk delight of battle with my peers,
Far on the ringing plains of windy Troy.
I am a part of all that I have met;
Yet all experience is an arch wherethrough
(20) Gleams that untravelled world, whose margin fades
For ever and for ever when I move.

(ca. 1860)

In the poem "Ulysses," the speaker reveals that he

(A) does not frequently leave his responsibilities as king
(B) considers himself an adventurer
(C) is not well liked among his people
(D) shuns battle and confrontation
(E) deeply respects his subjects

Explanation: Look for how the speaker's character is revealed. He "cannot rest from travel" and views experience as "an arch wherethrough / Gleams that untravelled world...."

Correct Answer: **B**

Example 12

Elegy

Read the first stanza of Thomas Gray's "Elegy Written in a Country Churchyard."

The curfew tolls the knell of parting day,
The lowing herd wind slowly o'er the lea,
The plowman homeward plods his weary way,
And leaves the world to darkness and to me.

(ca. 1760)

In the context of the poem, the emphasis is on

(A) curfew
(B) fear
(C) work
(D) loneliness
(E) nature

Explanation: In addition to recognizing an elegy, you need to look for its main elements, such as mourning, a solemn mood, meditation, and/or grief. In this stanza, curfew means people are getting off the streets, the day is parting, the cattle and plowman are going home, and the speaker is alone in the dark.

Correct Answer: **D**

Example 13

Ode

Here is "Ode on Solitude" by Alexander Pope (ca. 1700)

> Happy the man, whose wish and care
>   A few paternal acres bound,
> Content to breathe his native air,
>   In his own ground.
>
> *Line*
> (5) Whose herds with milk, whose fields with bread,
>   Whose flocks supply him with attire,
> Whose trees in summer yield him shade,
>   In winter fire.
>
> Blest, who can unconcern'dly find
> (10) Hours, days, and years slide soft away,
> In health of body, peace of mind,
>   Quiet by day,
>
> Sound sleep by night; study and ease,
>   Together mixed; sweet recreation;
> (15) And innocence, which most does please
>   With meditation.
>
> Thus let me live, unseen, unknown,
>   Thus unlamented let me die,
> Steal from the world, and not a stone
> (20)   Tell where I lie.

The theme of this poem revolves mainly around

(A) life
(B) self-sufficiency
(C) a solitary, natural life
(D) the balance of nature
(E) innocence

Explanation: What is the theme? The final stanza provides the answer: To be happy (line 1), live a solitary, natural life, and die unknown (last stanza). What is the subject of this theme? A solitary, natural life.

Correct Answer: **C**

Example 14

Sonnet

Notice Wordsworth's use of the sonnet form in "Nuns Fret Not."

	X / X / X / X / X /	
	Nuns fret not at their convent's narrow room;	a
	And hermits are contented with their cells;	b
	And students with their pensive citadels;	b
Line	Maids at the wheel, the weaver at his loom,	a
(5)	Sit blithe and happy; bees that soar for bloom,	a
	High as the highest Peak of Furness-fells,	b
	Will murmur by the hour in foxglove bells:	b
	In truth the prison, into which we doom	a
	Ourselves, no prison is: and hence for me,	c
(10)	In sundry moods, 'twas pastime to be bound	d
	Within the Sonnet's scanty plot of ground;	d
	Pleased if some Souls (for such there needs must be)	c
	Who have felt the weight of too much liberty,	c
	Should find brief solace there, as I have found.	d

(ca. 1807)

The main point of this poem is

(A) the sonnet form is beneficial
(B) a call to abandon what imprisons us
(C) we all sit in our own prisons
(D) we should break free from the sonnet
(E) life is made of choices

Explanation: First, in lines 1–9, Wordsworth tells the reader that some "imprison" themselves by choice (nuns, hermits, students). If by choice, they are not really in prison (lines 8–9). He concludes in lines 10–14 that the "prison" of the sonnet (the confines of structure required to write in this form) is actually a "solace" from "the weight of too much liberty," in other words, poems lacking the tight structure of a sonnet.

Correct Answer: **A**

Example 15

Ballad

For an example of the literary ballad, read these first four stanzas of Coleridge's *The Rime of the Ancient Mariner*, Part I (1798).

> It is an ancient Mariner
> And he stoppeth one of three.
> "By thy long gray beard and glittering eye,
> Now wherefore stopp'st thou me?
>
> *Line*
> *(5)* The Bridegroom's doors are opened wide,
> And I am next of kin;
> The guests are met, the feast is set:
> May'st hear the merry din."
>
> He holds him with his skinny hand,
> *(10)* "There was a ship," quoth he.
> "Hold off! unhand me, gray-beard loon!"
> Eftsoons his hand dropt he.
>
> He holds him with his glittering eye—
> The Wedding-Guest stood still,
> *(15)* And listens like a three years' child:
> The Mariner hath his will.

Why does the wedding guest listen to the mariner?

(A) The mariner physically restrains him.
(B) The wedding guest does not stop.
(C) The wedding was called off.
(D) The mariner restrains him by his will.
(E) The mariner follows him to the wedding.

Explanation: Notice the narrative elements in this poem. We have an unknown narrator and two principal characters (the mariner and the wedding guest), a conversation, and the beginning of conflict. At first the mariner held the guest with his "skinny hand"; however, "Eftsoons his hand dropt he. / He holds him with his glittering eye— … The Mariner hath his will."

Correct Answer: **D**

Example 16

Parody

A parody can be fun to write, especially when the original poem has a very pronounced rhythm or mood. Edgar Allan Poe's "The Raven" has such a distinctive rhythm pattern that it works well in parody. Here is the first stanza of the original poem:

> Once upon a midnight dreary, while I pondered, weak and weary,
> Over many a quaint and curious volume of forgotten lore,
> While I nodded, nearly napping, suddenly there came a tapping,
> *Line*   As of some one gently rapping, rapping at my chamber door.
> *(5)*   "'Tis some visitor," I muttered, "tapping at my chamber door—
> Only this and nothing more."

Here is a parody of the preceding stanza:

> Once upon a schoolday dreary, while I studied, weak and weary,
> Over many a quaint and curious volume of literature,
> Feeling grisly, grim and grumbling, suddenly there came a rumbling,
> *Line*   A gruesome gripping kind of rumbling, rumbling that was premature.
> *(5)*   "'Tis my stomach," then I muttered, "rumbling here so premature—
> Candy bars will be the cure."

The main point of the parody is to ridicule

  I. "The Raven"
 II. Poe
III. narrative poetry
 IV. literary study

(A) I only
(B) II only
(C) III only
(D) I, III, and IV only
(E) I, II, III, and IV

Explanation: The parody obviously is capitalizing on the style and mode of "The Raven" (I and III). The speaker of the parody is a weary student studying literature for a class or test. To select such a famous work to bewail studying "quaint and curious ... literature" also mocks literary study. The author of the original work is not in focus.

Correct Answer: **D**

Example 17

Concrete Poetry

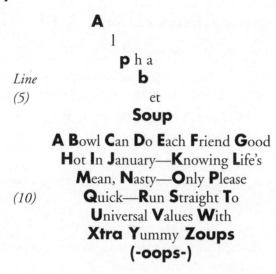

by L. E. Myers

The shape of this poem looks like its subject—a bowl of soup.

The meaning of this poem revolves around

(A) friends
(B) a conflict
(C) the nastiness of life
(D) an ironic situation
(E) mistakes

Explanation: Hot soup is traditionally viewed as a comfort food and an economical food to feed the hungry, such as in a "soup kitchen." Alphabet soup has been enjoyed by generations. Structuring the poem by placing the alphabet in sequence, then contrasting that traditional structure with a deliberate departure from traditional spelling (Xtra Yummy Zoups) to maintain the alphabetical sequence creates irony. This structural irony mirrors the irony in the poem's meaning: When life gets mean and nasty, the speaker goes to "Universal Values" (hot food that is traditionally thought to bring comfort) only to find by the bottom of the bowl that some breaks with tradition have to be made. The comfort food of tradition sometimes is not enough (-oops-).

Correct Answer: **D**

Example 18

Dramatic Structure

Here are a few lines from Shakespeare's *The Tempest* (1623).

  Miranda. Sir, are not you my father?

  Prospero. Thy mother was a piece of virtue, and
        She said thou wast my daughter; and thy father
Line   Was Duke of Milan; and his only heir
(5)   A princess—no worse issued.

  Miranda.   O the heavens!
        What foul play had we that we came from thence?
        Or blessed was't we did?

  Prospero.   Both, both, my girl!
(10)   By foul play, as thou say'st, were we heaved thence,
        But blessedly holp hither.

  Miranda.   O, my heart bleeds
        To think o' th' teen that I have turned you to,
        Which is from my remembrance! Please you, farther.

(15) *Prospero.* My brother and thy uncle, called Antonio—
        I pray thee mark me—that a brother should
        Be so perfidious!—he whom next thyself
        Of all the world I loved, and to him put
        The manage of my state, as at that time
(20)   Through all the signories it was the first
        And Prospero the prime duke, being so reputed
        In dignity, and for the liberal arts
        Without a parallel: those being all my study,
        The government I cast upon my brother
(25)   And to my state grew stranger, being transported
        And rapt in secret studies. Thy false uncle—
        Dost thou attend me?

Who are Prospero and Miranda?

(A) Duke of Milan and his daughter, a princess
(B) The uncle of the Duke and his niece
(C) Antonio's uncle and his daughter, a princess
(D) Antonio's nephew and his daughter
(E) A signory and his niece

The situation of the drama is that

(A) Prospero is telling a story about the Duke of Milan
(B) Prospero identifies himself as a servant of a prime duke and princess
(C) Prospero reveals his true identity and circumstances
(D) Prospero and Antonio are co-rulers of Milan
(E) Prospero declares Antonio to be Miranda's father

The point in the plot is best described as part of the

(A) exposition
(B) rising action
(C) climax
(D) falling action
(E) resolution

Explanation: In speaking to Miranda, Prospero says she is his daughter, a princess, and that he was the Duke of Milan (lines 1–5). The key to understanding the situation in this selection is to realize that Prospero shifts in lines 3–4 from first to third person, but is still referring to himself. From·that point on, he is revealing who he is and how he came to be in his current circumstances. Obviously, his struggle with his brother provides conflict for the story.

Correct Answers: **A, C**

Example 19

Validity

This passage is taken from Emily Brontë's *Wuthering Heights* (1847).

> He [Earnshaw] afterwards gathered the books and hurled them on the fire. I read in his countenance what anguish it was to offer that sacrifice to spleen—I fancied that as they consumed, he recalled the pleasure they had
> *Line*
> *(5)* already imparted; and the triumph and ever-increasing pleasure he had anticipated from them—and I fancied, I guessed the incitement to his secret studies, also. He had been content with daily labour and rough animal enjoyments, till Catherine crossed his path—Shame at her scorn, and hope of her approval were his first prompters to higher pursuits; and instead of guarding him from one, and winning him the other, his endeavours to raise
> *(10)* himself had produced just the contrary result.

The narrator's assessment of Earnshaw's motivation is probably based on

(A) careful analysis
(B) the opinions of others
(C) conjecture
(D) shared confidences
(E) trained observations

Explanation: There is no evidence of analysis, consultations with others, or training in observation on the part of the narrator. He does, however, confess to conjecture in "I fancied, I guessed." Only learning more about the unknown narrator, the other characters, and his relationship to them, in this case will help you determine whether his opinions could be valid. This question, however, illustrates the first step in establishing the validity of any point being made: Is the point an opinion or a statement of fact?

Correct Answer: **C**

Strategy for Analyzing Question Types

You may be unfamiliar with "spleen" as used in line 4, but <u>context</u> tells you that it must relate to emotions.

Test Taker → Test Maker

If you were writing SAT Literature tests, what questions about form would you ask? Here is an opportunity for you to approach form from the test writer's point of view. Henry Wadsworth Longfellow was an abolitionist whose wife died from a fire and whose son was injured during the Civil War. He is well known, of course, for his famous poem "The Song of Hiawatha." You may not realize, however, that he wrote "Christmas Bells" as well.

I heard the bells on Christmas Day
Their old, familiar carols play,
And wild and sweet
Line The words repeat
(5) Of peace on earth, good-will to men!

And thought how, as the day had come,
The belfries of all Christendom
Had rolled along
The unbroken song
(10) Of peace on earth, good-will to men!

Till, ringing, singing on its way,
The world revolved from night to day,
A voice, a chime,
A chant sublime
(15) Of peace on earth, good-will to men!

Then from each black, accursed mouth
The cannon thundered in the South
And with the sound
The carols drowned
(20) Of peace on earth, good-will to men!

It was as if an earthquake rent
The hearth-stones of a continent,
And made forlorn
The households born
(25) Of peace on earth, good-will to men!

And in despair I bowed my head;
"There is no peace on earth," I said:
"For hate is strong,
And mocks the song
(30) Of peace on earth, good-will to men!"

Then pealed the bells more loud and deep:
"God is not dead; nor doth he sleep!
The Wrong shall fail,
The Right prevail,
(35) With peace on earth, good-will to men!"

Do you recognize the words? Do you know the tune? As one of America's traditional Christmas carols, "Christmas Bells" stands out for its familiarity and its form.

Begin to think about a possible test question by identifying the poem's structure and mode:

The poem's mode is _____

The rhyme scheme is mostly _____

The foot is _____; meter:_____.

Discussion

Because it is meant to be sung, the poem is in the lyric mode, written in mostly couplets of iambic tetrameter.

Any one of these points would make an excellent test question. But let's tackle writing a question that's more challenging. Do you see a progression within the poem?

In Stanzas 1–3, the speaker's attitude is _____.

In Stanzas 4–5, the speaker's attitude is _____.

In Stanza 6, the speaker's attitude is _____.

In Stanza 7, the speaker's attitude is _____.

TIP

Use this activity to practice spotting relationships.

The speaker goes from contented complaisance in a world of "familiar carols" and "The unbroken song" (1–3) to the shock of war in Stanzas 4–5, to self-named "despair" in 6, then hope that "The Right prevail" in the final stanza.

Because the SAT STL might include relationship questions (questions about patterns, changes, contrasts, similarities, progressions, multiple themes, and structural parallelisms), try writing a relationship question about this poem.

You may have your own ideas, or you can use these ideas to write your answer choices:

1. The progression of the speaker's attitude

2. The contrast of the descriptive words used in Stanzas 1–3 to those used in stanzas 4–6

3. The changing meanings of the last line of each stanza

4. The effect of the lyric nature of the rhythm and rhyme scheme as they first harmonize, then contrast, with the meaning

5. The progression of singing (Stanza 3) to "accursed mouth" (4) to "mock the song" (6) to "more loud and deep" (7)

The LEAST accurate description of the poem's structure is

(A) _____

(B) * _____

(C) _____

(D) _____

(E) _____

Remember: In a LEAST question, all your answer choices will be correct but one.

FORM IN CONCLUSION

A writer's intended meaning determines what form the work will take, and the form of a work can enhance or destroy its meaning: a reciprocal relationship.

*Correct Answer

LITERARY ELE
(NARRATIVE) V

The voice of a literary

What terms do I ne
voice?

1. Perspective an

Definition: In any given s
rative) and an author. Ea
or events involved. That
opinions and attitudes. Vo
however, think of voice as
the reader and subject. Th

2. Point of view

Definition: The first step in
view is being used. In other
relate to the action of the pl
going on in the story and in
Pretend that the "world" o

The world
NARRA

4. Third-person unlimited (omni

Definition: In the omniscient or third-pe
knows everything about everyone in e
mation at will to the reader.

TERM ALERT

5. First-person poin

Definition: The first-pers
characters, or simply

TERM ALERT

6. Satire

Definition:
Why? T

TERM ALERT

TERM REVIEW

The place, time, characters, and events of the story all exist within "the world of the narrative." The "world outside the narrative" is where the readers exist. The narrator, then, stands between the reader and the story; and his or her aim is to tell the reader a story, to describe the characters and events as they move around within the confines of the world of the narrative while the reader watches and listens.

3. Third-person limited (limited omniscient point of view)   **TERM ALERT**

Definition: In the third-person limited point of view (also called limited omniscient point of view), the narrator tells the story using third-person pronouns (he, she, they, him, her, them) and is able to tell the reader the thoughts, opinions, motives, and inner feelings of *only one* of the characters in the story, someone who often is the main character or protagonist.

Sometimes the narrator reveals the main character's thoughts through **stream-of-consciousness** techniques, the flow of thoughts that people experience, thoughts that range from the unintelligible to the very rational and well articulated. One such technique is the *interior monologue* in which the main character's thoughts are reported as they occur—often in vague terms with sometimes (but not always) illogical order and a lack of grammatical clarity.

...scient point of view)

...son unlimited point of view, the narrator
...very situation and feels free to reveal this infor-

... of view

...son narrator might be the main character, one of the minor
...an observer. The story is written in the first-person "I".

...in general, satire makes a subject look ridiculous in order to make a point.
...stimulate change.

Persona

Definition: A persona is a narrator, speaker, or implied author created by the real writer as a "mask" to tell the story and/or express opinions in the first person. The attitude of the persona may or may not be the same as that of the author.

What else do I need to know about (narrative) voice?

1. Characterization of the Narrator

The point of view tells you whether the narrator is in the story or out of the story and to some degree how much he or she knows about the thinking of the characters. The narrator can also be characterized in three major areas:

- Does the narrator deliberately allow the reader to know that the work is a fictional account? Does he or she point out the elements of narration at work?

At the other extreme, you are almost totally unaware of the existence of some narrators because the stories are told objectively. Scenes are described, dialogue spoken, and action conveyed; but the narrator fades into the background, out of sight.

- Is the narrator reliable or unreliable? Although the reader may have a tendency to believe that the narrator is *always* credible and correct in his or her opinions, sometimes the narrator has an erroneous understanding of the situation.
- Does the narrator give opinions concerning the words and deeds, the personalities and motives, and the events and circumstances at work in the story?

2. The Narrator or Speaker Versus the Author

Some readers mistakenly assume that the writer and the narrator or speaker are the same. Sometimes the author and narrator or speaker are the same, but at other times they are two distinctly different voices. When the narrative is in the first person, with a character being the one telling the story, identifying the voice of the writer as different from that of the narrator can be difficult.

3. The Attitude of the Speaker

Speakers in nonnarrative works also project an attitude. Just as with narrators, sometimes the speaker and author share the same opinions, sometimes not.

4. Other Voices

- Lyric poems are nonnarrative works that express the speaker's feelings, state of mind, thoughts, and other expressions, and are written generally in the first person. The usage of the first person "I" in the lyric poem does not necessarily mean that the poet is the speaker (just as the first person narrator of a story is not always the author).
- Can a drama have a narrative voice? Critics and teachers vary on the subject. On one hand, plays have no narrator, no one to intervene between the audience and the events and conversations being acted out on stage and no true sense of the author's presence. From this view, narrative voice is not an element of drama. The opposing view would contend that you can catch glimpses of the writer, even in drama, from time to time.

To determine the narrative voice in a play, some look to the dramatist's use of dramatic conventions, especially the use of the chorus, the choral-character, the prologue, and the epilogue.

- Another voice writers use is grammatical voice.

You are probably familiar with active voice and passive voice. To review, when the subject does the action in a sentence or in the condition named by the verb, the voice of the verb is active. (I threw a ball.) When the subject receives the action, the voice of the verb is passive. (The ball was thrown by me.) Passive voice constructions are made with the past participle and a form of the verb *to be*: was thrown. Much of the writing done in English is in the active voice, and the occasional shift to passive voice can be very effective, particularly when emphasis is to be placed on the object, as in "The difficult test was passed by the student" (emphasis is on the test) or when the actors are not known, as in "Many books have been written this year" (Who wrote the books?).

To illustrate, compare these two versions of the same paragraph:

VERSION ONE:

> The ball was hit by Jim, but it was immediately caught by the outfielder. Roars were heard from the crowd. Tears streaming down his face were awkwardly wiped away by Jim's gloved hand. The truth was finally realized by him: the championship game was lost.

VERSION TWO:

> Jim hit the ball, but the outfielder caught it immediately. The crowd roared. Jim's gloved hand awkwardly wiped away the tears streaming down his face. He finally realized the truth: the championship game was lost.

In Version One, the narrator probably views the scene as

(A) merely a game
(B) active, loud, and sentimental
(C) the loss of a man's dream
(D) unexciting and regrettable
(E) just another part of sports

In Version Two, the narrator probably views the scene as

(A) merely a game
(B) active, loud, and sentimental
(C) the loss of a man's dream
(D) unexciting and regrettable
(E) just another part of sports

Explanation: In Version One, attention is on our descriptive senses: seeing the ball being hit, hearing the roar, seeing tears flow (emotionally centered). In Version Two, the attention is on Jim, the outfielder, and the crowd (people-centered).

Correct Answers: **B, C**

How could questions about (narrative) voice be worded?

The following selections and their questions illustrate some of the ways (narrative) voice might be tested.

Example 1

Stream of Consciousness

Both James Joyce and William Faulkner used stream-of-consciousness techniques in their writings. Here is a sample from Faulkner's short story "Barn Burning."

> They were running a middle buster now, his brother holding the plow straight while he handled the reins, and walking beside the straining mule, the rich black soil shearing cool and damp against his bare ankles, he
>
> *Line* thought *Maybe this is the end of it. Maybe even that twenty bushels that seems*
> *(5)* *hard to have to pay for just a rug will be a cheap price for him to stop forever and always from being what he used to be;* thinking, dreaming now, so that his brother had to speak sharply to him to mind the mule:
>
> *Maybe he even won't collect the twenty bushels. Maybe it will all add up and balance and vanish—corn, rug, fire; the terror and grief, the being pulled two*
> *(10)* *ways like between two teams of horses—gone, done with forever and ever.*
>
> (1939)

The nature of the person's thoughts makes him seem

(A) overworked
(B) worried
(C) conniving
(D) cynical
(E) enigmatic

Explanation: The narrator reveals the character's thoughts through an interior monologue, what he is thinking as he and his brother are plowing. Although we lack enough context to identify what is happening and who "he" might be, we can tell that the character's problem concerns a fire and a payment to be made. He is worried.

Correct Answer: **B**

Example 2

First-person Narrator

Examine again this selection taken from *Wuthering Heights* (1847).

> But his self-love would endure no further torment—I heard, and not alto-
> gether disapprovingly, a manual check given to her saucy tongue—The lit-
> tle wretch had done her utmost to hurt her cousin's sensitive though
> *Line* uncultivated feelings, and a physical argument was the only mode he had of
> *(5)* balancing the account, and repaying its effects on the inflicter.
> He [Earnshaw] afterwards gathered the books and hurled them on the fire.
> I read in his countenance what anguish it was to offer that sacrifice to
> spleen—I fancied that as they consumed, he recalled the pleasure they had
> already imparted; and the triumph and ever-increasing pleasure he had
> *(10)* anticipated from them—and I fancied, I guessed the incitement to his secret
> studies, also. He had been content with daily labour and rough animal
> enjoyments, till Catherine crossed his path—Shame at her scorn, and hope
> of her approval were his first prompters to higher pursuits; and instead of
> guarding him from one, and winning him the other, his endeavours to raise
> *(15)* himself had produced just the contrary result.

The narrator is best described as

(A) unlimited in knowledge
(B) able to read Earnshaw's mind
(C) able to read Catherine's mind
(D) a character in the story
(E) an observer outside the story

Which of the following pairs LEAST effectively describes the contrast of the narrator's attitude toward Catherine and Earnshaw?

(A) censorious, understanding
(B) angry, approving
(C) disapproving, sympathetic
(D) disapprobative, pitying
(E) critical, sensitive

Explanation: This account is obviously written in the first person ("I"). He is in the scene, observing the countenance of Earnshaw, which means the narrator is a character in the story. What are his attitudes? All five answers are possible (a LEAST question), but the subtle elements of B make it the least effective contrast. The speaker does not show real anger toward Catherine. That he was "not altogether" disapproving when she was slapped ("manual check ... to her saucy tongue") implies some element of disapproval over Earnshaw hitting a woman. He disapproves of Catherine's behavior (calling her a wretch) and sympathizes with Earnshaw's hurt feelings, but not to the point of complete approval of slapping her, even if (in the opinion of the narrator) she deserves it.

Here is the point: Because the first-person narrator is a character in the story, he cannot project an attitude based on really knowing what Catherine and Earnshaw are thinking, as a third-person unlimited or even third-person limited narrator might have done.

Correct Answers: **D, B**

Example 3

Characterization of the Narrator

Read this first paragraph of *The Posthumous Papers of the Pickwick Club* (1836) by Charles Dickens:

> The first ray of light which illumines the gloom, and converts into a daz-
> zling brilliancy that obscurity in which the earlier history of the public career
> of the immortal Pickwick would appear to be involved, is derived from the
> *Line* perusal of the following entry in the Transactions of the Pickwick Club,
> *(5)* which the editor of these papers feels the highest pleasure in laying before
> his readers, as a proof of the careful attention, indefatigable assiduity, and
> nice discrimination, with which his search among the multifarious docu-
> ments confided to him has been conducted.

The narrator's attitude toward his work is somewhat

(A) self-confident
(B) self-condemning
(C) belligerent
(D) uncaring
(E) relaxed

Explanation: The narrator describes himself as "the editor of these papers" in the third person and describes his work as done with "careful attention, indefatigable assiduity, and nice discrimination." He *knows* that his work is done well. He has a self-confident attitude.

Correct Answer: **A**

Example 4

Characterization of the Narrator

These paragraphs are found near the end of *Oliver Twist* (1838), in which the narrator talks of "this tale" and describes his writing of the conclusion:

> The fortunes of those who have figured in this tale are nearly closed. The little that remains to their historian to relate, is told in few and simple words.
>
> ...   ...
>
> And now, the hand that traces these words, falters, as it approaches the
> *Line* conclusion of its task: and would weave, for a little longer space, the thread
> *(5)* of these adventures.
>
> I would fain linger yet with a few of those among whom I have so long moved, and share their happiness by endeavouring to depict it. I would show Rose Maylie in all the bloom and grace of early womanhood, shedding on her secluded path in life such soft and gentle light, as fell on all who trod
> *(10)* it with her, and shone into their hearts. I would paint her the life and joy of the fireside circle and the lively summer group; I would follow her through the sultry fields at noon, and hear the low tones of her sweet voice in the moonlit evening walk; I would watch her in all her goodness and charity abroad, and the smiling untiring discharge of domestic duties at home; I
> *(15)* would paint her and her dead sister's child happy in their mutual love, . . .

What is the narrator's attitude toward Rose Maylie?

(A) Passionate
(B) Affectionate
(C) Amorous
(D) Zealous
(E) Dispassionate

Explanation: The narrator's affectionate attitude toward Rose Maylie is obvious in his choice of description. She was "the life and joy of the . . . summer group," one of "goodness and charity," and so forth.

Correct Answer: **B**

Example 5

The Unreliable Narrator

The following selection comes from *The Turn of the Screw,* written by Henry James in 1898. The narrator is a governess of two children. She is in love with her employer, the guardian of the children.

I scarce know how to put my story into words that shall be a credible picture of my state of mind; but I was in these days literally able to find a joy in the extraordinary flight of heroism the occasion demanded of me. I now
Line saw that I had been asked for a service admirable and difficult; and there
(5) would be a greatness in letting it be seen—oh, in the right quarter!—that I could succeed where many another girl might have failed. It was an immense help to me—I confess I rather applaud myself as I look back!—that I saw my service so strongly and so simply, I was there to protect and defend the little creatures [children], in the world the most bereaved and the most love-
(10) able,… We were cut off, really, together; we were united in our danger. They had nothing but me, and I—well, I had *them*. It was in short a magnificent chance. This chance presented itself to me in an image richly material. I was a screen—I was to stand before them. The more I saw, the less they would. I began to watch them in a stifled suspense, a disguised excitement that
(15) might well, had it continued too long, have turned to something like madness.

"It was…a magnificent chance" (lines 11–12) to do what?

(A) To escape danger
(B) To reminisce
(C) To bond with the children
(D) To impress "the right quarter"
(E) To tell an interesting story

The narrator sees herself as

(A) a superheroine
(B) a mad woman
(C) a simple servant
(D) a shield against injustice
(E) one of the children

Which of the following LEAST serves to make the narrator seem unreliable?

(A) Her view of the children
(B) Her struggle to make her story seem "credible"
(C) Her sense of isolation
(D) Her motives
(E) Her line of reasoning

Explanation: Without knowing the outcome of the story, the reader cannot determine whether the narrator is sane or not. However, her line of reasoning does give us reason to question her reliability as a participatory witness to and narrator of the events that follow this selection in the story. She views herself as a superheroine, who could do what others could not. Her motives (to impress "the right quarter") hint at a "danger" that might be contrived. For her to find "a joy in the extraordinary flight of heroism" seems questionable when she claims she is "cut off" or isolated and "united" with the children in a situation that is dangerous. Although even reliable people sometimes might struggle to make their accounts of an unusual event seem "credible," this narrator pursues a line of thinking that she confesses could turn into "madness."

Correct Answers: **D, A, B**

Example 6

The Narrator's Direct Opinions

Notice how the narrator interjects his opinions in this excerpt from *Oliver Twist* (1838):

Although I am not disposed to maintain that the being born in a workhouse, is in itself the most fortunate and enviable circumstance that can possibly befall a human being, I do mean to say that in this particular instance,
Line it was the best thing for Oliver Twist that could by possibility have occurred.
(5) The fact is, that there was considerable difficulty in inducing Oliver to take upon himself the office of respiration,—a troublesome practice, but one which custom has rendered necessary to our easy existence; and for some time he lay gasping on a little flock mattress, rather unequally poised between this world and the next: the balance being decidedly in favour of
(10) the latter. Now, if, during this brief period, Oliver had been surrounded by careful grandmothers, anxious aunts, experienced nurses, and doctors of profound wisdom, he would most inevitably and indubitably have been killed in no time. There being nobody by, however, but a pauper old woman, who was rendered rather misty by an unwonted allowance of beer; and a
(15) parish surgeon who did such matters by contract; Oliver and Nature fought out the point between them. The result was, that, after a few struggles, Oliver breathed, sneezed, and proceeded to advertise to the inmates of the workhouse the fact of a new burden having been imposed upon the parish, by setting up as loud a cry as could reasonably have been expected from a
(20) male infant who had not been possessed of that very useful appendage, a voice, for a much longer space of time than three minutes and a quarter.

Based on his general attitude, the narrator's opinion of life is

(A) respectful
(B) pessimistic
(C) optimistic
(D) sanguine
(E) zealous

Explanation: The narrator describes in a somewhat sarcastic tone the struggle between Nature and a newborn child, a struggle that the child wins, only to become "a new burden . . . on the parish"—a pessimistic attitude.

Correct Answer: **B**

Example 7

Identifying the Voice of the Author

Sometimes the speaker and the author can arguably be viewed as the same voice. For example, in Charles Dickens's *David Copperfield* (a story that Dickens based on some of his own life experiences and in which he expresses many of his own personal views), Dickens has written in the first person:

> In consideration of the day and hour of my birth, it was declared by the nurse, and by some sage women in the neighbourhood who had taken a lively interest in me several months before there was any possibility of our
>
> *Line* becoming personally acquainted, first, that I was destined to be unlucky in
> *(5)* life; and secondly, that I was privileged to see ghosts and spirits; both these gifts inevitably attaching, as they believed, to all unlucky infants of either gender, born towards the small hours on a Friday night.
>
> I need say nothing here, on the first head, because nothing can show better than my history whether that prediction was verified or falsified by the
> *(10)* result. On the second branch of the question, I will only remark, that unless I ran through that part of my inheritance while I was still a baby, I have not come into it yet. But I do not at all complain of having been kept out of this property; and if anybody else should be in the present enjoyment of it, he is heartily welcome to keep it.
>
> (1850)

The autobiographical elements of this story probably make David's attitude toward superstition

(A) in antithesis of Dickens's opinion
(B) unnecessary to the story
(C) indefensible
(D) a betrayal of trust
(E) a reflection of the author's view

Explanation: In this story Dickens is the author, David is the main character, and David is the narrator who tells the story using the first-person pronoun "I" as if he is the author. David is Dickens's **persona**: in other words, he is a character who narrates the story for the author. As Dickens's persona, David the narrator and Dickens the author have the same voice.

Correct Answer: **E**

In other situations, however, the narrator or speaker and author do not share the same attitude, as illustrated by Swift's "A Modest Proposal" that follows.

Example 8

When the Speaker and Author Do Not Share the Same Attitude

Read carefully the following excerpt from "A Modest Proposal," written in 1729 by Jonathan Swift at a time when English landowners were turning deaf ears to the suffering of homeless Irish who were victims of a three-year drought.

Line (5)

It is a melancholy object to those who walk through this great town or travel in the country, when they see the streets, the roads, and cabin doors, crowded with beggars of the female sex, followed by three, four, or six children, all in rags and importuning every passenger for an alms. These mothers, instead of being able to work for their honest livelihood, are forced to employ all their time in strolling to beg sustenance for their helpless infants, who, as they grow up, either turn thieves for want of work, or leave their dear native country to fight for the Pretender in Spain, or sell themselves to the Barbados. . . .

(10)

But my intention is very far from being confined to provide only for the children of professed beggars; it is of much greater extent, and shall take in the whole number of infants at a certain age who are born of parents in effect as little able to support them as those who demand our charity in the streets.

(15)

. . . [I]t is exactly at one year that I propose to provide for them in such a manner as instead of being a charge upon their parents or the parish,...they shall on the contrary contribute to the feeding, and partly to the clothing, of many thousands.

* * *

(20)

I am assured by our merchants that a boy or a girl before twelve years old is no salable commodity; and even when they come to this age they will not yield above three pounds, or three pound and half a crown at most on the Exchange; which cannot turn to account either to the parents or the kingdom, the charge of nutriment and rags having been at least four times that value.

(25)

I shall now therefore humbly propose my own thoughts, which I hope will not be liable to the least objection.

(30)

I have been assured by a very knowing American of my acquaintance in London, that a young healthy child well nursed is at a year old a most delicious, nourishing, and wholesome food, whether stewed, roasted, baked, or boiled; and I make no doubt that it will equally serve in a fricassee or a ragout....

The speaker's solution to his nation's poverty problems is

(A) a social welfare system
(B) social reform
(C) a system of cannibalism
(D) establishing a commodities market
(E) an expanded agricultural base

The speaker's solution is best characterized as

(A) communal
(B) concessional
(C) confiscatory
(D) larcenous
(E) macabre

Explanation: Lines 44–48 describe using children as an ingredient in recipes. The speaker's solution reflects a distorted view of humanity, making him naïve. His solution is obviously gruesome and horrible—macabre. This essay is a satire because Swift uses wit to censor or criticize society, <u>with the aim toward reform</u>. In satire, the writer's attitude often is one of condemnation or contempt.

Correct Answers: **C, E**

The speaker in "A Modest Proposal" is Swift's persona. Sometimes a character who narrates in the first person (as if he or she is the author) has opinions, actions, or thoughts that are so naïve or so obtuse (as in this case) they ironically make the point of the author.

Of the attitudes listed, which is the attitude of the speaker in "A Modest Proposal" toward his readers?

(A) Overbearing self-confidence
(B) Aggressive hostility
(C) Confident conviction
(D) Feigned sincerity
(E) Ribald frivolity

Explanation: Swift is the author; "I" is the speaker. Does this speaker, however, represent Swift's true opinions? Obviously not. Note the shocking nature of the speaker's proposal, particularly when he exposes his "plan" for turning children into a food source in the last paragraph of the excerpt, a totally alien concept to any civilized people. The writer might have directly said, "You are allowing these children to starve and to be treated like animals," but would such direct words have had the attention-getting effect and the same shame-producing impact that his proposal elicits? In the case of "A Modest Proposal," the author and the speaker do not share the same voice.

Correct Answer: **D**

Sometimes the speaker and the author are not of the same opinion, even when the work is written in the first person.

Example 9

Dramatic Monologue

The following excerpt is taken from the often referenced dramatic monologue by Robert Browning called "My Last Duchess." The lyric speaker is *not* Browning, but rather a sixth-century Italian duke named Alfonso II. He was married to a fourteen-year-old girl who died when she was just seventeen. Her death has been described as "suspicious"; however, Duke Alfonso went on to negotiate an arrangement to marry a member of Austrian royalty. He used an agent for these negotiations; that agent is the silent auditor to whom this lyric poem is addressed:

That's my last Duchess painted on the wall,
Looking as if she were alive. I call
That piece a wonder, now: Fra` Pandolf's hands
Line   Worked busily a day, and there she stands.
(5)   Will't please you sit and look at her? . . .
    . . . Sir, 'twas not
Her husband's presence only, called that spot
Of joy into the Duchess' cheek: . . .
    . . . She had
(10)   A heart—how shall I say?—too soon made glad,
Too easily impressed; she liked whate'er
She looked on, and her looks went everywhere.
Sir, 'twas all one! My favor at her breast,
The dropping of the daylight in the West,
(15)   The bough of cherries some officious fool
Broke in the orchard for her, the white mule
She rode with round the terrace—all and each
Would draw from her alike the approving speech,
Or blush, at least. She thanked men,—good! but thanked
(20)   Somehow—I know not how—as if she ranked
My gift of a nine-hundred-years-old name
With anybody's gift. Who'd stoop to blame
This sort of trifling? Even had you skill
In speech—which I have not—to make your will
(25)   Quite clear to such an one, and say, "Just this
Or that in you disgust me; here you miss,
Or there exceed the mark"—and if she let
Herself be lessoned so, nor plainly set
Her wits to yours, forsooth, and made excuse,
(30)   —E'en then would be some stooping; and I choose
Never to stoop. Oh sir, she smiled, no doubt,
Whene'er I passed her; but who passed without
Much the same smile? This grew; I gave commands
Then all smiles stopped together. There she stands
(35)   As if alive. Will't please you rise? We'll meet
The company below, then I repeat,

The Count your master's known munificence
Is ample warrant that no just pretense
Of mine for dowry will be disallowed;
(40) Though his fair daughter's self, as I avowed
At starting, is my object. Nay, we'll go
Together down, sir. Notice Neptune, though,
Taming a sea-horse, thought a rarity,
Which Claus of Innsbruck cast in bronze for me!

(1842)

In lines 9–33, the attitude of the speaker toward his late wife is best described as

(A) magnanimous
(B) indulgent
(C) meddlesome
(D) lenient
(E) petty

Why did the speaker never voice his objections to his wife?

(A) bashfulness
(B) shame
(C) pride
(D) insolence
(E) humility

The poet presents the speaker as a man who is

(A) grieving
(B) cold-blooded
(C) fickle
(D) dignified
(E) vulnerable

Explanation: The duke resented that his wife had the same youthful smile for everyone and everything that pleased her, including him. He wanted her to smile and blush only for him. His pettiness went so far as to criticize the excitement she felt over such innocent things as a sunset (line 14) and riding her mule (line 16). He did not tell her so that she could amend her actions, because to do so would be "stooping; and I choose / Never to stoop" (lines 30–31), projecting his attitude of pride. What is the poet's attitude toward this man? Condemning. Browning presents him as unreasonable, filled with pride, and capable of murdering a young girl (lines 33–35), then going on without regret to negotiate marriage to yet another (lines 35–41), in other words, a cold-blooded killer.

Correct Answers: **E, C, B**

Example 10

Voice Revealed in Dramatic Conventions

Here is the chorus from the Prologue before Act I Scene I of *Romeo and Juliet*.

> ACT I PROLOGUE
> [*Enter*] CHORUS
> CHORUS.
>
> Two households, both alike in dignity,
> In fair Verona, where we lay our scene,
> From ancient grudge break to new mutiny,
> Where civil blood makes civil hands unclean.
>
> *Line*
> (5) From forth the fatal loins of these two foes
>   A pair of star-crost lovers take their life;
>   Whose misadventured piteous overthrows
>   Doth with their death bury their parents' strife.
>   The fearful passage of their death-mark'd love,
> (10) And the continuance of their parents' rage,
>   Which, but their children's end, naught could remove,
>   Is now the two hours' traffic of our stage;
>   The which if you with patient ears attend,
>   What here shall miss, our toil shall strive to mend. [*Exit*]

The attitude projected by the chorus toward the lovers is best described as

(A) sympathetic
(B) lenient
(C) callous
(D) matter-of-fact
(E) inclement

Explanation: Although the lines do seem somewhat matter-of-fact, the connotations of some lines reveal sympathy for the lovers. They are "star-crost," their "overthrows" are "misadventured" and "piteous," and their "parents' rage" could be removed only by "their children's end."

Correct Answer: **A**

Test Taker → Test Maker

If you were writing SAT Literature tests, what questions about (narrative) voice would you ask? Here is an opportunity for you to approach (narrative) voice from the test writer's point of view.

The *Riddle of the Sands* by Erskine Childers was published in 1903 and is considered the first spy novel.

> 'It's not much use,' he said, 'on a falling tide, but we'll try kedging-off. Pay that warp out while I run out the kedge.'
>
> *Line* Like lightning he had cast off the dinghy's painter, tumbled the kedge-
> anchor and himself into the dinghy, pulled out fifty yards into the deeper
> *(5)* water, and heaved out the anchor. 'Now haul,' he shouted.
>
> I hauled, beginning to see what kedging-off meant.
>
> 'Steady on! don't sweat yourself,' said Davies, jumping aboard again.
>
> 'It's coming,' I spluttered, triumphantly.
>
> 'The warp is, the yacht isn't; you're dragging the anchor home. Never
> *(10)* mind, she'll lie well here. Let's have lunch.'
>
> The yacht was motionless, and the water round her visibly lower. Petulant
> waves slapped against her sides, but, scattered as my senses were, I realized
> that there was no vestige of danger. ...
>
> 'Lies quiet, doesn't she?' he remarked. 'If you do want a sit-down lunch,
> *(15)* there's nothing like running aground for it. And anyhow, we're as handy for
> work here as anywhere else. You'll see.'
>
> Like most landsmen I had a wholesome prejudice against 'running
> aground', so that my mentor's turn for breezy paradox was at first rather exas-
> perating. After lunch the large-scale chart of the estuaries was brought down,
> *(20)* and we pored over it together, mapping out work for the next few days. There
> is no need to tire the general reader with its intricacies, nor is there space to
> reproduce it for the benefit of the instructed reader. For both classes the gen-
> eral map should be sufficient....

As a test writer, you look for the ways the author uses the literary elements. Here are some ideas to guide you:

Do you see any context clues that make it easier to understand specialized vocabulary?

_____

Are there any literary terms used by the writer?

_____

From what point of view is the author telling this story?

_____

Discussion

Even the narrator must use the context of the situation to know what "kedging-off" means, so this word would most likely be the subject of a test question. Did you notice the way he highlighted "breezy paradox" in line 18? A test writer would expect you to know what a paradox is, spot the words or phrases that are used paradoxically, and understand why. Actually, the "sit-down lunch," in conjunction with "running aground" for lunch, can also be considered a play on words.

Because we have been examining (narrative) voice, however, let's focus on the point of view. The use of "I" tells you first person, of course. How involved is the narrator with his audience? Notice how he refers to us directly in lines 21–24. Do you see anything unusual? He divides his readership into two groups, the "general reader" and the "instructed reader."

Now, think about this situation for a moment. We cannot accurately speculate on whether the persona/narrator's attitudes are the same as the writer's without the context of the entire novel, but we can try to identify what those attitudes are.

A question for thought and discussion

Writers sometimes directly address or refer to the reader to create a confidential tone between writer and reader. Is a connection made in this selection? Why or why not?

A test writer very likely would (1) write the question so that the test taker must directly identify the attitude(s) of the narrator toward his audience or (2) focus on the fact that he divides the readership into two groups. A comparison/contrast question might work here.

Select one of these two options to write your question.

_____

(A) _____

(B) _____

(C) _____

(D) *_____

(E) _____

NARRATIVE VOICE IN CONCLUSION

The nonnarrative speaker, the narrator, and the writer all have attitudes. The secret to identifying the voice in a work is first to establish clearly who is speaking and what that person is saying. You can then determine the person's attitude. This element does not end here, however. The attitudes expressed in a work also give it a tone, the next literary element.

*Correct Answer

LITERARY ELEMENT NUMBER FOUR: TONE

Perhaps the best way for you to understand narrative voice and tone in preparation for the test is to concentrate not on separating tone from voice, but rather to focus on their relationship to each other.

TERM ALERT You should know this term: **Tone**

Definition: Tone is a product of voice.

> *Example:* **He has a dogmatic attitude (voice). It makes him sound overbearing (tone).**

In its most narrow sense, tone is a description of the attitude of the speaker. That attitude can be described in many ways: happy, sad, ironic, sincere, playful, formal (or informal), condescending, admiring, and so forth.

What terms do I need to know that relate to a work's tone?

TERM ALERT ### 1. Onomatopoeia

Definition: Onomatopoeia refers to words, lines, and passages whose sound, size, movement, and overall effect denote the sense or meaning. The sounds work together to carry the meaning. Tennyson's *The Princess* ("Come Down, O Maid"—1847):

> "…The moan of doves in immemorial elms,
> And murmuring of innumerable bees."

Notice how, in this first stanza of a poem written by Robert Burns in the late eighteenth century, the sounds work together to carry its meaning and to establish the tone:

Afton Water

> Flow gently, sweet Afton, among thy green braes,
> Flow gently, I'll sing thee a song in thy praise;
> My Mary's asleep by thy murmuring stream,
> Flow gently, sweet Afton, disturb not her dream.

The sounds here seem to have a "feel" about them that relates to the meaning and results in a tone.

TERM ALERT ### 2. Alliteration

Definition: Alliteration occurs when the initial consonant or consonant cluster sounds in stressed syllables are repeated (generally in successive or closely associated stressed syllables).

> Lo, <u>h</u>ow I <u>h</u>old mine arms abroad,
> <u>Th</u>ee <u>t</u>o <u>r</u>eceive <u>r</u>eady spread!

In its more extreme form, alliteration becomes the tongue twister "Peter Piper picked a peck of pickled peppers" and "She sells sea-shells by the sea-shore."

Once again, the sounds have a "feel" that relates to the meaning and results in a tone.

3. **Setting** and **pastoral**

Definition: Setting in a literary selection refers to geographical location, time, and socioeconomic conditions. For example, **pastorals**, poems with country life as the subject and shepherds as characters in rural settings, were popular between 1550 and 1750.

Although setting is generally associated with narrative writing, some aspects of setting, particularly those of socioeconomic conditions, can affect the tone even in nonnarrative works.

The effects on tone of some settings are dramatic and easy to identify: the romantic tone of a deserted island, the frightening tone of a lonely graveyard on a stormy night, the warm tone of a family gathering on Christmas Eve. Some, however, are more subtle, changing, or perhaps even unexpected, as when the romantic island becomes a place of fear and hardship when food and water supplies dwindle.

4. **Style**

Definition: Style is how the writer uses the literary elements to express his or her attitude.

Although a writer may try to emulate another author's style, like snowflakes, no two writers' styles are *exactly* alike. A writer's style can be based on a wide range of factors, such as purpose (a scientific style, a journalistic style, a didactic style); chosen genre (a romantic style or a swashbuckler style); or desires to emulate the work of a particular literary period, school, or favorite writer (a Shakespearean style, a New Formalism style). Readers tend to label the style of a writer based on their overall impression of the "sense" they get of his or her writing, such as imaginative (or unimaginative), exciting (or dull), sensitive (or insensitive). Once a writer has established a recognizable style, readers tend to talk about whether a new work is consistent with or is a departure from the writer's "style."

5. **Assonance**

Definition: Assonance occurs when the same (or similar) vowel sounds are repeated in nearby words (usually in stressed syllables). Unlike rhyme, which has similarity of both vowel and final consonant sounds (for example, "book" and "took"), assonance repeats only the vowel sounds and ends with different consonant sounds. Notice the use of elements of rhyme, alliteration ("w"), and assonance in this anonymous ballad:

Helen of Kirconnell

I wish I were where Helen lies,
Night and day on me she cries;
O that I were where Helen lies
On fair Kirconnell lea!

TERM WATCH

TERM WATCH

TERM WATCH

"I" and "night" both contain the long i sound. This assonance is emphasized in the rhyme of "lies" with "cries." You also may find assonance a popular substitution for end rhyme, especially in the ballad form:

> His hounds they lie downe at his *feete*,
> So well they can their master *keepe*.

TERM WATCH

6. Consonance

Definition: Consonance occurs when final consonant sounds of stressed syllables are repeated but the preceding vowels are different. Consonance is often used in conjunction with alliteration (as in *reader* and *rider*); however, initial alliteration is not always a factor (as in *learn, torn*). The aural appeal can be heard in George Wither's use of consonance in the last stanza of "Shall I Wasting in Despair" (ca. 1622) in which *d, r, v, l,* and *t* are repeated:

> Great, or good, or kind, or fair,
> I will ne'er the more despair,
> If she love me, this believe,
> I will die, ere she shall grieve.
> If she slight me when I woo,
> I can scorn, and let her go.
>   For, if she be not for me,
>   What care I for whom she be?

TERM REVIEW

7. Mood

Definition: Mood refers to an emotional state, especially as projected by the characters in the work: "Joyce is in a foul mood" or "Eric is in a happy mood." Moods, of course, can change (as can many of the other elements of tone) within the work.

Also, attitude and tone can be projected by the mood of the verb used. Here is a review:

Indicative mood is used for making statements or questioning fact (or probable fact).

The book is on the desk.

I think that he is here.

Do you own a car?

The indicative mood is generally neutral; the tone of the speaker's attitude must be determined by other elements, such as connotative word choice.

Imperative mood is used to make direct requests or commands and requires the use of a simple form of the verb. Usually, the subject of the verb is the unspoken "you" or an indefinite pronoun.

(You) Stop jumping on the bed.

(Everybody) Follow the path through the woods.

(Somebody) Please help me!

Because the speaker is making a request or command of someone, the imperative mood of the verb obviously affects the tone of the speaker's words. The verb choice plus the context determine varying degrees of urgency of the request, as well as the speaker's purpose. Does the request have an instructional tone? Is the tone of the command authoritative?

Subjunctive mood is used to make conditional statements of possibility, hypothesis, speculation, wishes, and so forth.

Present subjunctive uses present tense, first- and second-person singular:

Should I *be* home to meet him?
The teacher demands that *he stay* late tomorrow.

Past subjunctive uses the simple past tense. The verb "to be," however, requires "were" regardless of the number (singular, plural) or person (first, second, or third):

If I *were* to stay, I might eat too much.
I wish that *he were* here for the holidays.

Keep alert!

Conditional statements can contain clues to attitudes and motives.

A conditional statement can powerfully affect the tone in a variety of ways. It can imply that there is **an element of doubt** (ambiguity) about the situation or person in question:

If Elizabeth were to have left this morning, surely Justin would have told me.

The subjunctive might suppose that a change in certain conditions would lead to different results:

If they were to leave, Georgia Ann would become hysterical.
Unless we were to have a flat tire, we'll be there by seven.

Longings of the heart, unfulfilled dreams, wishes, suggestions, and indirect requests can all be conveyed using the subjunctive.

If I were a rich woman, I would buy that car.
We recommend that the applicant complete the form quickly because the firm is requesting that her follow-up interview be scheduled for this afternoon.

Notice the use of "that" in these constructions.

Some uses of the subjunctive mood are so commonplace that they have become cliché. For example: Be that as it may. Far be it from me. If I were in your shoes. So be it.

8. **Feeling** and **atmosphere**

TERM REVIEW

Definition: Feeling has been defined as an intellectual state: the attitude of the author toward his subject on an intellectual rather than on an emotional basis. Conversationally, this might be approached with the question, "What is your *feeling* on the subject?" to which the respondent would express his or her views.

The setting, the tone (of voice) of the author and speaker, the emotional moods of the author, the speaker, and/or the characters, and the feelings of the author blend together to give the work its **atmosphere**—that prevailing and pervasive ambience that gives the reader the basis for expectation.

Atmosphere is often described using such terms as "mysterious," "romantic," "gloomy," "horrifying," "intellectual," and other expressions depicting these types of effects. When movie critics label a motion picture as a "feel-good movie," they are referring to its atmosphere.

TERM REVIEW   ## 9. Euphony

Definition: Euphony refers to sounds that are pleasing and easy to pronounce, producing a pleasant tone. One poem that many consider "pleasant" to the tongue and ear is "The Raven," although the tone is very disquieting.

What else do I need to know about tone?

1. Elements That Contribute to Tone

- The speaker has an attitude toward the subject. *How* he or she expresses that attitude projects a tone.
- The author also has an attitude toward the subject. The speaker can be the author's persona, expressing the writer's own views. The speaker's words and actions might be *in contrast* to the views of the author, creating an ironic tone. Swift's "A Modest Proposal" is an example.
- Some themes or subjects carry with them intrinsic elements of tone. For instance, death usually has an unhappy tone and birth generally a happy tone. You should not assume, however, that a work about death is always in a negative tone: The tone is a product of many elements that work together, including the author's intent.
- The characters in a work (what they say and do) and how they are characterized (what is said about them) can significantly influence the tone of a work.
- How words are used in a selection, the connotations, the figurative language, all contribute directly to setting the tone.

2. Sound Effects

One element that has significant impact on the tone of a work is the sound of the language.

One needs to look no further than the limerick to probe the effect of rhythm and rhyme on tone. Meaning is at the root of a limerick's humorous impact (its funny tone), but the impact of the rhythm and rhyme scheme on its tone cannot be denied:

> There was a young fellow named Hall,
> Who fell in the spring in the fall;
>   'Twould have been a sad thing
> *Line*   If he'd died in the spring,
> *(5)*   But he didn't—he died in the fall.

Anon.

In songs, ballads, and other styles of poetry set to music, the tone is influenced greatly by the arrangement of the music itself. Poems not intended to be sung, however, can also rely on verbal and musical elements to project a tone. There is more to the "sound" of a poem as it relates to the tone it projects than just rhythm and rhyme. Tone in a poem is also a product of *sound effects* (their uses and tonal qualities), such as onomatopoeia, alliteration, consonance, and euphony.

How could questions about tone be worded?

The following selections and their questions illustrate some of the ways tone might be tested.

Example 1

The Speaker's Attitude Projecting a Tone

Look at the tone projected by this poem written in the mid-1600s.

Peace

My soul, there is a country
    Far beyond the stars,
Where stands a wingèd sentry
Line   All skilful in the wars;
(5) There above noise, and danger
    Sweet peace sits crowned with smiles,
And one born in a manger
    Commands the beauteous files;
He is thy gracious friend,
(10)   And (O, my Soul, awake!)
Did in pure love descend
    To die here for thy sake.

If thou canst get but thither,
    There grows the flower of peace,
(15) The rose that cannot wither,
    Thy fortress, and thy ease;
Leave then thy foolish ranges,
    For none can thee secure,
But one, who never changes,
(20)   Thy God, thy life, thy cure.

by Henry Vaughan

The speaker of this poem is

(A) a disembodied spirit
(B) in a dream
(C) in a state of self-contemplation
(D) in astral projection
(E) in a nightmare

The central contrast can be summarized as

(A) waking and sleeping
(B) friends and enemies
(C) love and hate
(D) war and peace
(E) silence and noise

The speaker's

(A) negative attitude toward death sounds discouraging
(B) boisterous attitude toward war sounds dangerous
(C) irascible attitude toward peace sounds contradictory
(D) complaisant attitude toward love sounds tranquil
(E) positive attitude toward peace sounds hopeful

The speaker's attitude toward his own soul gives the poem a sense of

(A) urgency
(B) remorse
(C) ominousness
(D) belligerence
(E) condescendence

Explanation: Lines 1 and 10 tell us that the speaker is talking to his own soul or spiritual self in a state of self-contemplation. What is he thinking? First, he meditates upon a "country / Far beyond the stars." The country has a sentry, "skilful in the wars"—military imagery. The country is "above noise, and danger" (line 5) where there is peace. Lines 7–12 contain a biblical allusion. (We will discuss allusion in more detail in a later chapter.) Context, then, pinpoints a country where the speaker will find his fortress (a symbol of protection from war). The references to "foolish ranges" (line 17) that cannot be secured here in this life again add to the war imagery. The speaker is contrasting war below with the peace above. Of course, such a positive attitude would be hopeful.

There is yet another attitude at work in this poem: the attitude of the speaker toward his own soul. He begins with a rather matter-of-fact tone of self-address in line 1, but he commands his soul to "awake!" in line 10 and to "Leave" in line 17. In conjunction with the hint of uncertainty of "If thou canst get but thither" in line 13, his commanding attitude gives a sense of urgency to the tone of the entire poem.

A concluding thought: Who is the speaker? Is he Vaughan, the poet? Perhaps. However, line 10 commands his soul to "awake!" Is his soul asleep (in death)? Consider this possibility: What if the speaker is a persona for Vaughan? If so, how would you describe him? Could he be someone dying on the field of battle?

Correct Answers: **C, D, E, A**

Example 2

The Tone Projected By Characters

The characters determine the tone in this excerpt of dialogue from *The Old Curiosity Shop* by Charles Dickens (1841).

"I can't see anything but the curtain of the bed," said Brass, applying his eye to the keyhole of the door. "Is he a strong man, Mr. Richard [Dick Swiveller]?"

Line
(5)

"Very," answered Dick.

"It would be an extremely unpleasant circumstance if he was to bounce out suddenly," said Brass. "Hallo there! Hallo, hallo!"

. . .

Suddenly the door was unlocked on the inside and flung violently open. Miss Sally dived into her own bedroom; Mr. Brass, who was not
(10) remarkable for personal courage, ran into the next street, and finding that nobody followed him, armed with a poker or other offensive weapon, put his hands in his pockets, walked very slowly all at once, and whistled.

Meanwhile Mr. Swiveller, on the top of the stool, drew himself into
(15) as flat a shape as possible against the wall and looked, not unconcernedly, down upon the single gentleman, who appeared at the door growling and cursing in a very awful manner, . . .

"Have *you* been making that horrible noise?" said the single gentleman.

(20) "I have been helping, sir," returned Dick, keeping his eye upon him.

"How dare you then," said the lodger. "Eh?"

To this, Dick made no other reply than by inquiring whether the lodger held it to be consistent with the conduct and character of a gentleman to go to sleep for six-and-twenty hours at a stretch, and whether
(25) the peace of an amiable and virtuous family was to weigh as nothing in the balance.

"Is my peace nothing?" said the single gentleman.

"Yes, sir, indeed," returned Dick, yielding, "but an equal quantity of slumber was never got out of one bed and bedstead, and if you're going
(30) to sleep in that way, you must pay for a double-bedded room."

Dick's attitude toward the cost basis of renting a bed is best described as

(A) illogical
(B) reasonable
(C) thoughtful
(D) intuitive
(E) cogent

The incident about the price of a bed has a

(A) fanatic sense
(B) comic tone
(C) preoccupied sense
(D) sagacious tone
(E) tragic tone

Explanation: First, examine the situation. Dick Swiveller, Miss Brass, and Mr. Brass are trying to get the single gentleman's attention. When he opens the door, Miss Brass "dived into her own bedroom," Mr. Brass runs away, then pretends nothing is wrong, and Dick flattens himself against the wall, perhaps instinctively to hide. This *Three Stooges*–type scene is obviously meant to be amusing.

In this context, we have Dick confronting the single gentleman with his complaint. Implied in the scene is that the stranger is a lodger who is paying rent for a single bed. We, at this point, learn Dick's mission in disturbing the man. He objects that the lodger slept for twenty-six hours straight and contends that the bed got so much use that the stranger should "pay for a double-bedded room." Such reasoning is illogical and contributes to the comic tone.

Correct Answers: **A, B**

Example 3

Use of Language and Meanings in Context

Look at how the meanings of the language in context sets the tone in this excerpt from a communication sent by Benjamin Franklin to Lord Kames of England in April of 1767.

> But America, an immense territory, favored by nature with all advantages
> of climate, soil, great navigable rivers and lakes, etc., must become a great
> country, populous and mighty; and will, in a less time than is generally con-
> *Line* ceived, be able to shake off any shackles that may be imposed on her, and
> *(5)* perhaps place them on the imposers. In the meantime, every act of oppres-
> sion will sour their tempers, lessen greatly, if not annihilate, the profits of
> your commerce with them, and hasten their final revolt; for the seeds of lib-
> erty are universally sown there, and nothing can eradicate them.

Franklin's tone implies all the following EXCEPT

(A) confidence
(B) nerve
(C) rashness
(D) a threat
(E) dauntlessness

Explanation: The context of the communication is the growing resistance of the American colonists to British rule. First, Franklin describes America as "immense … favored by nature … a great country, populous and mighty"—in other words, a formidable nation. Then he introduces the element of time and uses figurative language to say that "any shackles … imposed" on America may eventually be placed "on the imposers"—a very connotatively harsh metaphor that compares Britain's relationship to America as enslavement, and that the slaves may turn and enslave their masters. He then points out that "oppression" might even "annihilate, the profits of your commerce"—a threat to Britain's financial base in America. Again, he links the element of time ("hasten") to the impending "final revolt." He concludes the excerpt with another powerful metaphor comparing liberty to sown seeds that cannot be eradicated (another strongly connotative word).

In the context of the excerpt, what is Franklin's (the speaker's) attitude? Disapproving, unintimidated, one of warning. What is his tone (in what manner does he convey this attitude)? In a threatening tone … a bold tone … an uncompromising tone … a confident tone.

Correct answer: **C**

Example 4

Form, Figurative Language, and Sound Devices

Edward Taylor uses form, rhythm, rhyme, alliteration, and other sound devices to contribute to the tone with this excerpt from "Upon a Spider Catching a Fly":

> Thou sorrow, venom elf:
>   Is this thy play,
> To spin a web out of thyself
> *Line*   To catch a fly?
> *(5)*   For why?
>
> I saw a pettish wasp
>   Fall foul therein,
> Whom yet thy whorl-pins did not clasp
>   Lest he should fling
> *(10)*   His sting.
>   . . .

(ca. 1700)

The use of couplets and short lines to conclude each stanza makes the speaker sound

(A) rowdy
(B) roguish
(C) cunning
(D) unrestrained
(E) playful

Explanation: His subject is a spider. He observes that a spider spins webs to catch flies, but the spider does not tackle a wasp because of the sting. The speaker may have a very serious meaning behind this observation; however, the sound of the verses (particularly the couplets) is incongruent with a serious attitude. They create a playful tone.

Correct Answer: **E**

Example 5

Mood (of the verb) and Tone

These lines are taken from Frances S. Osgood's "To Labor Is to Pray."

> Work,—and pure slumbers shall wait on thy pillow;
> Work,—thou shalt ride o'er Care's coming billow;
> Lie not down 'neath Woe's weeping Willow,
>   Work with a stout heart and resolute will!

(ca. 1840)

How does the mood relate to the tone of these lines?

(A) Use of the indicative mood creates a formal tone.
(B) Use of the subjunctive mood creates a stressful tone.
(C) Use of the subjunctive creates a wishful tone.
(D) Use of the imperative mood creates an uncertain tone.
(E) Use of the imperative mood creates an urgent tone.

Explanation: These lines are a series of commands with an understood subject. In this case, the commands add a sense of urgency.

Correct Answer: **E**

Example 6

Style and Tone

The writer's style influences the tone of this selection.

Ivanhoe
by
Sir Walter Scott

In that pleasant district of merry England which is watered by the river Don, there extended in ancient times a large forest, covering the greater part of the beautiful hills and valleys which lie between Sheffield and the pleasant
Line town of Doncaster. The remains of this extensive wood are still to be seen at
(5) the noble seats of Wentworth, of Wharncliffe Park, and around Rotherham. Here haunted of yore the fabulous Dragon of Wantley; here were fought many of the most desperate battles during the Civil Wars of the Roses; and here also flourished in ancient times those bands of gallant outlaws whose deeds have been rendered so popular in English song.

(10) Such being our chief scene, the date of our story refers to a period towards the end of the reign of Richard I., when his return from his long captivity had become an event rather wished than hoped for by his despairing subjects, who were in the meantime subjected to every species of subordinate oppression. The nobles, whose power had become exorbitant during the

(15) reign of Stephen, and whom the prudence of Henry the Second had scarce reduced into some degree of subjection to the crown, had now resumed their ancient license in its utmost extent; despising the feeble interference of the English Council of State, fortifying their castles, increasing the number of their dependents, reducing all around them to a state of vassalage, and striv-

(20) ing by every means in their power to place themselves each at the head of such forces as might enable him to make a figure in the national convulsions which appeared to be impending.

(1819)

The tone of the first paragraph

(A) is unnecessary to the story
(B) contrasts to the second paragraph
(C) is continued in the second paragraph
(D) conflicts with the narrator's point
(E) is critical

The overall style of this selection relies heavily on

(A) lively dialogue
(B) figurative language
(C) romance
(D) connotative word choices
(E) journalistic technique

Explanation: The narrator has invested significant effort in establishing the tone of the setting in its historical context, giving the reader reason to *anticipate* that the focus of the narrative is on, not exclusively the characters, but also on how the events of the time and place (as they are historically significant) affect the lives of the characters and how, in turn, the lives of the characters may (or may fail to) affect historical events and outcomes.

In examining the style of the narrative, you will find that the writer relies heavily on connotative word choices, particularly in the contrast of the tone established in the first paragraph (the tone projected by the description of a beautiful place of fabulous events) with the following paragraph (the tone projected by introduction of a blight imposed upon that beautiful place by hated nobles).

Correct Answers: **B, D**

Example 7

Style, Rhyme Scheme, and Tone

Here is "That Sound," written by L. E. Myers.

> What fun camping out—
>   Wild animals all about.
> Then it gets dark
>   In the National Park.

Line

(5)
> And after all are fed,
>   You're tired and ready for bed.
> The tents are all in a row
>   And into bed you all go.

> You hear that sound

(10)
>   And out of bed you bound.
> It's still quite early—
>   Only about four-thirty.

> That sound came from who-o-o
>   Just in time to scare you.

(15)
> A quivering sound that's eerie;
>   The dark makes you leery.

> The others hear it, too—
>   That same sound that scared you.
> Please try to identify

(20)
>   That strange and scary cry.

(1996)

The tone of this poem is NOT the result of

(A) figurative language
(B) the subject
(C) the intended audience
(D) style
(E) rhyme scheme

Explanation: Obviously intended to entertain children, this riddle poem (describing campers encountering an owl) uses a style appropriate to the audience (simple words and sentence structure), as well as an uncomplicated rhyme scheme that keeps the emphasis on the subject—a mysterious sound in the woods.

Correct Answer: **A**

Example 8

Rhythm, Rhyme, and Alliteration

Edgar Allan Poe's "The Raven" follows. Teachers, critics, and anthology editors for generations have pointed to "The Raven" as an American classic because of its distinctive use of rhythm, rhyme, and alliterative elements that contribute to its tone.

First, read the poem for enjoyment. Notice the use of internal rhyme: "dreary" and "weary"; "napping," "tapping," and "rapping"; "remember," "December," and "ember"; "morrow," "sorrow," and "borrow." In the third stanza, listen to the effects of "silken, sad, uncertain rustling." But how do these elements work together to give the poem its atmosphere? How would you describe the atmosphere of "The Raven?"

The Raven

Stanza:

1   Once upon a midnight dreary, while I pondered, weak and weary,
      Over many a quaint and curious volume of forgotten lore,
    While I nodded, nearly napping, suddenly there came a tapping,
      As of some one gently rapping, rapping at my chamber door.
    "'Tis some visitor," I muttered, "tapping at my chamber door—
      Only this and nothing more."

2   Ah, distinctly I remember it was in the bleak December,
      And each separate dying ember wrought its ghost upon the floor.
    Eagerly I wished the morrow; vainly I had sought to borrow
      From my books surcease of sorrow—sorrow for the lost Lenore,
    For the rare and radiant maiden whom the angels name Lenore—
      Nameless *here* for evermore.

3   And the silken, sad, uncertain rustling of each purple curtain
      Thrilled me—filled me with fantastic terrors never felt before;
    So that now, to still the beating of my heart, I stood repeating,
      "'Tis some visitor entreating entrance at my chamber door—
    Some late visitor entreating entrance at my chamber door—
      This it is and nothing more."

4   Presently my soul grew stronger: hesitating then no longer,
      "Sir," said I, "or Madam, truly your forgiveness I implore;
    But the fact is I was napping, and so gently you came rapping,
      And so faintly you came tapping, tapping at my chamber door,
    That I scarce was sure I heard you"—here I opened wide the door—
      Darkness there and nothing more.

5   Deep into that darkness peering, long I stood there, wondering, fearing,
      Doubting, dreaming dreams no mortal ever dared to dream before;
    But the silence was unbroken, and the stillness gave no token,
      And the only word there spoken was the whispered word "Lenore!"
    This I whispered, and an echo murmured back the word "Lenore!"
      Merely this and nothing more.

6 Back into the chamber turning, all my soul within me burning,
  Soon again I heard a tapping, somewhat louder than before.
"Surely," said I, "surely that is something at my window lattice;
  Let me see, then, what thereat is, and this mystery explore—
Let my heart be still a moment and this mystery explore—
  'Tis the wind and nothing more."

7 Open here I flung the shutter, when, with many a flirt and flutter,
  In there stepped a stately Raven of the saintly days of yore.
Not the least obeisance made he, not a minute stopped or stayed he,
  But with mien of lord or lady perched above my chamber door—
Perched upon a bust of Pallas just above my chamber door—
  Perched and sat, and nothing more.

8 Then, this ebony bird beguiling my sad fancy into smiling
  By the grave and stern decorum of the countenance it wore,
"Though thy crest be shorn and shaven, thou," I said, "art sure no craven,
  Ghastly, grim, and ancient Raven, wandering from the nightly shore:
Tell me what thy lordly name is on the night's Plutonian shore!"
  Quoth the Raven, "Nevermore."

9 Much I marveled this ungainly fowl to hear discourse so plainly,
  Though its answer little meaning, little relevancy bore;
For we cannot help agreeing that no living human being
  Ever yet was blessed with seeing bird above his chamber door—
Bird or beast upon the sculptured bust above his chamber door—
  With such name as "Nevermore."

10 But the Raven, sitting lonely on the placid bust, spoke only
  That one word, as if his soul in that one word he did outpour.
Nothing further then he uttered, not a feather then he fluttered;
  Till I scarcely more than muttered, "Other friends have flown before:
On the morrow he will leave me, as my hopes have flown before."
  Then the bird said, "Nevermore."

11 Startled at the stillness broken by reply so aptly spoken,
  "Doubtless," said I, "what it utters is its only stock and store,
Caught from some unhappy master whom unmerciful Disaster
  Followed fast and followed faster till his songs one burden bore,
Till the dirges of his hope that melancholy burden bore
  Of 'Never—nevermore.'"

12 But the Raven still beguiling my sad fancy into smiling,
  Straight I wheeled a cushioned seat in front of bird and bust and door;
Then, upon the velvet sinking, I betook myself to linking
  Fancy unto fancy, thinking what this ominous bird of yore,
What this grim, ungainly, ghastly, gaunt, and ominous bird of yore
  Meant in croaking "Nevermore."

13   This I sat engaged in guessing, but no syllable expressing
    To the fowl, whose fiery eyes now burned into my bosom's core;
This and more I sat divining, with my head at ease reclining
    On the cushion's velvet lining that the lamplight gloated o'er,
But whose velvet-violet lining with the lamplight gloating o'er,
    She shall press, ah, nevermore!

14   Then, methought, the air grew denser, perfumed from an unseen censer
    Swung by seraphim whose foot-falls tinkled on the tufted floor.
"Wretch," I cried, "thy God hath lent thee—by these angels he hath sent thee
    Respite—respite and nepenthe from thy memories of Lenore!
Quaff, oh quaff this kind nepenthe, and forget this lost Lenore!"
    Quoth the Raven, "Nevermore."

15   "Prophet!" said I, "thing of evil! prophet still, if bird or devil!
    Whether Tempter sent, or whether tempest tossed thee here ashore,
Desolate yet all undaunted, on this desert land enchanted—
    On this home by Horror haunted—tell me truly, I implore:
Is there—is there balm in Gilead?—tell me—tell me, I implore!"
    Quoth the Raven, "Nevermore."

16   "Prophet!" said I, "thing of evil—prophet still, if bird or devil!
    By that Heaven that bends above us, by that God we both adore,
Tell this soul with sorrow laden if, within the distant Aidenn,
    It shall clasp a sainted maiden whom the angels name Lenore:
Clasp a rare and radiant maiden whom the angels name Lenore!"
    Quoth the Raven, "Nevermore."

17   "Be that word our sign of parting, bird or fiend!" I shrieked, upstarting:
    "Get thee back into the tempest and the Night's Plutonian shore!
Leave no black plume as a token of that lie thy soul hath spoken!
    Leave my loneliness unbroken! quit the bust above my door!
Take thy beak from out my heart, and take thy form from off my door!"
    Quoth the Raven, "Nevermore."

18   And the Raven, never flitting, still is sitting, *still* is sitting
    On the pallid bust of Pallas just above my chamber door;
And his eyes have all the seeming of a demon's that is dreaming,
    And the lamp-light o'er him streaming throws his shadow on the floor;
And my soul from out that shadow that lies floating on the floor
    Shall be lifted—nevermore!

                                        (1845)

The mood of the poem is best described as

(A) sad, yet hopeful
(B) a reflection of the speaker's grief
(C) influenced by Lenore's return
(D) constant throughout the work
(E) based on the role of the bird

The atmosphere of much of the poem is

(A) relaxed
(B) artificial
(C) desperate
(D) homey
(E) celebrative

Stanza 5, lines 1–2, contain all the following EXCEPT

(A) alliteration
(B) assonance
(C) consonance
(D) internal rhyme
(E) subjunctive mood

The significance of the onomatopoeia in Stanza 11, line 1, is that it

(A) breaks the mood established in Stanza 10
(B) begins a new alliterative pattern
(C) simply starts a new thought
(D) reinforces the mood of Stanza 10
(E) stresses the relationship of bird and man

The repetitive elements of each stanza's final line contribute LEAST to

(A) a sense of the meaning
(B) the atmosphere
(C) the overall tone
(D) character development
(E) a distinctive style

Explanation: Stanza 2 sets the speaker's mood. He is grieving over Lenore's death. The poem's atmosphere is desperate as he searches for "surcease of sorrow" first with books, then with the idea of forgetting her in stanza 14 or the idea of meeting her again in "distant Aidenn" (stanza 16). The desperation reaches its height in stanza 17, followed by defeat in the final stanza. Obviously, the lines are not in the subjunctive mood. The mood of the speaker's complaisant futility in stanza 10 is broken by the explosive "Startled" in line 1 of stanza 11. Although the speaker gives up hope by the final line, his character does not really change.

Correct Answers: **B, C, E, A, D**

Test Taker → Test Maker

If you were writing SAT Literature Tests, what questions about tone would you ask? Here is an opportunity to approach tone from the test writer's point of view.

Alonzo Delano left his wife and children in 1849 to go to the California gold fields. He kept a diary of his life, published in 1854 as *Life on the Plains and among the Diggings.* Here is an excerpt.

California proved to be a leveler of pride, and everything like aristocracy of employment; indeed, the tables seemed to be turned, for those who labored hard in a business that compared with digging wells and canals at home, and *Line* fared worse than the Irish laborer, were those who made the most money in
(5) mining. It was a common thing to see a statesman, a lawyer, a physician, a merchant, or clergyman, engaged in driving oxen and mules, cooking for his mess, at work for wages by the day, making hay, hauling wood, or filling menial offices. Yet false pride had evaporated, and if they were making money at such avocations, they had little care for appearances. I have often seen the
(10) scholar and the scientific man, the ex-judge, the ex-member of Congress, or the would-be exquisite at home, bending over the wash-tub, practicing the homely art of the washerwoman; or, sitting on the ground with a needle, awkwardly enough repairing the huge rents in his pantaloons; or, sewing on buttons *a la tailor*, and good-humoredly responding to a jest, indicative of his present employment—thus:
(15)   "Well, Judge, what is in the docket to-day?"

"Humph! a trial on an action *for rents*—the parties prick anew."

"Any rebutting testimony in the case?"

"Yes, a great deal of re-*button* evidence is to be brought in, and a *strong thread* will uphold the suit."
(20)   —Or, to the ex-Congressman at the wash-tub – "What bill is before the house now?"

"A purifying amendment, sir: one that will make a clean sweep of the vermin which infest the *precincts* of our constituents."

"Will not the bill be laid on the table?"

"At all events, a thorough *renovation* will take place; for the state of things
(25) requires a soap-orific modification of existing evils."

But I resume the regular course of my narrative from Lawson's.

As a test writer, do you see any uses of literary elements that would make good questions?

_____

_____

_____

Discussion

Did you notice the irony in the "tables seemed to be turned" (line 2)? What does he mean by "aristocracy of employment" (lines 1–2)? What makes the pride "false" in line 8?

Do you see the puns (plays on words), emphasized by italics by the writer to make his point?

You can see from these examples that this selection is full of potential test questions. For now, though, let's target its tone.

Here is something interesting: The serious tone of the introductory paragraph is different from the humorous tone of lines 15–26. Of course, these lines are illustrating his point, but they do provide a possible contrast question:

The humorous tone of the dialogue in lines 15–26 makes the narrator's attitude in lines 1–14 seem

(A) _____

(B) _____

(C) _____

(D) * _____

(E) _____

Here is another approach: Why is the dialogue funny?
The humorous tone of the dialogue in lines 15–26 is the result of

(A) _____

(B) _____

(C) * _____

(D) _____

(E) _____

> Test writers look for changes and/or contrasts in tone.

TONE IN CONCLUSION

The tones used by a speaker or writer greatly influence our perception of any given work. Tone also applies to the characters within a narrative, affecting interaction among characters, as well as how readers view each character. Consequently, the time is here to move on to Literary Element Number 5, Character.

*Correct answer

LITERARY ELEMENT

A character is a person (or a bei[ng] ...
in, acts and/or speaks in, narrate[d] ...

What terms do I need to kno[w]

1. Characterization

Definition: Characterization includes ...
(a character). To characterize someone ...
traits or features present, including mo ...

2. Hero(ine) or protagonist

Definition: The leading male (female) cha[racter] ...
ities or who simply is the main character.

3. Villain(ess) or antagonist

Definition: A character who is often charac ...
protagonist.

4. Antihero(ine) and tragic hero

Definition: An antihero(ine) is a protagonist wh ... [tra]ditional
hero(ine) or one who is somewhat villainous. A ... flaw in his character
that causes his defeat, even though he was origin[all]y of a noble family (tragic genre).

5. Foil

Definition: A *foil* is a contrasting character, who through that very contrast causes
the viewer to see more clearly the personality of another character.

6. Climate

Definition: A group of people (such as a family or community), a nation, or a literary work can have a prevailing attitude. Sometimes this is referred to as the "climate"—the political climate might be referred to as liberal or conservative; the intellectual climate might be referred to as decaying; the moral climate as strict; the climate of opinion as going against a particular stance; the climate of the stock market as "bullish." A prevailing attitude or climate can also sometimes be identified in a literary work.

7. Empathy

Definition: When readers empathize with a character, they experience a sense of participation in the story or situation, often based on vivid descriptions of experiences common to both the reader and the character.

8. Pathos

Definition: Pathos occurs when a passage (or scene) captures the heart of the reader or audience with intense feelings of sorrow and pity.

9. Flashback and foreshad[owing]

Definition: One method to give ...
dream sequences, recollectio ...
are recounted. Sometim ...
the story might beg ...
He sits "rememb[er] ...
with the jud ...
Anoth ...
of f ...

TERM REVIEW

TERM P[REVIEW]

TERM WATCH

TERM REVIEW

TERM REVIEW

TERM REVIEW

... readers more detail is the use of **flashback**, such as ... ons by a character, and other means in which past events ... es the flashback can be almost the entire story. For example, ... n with the main character awaiting sentencing after a jury trial. ... ering" the events that led to that point, and then the story concludes ... ge's pronouncement of sentence.

... er means a writer can use to achieve credibility for change is the effective use ... oreshadowing, a means of preparing the reader or audience for upcoming events. Foreshadowing devices include the clues in a mystery or a prevailing atmosphere, among others.

EVIEW **10.** **Superhero(ine)**

Definition: A larger-than-life, usually supernatural, hero(ine).

TERM REVIEW **11.** **Confidant** (or feminine, **confidante**)

Definition: A **confidant** is generally a friend, who "draws out" the person into talking about private matters.

What else do I need to know about character?

1. Distinctive Traits

- **Attitudes**

    A character's attitudes are his or her mental positions or feelings with regard to self, other people, objects, or a subject. Conversation often includes talk about a person's attitude as being "good" or "bad," as being "productive" or "unproductive," as being "responsive" or "unresponsive," and the list goes on.

    When test questions ask you to identify a character's posture, demeanor, or standpoint (to name a few), they may be asking you to identify his or her attitude.

- **Emotions**

    The emotions of a character are his or her intense feelings. Emotions, as with attitudes, can polarize to the "positive" or to the "negative." Affection, tenderness, zeal, and responsiveness are considered positive (for example), but sentimentality or melodrama are "too much." At the other extreme are those emotions connotatively regarded as "negative" because of their lack of feeling, such as heartlessness, cold-bloodedness, and apathy.

    The role of hope and of its opposite, hopelessness, on character development and revelation should not be underestimated. Hope is a powerful motivating force as seen in last-minute plays that win the championship game or in acts of heroism that save lives or win wars; and being in a state of hopelessness can be equally powerful, as seen in lives that have lost meaning, ending in suicides or unfulfilled dreams.

- **Response Mechanisms**

  How does the character respond physically and emotionally to life?

  When under pressure, does the character exhibit, for example, agitation and fury or even-temperedness and composure? How nervous does the character become? Is the character patient or impatient? Tolerant or intolerant? Resigned or anxious? When put to the test, is the character honest (dishonest), courageous (fearful), faithful (unfaithful), or giving (taking, envious, jealous, resentful)?

- **Intrinsic Values**

  Intrinsic values are those traits that result from the value judgments made in the heart of a person—what is really important (or not important) to him or her. At their core are fundamental concepts: home, family, country, religion, fellow man, self, and other value-type concepts. The reader may conclude that the character is trustworthy, a criminal, a proud man, a humble boy, a fastidious girl, an honorable woman, a shallow person, a devil—or a saint. "**Emotional state**" is connotative of that person's feelings *at a particular time*—his or her emotional state may be happy today, unhappy tomorrow. In contrast, a character's **disposition** is connotative of his or her feelings as well as *natural attitudes toward life* that are somewhat consistent throughout his or her life. Although we may say that George, for example, might be unhappy today, he generally has a "happy disposition," outlook on life, or temperament.

2. Methods of Characterization

Characterization (character development in a story) can be accomplished through many different methods or techniques.

- **Stereotyping**

  This method of characterization involves identifying a character with a group about which you have certain cultural assumptions (stereotypes).

  Look at the last paragraph in the Hawthorne passage in Example 1 that follows. The narrator describes Zenobia as an experienced woman who still has some "noble traits" (a derogatory stereotype). He also hints at her heart condition (symbolic of kindness) as "valuable when new," alluding to the stereotype of "a heart of gold."

- **Exposition**

  Sometimes, however, the author or narrator will simply tell the reader about the character.

- **Character's Actions**

  What does the character do at times of crisis? How does he or she react to conflict? To everyday situations? To extraordinary situations? You can learn a great deal about a character from the way in which he or she reacts in different circumstances and situations.

- **Character's Words**

  You can deduce a great deal about a character's personality from his or her own words. Sometimes a character will reveal significant hidden aspects of his or her personality from words spoken in an unguarded moment or during a heated argument.

- **Character's Thoughts**
  A character's own thoughts (through such devices as interior monologue and stream of consciousness) can be a rich source for insight into motivation and character; however, be alert for elements of self-delusion on the part of the character.
- **Words of Others**
  Much can be learned about a character by "listening in" on what other characters have to say about him or her.
- **Use of Setting**
  The setting can to varying degrees be a factor in determining character. In real life, people are constantly affected by their environment—the settings around them. Likewise, the setting can affect characters in literature.

Shakespeare's *Julius Caesar*

Act I Scene II

The same. A hall in Caesar's *palace.*

Thunder and lightning, Enter Julius Caesar, *in his nightgown.*

Julius Caesar.

[This sets the atmosphere and permits you to know it is a threatening situation for Caesar.]

→ Nor heaven nor earth have been at peace to-night: Thrice hath Calphurnia in her sleep cried out, "Help, ho! they murder Caesar!"—Who's within?

Enter a Servant.

Servant.   My lord?

Julius Caesar.   Go bid the priests do present sacrifice,

[Here you learn Caesar is superstitious, believing the priests can give him insight into his chances for success.]

→ And bring me their opinions of success.

- **The Humours**
  From the period of Elizabethan literature, the *humours* were used by various writers to describe the temperaments of characters, with the word "humour" (British spelling) referring to a person's mood. For example, we might say, "He's in good humor [American spelling] today!" The four humours include *melancholic* (depressed, gloomy, gluttonous, sentimental), *sanguine* (cheerful, hopeful, amorous), *choleric* (angry, vengeful, impatient), and *phlegmatic* (stoic, apathetic, impassive, dull, cowardly).
- **Eliciting Reader Responses**
  As pointed out by novelist Kit Reed in *Mastering Fiction Writing*, writers sometimes "become" the characters in their stories, just as actors may "become" the characters that they are portraying. This is a very interesting and useful perspective for the reader of literature as well as for the writer. The reader also brings his or her own experience to the work and, to greatly varying degrees, becomes the characters.

3. Character D[evelopment]

Character developme[nt] ...
narrative.

Character developm[ent] ...

- Did the charact[er] ...
- Was there suffici[ent] ... be realistic and p[lausible] ...
- Has the reader b[een] ... the change seem[s] ...

4. Conventional [Characters]

The roles of hero(ine) ...
antihero(ine), tragic hero ...
characters.

5. Character Roles

- **Flat characters** are ... view the characters a ...
- **Round characters** ar[e] ...
- **Stock characters** are ... Charming in fairy tal[es] ...
- **Type characters** repre[sent] ... people but still are un[...]
- **Stereotype characters** ....on from one story to the next; they [...]

The **character of places and things** refer[s] ...
- The **character of places and things** refer[s] ... For example: "That wonderful coun[...] "His essay is <u>characterized</u> by a [...] nature of the subject."

How could questions ab[out] ...

The following selectio[n] ...
might be tested.

Attit[...]

Example [...]

6. Dramatic Characters and Conventions

These characters and conventions are defined by how they reveal their thoughts:

- A **confidant(e)** is generally a friend who "draws out" the person into talking about private matters.
- A **foil** is a contrasting character who, through that very contrast, causes the viewer to see more clearly the personality of another character.
- An **aside** is a situation in which a character directly addresses the audience.
- A **soliloquy** is a situation in which a character, alone on stage, delivers a speech that reveals his or her thoughts.

7. Special Characters

In literary discussion, the word "character" can carry with it several meanings beyond those already discussed:

- The **character** is a brief, very descriptive essay that focuses on a person who embodies a particular virtue, vice, or character trait.
- The **character sketch** is a short essay that focuses on a person, describing all aspects of his or her personality.

... to the essential quality found there. ... ...try restaurant has a lot of <u>character</u>." ...omber tone that conflicts with the trivial

...ut character be worded?

...ns and their questions illustrate some of the ways character

...de, Climate, Emotions, Responses, and Intrinsic Values

The following passage is taken from Nathaniel Hawthorne's *The Blithdale Romance* (1852).

"Angry with you, child? What a silly idea!" exclaimed Zenobia, laughing. "No, indeed! But, my dear Priscilla, you are getting to be so very pretty that you absolutely need a duenna; and, as I am older than you, and have had my
Line own little experience of life, and think myself exceedingly sage, I intend to
(5) fill the place of a maiden aunt. Every day, I shall give you a lecture, a quarter of an hour in length, on the morals, manners, and proprieties of social life. When our pastoral shall be quite played out, Priscilla, my worldly wisdom may stand you in good stead."

"I am afraid you are angry with me!" repeated Priscilla, sadly; for, while
(10) she seemed as impressible as wax, the girl often showed a persistency in her own ideas as stubborn as it was gentle.

"Dear me, what can I say to the child!" cried Zenobia, in a tone of humorous vexation. "Well, well; since you insist on my being angry, come to my room, this moment, and let me beat you!"

(15) Zenobia bade Hollingsworth good night very sweetly, and nodded to me with a smile. But, just as she turned aside with Priscilla, into the dimness of the porch, I caught another glance at her countenance. It would have made the fortune of a tragic actress, could she have borrowed it for the moment when she fumbles in her bosom for the concealed dagger or the exceedingly
(20) sharp bodkin, or mingles the ratsbane in her lover's bowl of wine or her rival's cup of tea. Not that I in the least anticipated any such catastrophe—it being a remarkable truth that custom has in no one point a greater sway than over our modes of wreaking our wild passions. And besides, had we been in Italy, instead of New England, it was hardly yet a crisis for the dag-
(25) ger or the bowl.

It often amazed me, however, that Hollingsworth should show himself so recklessly tender towards Priscilla, and never once seem to think of the effect which it might have upon her heart. But the man, as I have endeavored to explain, was thrown completely off his moral balance, and quite bewildered

(30) as to his personal relations, by his great excrescence of a philanthropic scheme. I used to see, or fancy, indications that he was not altogether obtuse to Zenobia's influence as a woman. No doubt, however, he had a still more exquisite enjoyment of Priscilla's silent sympathy with his purposes, so unalloyed with criticism, and therefore more grateful than any intellectual

(35) approbation, which always involves a possible reserve of latent censure. A man—poet, prophet, or whatever he may be—readily persuades himself of his right to all the worship that is voluntarily tendered. In requital of so rich benefits as he was to confer upon mankind, it would have been hard to deny Hollingsworth the simple solace of a young girl's heart, which he held in his

(40) hand, and smelled to, like a rosebud. But what if, while pressing out its fragrance, he should crush the tender rosebud in his grasp!

As for Zenobia, I saw no occasion to give myself any trouble. With her native strength, and her experience of the world, she could not be supposed to need any help of mine. Nevertheless, I was really generous enough to feel

(45) some little interest likewise for Zenobia. With all her faults (which might have been a great many besides the abundance that I knew of), she possessed noble traits, and a heart which must, at least, have been valuable while new. And she seemed ready to fling it away as uncalculatingly as Priscilla herself. I could not but suspect that, if merely at play with Hollingsworth, she was

(50) sporting with a power which she did not full estimate. Or, if in earnest, it might chance, between Zenobia's passionate force and his dark, self-delusive egotism, to turn out such earnest as would develop itself in some sufficiently tragic catastrophe, though the dagger and the bowl should go for nothing in it.

The narrator characterizes Priscilla as

(A) psychologically unbalanced
(B) a clever little actress
(C) simpleminded
(D) naïve and unsophisticated
(E) stubborn and self-centered

Explanation: Be sure to read all the answer choices. Priscilla is stubborn; however, there are no indications that she is self-centered. She is naïve (she gave her heart "like a rosebud" in an implied state of worship) and so unsophisticated that Zenobia presumes she needs someone worldly to teach her.

Correct Answer: **D**

The "dagger and the bowl" come to represent in the passage

(A) tragic acting
(B) suicidal tendencies
(C) homicidal jealousy
(D) a drunken rage
(E) martyrdom

The general climate of this passage serves to

(A) make philanthropy seem selfish
(B) foreshadow trouble
(C) cast a shadow on the value of experience
(D) reveal the best in the characters
(E) conceal true motives

Explanation: In classical literature, a romantic triangle often ends with murder committed by violence (symbolized by a dagger) or poison (symbolized by the bowl). The general climate of the passage is a product of the words and actions of the characters and the observations of the narrator. Three people are living together. One is a young, impressionable girl who worships the much older man, who has a "self-delusive egotism." The third character is an experienced woman (with many faults) who is "ready to fling" her heart at the man. Such conditions would naturally produce a climate that is emotionally stressful. Add to this mix the repeated allusions to the dagger and bowl and an element of danger is injected into the scene. This climate hints at future trouble. Notice: Both times the narrator mentions dagger and bowl, he denies that he really believes that a "tragic catastrophe" will actually happen; however, the fact that he does mention them plants the idea in the reader's mind.

Correct Answers: **C, B**

According to the narrator, the greatest influence on how people express extreme emotion is

(A) the law
(B) a sense of duty
(C) social convention
(D) habit
(E) fear

Explanation: "—it being a remarkable truth that custom has in no one point a greater sway than over our modes of wreaking our wild passions" (fourth paragraph).

Correct Answer: **C**

Context suggests that in the third paragraph, Zenobia's choice of words

(A) marks the beginning of a joke
(B) makes her seem like a child abuser
(C) reveals her true intentions
(D) renders her role as the "maiden aunt" unbelievable
(E) conceals, yet ironically reveals, her genuine reactions

Explanation: Of course, Zenobia is joking. The next paragraph, however, reveals that she also is dealing with jealousy concealed by her joking tone, but revealed by choice of humor. She is responding with jealousy toward the girl.

Correct Answer: **E**

> In the Hawthorne passage, Hollingsworth is portrayed as
>
> (A) dangerous
> (B) generous
> (C) moral
> (D) obsequious
> (E) unpretentious

Explanation: Look for clues to his intrinsic values. Normally, an act of philanthropy is associated with a generous heart. In Hollingsworth's case, his "philanthropic scheme" is an "excrescence," contextually meaning an abnormal outgrowth that, according to the narrator, has made Hollingsworth "thrown completely off his moral balance." Also, he is capable of emotionally crushing a person "like a rosebud" (Priscilla), and he is a "power" with a "dark, self-delusive egotism." We can conclude from these statements that he is a potentially dangerous man.

Correct Answer: **A**

Example 2

Exposition

An example of characterization through exposition can be seen in this paragraph taken from the early nineteenth-century American short story "Rip Van Winkle" by Washington Irving (1820):

> The great error in Rip's composition was an insuperable aversion to all kinds of profitable labor. It could not be from the want of assiduity or perseverance; for he would sit on a wet rock, with a rod as long and heavy as a
>
> *Line* Tartar's lance, and fish all day without a murmur, even though he should not
> *(5)* be encouraged by a single nibble. He would carry a fowling-piece on his shoulder for hours together, trudging through woods and swamps, and up hill and down dale, to shoot a few squirrels or wild pigeons. He would never refuse to assist a neighbor even in the roughest toil, and was a foremost man at all country frolics for husking Indian corn, or building stone fences; the
> *(10)* women of the village, too, used to employ him to run their errands, and to do such little odd jobs as their less obliging husbands would not do for them. In a word, Rip was ready to attend to anybody's business but his own; but as to doing family duty, and keeping his farm in order, he found it impossible.

What irony does the speaker use to characterize Rip Van Winkle?

(A) Rip liked to fish.
(B) Rip worked for his family, but not others.
(C) Rip would work for others, but not for his own family.
(D) Rip refused to help neighbors.
(E) Rip had a kind nature and conciliatory disposition.

Explanation: In this case, the narrator uses examples to disclose Rip's character. The contradictory nature of Rip's behavior produces irony and insight into his character.

Correct Answer: **C**

Example 3

Exposition

At about the same time Irving was writing in America, Jane Austen (a writer of the Romantic Period) was in England writing this characterization in her novel of manners *Persuasion* (1818):

> . . . Lady Elliot had been an excellent woman, sensible and amiable; whose judgement and conduct, if they might be pardoned the youthful infatuation which made her Lady Elliot, had never required indulgence
> *Line* afterwards.—She had humoured, or softened, or concealed his failings, and
> *(5)* promoted his real respectability for seventeen years; and though not the very happiest being in the world herself, had found enough in her duties, her friends, and her children, to attach her to life, and make it no matter of indifference to her when she was called on to quit them.

Lady Elliot's character is largely

(A) silly
(B) infatuated
(C) disrespectful
(D) vain
(E) pragmatic

Explanation: The narrator tells us that Lady Elliot is sensible and did not indulge herself once married. Even though she married a man with failings, she grounded herself in her duties, friends, and children (a practical response to life).

Correct Answer: **E**

Example 4

Characters' Actions

Here is an excerpt from Jane Austen's *Persuasion*.

> Something occurred, however, to give her a different duty. Mary, often a little unwell, and always thinking a great deal of her own complaints, and always in the habit of claiming Anne when any thing was the matter, was
> *Line* indisposed; and foreseeing that she should not have a day's health all the
> *(5)* autumn, entreated, or rather required her, for it was hardly entreaty, to come to Uppercross Cottage, and bear her company as long as she should want her, instead of going to Bath.

Mary's treatment of Anne is best described as

(A) virtuous
(B) self-abnegatory
(C) selfish
(D) magnanimous
(E) impersonal

Explanation: By changing the word choice from "entreated" to "or rather required" and by describing her "habit of claiming Anne," the narrator portrays a character used to self-indulgence and attention, regardless of the feelings of others.

Correct Answer: **C**

Example 5

Characters' Words

Here is a conversation that takes place in *Persuasion*.

'Oh! he talks of you,' cried Charles, 'in such terms,'—Mary interrupted him. 'I declare, Charles, I never heard him mention Anne twice all the time I was there. I declare, Anne, he never talks of you at all.'

Line
(5)
'No,' admitted Charles, 'I do not know that he ever does, in a general way—but however, it is a very clear thing that he admires you exceedingly. . . . No Mary, I declare it was so, I heard it myself, and you were in the other room.—"Elegance, sweetness, beauty," Oh! there was no end of Miss Elliot's charms.'

. . .

'Oh! as to being Anne's acquaintance,' said Mary, 'I think he is rather my
(10) acquaintance, for I have been seeing him every day this last fortnight.'

'Well, as your joint acquaintance, then, I shall be very happy to see Captain Benwick.'

'You will not find any thing very agreeable in him, I assure you, ma'am. He is one of the dullest young men that ever lived. He has walked with me,
(15) sometimes, from one end of the sands to the other, without saying a word. He is not at all a well-bred young man. I am sure you will not like him.'

Mary's reaction to Charles reveals she is

(A) plaintive
(B) exuberant
(C) genial
(D) competitive
(E) jocular

Explanation: Her petty attitude in claiming Benwick as her acquaintance and not Anne's, yet defaming his character, reveals a self-centered, competitive nature. In her view, he is *her* friend, not Anne's; he sees *her* every day, but never mentions Anne.

Correct Answer: **D**

Example 6

Characters' Thoughts

Again, examine an excerpt from *Persuasion.*

> . . . He had been engaged to Captain Harville's sister, and was now mourning her loss. . . . Captain Wentworth believed it impossible for man to be more attached to woman than poor Benwick had been to Fanny Harville, or to be more deeply afflicted under the dreadful change. . . .
>
> *Line*
> (5) 'And yet,' said Anne to herself, as they now moved forward to meet the party, 'he has not, perhaps, a more sorrowing heart than I have. I cannot believe his prospects so blighted for ever. He is younger than I am; younger in feeling, if not in fact; younger as a man. He will rally again, and be happy with another.'

Anne views Captain Benwick's situation with

(A) optimism
(B) Pollyannaism
(C) aggravation
(D) palliation
(E) drollness

Explanation: Anne reveals a sense of optimism that he will "rally again"; however, she is not optimistic to the extreme of a Pollyanna. FYI: Pollyanna is the name of the heroine of a book by Eleanor Porter. No longer just a literary reference, you will find the name in many dictionaries as a vocabulary word meaning an excessively optimistic person.

Correct Answer: **A**

Example 7

Words of Others

In this excerpt, the reader learns something of the character of Captain Wentworth (in *Persuasion*):

> 'Miss Elliot,' said he [Captain Harville], speaking rather low, 'you have done a good deed in making that poor fellow talk so much. . . . I was at Plymouth, dreading to hear of him; he sent in letters, but the *Grappler* was
> *Line* under orders for Portsmouth. There the news must follow him, but who was
> (5) to tell it? not I. I would as soon have been run up to the yard-arm. Nobody could do it, but that good fellow, (pointing to Captain Wentworth). The *Laconia* had come into Plymouth the week before; no danger of her being sent to sea again. He stood his chance for the rest—wrote up for leave of absence, but without waiting the return, travelled night and day till he got
> (10) to Portsmouth, rowed off to the *Grappler* that instant, and never left the poor fellow for a week; that's what he did, and nobody else could have saved poor James. You may think, Miss Elliot, whether he is dear to us!'

Harville sees Wentworth's character as a(n)

(A) chivalrous rival
(B) self-abasing knight
(C) unpardonable tyrant
(D) magnanimous hero
(E) diabolic fiend

Explanation: First, Wentworth accomplished a job Harville would not do: telling James that his fiancée is dead. Secondly, he rushed to be with James through the first week of grief ("nobody else could have saved poor James"). He acted the role of a hero in Harville's eyes: noble, honorable, generous.

Correct Answer: **D**

Use caution, however, in accepting the words of other characters—be sure to examine their motives (and the possibility of differences in their perceptions) for how their personal interests might affect their words about the character in question.

Example 8

The Humours

Jane Austen refers to his "sanguine temper" in this description of Captain Wentworth in *Persuasion*:

> Captain Wentworth had no fortune. He had been lucky in his profession, but spending freely, what had come freely, had realized nothing. But, he was confident that he should soon be rich;—full of life and ardour, he knew that
> *Line* he should soon have a ship, and soon be on a station that would lead to
> (5) every thing he wanted. He had always been lucky; he knew he should be so still.—Such confidence, powerful in its own warmth, and bewitching in the wit which often expressed it, must have been enough for Anne; but Lady Russell saw it differently.— His *sanguine temper, and fearlessness of mind, operated very differently on her. . . .

Based on context, Captain Wentworth's "sanguine temper" is what personality type?

(A) Sentimental
(B) Hopeful
(C) Vengeful
(D) Apathetic
(E) Cowardly

Explanation: A sanguine person is hopeful. Even without knowing this definition, however, context (line 6) tells you the answer.

Correct Answer: **B**

Example 9

Empathy

Here is the first stanza of John Keats's "The Eve of St. Agnes."

> St. Agnes' Eve—Ah, bitter chill it was!
> The owl, for all his feathers, was a-cold;
> The hare limped trembling through the frozen grass,
> *Line* And silent was the flock in woolly fold:
> *(5)* Numb were the Beadsman's fingers, while he told
> His rosary, and while his frosted breath,
> Like pious incense from a censer old,
> Seemed taking flight for heaven, without a death,
> Past the sweet Virgin's picture, while his prayer he saith.

(ca. 1800)

To empathize with the Beadsman would be to

(A) participate in a rosary
(B) vicariously feel the cold
(C) outline his actions
(D) meditate on cold weather
(E) become emotionally detached

Explanation: The vivid descriptions of the cold, especially the Beadsman's cold fingers and breath, make the scene seem real for the reader.

Correct Answer: **B**

The reader's *sympathy* in this context includes a sense of emotional agreement (empathy).

In "Lord Randal," the anonymous fifteenth-century ballad, the reader can certainly feel pity and grief both for the poisoned son and for his mother; however, the reader generally does not identify with them or feel what they are feeling, although the emotion of the last stanza is very moving:

> "O I fear ye are poisond, Lord Randal, my son!
> O I fear ye are poisond, my handsome young man!"
> "O yes! I am poisond; mother, make my bed soon,
> For I'm sick at the heart, and I fain wald lie down."

(Note: "Make my bed soon" is an expression said to refer to making a coffin—a bed for the sleep of death, with *bed* also referring to the grave.)

Of course, the character can also elicit feelings of antipathy from the reader—aversion, dislike, distrust, disassociation, and as a result, distance from the reader.

Example 10

Pathos

The Old Curiosity Shop by Charles Dickens (1841):

> "You plot among you to wean my heart from her. You never will do that—never while I have life. I have no relative or friend but her—I never had—I never will have. She is all in all to me. It is too late to part us now."

> . . .

Line   For she was dead. There, upon her little bed, she lay at rest. The solemn
(5)   stillness was no marvel now.

> Her couch was dressed with here and there some winter berries and green leaves, gathered in a spot she had been used to favour. "When I die, put near me something that has loved the light, and had the sky above it always." Those were her words.

(10)   The old man held one languid arm in his, and had the small hand tight folded to his breast, for warmth. It was the hand she had stretched out to him with her last smile—the hand that had led him on through all their wanderings. Ever and anon he pressed it to his lips; then hugged it to his breast again, murmuring that it was warmer now; and as he said it he
(15)   looked, in agony, to those who stood around, as if imploring them to help her.

> But she was dead, and past all help, or need of it.

Holding the dead girl's hand serves to

(A) make the scene macabre
(B) add a bitter tone to the scene
(C) introduce an element of insanity
(D) instill a sense of unreality to the situation
(E) intensify the sense of the old man's grief

Explanation: Pathos, fundamentally, is a response from the heart of the individual, yet pathos or the lack of pathos is also often a reflection of society and the norms and cultures of the age. Dickens and the readers of his day lived in a world without television, action news reports, and big-screen movie theaters. As a result, stage productions, concerts, and reading were major outlets for the feelings and interests of the people. Serial publications were especially popular. Monthly magazines would publish sequential chapters of novels so that readers would buy the next issue to see what happened in the story. Often, the chapters would end with "cliffhangers," much like television series do today. Emotions over special characters sometimes were very high, as was the case of Little Nell in *The Old Curiosity Shop*. The readers of *The Old Curiosity Shop* during the period when it was first written reacted strongly to Little Nell's death. According to one historian, a reader wrote in his diary that he had never read such painful words, and another reader threw his copy of the book out a train window in his grief. Writers of the time record that American readers were also deeply affected—a crowd of concerned people gathered at a New York pier to shout questions at an arriving ship concerning Little Nell's fate. These reactions show that they had become personally involved with the character Little Nell as if she were a real person.

Correct Answer: **E**

<hr>

Example 11

Character Traits and Foreshadowing

Read the following selection from William Makepeace Thackeray's *Vanity Fair* (1847–8).

When Rebecca saw the two magnificent Cashmere shawls which Joseph Sedley had brought home to his sister, she said, with perfect truth, "that it must be delightful to have a brother," and easily got the pity of the tender-hearted Amelia, for being alone in the world, an orphan without friends or kindred.

Line
(5)

"Not alone," said Amelia; "you know, Rebecca, I shall always be your friend, and love you as a sister—indeed I will."

"Ah, but to have parents, as you have—kind, rich, affectionate parents, who give you everything you ask for; and their love, which is more precious than all! My poor papa could give me nothing, and I had but two frocks in all the world! And then, to have a brother, a dear brother! Oh, how you must love him!"

(10)

Amelia laughed.

"What! *don't* you love him? You, who say you love everybody?"

"Yes, of course, I do—only—"

(15)

"Only what?"

"Only Joseph doesn't seem to care much whether I love him or not.

He gave me two fingers to shake when he arrived after ten years' absence! He is very kind and good, but he scarcely ever speaks to me; I think he loves his pipe a great deal better than his"—but here Amelia checked herself, for why should she speak ill of her brother? "He was very kind to me as a child," she added; "I was but five years old when he went away."

(20)

"Isn't he very rich?" said Rebecca. "They say all Indian nabobs are enormously rich."

"I believe he has a very large income."

(25)

"And is your sister-in-law a nice pretty woman?"

"La! Joseph is not married," said Amelia, laughing again.

Perhaps she had mentioned the fact already to Rebecca, but that young lady did not appear to have remembered it; indeed, vowed and protested

(30) that she expected to see a number of Amelia's nephews and nieces. She was quite disappointed that Mr. Sedley was not married; she was sure Amelia had said he was, and she doted so on little children.

"I think you must have had enough of them at Chiswick," said Amelia, rather wondering at the sudden tenderness on her friend's part; and indeed

(35) in later days Miss Sharp would never have committed herself so far as to advance opinions, the untruth of which would have been so easily detected. But we must remember that she is but nineteen as yet, unused to the art of deceiving, poor innocent creature! And making her own experience in her own person. The meaning of the above series of queries, as translated in the

(40) heart of this ingenious young woman, was simply this:—"If Mr. Joseph Sedley is rich and unmarried, why should I not marry him? I have only a fortnight, to be sure, but there is no harm in trying."

Rebecca can be characterized as all the following EXCEPT

(A) perceptive
(B) sophisticated
(C) clever
(D) artful
(E) opportunistic

The narrator's comment that Rebecca is "unused to the art of deceiving" (lines 37–38) probably

(A) betrays a kindness of spirit in Rebecca
(B) sarcastically foreshadows Rebecca's future conduct
(C) provides a basis for her friendship
(D) reduces her to a thief
(E) reinforces Amelia's good opinion of her

Rebecca's character is best summarized as

(A) opportunistic
(B) unresponsive
(C) indifferent
(D) disconsolate
(E) antagonistic

Amelia's feelings toward her brother are NOT the result of

(A) his absence
(B) the gifts he sends her
(C) his kindness as a child
(D) his being single
(E) his coldness toward her

Explanation: Amelia Sedley and Rebecca Sharp are the main characters in this excerpt; however, a third character, Joseph Sedley (Amelia's brother), is also mentioned.

From the context, you can gather many clues about each person's identity as a character and insight into his or her personality.

Amelia Sedley: 1. wealthy,   2. both parents alive,   3. has a brother named Joseph,   4. "tender-hearted,"   5. perhaps naïve,   6. five years old when brother left + 10 years he was away = 15 years old,   7. claims to love her brother,   8. feels hurt because of her brother's actions and demeanor,   9. loyal to family and friends,   10. misinterprets Rebecca's conduct, except perhaps at an intuitive level,   11. affectionate.

Rebecca Sharp: 1. now an orphan,   2. poor heritage,   3. knew her father,   4. implications of being manipulative,   5. interested in wealth,   6. nineteen years old,   7. inexperienced at deception, but learning—foreshadowing trouble ahead,   8. intends to try to marry the rich Mr. Joseph Sedley,   9. has little time to implement her plans,   10. has no friends except Amelia.

Joseph Sedley: 1. just returned from India,   2. wealthy,   3. smokes a pipe,   4. has been away for ten years,   5. single,   6, brought presents for his sister,   7. was kind as a child, but has changed and is reserved with his sister now.

Correct Answers: **B, B, A, D**

Example 12

Special Characterizations

The following selections illustrate four additional ways you may encounter "character" on the test.

- **Characterization of a written work**

  These words are taken from Benjamin Franklin's *Autobiography* (ca. 1800).

  It was about this time I conceiv'd the bold and arduous project of arriving at moral perfection. I wish'd to live without committing any fault at any time; I would conquer all that either natural inclination, custom, or company might lead me into. As I knew, or thought I knew, what was right and wrong, I did not see why I might not always do the one and avoid the other. But I soon found I had undertaken a task of more difficulty than I had imagined. While my care was employ'd in guarding against one fault, I was often surprised by another; habit took the advantage of inattention; inclination was sometimes too strong for reason. I concluded, at length, that the mere speculative conviction that it was our interest to be completely virtuous, was not sufficient to prevent our slipping; and that the contrary habits must be broken, and good ones acquired and established, before we can have any dependence on a steady, uniform rectitude of conduct. For this purpose I therefore contrived the following method.

Line (5) ... *(10)*

This passage can best be characterized as

(A) comic, with a silly tone
(B) tragic, with a circumspective tone
(C) farcical, with a careless tone
(D) melodramatic, with a dogmatic tone
(E) serious, with a pragmatic tone

• Characterization of setting

"A Descent into the Maelström" by Edgar Allan Poe:

> As the old man spoke, I became aware of a loud and gradually increasing sound, like the moaning of a vast herd of buffaloes upon an American prairie; and at the same moment I perceived that what seamen term the *chopping* character of the ocean beneath us, was rapidly changing into a current which set to the eastward.

Line (5)

The *chopping* character of the ocean refers to which of the following?

I. The nature of its sound
II. The nature of its movement
III. The nature of its changes

(A) I only
(B) II only
(C) III only
(D) I and II only
(E) I, II, and III

• Conventional characters

Return to Poe's "The Man of the Crowd" on page 92 to answer the next question.

Based on the passage, the narrator is best described as

(A) the antagonist
(B) a villain
(C) the protagonist
(D) a superhero
(E) an antihero

• Character roles

These lines come from Anthony Trollope's *The Warden*:

> Do we not all know some reverend, all but sacred, personage before whom our tongue ceases to be loud, and our step to be elastic? But were we once to see him stretch himself beneath the bedclothes, yawn widely, and bury his face upon his pillow, we could chatter before him as glibly as before a doctor or a lawyer.

Line (5)

The narrator's underlying premise is based on

(A) boring aspects of flat characters
(B) the unpredictability of round characters
(C) the predictability of type characters
(D) the sensible aspects of stereotyping people
(E) the fallacy of stereotyping people

Explanation: These four examples illustrate some of the ways "special characters" can work within literary selections. Franklin's serious (though unsuccessful) first attempt at self-improvement is followed by a sensible idea: making a plan. The *chopping* character of Poe's water refers to its up-and-down movement. It then changes in character to become a current. Poe's narrator in "The Man of the Crowd" is clearly the main character or protagonist; however, an excellent case could be made to label him an antihero because of his somewhat peculiar behavior. Trollope's narrator first gives a stereotypical description of a person held in high esteem (people use hushed tones and subdued movements when in his or her presence), then points out that such a person is human; the basis for the stereotype is not grounded in reality.

Correct Answers: **E, B, C, E**

Test Taker → Test Maker

If you were writing SAT Literature tests, what questions about character would you ask? Here is an opportunity for you to approach character from a test writer's point of view.

John Bunyan's *The Pilgrim's Progress* is a classic example of allegory. His "Apology" for the book, however, is sometimes overlooked. Following are the first three stanzas (of irregular lengths) of this lengthy work.

> When at the first I took my pen in hand
> Thus for to write, I did not understand
> That I at all should make a little book
> *Line*   In such a mode; nay, I had undertook
> *(5)*   To make another; which, when almost done,
> Before I was aware I this begun.
>   And thus it was: I writing of the way
> And race of saints, in this our gospel day,
> Fell suddenly into an allegory
> *(10)*   About their journey, and the way to glory,
> In more than twenty things which I set down;
> This done, I twenty more had in my crown;
> And they again began to multiply,
> Like sparks that from the coals of fire do fly.
> *(15)*   Nay, then, thought I, if that you breed so fast
> I'll put you by yourselves, lest you at last
> Should prove ad infinitum, and eat out
> The book that I already am about.
> Well, so I did, but yet I did not think
> *(20)*   To show to all the world my pen and ink
> In such a mode, I only thought to make
> I knew not what: nor did I undertake
> Thereby to please my neighbor: no, not I;
> I did it mine own self to gratify.
> *(25)*   Neither did I but vacant seasons spend
> In this my scribble: nor did I intend
> But to divert myself in doing this,
> From worser thoughts which make me do amiss.

Of course, narrative works that include dialogue, action, and so forth are obvious sources for examining character. But this selection shows that elements of character can show up in surprising places.

Begin by making sure you understand what the author is saying by putting it into your own words (MOW the selection). The poem is written from what point of view?

_____

Lines 1–6   _____

Lines 7–10   _____

Lines 11–18 _____

Lines 19–24 _____

Lines 24–28 _____

Discussion

Writing in the first person, Bunyan tells us that he was writing a book when he got the idea for another one (lines 1–6), an allegory about the saints' journey to glory (lines 7–10). The ideas for the allegory came to him so quickly that he had to jot them down and put them aside to keep them from interfering with the book he was currently writing (lines 11–16). He did write the allegory, not for others but to please himself (lines 19–24). He wrote the allegory in his spare time to keep himself out of trouble (lines 25–28).

Next, underline the phrases in the poem that reveal Bunyan's character.

Here are some possibilities:

MOWing can help you better understand more challenging poetry. (See page 15 for details on MOWing.)

1. "before I was aware" (line 6)
2. thoughts "in my crown (line 12)...like sparks that from the coals of fire do fly" (line 14)
3. "did it mine own self to gratify" (line 24)
4. "to divert myself ...From worse thoughts which make me do amiss" (lines 27–28)
5. "I only thought to make/I knew not what" (lines 21–22)

As a test writer, you could use any of these ideas to ask questions about Bunyan's character. The questions might contain the word "character," for example:

What does the author reveal about his own character in lines 27–28?

You do not have to include the word "character," however:

The rapidity of the speaker's thought in lines 12–13 makes him seem....

Or you could write a question about the character of the entire selection:

These lines could be characterized as ....

With these ideas in mind, write a question about character for this selection.

Question

_____

_____

(A) *_____

(B) _____

(C) _____

(D) _____

(E) _____

CHARACTER IN CONCLUSION

Character concludes the first five literary elements that, to a great degree, deal with a selection as a whole: What is the work's meaning, form, overall voice, and tone, and how is it characterized? There are details within these elements, of course, but understanding how they work in the big picture is an important step in critical reading. The next two elements, in contrast, deal almost exclusively with details, where understanding can hinge on a single word.

*Correct Answer

LITERARY ELEMENT NUMBER SIX: USE OF LANGUAGE

You are traveling in the American Midwest and open the newspaper to learn about the area. There are the grocery store ads: This week's featured item in the bakery—apple pie.

A crust, cooked apples, cinnamon.

You can see it in your mind's eye now: hot apple pie, rich pastry crust that flakes apart when your fork hits it. Steam rises from the slice and softly brushes your cheek as the slice is lifted from the rest of the pie—and it smells *so-o-o* good. You begin to breathe deeper: Aromas of hot cinnamon and vanilla and baked apples swirl around your head. Maybe add a thick slice of American cheese that melts down into the apples and sauce. No, better yet—a big scoop of rich vanilla ice cream that melts and makes a creamy, thick sauce all around the chunks of steamy apples, mixing with the cinnamon in great big swirls of flavor. Your mouth waters in anticipation of that first bite. After all, it's your duty to eat a slice of fresh-baked apple pie, because what represents America better than the flag, Mom, and apple pie?

Welcome to the world of **imagery**.

TERM ALERT To refresh your memory review this term: **Imagery**

Definition: Roughly defined, imagery (the use of images) refers to the mental pictures you get as a result of words.

An image can be **literal**, a standard meaning like the mental picture of apples and cinnamon baked in a pastry crust for an apple pie, or it can be **figurative**, like the American love of country associated with apple pie. Imagery can refer to visual pictures that come to mind, or it can also include all the sensual qualities (kinesthetic/motion, auditory/hearing, thermal/heat, tactile/touch, gustatory/taste, and olfactory/smell). Imagery can also refer to abstract, nonsensual qualities, such as love, hate, peace, fear, and other emotions.

Imagery is a collection of images. Look at the collection of images used in the preceding apple pie illustration. You see the pie (visual), smell the pie (olfactory), feel the steam (tactile), and taste the pie (gustatory). Sometimes one sense is described by terms usually associated with another sense, such as "a red-hot candy." Imagery can also take on patterns as the images are used throughout a work.

To summarize: Words create images in people's minds, some of which are literal and some of which are figurative.

What terms do I need to know that relate to the use of language in a work?

TERM ALERT ### 1. Simile

Definition: Simile is a comparison using "like" or "as." A person who has never tasted buffalo meat might ask someone who just ate a buffalo burger, "What does it taste *like*?" The answer, "It tastes *like* a very strong beef burger," is a simile.

Similes are characterized by their directness, as in the first stanza of "The Blood Horse" by Barry Cornwall, a.k.a. Bryan W. Procter:

Gamarra is a dainty steed,
Strong, black, and of a noble breed,
Full of fire, and full of bone,
Line With all his line of fathers known;
(5) Fine his nose, his nostrils thin,
But blown abroad by the pride within!
His mane is like a river flowing,
And his eyes like embers glowing
In the darkness of the night,
(10) And his pace as swift as light.

The speaker compares the horse's mane to a flowing river (line 7) and his eyes to embers (line 8). What is the simile in the last line? He compares the horse's pace to the speed of light.

2. Metaphor

TERM ALERT

Definition: Metaphor, unlike the direct nature of the simile, is an *implied* comparison: rosy-red lips (tenor—lips; vehicle—a red rose).

3. Personification

TERM ALERT

Definition: Personification occurs when inanimate objects, animals, or abstract ideas are given human characteristics.

4. Allusion

TERM ALERT

Definition: Allusion is a direct or indirect reference in a literary work to some person, place, thing, or event outside the work, or to some other literary work.

5. Hyperbole (overstatement or exaggeration)

TERM ALERT

Definition: Hyperbole can be especially comic: Texans, as a case in point, are noted for their use of hyperbole, exaggeration, in a state where "the men are braver, the sky is bluer, the steaks are bigger, and the women are prettier than anywhere else in the world." **Meiosis**, or understatement, treats a serious subject as though it is much less important than it is. Often meiosis projects a derogatory tone; however, context may dictate any number of effects, such as irony.

This example is from *Oliver Twist* by Dickens.

The fact is, that there was considerable difficulty in inducing Oliver to take upon himself the office of respiration,—a troublesome practice, but one which custom has rendered necessary to our easy existence;…

TIP

The SAT Literature test does not require you to have background knowledge about literary periods, authors' lives, or literary criticism. However, there are some allusions that you should recognize and understand because they are used so frequently. Most of these allusions are **literary** (alluding to works of literature), **mythical** (alluding to classical myths), **biblical** (alluding to Bible stories and characters), and **historical** (alluding to events and people of the past).

You will not be tested about obscure allusions; however, you are expected to be familiar with allusions that are considered part of the common knowledge of British and American cultures. For example, you should know that there is a rabbit that talks in *Alice in Wonderland.*

6. Paradox

TERM ALERT

Definition: Paradox is a statement that seems to contradict itself, yet is actually true. Statements of paradox occur in conversations in everyday life: a couple may look at a pug-faced dog in a store window and exclaim, "He's so ugly he's cute!"

TERM ALERT

7. Irony

Definition: Irony is a concept that involves opposites. In **situational** or **dramatic irony**, the result following a sequence of events is the opposite of what is expected.

Verbal irony occurs when the speaker says the opposite of what he or she means. When the intent of the irony is to criticize by use of praise, the form is called **sarcasm**. (The sarcastic tone of Robert Browning's "Soliloquy of the Spanish Cloister" is an oft-cited example, as is Swift's "A Modest Proposal.")

Verbal irony, although sometimes described as "tongue in cheek," is not always sarcastic in tone or intent. The irony may be the result of **understatement**, also called **meiosis**, ("I think we have a little water in the basement"—when the basement contains a 3-foot-deep flood), in which the irony intensifies the meaning of what is said; the result of **overstatement**, also known as **hyperbole** ("This pimple outshines a neon sign!"), in which the irony lessens the importance of the meaning of what is said; or the result of **contradiction in context** (such as describing a cruel, uncaring person in terms that are endearing).

TERM ALERT

8. Diction

Definition: Diction will be discussed in greater detail in the next chapter, but as a use of language, diction (defined as word choice) plays an obvious role, particularly in imagery and figures of speech.

To some degree, diction can be viewed as isolated word choices, for example, the use of a word that is inappropriate for the context but that resembles a word that is appropriate. The effect, of course, of using the incorrect word can be amusing or it can be embarrassing when the error in word choice is unintentional. Richard Brinsley Sheridan's Mrs. Malaprop in *The Rivals* (1775) is the character whose constant misuse of words, such as "a progeny of learning," gave rise to the expression "**malapropism**." In the case of Mrs. Malaprop, she was trying to display mastery of a large vocabulary.

TERM WATCH

9. Figure of speech and figurative language

Definition: A figure of speech is a use of language in which a figurative (associated, connotative), rather than literal, meaning is conveyed. A figure of speech can change the meanings of words or change the way words are used without changing the meanings.

TERM WATCH

10. Anthropomorphism

Watch Out

Definition: **Do not confuse personification** (figurative language in which human characteristics are given to inanimate objects or abstract ideas) **with *anthropomorphism***, which is presenting a nonhuman (such as an animal or mythical god) as a human. The rabbit who <u>declares</u> he is "late" in *Alice in Wonderland* is an anthropomorphism; the rabbit <u>described by</u> the hunter as "a worthy opponent who planned his strategy well, laughing at my clumsiness and disdaining the sophistication of my weapons" is being personified.

TERM WATCH

11. Metonymy

Definition: Metonymy occurs when a closely associated name of an object is used in place of a word, such as referring to a king as "the ring giver" or "the crown," or to his position of authority as "the throne." In the United States, people often refer to

UNIVERSAL SYMBOLS

Symbol	Meaning Level one	Meaning Level two	*Possible Emotions
1. National flag	Cloth with pattern	Represents country	Pride, patriotism
2. Sea	Large body of water	Represents countless people	Fear of invasion, pity on the masses
3. Red rose	Flower	Represents love	Sentimentalism, special person
4. Purple	Color	Represents royalty	Respect, honor
5. Wedding ring	Gold band worn on left hand	Represents a state of being married	Fidelity, loyalty
6. Longhorned steer	Steer with long, curved horns	Represents football team at a Texas school	School loyalty and rivalry
7. Yellow	Color	Represents cowardice and fear also Slow down and Homecoming, reunion (ribbons) and survival, winning	Shame, dishonor Caution Support, honor, and happiness Pride, courage, hope

*Notice that the same symbol can have both negative or positive connotations depending on usage or context.

the executive branch of the federal government or to the president as "the White House."

12. Synecdoche

TERM WATCH

Definition: In a synecdoche, the name of a part represents the whole or the name of the whole represents the part. Workers may be referred to as "hands." A country's "ears and eyes" are its spies. A "roof over your head" is a home, and a musical producer might refer to the lead singer as "the voice."

13. Symbol

TERM WATCH

Definition: A symbol (in contrast to metaphor that serves to illustrate) is a type of image. It begins with some objective thing that calls to mind a second level of meaning. Oftentimes, the symbol embodies abstract concepts that elicit from the reader a range of emotions. (See chart above for examples.)

14. Rhetorical question

TERM WATCH

Definition: Rhetorical questions are those asked, not for the purpose of eliciting an expressed answer, but rather for their rhetorical effect: an emphasis of the speaker's point.

TERM WATCH

15. Anachronism

Definition: Anachronism refers to violations of time and space in which an event or person is placed in the wrong time. When these violations appear in movies and television, viewers include them in a broad category of cinematic error called "bloopers." Examples of anachronistic-type bloopers are when the soldiers defend the fort against an Indian attack in 1855 by setting up a Gatling gun (not invented until 1861) or when Geronimo (not born until 1829) attacks a fort in 1820. Such anachronisms can be found in prose, poetry, and drama.

TERM WATCH

16. Oxymoron

Definition: An oxymoron occurs when words, terms, or expressions appear to be self-contradicting: bittersweet, a dry martini, sweet-and-sour, love-hate relationships, passive resistance, jumbo shrimp, or a kind ogre. Sometimes you will find passages in which the speaker makes extensive use of oxymorons, as Romeo's speech in *Romeo and Juliet* (Act I Scene I) "loving-hate" and "cold fires."

TERM WATCH

17. Antithesis

Definition: Antithesis is a balance of contrasting terms with parallel grammatical structure. Example: O, change thy thought, that I may change my mind! Turn to the "Elegy" by Chidioch Tichborne on page 179. This conceit consists of a series of ideas that are antithetical (in antithesis to one another).

TERM WATCH

18. Apostrophe

Definition: Apostrophe is a direct address to a thing, person (real or imaginary), or abstraction (such as love or envy), who is usually absent. You may encounter apostrophe, however, when the auditor is present, such as My pen, take pain a little space. To follow that which doth me chase. The apostrophe is called an **invocation** if to a muse (a spirit of inspiration).

TERM WATCH

19. Allegory

Definition: When metaphors are extended into narrative form in which the actual story and its elements (actions, places, people, and things) represent elements outside the story, often with the characters and events representing ideas, the work is called an **allegory**. John Bunyan's *Pilgrim's Progress* is a famous allegory in which the journey of "Christian" (a character in the story) from the City of Destruction to the Celestial City allegorizes the Christian doctrine of salvation.

TERM REVIEW

20. Epithet

Definition: An epithet is an adjective, noun, or noun phrase describing a particular characteristic of a person or thing. An epithet might be to describe a puzzle as a "brain-twister," a home as a "sanctuary from the storm," or an admired leader as a "shining beacon of light." An epithet is often used as a substitution for a proper name, such as when, in referring to Elvis Presley, tabloid headlines read "The King of Rock 'n' Roll Spotted in White House Tour Group."

Note that the epithet is not restricted to just the negative name-calling normally associated with the term.

21. Pun

TERM REVIEW

Definition: A pun is a word choice that is referred to as a "play on words"—two words have the same sound but very different meanings.

Puns rely, of course, on context for their witty overtones because context gives significance to *both* meanings.

22. Euphemism

TERM REVIEW

Definition: Some choices of words are considered offensive to readers. Consequently, writers sometimes replace those words with inoffensive synonyms called euphemisms. What is considered offensive diction, of course, is based on the culture of the age when the work is being written.

Examples of euphemism include "G-rated" alternatives to "swear words" or "four-letter words," references to death as "passing away," and troubles or problems being called "issues."

Euphemisms were used extensively in the 1800s. The selection that follows contains a good example of euphemism from that period.

> from *Diary in America*, written by Frederick Marryat:
> When at Niagara Falls I was escorting a young lady with whom I was on friendly terms. She had been standing on a piece of rock, the better to view the scene, when she slipped down, and was evidently hurt by the fall: she had, in fact, grazed her shin. As she limped a little in walking home, I said, "Did you hurt your leg much?" She turned from me, evidently much shocked, or much offended,—and not being aware that I had committed any very heinous offence, I begged to know what was the reason of her displeasure. After some hesitation, she said that as she knew me well, she would tell me that the word leg was never mentioned before ladies. I apologized for my want of refinement, which was attributable to having been accustomed only to *English* society; and added, that as such articles must occasionally be referred to, even in the most polite circles in America, perhaps she would inform me by what name I might mention them without shocking the company. Her reply was, that the word limb was used; "nay," continued she, "I am not so particular as some people are, for I know those who always say limb of a table, or limb of a piano-forte."
>
> There the conversation dropped; but a few months afterwards I was obliged to acknowledge that the young lady was correct when she asserted that some people were more particular than even she was.
>
> I was requested by a lady to escort her to a seminary for young ladies, and on being ushered into the reception-room, conceive my astonishment at beholding a square piano-forte with four *limbs*. However, that the ladies who visited their daughters might feel in its full force the extreme delicacy of the mistress of the establishment, and her care to preserve in their utmost purity the ideas of the young ladies under her charge, she had dressed all these four limbs in modest little trousers, with frills at the bottom of them!

Do not confuse euphemism with euphony. Both affect the tone of a work, but euphemism is based on the meaning of a word and euphony relates to the sound. This little poem may help you differentiate the two literary terms:

Is It Euphemism or Euphony?

Is it euphemism or euphony?
   The answer has evaded me.
Euphemism, they say, is to render
   A harsh word into one kind and tender.
We don't say "leg"; we say a "limb."
   Don't call him "skinny," instead say "trim."
But when a poem has euphony,
   It simply "sounds" pleasant to you and me.
Now all your doubts should flee when you see:
   Is it euphemism or euphony?

Line

(5)

(10)

by L. E. Myers

What else do I need to know about use of language?

1. Figures of Speech Based on Analogy

Analogies are comparisons. The **tenor** is the subject or idea you are trying to explain, and the **vehicle** is the means by which you explain it. If you try to describe a zebra by comparing it to a horse with stripes, the zebra is the tenor and the horse is the vehicle. Likewise, if you wanted to explain some abstract concept, such as rage, you might compare it to a consuming fire: Tenor? Rage. Vehicle? Fire.

   Analogies include simile, metaphor, allegory, personification, anthropomorphism, allusion, metonymy, synecdoche, epithet, and symbols (in their many forms).

2. Figures of Speech Based on Rhetoric

In its broadest sense, rhetoric is use of language for the purpose of persuading the readers or hearers. In verbal communication, we can use rhetorical accent. (When the accent is determined by the intent or meaning, for example, "She gave the keys to <u>you</u>?" implies that the speaker is surprised at who is the recipient of the keys. Compare: "She <u>gave</u> the keys to you?" questions whether she really did give the keys or "<u>She</u> gave the keys to you?" questions who actually gave the keys.) However, in the written word, other means are needed.

   Rhetoric includes rhetorical questions, anachronisms, hyperbole, paradox, oxymoron, and irony (in their many forms).

3. Figures of Speech Based on Syntax and Diction

Syntax refers to the arrangement of words into patterns; **diction** refers to the word choices being arranged into those patterns. Four of the most widely used figures of speech based on syntax and diction are the pun, euphemism, antithesis, and apostrophe.

How could questions about use of language be worded?

The following selections and their questions illustrate some of the ways use of language might be tested.

Example 1

Simile

Sometimes the simile is sustained for an entire stanza or even an entire poem. Here is the first stanza of Thomas Lodge's "Love in My Bosom."

Love in my bosom like a bee
   Doth suck his sweet;
Now with his wings he plays with me,
Line   Now with his feet.
(5) Within mine eyes he makes his nest,
His bed amidst my tender breast;
My kisses are his daily feast,
And yet he robs me of my rest.
   Ah, wanton, will ye?

(ca. 1600)

The speaker compares love to a

(A) bosom
(B) bee
(C) wing
(D) kiss
(E) bed

The simile in this poem makes love seem

(A) dangerous
(B) annoying
(C) delightful
(D) thrilling
(E) burdensome

Explanation: "Love…like a bee" (line 1): This bee of love is playful, rests in the speaker's eyes and heart (emotions), and ultimately "robs" the speaker of his rest.

Correct Answers: **B, B**

Example 2

Metaphor

Thomas Nashe's sixteenth-century "Adieu, Farewell Earth's Bliss":

> Beauty is but a flower
> Which wrinkles will devour;
> Brightness falls from the air,
> *Line* Queens have died young and fair,
> *(5)* Dust hath closed Helen's eye.
> I am sick, I must die.
>   Lord, have mercy on us!

"A flower" in line 1 is used as a vehicle to describe

(A) brightness
(B) queens
(C) beauty
(D) Helen
(E) wrinkles

"A flower" in line 1 relates to

(A) time
(B) love
(C) personality
(D) appearance
(E) royalty

An important approach to understanding any use of language is to determine the *effects* of its use.

Comparing beauty to a flower in line 1 has the effect of

(A) emphasizing the natural elements of beauty
(B) making beauty seem fragile
(C) elevating beauty to a higher symbolic level
(D) limiting beauty to natural elements
(E) exaggerating beauty's impact

Explanation: "Beauty is…a flower" (line 1); beauty, as it relates to a flower, is based on appearance because "wrinkles will devour" it, as opposed to inner beauty. In the third question, context will help you select answer B (the correct answer) over A (an answer that may seem to be correct): use of "but" in the sense of "nothing more than" or "merely" and the clear reference to a flower's fragility in line 2— "wrinkles will devour."

Correct Answers: **C, D, B**

TIP

On the test, you may find use of metaphor in which the tenor is not directly named but only implied; and you must rely on context for meaning. In a work about a young woman's growing affection for a young man, a descriptive line might read "The bud drowned in the seas of distrust and envy." The *bud* is a vehicle for an implied tenor that can only be determined by the situation: undeveloped love. In contrast, the second metaphor at work here has directly stated tenors (distrust and envy) for its vehicle (seas).

Example 3

Controlling Image

At other times the metaphor (like simile) can be a **controlling image**. A controlling (or main) image is an image that runs throughout a work. Consider Shakespeare's "Sonnet 97":

> How like a winter hath my absence been
> From thee, the pleasure of the fleeting year!
> What freezings have I felt, what dark days seen!
> *Line*   What old December's bareness everywhere!
> *(5)*   And yet this time removed was summer's time,
> The teeming autumn, big with rich increase,
> Bearing the wanton burden of the prime,
> Like widowed wombs after their lords' decease:
> Yet this abundant issue seemed to me
> *(10)*   But hope of orphans and unfathered fruit;
> For summer and his pleasures wait on thee,
> And, thou away, the very birds are mute.
> Or, if they sing, 'tis with so dull a cheer,
> That leaves look pale, dreading the winter's near.

The main image compares

(A) winter to widowed wombs
(B) pleasure to the fleeting year
(C) autumn to abundant issue
(D) absence to summer's time
(E) absence to the winter season

Explanation: The first simile is presented in line 1: his absence has been "like a winter." A different simile appears in line 8; however, he returns to the winter image by line 11, using "For" to establish a causal relationship and ending with "winter's near."

Correct Answer: **E**

Example 4

Multiple Vehicles

Sometimes a tenor will have more than one vehicle: "His attitude was ice-cold, rock-hard, and knife-sharp." Anthony Munday uses more than twenty vehicles in "I Serve a Mistress":

> I serve a mistress whiter than the snow,
>   Straighter than cedar, brighter than the glass,
> Finer in trip and swifter than the roe,
> *Line*   More pleasant than the field of flowering grass;
> (5)   More gladsome to my withering joys that fade,
>   Than winter's sun or summer's cooling shade.
>
> Sweeter than swelling grape of ripest wine,
>   Softer than feathers of the fairest swan,
> Smoother than jet, more stately than the pine,
> (10)   Fresher than poplar, smaller than my span,
> Clearer than beauty's fiery pointed beam,
> Or icy crust of crystal's frozen stream.
>
> Yet is she curster than the bear by kind,
>   And harder-hearted than the agèd oak,
> (15)   More glib than oil, more fickle than the wind,
>   Stiffer than steel, no sooner bent but broke.
> Lo! thus my service is a lasting sore;
> Yet will I serve, although I die therefore.

(ca. 1600)

The change in imagery in this poem describes

(A) mental instability
(B) seasonal changes
(C) primeval hatred
(D) a love-hate relationship
(E) a reversal of fortune

Explanation: Notice the change in vehicles in the last stanza from how wonderful she is to how horrible, to the point of making his "service ... a lasting sore."

Correct Answer: **D**

Example 5

Conceit

A *conceit* is a very intricate parallel (metaphor) drawn between two otherwise *dissimilar* concepts or things:

Elegy

My prime of youth is but a frost of cares,
My feast of joy is but a dish of pain,
My crop of corn is but a field of tares,
Line And all my good is but vain hope of gain;
(5) The day is past, and yet I saw no sun,
And now I live, and now my life is done.

by Chidiock Tichborne
(ca. 1580)

The speaker sees his life as

(A) comic
(B) too short
(C) tragic
(D) too long
(E) too busy

Explanation: Youth is generally associated with spring's warmth, not fall's frost; joy is not associated with pain; tares have invaded his corn crop (the product of his work is worthless); even his good was only "vain hope." His life is about over—a day without sun. What a tragic situation!

Correct Answer: **C**

Example 6

Personification

In the third stanza of "The Aged Lover Renounceth Love" (Lord Thomas Vaux's sixteenth-century work), age and "lusty life" are both personified:

For age with stealing steps
Hath clawed me with his crutch,
And lusty life away she leaps
As there had been none such.

Age is given the human characteristics of walking with a crutch. Lusty life—youth—is given the human characteristic of leaping.

In a testing situation, you may be asked to identify that the object or idea is being personified. Tests also may include questions concerning the effects of the personification:

"Lusty life," as a character in lines 3–4, of the above stanza seems

(A) uncaring
(B) happy
(C) athletic
(D) an illusion
(E) deceptive

The personification of "age" in lines 1–2 emphasizes

(A) that no one escapes age
(B) the speaker's acceptance of age
(C) universal carnality
(D) age's feeble condition
(E) age's furtive nature

Explanation: The lusty life of youth does not even look back; age has used stealth, coming on the speaker unexpectedly.

Correct Answers: **A, E**

Example 7

Personification

In Sir Phillip Sidney's sixteenth-century poem "Loving in Truth," he personifies Invention, Nature, and Study:

> Loving in truth, and fain in verse my love to show,
> That she, dear she, might take some pleasure of my pain,
> Pleasure might cause her read, reading might make her know,
> Knowledge might pity win, and pity grace obtain,
> I sought fit words to paint the blackest face of woe,
> Studying inventions fine, her wits to entertain,
> Oft turning others' leaves, to see if thence would flow
> Some fresh and fruitful showers upon my sunburnt brain.
> But words came halting forth, wanting Invention's stay;
> Invention, Nature's child, fled step-dame Study's blows;
> And others' feet still seemed but strangers in my way.
> Thus great with child to speak, and helpless in my throes,
> Biting my truant pen, beating myself for spite:
> "Fool," said my Muse to me, "look in thy heart and write."

Line (5) ... (10) appear at lines 4 and 10.

The effect of personifying Invention, Nature, and Study (lines 9–10) is to

(A) contrast the natural to the artificial
(B) emphasize love
(C) imitate other poets
(D) confirm his love for his auditor
(E) compare his work to that of others

Explanation: What is the *effect* of this personification? The first four lines set up the situation: The speaker wants to write a poem that will show the woman he loves how much he loves her. Lines 5–8 outline that he studied "inventions" and "others' leaves" (other poets' writings) for ideas, but his brain is "sunburnt"—what today might be called "writer's block" or "burnout." Lines 9–10 (the lines that contain the personification) reveal that although he wanted "Invention" (originality) which is "Nature's child" (unlearned, natural) to stay, it "fled" from "step-dame Study's blows." Line 11 confirms that copying the style of others' works did not help him. He compares himself to a pregnant woman in line 12, his message wants so to be delivered; he is desperate by line 13. But line 14 makes his point: originality must come from within.

Within this context, what is the *effect* of personifying Invention and Nature? One possible effect is to make originality, as "Nature's child" seem innocent (as a child), nonthreatening and desirable. The personification of Study, on the other hand, heightens the perception that the speaker has lost his fresh approach (perhaps) to imitation of others' works (a "step-dame" relationship to Invention in contrast to Invention as "Nature's child"—a natural relationship). The effect of the personification of Invention, Nature, and Study is to emphasize that writing a poem is a natural process from within rather than an artificial process.

Correct Answer: **A**

Example 8

Allusion

Some allusions are popular among writers and are used over the centuries. The Trojan War, its characters and circumstances, has remained a rich source of allusion for both prose and poetry for many generations. These two stanzas from Thomas Nashe's "Adieu, Farewell Earth's Bliss" (1592) are characteristic:

> Beauty is but a flower
> Which wrinkles will devour,
> Brightness falls from the air,
> Queens have died young and fair,
> (5) (allusion) → Dust hath closed Helen's eye.
> I am sick, I must die.
> Lord, have mercy on us!

> Strength stoops unto the grave,
> (allusion) → Worms feed on Hector brave,
> (10) Swords may not fight with fate,
> Earth still holds ope her gate.
> Come! come! the bells do cry.
> I am sick, I must die.
> Lord, have mercy on us!

In line 5, "Helen" is presented as

(A) a woman who became ill and died
(B) famous for growing flowers
(C) a woman symbolic of beauty
(D) the speaker's lover
(E) the victim of a dust storm

Explanation: The allusion to Helen as beautiful and Hector as brave has been used so extensively as to become traditional "types" of beauty and bravery.

Correct Answer: **C**

Example 9

Mythical Allusion

A common source for allusion that might be tested is the systems of Greek and Roman mythology. For example, Matthew Arnold's "Memorial Verses," for the day that William Wordsworth died (April 27, 1850):

> When Byron's eyes were shut in death,
> We bowed our head and held our breath.
> He taught us little; but our soul
Line > Had *felt* him like the thunder's roll.
(5) > With shivering heart the strife we saw
> Of passion with eternal law;
> And yet with reverential awe
> We watched the fount of fiery life
(allusion) → Which served for that Titanic strife.

The allusion in the last line ("Titanic strife") serves to

(A) confound the issue
(B) emphasize the size of the strife
(C) reinforce the speaker's trauma
(D) contrast the "fiery life"
(E) diminish the size of the strife

Explanation: The Titans of Greek myth were known for their enormous size and strength. *The Titanic,* a ship that sank when it hit an iceberg in 1912, was notable at the time for its large size.

Correct Answer: **B**

Example 10

Allusion

Leave Me, O Love

Leave me, O Love, which reachest but to dust,
And thou, my mind, aspire to higher things;
Grow rich in that which never taketh rust:
Line Whatever fades but fading pleasure brings.
(5)   Draw in thy beams, and humble all thy might
To that sweet yoke where lasting freedoms be;
Which breaks the clouds and opens forth the light
That doth both shine and give us sight to see.
   O take fast hold; let that light be thy guide
(10) In this small course which birth draws out to death,
And think how evil becometh him to slide,
Who seeketh heav'n, and comes of heav'nly breath.
   Then farewell, world, thy uttermost I see;
Eternal Love, maintain thy life in me.

by Sir Philip Sidney

This poem does NOT include

(A) sonnet form
(B) biblical allusion
(C) alliteration
(D) allusion to love poetry
(E) a concluding couplet

The central contrast is seen in which of the following?

(A) Love (line 1) and Eternal Love (line 14)
(B) mind (line 2) and world (line 13)
(C) Grow rich (line 3) and evil (line 11)
(D) birth (line 10) and farewell (line 13)
(E) clouds (line 7) and light (line 7)

Explanation: This poem is fourteen lines written in iambic pentameter (a sonnet) with a concluding couplet. Alliteration? "Leave . . . Love (line 1), "fades . . . fading" (line 4). Seeking Heaven and Eternal Love is a frequently used biblical allusion. In the context of this poem, "Love, which reachest but to dust" obviously is finite, carnal, and earthbound in contrast to Eternal Love.

Correct Answers: **D, A**

Example 11

Biblical Allusion

The Bible is a source of literary allusion that might be tested because of its prevalence in terms of numbers of references in English and American literature.

According to Professor Northrup Frye in *The Great Code*, ". . . a student of English literature who does not know the Bible does not understand a good deal of what is going on in what he reads: the most conscientious student will be continually misconstruing the implications, even the meaning."

A few of the many biblical phrases and concepts often used in literature include:

- The apple of my eye
- A Judas
- A prophet has no honor in his own country
- The salt of the earth
- Hiding your light under a bushel
- Man does not live by bread alone
- Turning water into wine
- Walking on water
- Casting the first stone
- My brother's keeper
- A house divided cannot stand
- Standing against a Goliath
- Forty years in the wilderness
- Being thrown to the lions
- Being thrown into the fiery furnace
- Trying to pass a camel through the eye of a needle
- The patience of Job
- Wisdom of Solomon
- A coat of many colors
- A leopard changing its spots

This list could go on and on.

For example, most Americans are familiar with Patrick Henry's most famous speech (in 1775) in which he challenged, "Give me liberty, or give me death!" Notice his use of biblical allusion (highlighted by underscore) in these excerpts from the speech:

Liberty or Death
a speech by Patrick Henry

Mr. President, it is natural to man to indulge in the illusions of hope. We are apt to shut our eyes against a painful truth and listen to the song of that siren, till she transforms us into beasts. Is this the part of wise men, engaged *Line* in a great and arduous struggle for liberty? Are we disposed to be of the *(5)* number of those, who, <u>having eyes, see not, and having ears, hear not</u>, the things which so nearly concern their temporal salvation? For my part, whatever anguish of spirit it may cost, I am willing to know the whole truth, to know the worst and to provide for it.

I have but one lamp by which my feet are guided, and that is the lamp of experience. I know of no way of judging of the future but by the past. And (10) judging by the past, I wish to know what there has been in the conduct of the British ministry for the last ten years to justify those hopes with which gentlemen have been pleased to solace themselves and the House? Is it that insidious smile with which our petition has been lately received? Trust it not, sir; it will prove a snare to your feet. Suffer not yourselves <u>to be betrayed</u> (15) <u>with a kiss</u>. Ask yourselves how this gracious reception of our petition comports with these warlike preparations which cover our waters and darken our land. Are fleets and armies necessary to a work of love and reconciliation? Have we shown ourselves so unwilling to be reconciled that force must be called in to win back our love? Let us not deceive ourselves, sir. These are the (20) implements of war and subjugation, the last arguments to which kings resort....If we wish to be free—if we mean to preserve inviolate those inestimable privileges for which we have been so long contending—if we mean not basely to abandon the noble struggle in which we have been so long engaged, and which we have pledged ourselves never to abandon until the (25) glorious object of our contest shall be obtained, we must fight! I repeat it, sir, we must fight! An <u>appeal to arms and to the God of Hosts</u> is all that is left us!

* * *

(30) It is in vain, sir, to extenuate the matter. <u>Gentlemen may cry, peace,</u> <u>peace!—but there is no peace</u>. The war is actually begun! The next gale that sweeps from the north will bring to our ears the clash of resounding arms! Our brethren are already in the field! Why stand we here idle? What is it that gentlemen wish? What would they have? Is life so dear, or peace so sweet, as (35) to be purchased at the price of chains and slavery? Forbid it, Almighty God! I know not what course others may take, but as for me: *Give me liberty, or give me death!*

Having eyes, but not seeing, and ears, but not hearing, refers to

   I. being deaf and mute
  II. understanding
 III. attitudes
 IV. being deaf and blind

(A) I only
(B) II only
(C) IV only
(D) II and III only
(E) I, II, III, and IV

Being "betrayed with a kiss" (line 14–15) is an allusion to

(A) the murder of Caesar by Mark Anthony
(B) the suicide of Cleopatra
(C) Hitler's death orders during World War II
(D) warnings that the "British are coming!"
(E) Judas identifying Jesus Christ to be arrested

"An appeal to arms and to the God of Hosts" (line 26) is to

(A) watch and listen
(B) recruit men and be hospitable
(C) fight and pray
(D) challenge and capitulate
(E) carry and enlist

According to the speaker, the gentlemen who cry peace are

(A) mistaken
(B) peacemakers
(C) reliable
(D) true prophets
(E) politicians

Explanation: In this often-referenced biblical allusion, those who have eyes (physically to see), but do not see (spiritual discernment) and who have ears to listen with, but do not hear the message, lack understanding because of their attitudes. A modern key to understanding this allusion is the expression "Oh, I see!" when we finally understand something or "I hear you" said when we understand and are in agreement. In contrast, people sometimes say, "I hear you talking" to indicate that they understand what is being said, but do not agree with it (by implication, the hearer views what is being said as simply "talk"). Based on the account of Judas Iscariot kissing Jesus on the cheek to identify him to the armed crowd, "betrayed by a kiss" is a traditional symbol of betrayal by those once thought to be friends. Also, the name "Judas" is a related symbol. To call someone a "Judas" is to accuse the person of betrayal. "An appeal to arms" or weapons is to fight. The men who cry peace are mistaken because "The war is actually begun!"

Correct Answers: **D, E, C, A**

Example 12

Metonymy

James Shirley uses metonymy in this seventeenth-century poem "The Glories of Our Blood and State":

> The glories of our blood and state
>   Are shadows, not substantial things;
> There is no armour against fate;
>   Death lays his icy hand on kings:

Line
(5)   metonymy →   Sceptre and crown
>   Must tumble down,
> And in the dust be equal made

metonymy →   With the poor crooked scythe and spade.

"Scythe and spade" in the last line contextually refers to

(A) damaged equipment
(B) death
(C) farm implements
(D) the working man
(E) fate

Explanation: "Sceptre and crown" is a metonymy for the king, and "scythe and spade" is a metonymy for the working man.

Correct Answer: **D**

Example 13

Epithet

This selection is found in *The Pilot* by James Fenimore Cooper (1823).

> "No man—I speak not of women, who cannot be supposed so well versed in human nature—but no man who has reached the time of life that enti-
> tles him to be called by that name, can consort with these disorganizers, who
Line would destroy everything that is sacred—these levellers who would pull
(5) down the great to exalt the little—these Jacobins, who—who—"

> "Nay, sir, if you are at a loss for opprobrious epithets," said Katherine, with provoking coolness, "call on Mr. Christopher Dillon for assistance; he waits your pleasure at the door."

The best understanding of "opprobrious epithets" as used in the passage is

(A) high-sounding praise
(B) contemptuous names
(C) burdensome directives
(D) convenient titles
(E) harsh orders

Explanation: By definition and supported by context, to be opprobrious is to be contemptuous in an abusive or shameful manner. An epithet refers to, in this context, negative name-calling.

Correct Answer: **B**

Example 14

Symbols

Here is the third stanza of "The Canonization," by John Donne (ca. 1600)

> Call us what you will, we are made such by love.
>   Call her one, me another fly,
> We're tapers too, and at our own cost die;

Line → And we in us find th'eagle and the dove.
(5)   The phoenix riddle hath more wit
>   By us; we two, being one, are it.
> So to one neutral thing both sexes fit,
>   We die and rise the same, and prove
>   Mysterious by this love.

The eagle and dove could represent which of the following in this context?

 I. Strength
 II. Purity
III. Peace
IV. National pride

(A) I only
(B) II only
(C) III only
(D) I, II, and III only
(E) I, II, III, and IV

Explanation: Generally, symbols depend for their associated meanings on the context of the literary work in which they are used. A deeper analysis would be needed to explore the levels of meaning of "th' eagle and the dove" in this poem; however, traditionally, an eagle symbolizes strength and the dove represents purity and peace. The eagle is a symbol of America, but within the context of this stanza, national pride does not fit.

Correct Answer: **D**

Example 15

Rhetoric

In this excerpt from James Madison's June 6, 1788, speech, Madison (who favored a federal constitution) is arguing against a speech made the previous day by Patrick Henry in which Henry spoke against ratification:

> I must confess I have not been able to find his usual consistency in the gentleman's argument on this occasion. He informs us that the people of the country are at perfect repose; that is, every man enjoys the fruits of his labor
>
> *Line* peaceably and securely, and that everything is in perfect tranquility and
> *(5)* safety. I wish sincerely that this were true. If this be their happy situation, why has every state acknowledged the contrary? Why were deputies from all the states sent to the general convention? Why have complaints of national and individual distresses been echoed and reechoed throughout the conti- nent? Why has our general government been so shamefully disgraced and
> *(10)* our Constitution violated? Wherefore have laws been made to authorize a change, and wherefore are we now assembled here? A federal government is formed for the protection of its individual members. Ours has attacked itself with impunity. Its authority has been disobeyed and despised.

The effect of the speaker's series of rhetorical questions is to

(A) cast doubt on another speaker's argument
(B) reinforce the other speaker's ideas
(C) reveal a certain gullibility
(D) give grounds for an act of war
(E) attest to the lack of need for action

Madison amplifies which of the following?

(A) "usual consistency" (line 1)
(B) "perfect repose" (line 3)
(C) "their happy situation" (line 5)
(D) "complaints" (line 7)
(E) "authorize a change" (lines 10–11)

Madison uses repetition to

(A) keep an even tone
(B) keep from revealing his anger
(C) emphasize his point
(D) reveal his anger
(E) take attention from Henry

Explanation: Madison uses three different rhetorical devices in the passage:

1. He uses rhetorical questions to cast doubts on Henry's argument. "If" (line 5) what he says is true, then "why" (lines 6–11) does the evidence not support it?
2. He amplifies "perfect repose" in lines 3–5. Amplification occurs when a word, concept, point, or idea is defined or explained, then is followed by even more explanation. Amplification is rhetorically effective to emphasize the importance of an idea, clarify it, and help the reader retain the idea.
3. He keeps repeating "Why…? Why …?" in lines 6–10. Generally, such repetition serves to emphasize. In this case, it creates an emotionally driving tone of doubt.

Correct Answers **A, B, C**

Example 16

Anachronism

Here are some lines from Shakespeare's *Julius Caesar*.

MARCUS BRUTUS.	Alas, good Cassius, do not think of him:
	If he love Caesar, all that he can do
	Is to himself,—take thought, and die for
Line	Caesar:
(5)	And that were much he should; for he is
	given
	To sports, to wildness, and much company.
TREBONIUS.	There is no fear in him; let him not die;
	For he will live, and laugh at this hereafter.
	[*Clock strikes.*]
(10) MARCUS BRUTUS.	Peace! count the clock.
CASSIUS.	The clock hath stricken three.
TREBONIUS.	'Tis time to part.

An anachronism occurs when

(A) sports is mentioned
(B) Caesar has already died
(C) the clock strikes
(D) Brutus counts the clock
(E) Cassius has already died

Explanation: A clock that can strike the hour? In Caesar's Rome?

Correct Answer: **C**

Example 17

Hyperbole

Read this first stanza of Andrew Marvell's "To His Coy Mistress":

→   Had we but world enough, and time,
     This coyness, Lady, were no crime.
     We would sit down, and think which way

Line   To walk, and pass our long love's day.
(5)   Thou by the Indian Ganges' side
     Should'st rubies find: I by the tide
     Of Humber would complain. I would

→   Love you ten years before the Flood:
     And you should if you please refuse

(10) →   Till the conversion of the Jews.
     My vegetable love should grow

→   Vaster than empires, and more slow.

→   And hundred years should go to praise
     Thine eyes, and on thy forehead gaze.

(15) →   Two hundred to adore each breast:

→   But thirty thousand to the rest.
     An age at least to every part,
     And the last age should show your heart.
     For, Lady, you deserve this state;

(20)   Nor would I love at lower rate.

(ca. 1660)

The speaker's use of hyperbole is intended to create a sense of

(A) absurdity
(B) sincerity
(C) irony
(D) urgency
(E) affirmation

Explanation: The speaker exaggerates a period of endless time in order to emphasize time's brevity in reality. This overstatement creates an urgent tone.
Correct Answer: **D**

Example 18

Paradox

The second stanza of Chidiock Tichborne's sixteenth-century "Elegy" is built upon paradoxical relationships:

> My tale was heard and yet it was not told,
> My fruit is fallen and yet my leaves are green,
> My youth is spent and yet I am not old,
Line I saw the world and yet I was not seen;
(5) My thread is cut and yet it is not spun,
> And now I live, and now my life is done.

Which of the following words best summarizes the speaker's view of his life?

(A) Confused
(B) Inconsequential
(C) Unfulfilled
(D) Imitative
(E) Immutable

Explanation: How can a tale be heard, but not told? A youth gone, but the person not be old? In this stanza, viewed apart from the rest of the poem, the speaker is expressing dissatisfaction over a life that is unfulfilled. Perhaps an event has happened to make him believe his "life" is over even if his biological life continues.

Correct Answer: **C**

Example 19

Oxymoron

The fourth stanza of Sir Thomas Wyatt's "Marvel No More" ends with an oxymoron.

> Play who that can that part:
> Needs must in me appear
> How fortune, overthwart,
> Doth cause my mourning cheer.

The oxymoron in the last line is based on

(A) rhyme scheme
(B) a play on words
(C) a reversal of thought
(D) sentimentality
(E) an allusion to coffee

Explanation: Morning/mourning is a play on words (pun).

Correct Answer: **B**

Example 20

Irony

The following paragraph comes from Samuel Johnson's "On Self-love and Indolence."

> It seems generally believed, that, as the eye cannot see itself, the mind has no faculties by which it can contemplate its own state, and that therefore we have not means of becoming acquainted with our real characters; an opin-
> *Line* ion which, like innumerable other postulates, an inquirer finds himself
> *(5)* inclined to admit upon very little evidence, because it affords a ready solution of many difficulties. It will explain why the greatest abilities frequently fail to promote the happiness of those who possess them; why those who can distinguish with the utmost nicety the boundaries of vice and virtue, suffer them to be confounded in their own conduct; why the active and vigilant
> *(10)* resign their affairs implicitly to the management of others; and why the cautious and fearful make hourly approaches toward ruin, without one sigh of solicitude or struggle for escape.

(ca. 1755)

The speaker's main point revolves around the ironic situation that

(A) "the eye cannot see itself"
(B) "the mind [cannot]…contemplate its own state"
(C) "the greatest abilities…fail to promote…happiness"
(D) "the active and vigilant resign their affairs…to others"
(E) "the cautious and fearful make hourly approaches toward ruin"

In line 1, "…as the eye cannot see itself" is

  I. the vehicle in an ironic simile
 II. a comparison of conditions
III. the tenor in an ironic metaphor

(A) I only
(B) II only
(C) III only
(D) I and II only
(E) I, II, and III

Explanation: This paragraph contains all the ironies listed in the first question and more; however, the central irony is B. Answer choice A serves only to introduce it, and all the other ironies illustrate it. In "…as the eye cannot see itself," use of "as" makes it a simile, not a metaphor. Its tenor is that the mind cannot "contemplate its own state." Both the eye and the mind are in the ironic condition of not being able to apply their primary functions to themselves.

Correct Answers: **B, D**

Example 21

Irony

The following paragraph comes from Thackeray's *Vanity Fair* (1847–8).

> "We don't care a fig for her," writes some unknown correspondent with a pretty little hand-writing and a pink seal to her note. "She is *fade* and insipid," and adds some more kind remarks in this strain, which I should
>
> *Line* never have repeated at all, but that they are in truth prodigiously compli-
> (5) mentary to the young lady whom they concern.

Which of the literary devices listed below is used to describe the remarks of the "unknown correspondent"?

(A) Situational irony
(B) Metaphoric prose
(C) Paradoxical amplification
(D) Verbal irony
(E) Personification

The situational irony presented by this narrator can best be seen in which of the following?

(A) "*fade* and insipid…prodigiously complimentary"
(B) "don't care a fig…more kind remarks"
(C) "unknown correspondent…the young lady"
(D) "kind remarks…repeated"
(E) "pretty little hand-writing and a pink seal"

Explanation: "*Fade* and insipid" are, in this context, insulting rather than kind remarks. This paragraph provides examples of both verbal and situational irony. To call insults "kind" is verbally ironic, and it is an ironic situation when insults reveal jealousy and become a compliment.

Correct Answers: **D, A**

Example 22

Malapropism

Romeo and Juliet, Act II Scene III

NURSE.	By my troth, it is well said;—'for himself to mar,' quoth a'?—Gentlemen, can any of you tell me where I may find the young Romeo?
Line ROMEO. (5)	I can tell you; but young Romeo will be older when you have found him than he was when you sought him: I am the youngest of that name, for fault of a worse.
NURSE.	You say well.

> MERCUTIO. Yea, is the worst well? very well took, i'faith; wisely, wisely.

(10) NURSE. If you be he, sir, I desire some confidence with you.

> BENVOLIO. She will indite him to some supper.

> MERCUTIO. A bawd, a bawd, a bawd! So-ho!

As used in the selection, which of the following contains misuses of diction?

(A) Nurse: troth; Romeo: worse
(B) Nurse: confidence; Benvolio: indite
(C) Benvolio: indite; Mercutio: bawd
(D) Nurse: quoth; Mercutio: i'faith
(E) Romeo: fault; Mercutio: worst well

Explanation: The first malapropism is the nurse's use of "confidence" where she most likely means "conference." The effect this malapropism has on Benvolio is to cause him to mock her by deliberately using a malapropism: "indite" for "invite."

Correct Answer: **B**

Example 23

Pun

An often quoted pun appears in *Romeo and Juliet*, Act III Scene I when Mercutio is wounded:

> ROMEO. Courage, man; the hurt cannot be much.

> MERCUTIO. No, 'tis not so deep as a well, nor so wide as a church-door; but 'tis enough, 'twill serve: ask for me to-morrow, and you shall find me a grave man.

Which of the following words is used as a pun in this passage?

(A) Courage
(B) Hurt
(C) Well
(D) Serve
(E) Grave

Explanation: What is the pun at work here? "Grave" can refer either to a "serious" man (as, indeed, his wound is a serious situation) and to a man in his grave.

Correct Answer: **E**

Example 24

Pun

Here is a stanza from John Donne's "A Hymn to God the Father."

> I have a sin of fear, that when I have spun
>   My last thread, I shall perish on the shore;
>   But swear by Thy self, that at my death Thy Son
> *Line*   Shall shine as he shines now, and heretofore;
> *(5)*   And, having done that, Thou hast done;
>   I fear no more.
>
>   (ca. 1600)

Which of the following words is used as a pun in this stanza?

(A) Fear
(B) Spun
(C) Thread
(D) Shore
(E) Son

Explanation: A very obvious pun "Son" and "sun." (Keep in mind that the pun as a literary device can be very serious.) There is another pun at work throughout this poem. Hint: Look again at the poet's name.

Line 5: "And, having done that, Thou hast done;…"

Correct Answer: **E**

Example 25

Practice Thinking on a Figurative Level

Here is John Donne's "The Legacy."

> When last I died, and, dear, I die
>   As often as from thee I go,
>   Though it be but an hour ago
> *Line* —And lovers' hours be full eternity—
> *(5)*   I can remember yet, that I
>   Something did say, and something did bestow;
> Though I be dead, which sent me, I might be
> Mine own executor, and legacy.
> I heard me say, "Tell her anon,
> *(10)*   That myself," that is you, not I,
>   "Did kill me," and when I felt me die,
> I bid me send my heart, when I was gone;
> But I alas! could there find none;
>   When I had ripp'd, and search'd where hearts should be
> *(15)* It kill'd me again, that I who still was true
> In life, in my last will should cozen you.

Yet I found something like a heart,
　　But colors it and corners had;
　　It was not good, it was not bad,
(20) It was entire to none, and few had part;
　　As good as could be made by art
　　　It seemed, and therefore for our loss be sad.
　　I meant to send that heart instead of mine,
　　But O! no man could hold it, for 'twas thine.

1. Of the following definitions and illustrative phrases, which best reflects the meaning of "corners" as used in line 18?

   (A) Geometric angles
   (B) Critical points
   (C) Secret places
   (D) Shortest routes
   (E) Awkward positions

2. That the speaker intended to "send" his heart but "could there find none" in the second stanza is

   (A) sarcastic rhetoric
   (B) symbolic of the nature of love
   (C) a structural pun describing discouragement
   (D) a parody of the first stanza
   (E) the vehicle for the legacy

3. The theme of the poem is mostly developed by

   (A) narrative accounts
   (B) paradoxical relationships
   (C) love lyrics
   (D) comparison and contrast
   (E) legal analogies

4. In line 24, "no man could hold it, for 'twas thine" projects an attitude of

   (A) congeniality
   (B) intimacy
   (C) devotion
   (D) isolation
   (E) disillusionment

5. What is the intended "legacy" in line 8?

   (A) "my heart" (line 12)
   (B) "executor" (line 8)
   (C) "Eternity" (line 4)
   (D) "something like a heart" (line 17)
   (E) "art" (line 21)

6. The central irony of the poem can be seen in which of the following lines?

(A) Line 4
(B) Line 9
(C) Line 14
(D) Line 17
(E) Line 24

Answers and Explanations

1. **(C)** They are secret places (the corners of the heart and mind) rather than geometric angles (the corners of the room), critical points (to turn a corner), shortest routes (to cut corners), or awkward positions (backed into a corner). Hint: When reading this poem, explore the figurative meanings of "heart" and "death."

2. **(C)** The speaker lost his heart (line 13), which also can mean that he "lost heart," an expression meaning discouragement.

3. **(B)** Some of the paradoxical elements in this poem include the following: an hour equals an eternity; a dead person being his own executor and legacy; the speaker finding his lover's heart in his own body. The seemingly contradictory concepts rely upon the figurative meanings of death and the heart.

4. **(E)** Look closely at the poet's description of his lover's heart: "something like a heart" (line 17), "not good…not bad" (line 19), and particularly note the description in lines 20–21. The speaker has taken a revealing look at his lover to find that "our loss be sad" (line 22). He feels disillusionment.

5. **(A)** The speaker, on a figurative level, plans upon death to send his legacy or heart to his lover (line 12).

6. **(E)** After a killing inner search of his own feelings or heart in the second stanza, he finds that he has already lost his heart to his lover and has lost heart in the process. As we read the third stanza, however, he does find and describe a heart that is less than perfect. Does it belong to him? Are his feelings less deep than those implied in the first stanza? No. Ironically, it belongs to his lover.

Test Taker → Test Maker

If you were writing SAT Literature tests, what questions about use of language would you ask? Here is an opportunity for you to approach use of language from a test writer's point of view.

"The Frost" was written by Hannah Flagg Gould of Lancaster, Massachusetts, sometime before 1870.

<blockquote>

The Frost looked forth, one still, clear night,
And he said, "Now I shall be out of sight;
So through the valley and over the height

Line In silence I'll take my way.
(5) I will not go like that blustering train,
The wind and the snow, the hail and the rain,
Who make so much bustle and noise in vain,
  But I'll be as busy as they!"

Then he went to the mountain, and powdered its crest,
(10) He climbed up the trees, and their boughs he dressed
With diamonds and pearls, and over the breast
  Of the quivering lake he spread
A coat of mail, that it need not fear
The downward point of many a spear
(15) That he hung on its margin, far and near,
  Where a rock could rear its head.

He went to the windows of those who slept,
And over each pane like a fairy crept,
Whenever he breathed, wherever he stepped,
(20) By the light of the moon were seen
Most beautiful things. There were flowers and trees,
There were bevies of birds and swarms of bees,
There were cities, thrones, temples, and towers, and these
  All pictured in silver sheen!

(25) But he did one thing that was hardly fair,—
He peeped in the cupboard, and, finding there
That all had forgotten for him to prepare,—
  "Now, just to set them a-thinking,
I'll bite this basket of fruit," said he;
(30) "This costly pitcher I'll burst in three,
And the glass of water they've left for me
  And *'tchick!'* to tell them I'm drinking."

</blockquote>

What uses of language do you see in this poem? List them below:

_____

_____

_____

_____

_____

_____

Discussion

1. Talking "Frost"—definitely a case of anthropomorphism. Why not personification? Because the poet is presenting "Frost" not just with human characteristics but as if Frost really is a human capable of talking, reasoning, eating, and drinking.

2. "Like" in line 5 is a clue to the simile. She is comparing wind, snow, hail, and rain (line 6) to what? A blustering train.

3. More personification:
   - dressed trees and boughs (line 10)
   - a lake with a breast (line 11)

4. Any metaphors? Notice that Frost has hung "many a spear" with "The downward point"—in other words, icicles (lines 14–16). Look at lines 17–24. The poet sees flowers, cities, and so forth, pictured in the frost on the windows—very similar to seeing shapes of animals and other things in clouds.

5. Another simile ("like") in line 18: Frost is compared to a fairy.

This poem contains much more, such as elements of tone (Did you notice the "tchick!" in the last line—onomatopoeia?) and character (Why isn't Frost being fair in lines 25–31?). We'll concentrate on the poet's use of language, however, for writing a question.

A Question for Thought and Discussion

The poet makes Frost seem like a person. Why, then, does she begin by naming Frost with a definite article ("The Frost" in line 1) rather than Mr., Mrs., Miss, or Ms. Frost?

Based on one of the five ideas just listed (or perhaps one of your own), write a question about this poem.

Lines _____ – _____ contain elements of

I.   _____

II. _____

III. _____

IV. _____

(A) I only
(B) II only
(C) I and III only
(D) I, II, and III only
(E) I, II, III, and IV

The correct answer will depend on what you select for the Roman Numeral answer choices.

USE OF LANGUAGE IN CONCLUSION

This chapter dealt with images that go beyond the written page and the figures of speech used to create those images. The last literary element will take a magnifying glass to look at the sentences, lines, phrases, and words as they relate to the context of the work.

LITERARY ELEMENT NUMBER SEVEN: MEANING(S) IN CONTEXT

Some questions on the literature test deal with the meanings of words, phrases, lines, or sentences as they are used in context (the ideas and information that come before or after the words in question).

What terms do I need to know that relate to the meaning(s) in context in a work?

TERM ALERT

1. **Syntax**

Definition: Diction is the choice of words used; syntax is their arrangement into patterns. Understanding syntax can provide context for understanding the meaning.

TERM WATCH

2. **Parallelism**

Definition: Parallelism occurs when similar ideas, structures, or sounds are repeated. Repetition can come in several forms, such as

a. Repetition of structure, for example:

"In short, our words to men are as empty sounds; our sighs, as puffs of winds; and our tears, as fruitless showers;... (Margaret Cavendish, Duchess of Newcastle, 1662)

b. Repetition of words for rhetorical effect (**palilogy**), for example:

"It is rather for us to be here dedicated to the great task remaining before us—that from these honored dead we take increased devotion to that cause for which they gave the last full measure of devotion—that we here highly resolve that these dead shall not have died in vain—that this nation, under God, shall have a new birth of freedom—and that government of the people, by the people, for the people, shall not perish from the earth." (Abraham Lincoln, 1863)

c. Repetition of words at the beginnings of sentences or clauses (**anaphora**)—a favorite of poets and expressive writers for example:

Stanza 11   And her voice, it murmurs lowly,
As a silver stream may run,
Which yet feels, you feel, the sun.

Stanza 12   And her smile, it seems half holy,
As if drawn from thoughts more far
Than our common jestings are.

Stanza 13   And if any poet knew her
He would sing of her with falls
Used in lovely madrigals.

Each of the concluding seven stanzas begins with the same pattern:

> And if any painter drew her...
> And if reader read the poem...
> And a dreamer (did you show him...
> And a stranger, when he sees her...
> And all voices that address her...
> And all fancies yearn to cover...
> And all hearts do pray, "God love her!"...

(Elizabeth Barrett Browning, "A Portrait")

3. Denotation

TERM REVIEW

Definition: Denotation is the basic or literal meaning or meanings of a word.

You need to develop your sight vocabulary to include as many words as possible. However, often you can use context to determine the intended meaning for words that have more than one denotation (literal meaning). For example, the verb "cover" has more than twenty definitions in some unabridged dictionaries. When a writer has a character decide to "cover" a bill on her desk, only context can tell you whether "cover" means she is protecting this bill from damage by children playing with water pistols nearby, hiding the amount of the bill from the prying eyes of another worker, or deciding to pay the bill herself rather than letting the company pay for it.

4. Connotation

TERM REVIEW

Definition: Denotations are the literal meanings of words; *connotations* are their emotional meanings. Sometimes *associations* result from a person's own nonverbal experiences. Such associations can be very powerful. A particular song might be associated with a first love. Certain foods can remind you of a person, an enjoyable vacation, or a particular place. Events in your life may be brought to mind when you hear a name, smell a fragrance, or experience a familiar feeling. Such associations can be positive or negative, but seldom without some type of emotional response.

Similarly, words can gain connotative meaning for a person through his or her personal experiences. Connotative meanings also can be universal (shared by most people) or shared by some group (such as a nation, an organization, a race, a religion, or a profession or trade).

A writer can elicit emotions from his or her readers simply by selecting connotatively charged words.

TIP

Positive connotation
an antique

Neutral
an old chair

Negative connotation
junk

5. Aphorism

TERM REVIEW

Definition: An aphorism is a pointed or concise statement of principle. Also called *maxims*, these statements combine denotation and syntax to achieve concise expression.

Examples: To the victor belong the spoils.
To err is human, to forgive, divine.
An apple doesn't fall far from the tree.
The proof of the pudding is in the eating.

TERM REVIEW ## 6. Cliché

Definition: A cliché is an expression that, although once considered clever, has been overused.

> Examples: Don't put the cart before the horse.
> To make a long story short …
> Fingers on the pulse of …
> Not worth a plugged nickel.
> Don't rock the boat.

Sometimes an aphorism can also be considered a cliché.

TERM REVIEW ## 7. Idiom

Definition: An idiom is an expression that does not make sense on a literal level, such as "to hang around" or "to fall off the wagon."

TERM REVIEW ## 8. Implication

Definition: **Implication and inference are two easily confused words that have related meanings.** An *implication* is an involvement or indication that is made indirectly by association; an *inference* is a conclusion drawn from facts or premises. The speaker implies (hints at, suggests) some idea from which the hearer or reader infers (receives, draws) a conclusion.

Do you see any implications in these lines from Joseph Conrad's "An Outpost of Progress"?

> He had charge of a small clay storehouse with a dried-grass roof, and pretended to keep a correct account of beads, cotton cloth, red kerchiefs, brass wire, and other trade goods it contained.

What are the implications in the statement that he "pretended to keep a correct account"? The obvious answer is that although he led others to believe the accounts were accurate, they were not; and he knew that they were not. This much can be learned from the implications of "pretended." From these implications, can an inference be made concerning <u>why</u> he did this? Perhaps he did not have the ability to keep accurate books and as a result tried to cover careless and perhaps unintended errors. Maybe he deliberately misled others to cover embezzlement or to harm them financially.

You can discover whether these conclusions are accurate only if the context reveals more information. Although the verbs "authenticate," "confirm," "corroborate," "substantiate," "validate," and "verify," for example, all mean to establish the truth of a situation or some information, each word choice carries with it a distinctive connotation that can imply a greater meaning in a given context.

You might *authenticate* someone's signature, proving it to be real; a traveler can *confirm* a hotel reservation, assuring the manager that he will be there by a certain time and proving his intentions by prepaying the bill; a witness might *corroborate* a defendant's alibi by swearing to have been with her at the time in question; fingerprints at a crime scene can *substantiate* the prosecution's theory that a defendant was there; city parking lot rules require patrons to *validate* their parking tickets, proving they were in the designated office or store; and a researcher might *verify* a project's conclusions by duplicating a key experiment several times and comparing the results.

Example

> "Can you authenticate that this is a genuine Monet?" Andre paused, waiting for Joseph to answer. Finally, he repeated the question, sounding out each syllable of "authenticate" as if Joseph might not understand the meaning of the word.

That Andre expected Joseph to authenticate the painting implies that

(A) Andre is an art expert
(B) Joseph forged the painting
(C) Andre does not believe Joseph owns the painting
(D) Joseph should have documentation to prove Monet painted it
(E) Joseph is an art expert

Explanation: At first glance, you might select E as the correct answer choice. However, that Andre decided "Joseph might not understand the meaning of the word" implies that Joseph is not an art expert, although Andre does expect him to have some type of proof that the painting is genuine.

Correct Answer: **D**

> "Can you corroborate that this is a genuine Monet?" Andre paused, waiting for Joseph to answer. Joseph looked nervously at his partner, Norton, then resettled his gaze on his feet. "Can you corroborate that this is a genuine Monet?" Andre repeated impatiently.

That Andre asked Joseph to corroborate that the painting is genuine implies that

(A) Norton and Joseph are fighting
(B) Norton has already claimed the painting is a Monet
(C) Norton is the sole owner of the painting
(D) Joseph is covering for his partner
(E) the painting is a forgery

Explanation: Indeed, Norton's reluctance to answer may mean that the painting is a forgery; however, within the limits of the context, use of "corroborate," together with Joseph's look toward Norton, strengthens the implication that Norton has already claimed the painting is genuine. One person is being asked to confirm the word of another.

Correct Answer: **B**

What else do I need to know about meaning(s) in context?

1. Denotation

Writers can use multiple denotative meanings of words to construct figures of speech, such as puns.

- Lack of precision in day-to-day conversations has resulted in confusion over words that are similar both in their individual meanings and in their shades of meaning. The words <u>assure</u>, <u>ensure</u>, and <u>insure</u> are examples. These three words tend to be used interchangeably, yet each has its own meaning:

  <u>Assure</u> means to give a promise to a person— "Let me assure you that I'll be there on time."
  <u>Ensure</u> means to make sure— "Your participation will ensure the success of the program."
  <u>Insure</u> means to protect with insurance— "I must insure the house against flood damage."

- Another element of denotation (the literal meanings of words) involves diction (the writer's or speaker's choice of words): the degree to which the words used are **specific** or **general**, and **concrete** or **abstract**.

  1. General words denote a group or class: <u>cat</u>
  2. Specific words denote members of a group or class: <u>Siamese</u>, <u>tabby</u>
  3. Concrete words denote people and things that are perceived by the five senses: <u>a warm coat</u>
  4. Abstract words denote concepts and ideas: <u>pride</u>, <u>responsibility</u>

  Concrete words are easily defined; abstract words, however, often defy universally accepted definitions because they cannot be measured or described by physical senses.

2. Syntax

Four different types of sentences and the effects of each:

- The loose, common, or cumulative sentence

  The loose or common sentence is the most used sentence structure in the English language. It generally is written in one of three basic patterns, each of which can be expanded by coordinating similar structures into the sentence or by modifying parts of or the entire sentence with more information:

TIP

Reminder: You need to know grammar and basic punctuation. The literature test might require you to identify the subject or main verb of a sentence, recognize a pronoun-antecedent relationship, and so forth. Often, you must understand word functions to understand fully the meaning of a selection.

Subject	Transitive Verb	Object
The car	hit	a tree.

Subject	Intransitive Verb
Susan	cried.

Subject	Linking Verb	Complement
Roger	was	a student.
The dog	is	happy.
The book	is	there.

Once the independent clause is written, modifiers are placed after the subject and verb. For example: I will hire him, despite his lack of references.

Effect: As the most common sentence structure used, there is a sense of met expectation (comfortable style caused by familiarity). The writing tends to be "choppy" if most of the sentences contain little coordination or modification. Too much elaboration, however, results in a difficult, wordy style.

- The periodic or climactic sentence

In contrast to the loose sentence in which the subject often appears early in the sentence, in the periodic sentence the subject and its verb come much later and serve as a climactic statement to a series of subordinate clauses or phrases. For example: Despite his lack of references, I will hire him. The rhetorical benefits of building to the main point can clearly be seen:

> Reaching deep within herself for some type of consolation, some small reflection of the pride and dignity that had once been the fighting edge of her courage, some reassurance that all was not lost, the *destitute woman opened the courtroom door.*

The defining element of a periodic sentence is that you must read to the end of the sentence to find the complete subject and verb (the independent clause).

Effect: The rhetorical buildup to the main point is dramatic.

- The parallel sentence

Parallel sentences consist of a series of phrases, main clauses, or subordinate clauses:

> The mother was *always laughing at his jokes, crying over his heartbreaks, and justifying his faults.*

> *The children laughed; the dog yelped; the young girl cried.*

> You should always remember *which key unlocks the chain, which chain binds the heart, and which heart breaks for you.*

Effect: The parallel sentence appeals to the reader's sense of logic in sequencing similar ideas or items and provides a sense of rhythm to the writing.

- The balanced sentence

The balanced sentence is a type of parallel construction in which two major sentence elements that contrast with one another are balanced between a coordinating conjunction:

> The river's ravishes stunned the older onlookers, *but* the water's pull mesmerized the younger ones.

> Working on the project satisfied his sense of justice, *but* destroyed his sense of independence.

Effect: The balanced sentence, as a type of parallel sentence, provides a sense of rhythm to the sentence, but also provides emphasis or contrast—an element of logic.

3. Poetic Syntax

- **Poetic syntax** includes language that speaks to the reader's emotions and a use of syntax that focuses on its effect over its conformity to rules. This freedom in the use of syntax is a major line drawn between prose and poetry. How do poets use syntax?

  Sometimes words that are normally assigned one function are used in an unusual function in a syntactical structure. For example, <u>was</u> normally functions as a verb and <u>lifetime</u> as a noun. The poet might assign <u>was</u> to the role of subject and use <u>lifetime</u> as a verb.

  > <u>Was</u> is a lifetime ago…
  > And she has <u>lifetimed</u> her existence away.

- **Anastrophe** is the inversion of normal syntactical patterns, such as placing the modifier after rather than before the word it modifies:

  > This <u>Hermit good</u> lives in that wood
  > Which slopes down to the sea. [emphasis added]

  Or placing the predicate modifier first in the sentence:

  > <u>Silent</u> is the house: all are laid asleep. [emphasis added]

  What would be the normal syntactical pattern for this structure?

  > With olives ripe the sauces
  >   Were flavored, without exception.

  Poetic syntax also includes the repetition of syntactical patterns:

My Mind to Me a Kingdom Is

Some have too much, yet still do crave;
    I little have, and seek no more.
They are but poor, though much they have,
    And I am rich with little store.
<u>They poor, I rich; they beg, I give;</u>
<u>They lack, I lend; they pine, I live.</u>

[emphasis added]

by Sir Edward Dyer   (fifth stanza)

4. Poetic Diction

Poetic diction refers to language that is normally associated with poetry and that has a poetic effect. See example 12 that follows.

5. Historical References

You do not need to memorize literary or historical periods for the test beyond recognizing allusions that are part of our common knowledge. Some literary works might contain references and allusions that you do not recognize. The test sometimes includes a marginal note for readers that will explain a given reference, allusion, or use of period diction; but even without such help, many times you can use context to determine correct answers.

6. Dialects

Dialect is the speech of a region; *accents* are the ways words are actually pronounced. Using context is very important when dealing with dialects. See Example 14.

7. Period Vocabulary

Words change over time and space. They change in spelling and meaning, and words can even shift functions as they are used syntactically. Test selections can be taken from works written more than four hundred years ago. Much has changed since then.

You will not be expected to be fluent in period vocabulary; however, if you do encounter a word or phrase that may have changed meaning, be sure to use context to determine what the speaker means rather than what you understand the word or phrase to mean in today's culture.

How could questions about meaning(s) in context be worded?

The following selections and their questions illustrate some of the ways meaning(s) in context might be tested.

Example 1

Denotation

"The Author to Her Book" is by Anne Bradstreet (1678).

> Thou ill-form'd offspring of my feeble brain,
> Who after birth did'st by my side remain,
> Till snatcht from thence by friends, less wise then true
> *Line* Who thee abroad, expos'd to publick view,
> *(5)* Made thee in raggs, halting to th' press to trudge,
> Where errors were not lessened (all may judg).
> At thy return my blushing was not small,
> My rambling brat (in print) should mother call,
> I cast thee by as one unfit for light,
> *(10)* Thy Visage was so irksome in my sight;
> Yet being mine own, at length affection would
> Thy blemishes amend, if so I could:
> I wash'd thy face, but more defects I saw,
> And rubbing off a spot, still made a flaw.
> *(15)* I stretcht thy joynts to make thee even feet,
> Yet still thou run'st more hobling then is meet;
> In better dress to trim thee was my mind,
> But nought save home-spun Cloth, i'th' house I find.
> In this array, 'mongst Vulgars mayst thou roam,
> *(20)* In Criticks hands, beware thou dost not come;
> And take thy way where yet thou art not known,
> If for thy Father askt, say, thou hadst none:
> And for thy Mother, she alas is poor,
> Which caus'd her thus to send thee out of door.

The word "blemishes" in line 12 contextually means which of the following?

(A) Deformities
(B) Stains
(C) Pimples
(D) Disfigurements
(E) Errors

Explanation: All five answer choices are denotations (literal definitions) of "blemishes." How is the word used in *this* selection? What is the context? A metaphor in which the author compares her book to a crippled child. Her friends gave her book to the public (lines 4–5), "Where errors were not lessened…" (line 6). Upon return of the book, she "cast" it by for a while (line 9) and then tried to correct its errors.

Correct Answer: **E**

Line 15 probably refers to

(A) physical therapy
(B) rehabilitation
(C) rhythm
(D) illusion
(E) allusion

Explanation: In her structural metaphor, she compares her book to a crippled child. "Feet" can be stretched on a child literally in physical therapy; however, in a book of verse (the real subject of the poem), she is stretching the poetic "feet" of rhythm. Notice that this poem consists of couplets written in iambic pentameter (heroic couplets).

Correct Answer: **C**

Example 2

Denotation and Syntax

This selection comes from Sir Philip Sidney's "An Apology for Poetry," in which he attempts to explain the significance of the abstract world of poetry (1595).

> But truly I imagine it falleth out with these poet-whippers, as with some good women, who often are sick, but in faith they cannot tell where. So the name of poetry is odious to them, but neither his cause nor effects, neither
> *Line* the sum that contains him nor the particularities descending from him, give
> *(5)* any fast handle to their carping dispraise.
>
> Since then poetry is of all human learning the most ancient and of most fatherly antiquity, as from whence other learnings have taken their beginnings, since it is so universal that no learned nation doth despise it, nor no barbarous nation is without it; since both Roman and Greek gave divine
> *(10)* names unto it, the one of *prophesying*, the other of *making*, and that indeed that name of *making* is fit for him, considering that whereas other arts retain themselves within their subject, and receive, as it were, their being from it, the poet only bringeth his own stuff, and doth not learn a conceit out of a matter, but maketh matter for a conceit; since neither his description nor his
> *(15)* end containeth any evil, the thing described cannot be evil; since his effects be so good as to teach goodness and to delight the learners; since therein (namely in moral doctrine, the chief of all knowledges) he doth not only far pass the historian, but, for instructing, is well-nigh comparable to the philosopher, and, for moving, leaves him behind him; since the Holy
> *(20)* Scripture ... hath whole parts in it poetical...; since all his kinds are not only in their united forms but in their severed dissections fully commendable; I think (and think I think rightly) the laurel crown appointed for triumphing captains doth worthily (of all other learnings) honor the poet's triumph.

1. What is the poet "moving" in line 19?

   (A) Philosophers' opinions
   (B) Historians' facts
   (C) Knowledge
   (D) Doctrines
   (E) Emotions

2. As used in line 5, "any fast handle to their carping dispraise" could be para-phrased to mean

   (A) help in understanding poetry
   (B) solid reason for censure
   (C) misunderstandings of the issue
   (D) reasonable clues to faithfulness
   (E) a cause and effect of poetry

3. The phrase "carping dispraise" is somewhat

   (A) paradoxical
   (B) redundant
   (C) anachronistic
   (D) analytical
   (E) flattering

4. As used in lines 13–14, "matter" versus "conceit" can be thought as

   (A) what is important versus imaginations or fancy
   (B) substance versus self-flattery
   (C) a document versus figure of speech
   (D) what occupies space versus fanciful expression
   (E) what is spoken or written versus an idea or understanding

5. Based on syntax, the speaker's conclusion that poets deserve the laurel crown is based upon how many proofs?

   (A) 7
   (B) 8
   (C) 9
   (D) 10
   (E) 11

Answers and Explanations:

1. (**E**) The speaker establishes a contrast as he builds to his main point that poetry surpasses "all other learnings" (line 23). He claims that the poet is "comparable to the philosopher" (lines 18–19) for "instructing," but "leaves him behind" for "moving" (a play on words). Philosophers can instruct in ideas, attitudes, opinions, facts; however, "moving" speaks to our emotions, an abstract concept. Today, we might say, "That story is moving" when the outcome "touches" our hearts or stirs emotions within us.

2. **(B)** "Fast" as an adjective can be meant to be firm or solid, with "dispraise" meaning "censure."

3. **(B)** Both "to carp" and "to dispraise" mean "to censure."

4. **(E)** "Matter" and "conceit" could mean any of the answer choices, but only E is supported by the context. In contrast to "other arts," poetry is the expression (written or spoken) of the poet's ideas or thoughts (expressions of the abstract).

5. **(B)** The speaker uses eight dependent clauses, each beginning with "since," to support his conclusion.

Example 3

Parts of Speech

The following stanza is taken from "Day, in Melting Purple Dying" by Maria Brooks (ca. 1840).

> Tell to thee the high-wrought feeling,
> Ecstasy but in revealing;
> Paint to thee the deep sensation,
> *Line* Rapture in participation;
> *(5)*   Yet but torture, if comprest
>   In a lone, unfriended breast.

In the context of line 2, "but" is

(A) a conjunction meaning *exact*
(B) an adverb meaning *merely*
(C) a conjunction meaning *that*
(D) an adverb meaning *only*
(E) a conjunction meaning *however*

Explanation: Context will help you determine the answer. Lines 2–4 reveal that the speaker's "sensation" is "rapture in participation." In other words, if she tells the auditor of her feelings (line 1), "rapture"; if she does not, the result is "torture" (line 5). Her feelings are "Ecstasy but [or only] in revealing."

Correct Answer: **D**

Example 4

Syntax

The introductory paragraph of *A Tale of Two Cities* by Charles Dickens further illustrates the point:

> It was the best of times, it was the worst of times, it was the age of wisdom, it was the age of foolishness, it was the epoch of belief, it was the epoch of incredulity, it was the season of Light, it was the season of Darkness, it
>
> *Line* was the spring of hope, it was the winter of despair, we had everything before
> (5) us, we had nothing before us, we were all going direct to Heaven, we were all going direct the other way —in short, the period was so far like the present period, that some of its noisiest authorities insisted on its being received, for good or for evil, in the superlative degree of comparison only.

Structurally, lines 1–6 contain elements that are which of the following?

I. Allusive
II. Antithetical
III Paradoxical

(A) I only
(B) II only
(C) III only
(D) II and III only
(E) I, II, and III

In line 6, "in short" is significant because it

(A) marks a change in structure
(B) is a misuse of an absolute
(C) negates the speaker's meaning
(D) contrasts times and periods
(E) balances two opposing elements

What is the effect of the change in the subject pronoun in lines 4–5?

(A) It has no real effect.
(B) It emphasizes superiority of the narrator's times.
(C) It shifts the tone from impersonal to personal.
(D) It affects the characterization of the narrator.
(E) It diminishes the sense of connection to the times.

Explanation: The bulk of the paragraph consists of a series of main clauses that are structured as loose or common sentences using a very simple, plain, easy-to-understand level of diction. This gives the reader a comfortable, nonthreatening beginning. Although so many short sentences would normally be "choppy," they have been joined together **mechanically** with commas (representing "and") and have been joined together **structurally** with parallel sentence construction.

	We had:	It was:	the best of times
	everything before us		the worst of times
	nothing before us		the age of wisdom
Line			the age of foolishness
(5)			the epoch of belief
	We were:		the epoch of incredulity
	all going direct to Heaven		the season of Light
	all going direct the other way		the season of Darkness
			the spring of hope
(10)			the winter of despair

The result is a rhythm that literally pulls the reader along, far outweighing any staccato effect the short, loose sentences might have otherwise produced.

Next, examine the contents of the syntactical structure used in the excerpt. "It was" is the subject-verb for the first ten independent clauses. The subject-verb changes to "We had" and "We were" respectively in the final four independent clauses. What is the effect of this change? One possible effect is that the momentum builds with a series of paradoxical statements with "it"—a neutral, *third-person* pronoun—as the subject. The change to "we"—a *first-person* pronoun—is startling; it jars the reader from any "lull" the otherwise comfortable rhythm might have given. Notice also how the paradoxes change from "time," "ages," "epochs," "seasons," "spring…winter," to "everything … nothing <u>before us</u>" and to the promise, "We were all going direct to Heaven" countered by the threat, "We were all going direct the other way." The syntactical structure makes the reader comfortable, appeals to our sense of logic through parallel sentence structure, then gains the reader's attention first with a change in pronoun usage, followed by the abrupt break in syntax with the use of an absolute: "in short." What is the significance of the use of this absolute to the meaning of the paragraph? It divides the paragraph structurally into two parts: The first part is a series of paradoxical relationships of a period that at first seems impersonal, but eventually comes to be on a more personal level as it relates to the "we" of the story. The second part summarizes that these paradoxes of that period are "like the present period"—a meaning that personally involves the reader.

Correct Answers: **D, A, C**

Example 5

Syntax

What sentence structures does Shakespeare use in his "Sonnet 64" and how do they affect meaning?

> When I have seen by Time's fell hand defaced
> The rich proud cost of outworn buried age;
> When sometime lofty towers I see down razed,
> *Line*   And brass eternal slave to mortal rage;
> *(5)*   When I have seen the hungry ocean gain
> Advantage on the kingdom of the shore,
> And the firm soil win of the watery main,
> Increasing store with loss, and loss with store;
> When I have seen such interchange of state,
> *(10)*   Or state itself confounded to decay,
> Ruin hath taught me thus to ruminate,
> That Time will come and take my love away.
> This thought is as a death, which cannot choose
> But weep to have that which it fears to lose.

by William Shakespeare

Lines 1–11 consist mostly of

(A) simple sentences
(B) subordinate clauses
(C) balanced sentences
(D) absolutes
(E) subject-verb constructions

Explanation: The first sentence is lines 1 through 12. Notice the parallel constructions:

Line 1 "When I have seen…"
Line 3 "When sometime lofty towers I see…"
Line 5 "When I have seen…"
Line 9 "When I have seen…"

These are subordinate clauses—so where are the subject and the verb of the sentence? They do not appear until line 11: "Ruin hath taught." Lines 1 through 12 consist of a periodic sentence in which the speaker "builds" to his point. This heightens the impact, then, of the meaning of the concluding couplet that is a loose sentence, in structural contrast to the preceding periodic sentence.

Correct Answer: **B**

Example 6

Transitional Markers

As these few illustrations show, the transitional marker can affect meaning. To demonstrate, read this first stanza of "Oft, in the Stilly Night" by Thomas Moore (ca. 1840). How would the meaning of the last four lines change if the speaker had used "Thence" rather than "Thus" in line 11?

> Oft, in the stilly night,
>   Ere Slumber's chain has bound me,
> Fond Memory brings the light
> *Line*   Of other days around me;
> *(5)*   The smiles, the tears,
>   Of boyhood's years,
>   The words of love then spoken;
>   The eyes that shone,
>   Now dimmed and gone,
> *(10)*   The cheerful hearts now broken!
>   Thus, in the stilly night,
>   Ere Slumber's chain hath bound me,
>   Sad Memory brings the light
>   Of other days around me.

In line 11, "Thus" points the reader to

(A) the element of time at work
(B) a degree of intensity of the speaker's emotion
(C) in what manner the speaker's night is spent
(D) new information concerning the speaker
(E) emotion beyond that previously expressed

Explanation: "Thus" generally marks a reason, a method, or what has happened.

NOTE: Transitional markers are relationship words that somehow establish some type of meaning between the words that appear before the marker to those that follow. Naturally, these include that large group called the **conjunction**. Most readers are aware that <u>and</u> signals combining relationships or addition, whereas <u>but</u> signals an exception. Some transitional markers carry obvious meaning, others have more subtle shades of meaning that although they may be similar, are not exactly the same:

Some Common Transitional Markers

<u>Thus</u> involves how, why, or to what extent something is done and suggests results.

<u>Thence</u> implies a forward progression from a specified point in space or time.

<u>Also</u> is a marker for additional information.

<u>Moreover</u> indicates an excess beyond that designated previously.

<u>Nevertheless</u> means despite the circumstances.

<u>However</u> marks relationships of manner, degree, or exception.

Correct Answer: **C**

Example 7

Syntax

This selection is from Samuel Johnson's "The Rambler, No. 4."

> These books are written chiefly to the young, the ignorant, and the idle, to whom they serve as lectures of conduct, and introduction into life. They are the entertainment of minds unfurnished with ideas, and therefore easily susceptible of impressions; not fixed by principles, and therefore easily following the current of fancy; not informed by experience, and consequently open to every false suggestion and partial account.

*Line
(5)*

These lines exhibit a sense that is

(A) apologetic
(B) apathetic
(C) apocalyptic
(D) aphoristic
(E) apostrophic

Explanation: Look at the sentence structure. They ("These books") are the entertainment of minds unfurnished with ideas, and therefore easily susceptible of impressions. They ("These books") are the entertainment of minds not fixed by principles, and therefore easily following the current of fancy. They ("These books") are the entertainment of minds not informed by experience, and consequently open to every false suggestion and partial account. Each of these constructions could stand as a one-sentence statement of principle.

Correct Answer: **D**

Example 8

Syntax

As far as the eye could reach, a line of white buildings extended along the bank, their background formed by the purple hue of the dense, interminable forest.

(from Susanna Moodie's "A Visit to Grosse Isle")

"As far as the eye could reach" is best described as which of the following?

I. A maxim
II. An aphorism
III. An idiom
IV. A cliché

(A) I only
(B) II only
(C) III only
(D) III and IV only
(E) I, II, III, and IV

Explanation: How far can an eye reach? This idiom has been well used over generations.

Correct Answer: **D**

Example 9

Connotation

These words are taken from George Eliot's *Silas Marner*.

> 'Well, my meaning is this, Marner,' said Godfrey, determined to come to the point. 'Mrs Cass and I, you know, have no children—nobody to be the better for our good home and everything else we have—more than enough
> *Line* for ourselves. And we should like to have somebody in the place of a daugh-
> *(5)* ter to us—we should like to have Eppie, and treat her in every way as our own child. It'ud be a great comfort to you in your old age, I hope, to see her fortune made in that way, after you've been at the trouble of bringing her up so well. And it's right you should have every reward for that. And Eppie, I'm sure, will always love you and be grateful to you: she'd come and see you very
> *(10)* often, and we should all be on the look-out to do everything we could towards making you comfortable.'
>
> A plain man like Godfrey Cass, speaking under some embarrassment, necessarily blunders on words that are coarser than his intentions, and that are likely to fall gratingly on susceptible feelings. While he had been speak-
> *(15)* ing, Eppie had quietly passed her arm behind Silas's head, and let her hand rest against it caressingly: she felt him trembling violently. . . .

"Susceptible feelings," as used in the second paragraph, connotes

(A) that Cass is feeling very emotional
(B) that Marner would agree to anything
(C) Eppie's insignificant role in Marner's life
(D) a vulnerability in Marner
(E) that Marner felt anger at Cass's manner

Explanation: To be susceptible denotes feelings that are easily affected and sensitive. Susceptible feelings, as a result, connote a sense that Marner is vulnerable at this point.

Correct Answer: **D**

Example 10

Connotation

Nonnarrative prose writers also use connotative word choices to project or intensify meaning. Here is a sentence from a letter written by Lord Chesterfield to his son.

> But there is no living in the world without a complaisant indulgence for people's weaknesses, and innocent, though ridiculous vanities.

The speaker's use of "complaisant" in this context connotes a sense of

(A) annoyance and resentment
(B) smugness and condescension
(C) rivalry and contention
(D) obedience and yielding
(E) compunction and regret

Explanation: "Complaisant" denotes having pleasing manners. Its connotative meaning is associated with a patronizing, condescending attitude *in this context*. The speaker indulges the "ridiculous vanities" and weaknesses of others, making him seem smug.

Correct Answer: **B**

Poets, too, use connotative language. Return to "The Author to Her Book" by Anne Bradstreet on page 210 to answer this question.

> Using the more specific word "Vulgars" (line 19) rather than the more general "common people" has which of these effects?

(A) Connotatively emphasizes that the work lacks refinement
(B) Illustrates the speaker's sense of drama
(C) Varies the tone of the poem
(D) Insults the readers of her work
(E) Reinforces the reader's sense of sympathy for the child

Explanation: Although synonyms by definition, "Vulgars" carries with it a connotation emphasizing that only those without culture or refinement would appreciate her work.

Correct Answer: **A**

Example 11

Poetic Syntax

You probably can easily spot poetic syntax in a selection. The real challenge in dealing with poetic syntax (particularly anastrophe) is deciding what the speaker is saying. Look at these lines taken from Alexander Pope's "An Essay on Criticism."

> A perfect judge will read each work of wit
> With the same spirit that its author writ:
> Survey the whole, nor seek slight faults to find
> *Line* Where Nature moves, and rapture warms the mind;
> *(5)* Nor lose, for that malignant dull delight,
> The generous pleasure to be charmed with wit.
> But in such lays as neither ebb nor flow,
> Correctly cold, and regularly low,
> That, shunning faults, one quiet tenor keep,
> *(10)* We cannot blame indeed—but we may sleep.
> In wit, as nature, what affects our hearts
> Is not the exactness of peculiar parts;
> 'Tis not a lip, or eye, we beauty call,
> But the joint force and full result of all.
> *(15)* Thus when we view some well-proportioned dome
> (The world's just wonder, and even thine, O Rome!),
> No single parts unequally surprise,
> All comes united to the admiring eyes:
> No monstrous height, or breadth, or length appear;
> *(20)* The whole at once is bold and regular.

(1711)

1. The speaker sees the pleasures of being "charmed with wit" (line 6)

   (A) as a result of "shunning faults"
   (B) as a reason to keep "quiet tenor"
   (C) as greater than enjoying finding "slight faults" (line 3)
   (D) as an unworthy goal compared to seeking faults
   (E) as a shallow endeavor, putting him to "sleep"

2. "We cannot blame" whom in line 10?

   (A) Judges
   (B) Nature
   (C) Wit
   (D) Authors
   (E) Rome

3. Lines 7–9 describe

   (A) an author sacrificing technical precision for wit
   (B) judges justly demanding precise writing
   (C) the role of nature's "ebb" and "flow"
   (D) an author sacrificing wit for technical precision
   (E) the character of the perfect judge

4. A "perfect judge" (line 1) would NOT

   (A) label "the joint force" (line 14) as beautiful
   (B) be "charmed with wit" (line 6)
   (C) share the author's "spirit" (line 2)
   (D) seek "exactness of peculiar parts" (line 12)
   (E) admire the structural unity of "some well-proportioned dome" (line 15)

5. The "sleep" in line 10 probably represents

   (A) satisfaction with works that warm the mind
   (B) escape from perfect judges
   (C) boredom with witless, cold works
   (D) illness of judges with malignant intents
   (E) fatigue of the author after seeking wit

Answers and Explanations

The poetic syntax of lines 3, 13, and especially lines 9–10 is obvious. Now, examine what the syntax means.

1. **(C)** To answer this question, you need to work through the poetic syntax of lines 1–10, picking up on key words. The perfect judge (line 1) will survey the whole, not seeking slight faults (line 3) and not losing "for that malignant dull delight," referring to the pleasure of finding slight faults (line 5), the pleasure of being charmed with wit (line 6). Also, note the connotative effects of "malignant."

2. **(D)** Again, delve into the structure of the poetic syntax. First, you can surmise from context that "lays" that do not "ebb nor flow" and are correct and regular (lines 7–8) are in contrast to a work "Where Nature moves, and rapture warms the mind" (line 4). A lay, by definition, is a type of poem. Who, then, would shun faults and keep a "quiet" tenor or direction (line 9)? Can we blame an author (line 2) for avoiding fault seekers (line 3)?

3. **(D)** This question requires drawing a conclusion based on restructuring the poetic syntax. If we cannot blame the author for keeping a quiet tenor, then we can conclude that he or she did sacrifice wit for technical precision.

4. (**D**) NOT questions can be especially tricky. One technique is to turn each answer choice into a true-false: The only true answer choice in this question is (D). A "perfect judge" would NOT seek "exactness of peculiar parts" (line 12).

5. (**C**) Context links sleep with a response to cold, low poems that "neither ebb nor flow" (lines 7–8), in other words, poems that are boring.

Example 12

Poetic Diction and Archaic Words

These lines are taken from Christina Rossetti's "A Bed of Forget-Me-Nots":

> Is LOVE so prone to change and rot
> We are fain to rear Forget-me-not
> By measure in a garden-plot?—

The central contrast in these lines makes boundaries seem

(A) unnecessary
(B) superior
(C) a necessary evil
(D) predictable
(E) desirable

Explanation: About now you may be asking whether this question belongs with this quote. Yes, it does. This question demonstrates how you can use what you have learned so far about the literary elements and context clues to overcome even poetic diction used more than 150 years ago.

First, look at the sentence structure: a rhetorical question. The speaker does not expect an answer, but is using the question to make her point. Now, search for the central contrast. Obviously, she is comparing LOVE with Forget-me-nots (flowers), a metaphor. She is using growing flowers as a vehicle to describe growing LOVE. What does "By measure in a garden-plot" mean? Look at the context of the sentence: raising flowers (Forget-me-nots) in a garden-plot. What would "By measure" mean in relation to a flower garden? Gardeners often measure the area for a garden and place boundaries (stones or some type of edging) to keep the flowers from spreading onto the walkways or into other garden-plots. According to the speaker, then, flowers are grown within boundaries ("by measure") in "garden-plots."

Look again at the diction used. Do you know what "fain" means? "Fain" is an archaic word labeled by some unabridged dictionaries as "poetic." How can you discover the contrast without knowing what "fain" means? You have a context clue to help you. Look at the first line: "Is LOVE so *prone* to change and rot…." In this context, "so" is an adverb showing degree. It directly points to the contrast: Is LOVE so prone (in such a condition) that we are "fain" to rear it (LOVE like flowers) within boundaries? LOVE without boundaries is contrasted to LOVE (like flowers) in boundaries. Using a rhetorical question implies that the speaker believes boundaries are unnecessary because (again, by implication) LOVE is not "so prone to change and rot" that it must be confined within boundaries like Forget-me-nots are confined in garden-plots. A modern illustration of this sentence construction would be "Is Jerry *so afraid* of a plane crash that he is fain to drive two thousand miles to reach home?" When you use context in this case, you do not need to know what "fain" means to understand the question.

FYI: "Fain" is used often in period poetry. As a verb, it is now obsolete; as an adverb it is used with *would* (She *would fain* have come with him tonight). "Fain" as an adjective can mean "pleased" or "making do." When it means accepting less-than-desired circumstances, it is usually accompanied by the infinitive form of the verb: Is LOVE so prone to change and rot / We are fain to rear [willing to settle for rearing] Forget-me not [LOVE] / By measure in a garden-plot?—

Correct Answer: **A**

Example 13

Historical References

The following poem was written by Phillis Wheatley (1773). Use context clues to answer the questions that follow.

To the Right Honourable William, Earl of Dartmouth, His Majesty's Principal Secretary of State for North America, Etc.[1]

> Hail, happy day, when, smiling like the morn,
> Fair Freedom rose New England to adorn:
> The northern clime Beneath her genial ray,
> *Line* Dartmouth, congratulates thy blissful sway:
> *(5)* Elate with hope her race no longer mourns,
> Each soul expands, each grateful bosom burns,
>
> While in thine hand with pleasure we behold
> The silken reins, and Freedom's charms unfold.
> Long lost to realms beneath the northern skies
> *(10)* She shines supreme, while hated Faction dies;
> Soon as appeared the goddess long desired,
> Sick at the view, she languished and expired;
> Thus from the splendors of the morning light
> The owl in sadness seeks the caves of night.
>
> *(15)* No more, America, in mournful strain
> Of wrongs, and grievance unredressed complain,
> No longer shalt thou dread the iron chain
> Which wanton Tyranny with lawless hand
> Had made, and with it meant to enslave the land.

---

[1] *This poem was written for William, Earl of Dartmouth, who was appointed the "Principal Secretary of State" over the American colonies in 1773. He replaced Lord Hillsborough.*

(20)   Should you, my lord, while you peruse my song,
Wonder from whence my love of Freedom sprung,
Whence flow these wishes for the common good,
By feeling hearts alone best understood,
I, young in life, by seeming cruel fate,
(25) Was snatched from Afric's fancied happy seat:
What pangs excruciating must molest,
What sorrows labour in my parents' breast?
Steeled was that soul and by no misery moved
That from a father seized his babe beloved:
(30) Such, such my case, And can I then but pray
Others may never feel tyrannic sway?

     For favours past, great Sir, our thanks are due,
And thee we ask thy favours to renew,
Since in thy power, as in thy will before.
(35) To soothe the griefs which thou didst once deplore.
May heavenly grace the sacred sanction give
To all thy works, and thou forever live
Not only on the wings of fleeting Fame,
Though praise immortal crowns the patriot's name,
(40) But to conduct to heaven's refulgent fane,
May fiery coursers sweep the ethereal plain,
And bear thee upwards to that blessed abode;
Where, like the prophet, thou shalt find thy God.

1. The second stanza is marked by a major change in

    (A) subject
    (B) rhyme scheme
    (C) rhythm
    (D) speaker
    (E) expressed auditor

2. Based on context, "The owl" in line 14 probably represents

    (A) slavery
    (B) the speaker
    (C) the new secretary (Dartmouth) and increasing freedom
    (D) the former secretary (Hillsborough) and partisan conflict
    (E) freedom

3. The purpose of the third stanza is to

    (A) elicit the auditor's sympathy
    (B) redirect the subject to slavery issues
    (C) explain the speaker's depths of emotion concerning the subject
    (D) persuade the auditor to abolish slavery in the colonies
    (E) change the tone of the work as a whole

4. Why does the speaker repeat "Such," in line 30 rather than complete the sentence with "Such was my case?"

   (A) The repetition serves to avoid an anachronism.
   (B) The amplification that follows depends upon an emphasis on "Such."
   (C) The repetition better suits the rhyme scheme.
   (D) The repetition makes "Such" become symbolic of Freedom.
   (E) The repetition rhetorically emphasizes the personal nature of lines 24–29.

5. For Fame to be "fleeting," yet praised to be "immortal" (lines 38–39) is a(n)

   (A) implicit metaphor
   (B) allegory
   (C) forensic rhetoric
   (D) oxymoron
   (E) paradox

6. The use of Freedom, Faction, Tyranny, and Fame results in which of the following effects?

   (A) It makes these ideas seem more fleeting.
   (B) It emphasizes the contrast of America's "mournful strain" line (15).
   (C) It enlarges the speaker's sense of loss.
   (D) It makes these abstract ideas seem more tangible.
   (E) It symbolizes mourning.

7. The speaker's attitude toward the poem's main auditor is best described as one of

   (A) assertive disapproval
   (B) defensive sympathy
   (C) hopeful anticipation
   (D) petulant disrespect
   (E) censorious foreboding

8. The central subject of this poem is

   (A) freedom
   (B) tyranny
   (C) slavery
   (D) Africa
   (E) faction

9. Lines 14–29 say that

   (A) the speaker's parents suffered coronary problems
   (B) the speaker was stolen from her parents
   (C) her father labored for her passage to America
   (D) the speaker's child was stolen
   (E) her entire family was seized

Answers and Explanations

1. **(E)** Although there is a change in rhyme scheme in line 17, the major change is from addressing the new secretary to addressing America. She returns to addressing Dartmouth in line 20.

2. **(D)** Identify the pronouns and symbols: In line 10 "she" is Freedom (line 8). The goddess (Freedom) appears (line 11). In line 12 she is Faction (line 10), who is sick and dying. "Thus" (line 13), or as a result, the owl is in sadness. The owl represents Faction or the old ways of the former secretary.

3. **(C)** The speaker reveals firsthand knowledge of Tyranny, giving reason for her love of Freedom (lines 21, 30–31).

4. **(E)** There is no anachronism, and a rhetorical question follows. The couplets are not affected. To decide between D and E, determine what "such" refers to: the speaker's personal account.

5. **(E)** In its positive sense, praise is an element of fame, making the ideas seem somewhat contradictory.

6. **(D)** Describing abstract ideas as if they are concrete things (reification) makes them seem more tangible.

7. **(C)** The speaker is hopeful (line 5) and has a sense of anticipation (lines 32–33).

8. **(A)** All five answer choices are mentioned in the work. Look for relationship to determine which subject is central. Tyranny and slavery are the absence of freedom. Africa is where the speaker lost her freedom. Faction is the enemy of Freedom (first stanza).

9. **(B)** "I…Was snatched" (lines 24–25) "…from a father seized his babe beloved" (line 29).

Example 14

Dialects

This paragraph comes from Susanna Moodie's description of Grosse Isle (ca. 1853):

> Turning to the south side of the St. Lawrence, I was not less struck with its low fertile shores, white houses, and neat churches, whose slender spires and bright tin roofs shone like silver as they caught the first rays of the sun.
> *Line* As far as the eye could reach, a line of white buildings extended along the
> (5) bank, their background formed by the purple hue of the dense, interminable forest. It was a scene unlike any I had ever beheld, and to which Britain contains no parallel. Mackenzie, an old Scotch dragoon, who was one of our passengers, when he rose in the morning and saw the parish of St. Thomas for the first time, exclaimed: "Weel, it beats a'! Can thae white clouts be a'
> (10) houses? They look like claes hung out to drie!" There was some truth in this odd comparison, and for some minutes I could scarcely convince myself that the white patches scattered so thickly over the opposite shore could be the dwellings of a busy, lively population.

A "dragoon" is a(n)

(A) sailor
(B) musket
(C) infantryman
(D) marine
(E) colonial

Mackenzie makes a comparison between

(A) houses and clouds
(B) clouds and wet clothes
(C) clouds and white patches
(D) white patches and people
(E) houses and wet clothes

Explanation: By definition, a dragoon is an infantryman. The speaker identifies him as Scotch. What is his "odd comparison?" "They look like claes hung out to drie." First, what are "They?" "Can these white clouts be a' houses?" "They" refers to houses. Now, what would "claes hung out to drie" be? Look for clues in the speaker's description. She describes the houses as "a line of white buildings" and "white patches scattered so thickly...." What would be hung out to dry? When not using electric clothes dryers, people sometimes hang their wet clothing (white sheets and white shirts) on clotheslines to dry in the wind and sun.

Correct Answers: **C, E**

Example 15

Period Vocabulary

Here is a paragraph taken from Thackeray's *Vanity Fair* (1848).

Has the beloved reader, in his experience of society, never heard similar remarks by good-natured female friends; who always wonder what you can see in Miss Smith that is so fascinating; or what *could* induce Major Jones to
Line propose for that silly insignificant simpering Miss Thompson, who has
(5) nothing but her wax-doll face to recommend her? What is there in a pair of pink cheeks and blue eyes forsooth? These dear Moralists ask....

As used in context, "forsooth" means

(A) in fact, in a persuasive tone
(B) in truth, in a sarcastic tone
(C) today, in an argumentative tone
(D) today, in an angry tone
(E) in truth, in a complimentary tone

Explanation: "Forsooth" is an archaic term meaning "in fact" or "in truth" and can be used as a grammatical absolute. Without knowing this definition, however, you can tell from the context that "today" has nothing to do with the discussion, eliminating C and D. Look at the speaker's tone. His sarcasm toward "dear Moralists" should catch your attention.

Correct Answer: **B**

Test Taker → Test Maker

If you were writing SAT Literature tests, what questions about meaning(s) in context would you ask? Here is an opportunity for you to approach meaning(s) in context from a test writer's point of view.

We'll begin with a selection from Mrs. Henry J. Thomas's *The Prairie Bride* or *The Squatter's Triumph*. Published in 1869 by Beadle and Company, this little book is part of series of books called "dime novels." They were written by women and featured heroines who fearlessly moved to the Wild West.

> "After we arrived at the diggings and began work, I seemed to be specially favored with good 'luck'. Scarcely a day but something unusual came in my way, so that when we came together to count out gains and divide them, I
>
> *Line* was almost certain to have something about the average to show. For a time
> *(5)* the men seemed pleased, and called me their 'lucky partner', and appeared to think themselves fortunate in having such a clever fellow among their number, but after a while they began to display feelings of jealousy and dislike toward me, and seemed to suspect that I was secreting a part of my gains, and did not throw into the common stock all that I found. This made me indig-
> *(10)* nant, and I determined to leave them and strike out for myself.
>
> "I had noticed, not more than half a mile from our camp, a little rocky ravine, through which a tiny brook trickled, which I knew must, at some season of the year, swell into a considerable torrent. It struck me that, amid the crevices of the rocks over which the stream dashed when swollen, there might
> *(15)* be deposits worth looking for. So after a formal 'dissolving of partnership', I started off with my "pick" upon my shoulder, and my knapsack of provisions on my back, and taking a course calculated to mislead my whilom partners if they should be disposed to watch me, I eventually made my way to the place.

As a test writer, circle any words or phrases that you think are dependent on the context for full meaning.

Discussion

(Here is a possible list of words and phrases.)

    diggings (line 1)
    secreting (line 8)
    common stock (line 9)
    dissolving of partnership (line 15)
    whilom (line 17)

Each of these words and phrases has potential. "Whilom" is perhaps most interesting, however, because you can write a question that requires the test takers to use both context clues and test-taking strategies (assuming they may not know what "whilom" means as a vocabulary word).

"Whilom" as an adjective means "former," so the speaker is saying "to mislead my whilom [or former] partners." The question can be stated directly:

In the context of line 17, "whilom" means

(A) _____

(B) * _____

(C) _____

(D) _____

(E) _____

Obviously, you would assign one answer as correct: "former."

The challenge is to make the incorrect answers really test the readers' abilities. For example, "secret" works as an incorrect answer because even though the speaker was suspected of "secreting a part of my gains," the selection does not describe the partnership as "secret." Be sure to include at least one very obviously incorrect answer choice to give the test takers a chance to strike it out immediately (a test-taking strategy) and to gain momentum into answering the question.

Flip Vocabulary Questions

What does a word or phrase mean in a specific context? This is an obvious test question. You may encounter, however, a case in which something is described and you must label it with the correct vocabulary choice—a flip vocabulary question. An example follows.

Physicist Michael Faraday is best known for his work in electricity and magnetism. The following selection comes from Paragraph 399 of his *Experimental Researches in Electricity*, first published in 1914.

> 399. ...Wishing for a natural standard of electric direction to which I might refer these, expressive of their difference and at the same time free from all theory, I have thought it might be found in the earth. If the magnetism of
> *Line* the earth be due to electric currents passing round it, the latter must be in a
> *(5)* constant direction, which, according to present usage of speech, would be from east to west, or, which will strengthen this help to the memory, that in which the sun appears to move. If in any case of electro-decomposition we consider the decomposing body as placed so that the current passing through it shall be in the same direction, and parallel to that supposed to exist in the
> *(10)* earth, then the surfaces at which the electricity is passing into and out of the substance would have an invariable reference, and exhibit constantly the same relations of powers. Upon this notion we purpose calling that towards the east the *anode*,[1] and that towards the west the *cathode*;[2] . . .
>
> 1...; the way which the sun rises.
> 2...; the way which the sun sets.

Do you recognize what Faraday is doing when he compares the direction of electric currents around the earth to "that in which the sun appears to move"? He directly tells us his intent: to "strengthen this help to the memory."

What is something that assists memory called? _____

Discussion

Faraday is giving his readers a **mnemonic**—a way to help them remember the direction electric currents move (from east to west). He even reinforces this mnemonic with his footnotes. Now, let's write a possible flip vocabulary question.

Lines 5–7 contain which of the following?

(A) _____

(B) _____

(C) _____

(D) _____

(E) * _____

Don't be afraid to think beyond the obvious. In this selection, for example, on what is Faraday's mnemonic based? He is <u>comparing</u> one thing to another—a metaphor.

Consequently, a test writer could combine these elements for the correct answer:

A mnemonic based on a metaphor

Of course, the incorrect answer choices could be written with other combinations of elements.

MEANING (IN CONTEXT) IN CONCLUSION

This chapter marks the end of our examination of the seven literary elements. Each has distinctive traits, yet you can see how the elements ultimately depend on one another. Check your progress at this point by taking Diagnostic Test II.

*Correct Answer

How Are These Elements Tested?

CHAPTER 7

As an overview, the following practice set contains five selections (two prose, two poetry, and one drama). Following each selection, you will find seven questions (one question for each of the seven literary elements), the correct answers, and explanations.

The seven literary elements, however, are very <u>interdependent</u>. As a result, labeling a particular test question as testing any single literary element should not be construed to mean that the test question is testing only one literary element.

Selection One

A stern smile curled the Prince's lip as he spoke. Waldemar Fitzurse hastened to reply that Ivanhoe was already removed from the lists, and in the custody of his friends.

Line
(5) 'I was somewhat afflicted,' he said, 'to see the grief of the Queen of Love and Beauty, whose sovereignty of a day this event has changed into mourning. I am not a man to be moved by a woman's lament for her lover, but this same Lady Rowena suppressed her sorrow with such dignity of manner that it could only be discovered by her folded hands and her tearless eye, which trembled as it remained fixed on the lifeless form before her.'

(10) 'Who is this Lady Rowena,' said Prince John, 'of whom we have heard so much?'

'A Saxon heiress of large possessions,' replied the Prior Aymer; 'a rose of loveliness, and a jewel of wealth; the fairest among a thousand, a bundle of myrrh, and a cluster of camphire.'

(15) 'We shall cheer her sorrows,' said Prince John, 'and amend her blood, by wedding her to a Norman. She seems a minor, and must therefore be at our royal disposal in marriage. How sayst thou, De Bracy? What thinkst thou of gaining fair lands and livings, by wedding a Saxon, after the fashion of the followers of the Conqueror?'

(20) 'If the lands are to my liking, my lord,' answered De Bracy, 'it will be hard to displease me with a bride; and deeply will I hold myself bound to your Highness for a good deed, which will fulfil all promises made in favour of your servant and vassal.'

(1819) *Ivanhoe*
by Sir Walter Scott

Questions based on literary elements as indicated.

1. (Meaning) The purpose of the passage is to describe a situation in which

    (A) Lady Rowena is a beautiful Norman woman
    (B) Prince John has no control over the Saxons
    (C) Lady Rowena refuses to see Prince John
    (D) a Saxon heiress is given to a Norman for marriage as a favor from Prince John
    (E) the Saxons and Normans are at war

2. (Form) How does Fitzurse know that Lady Rowena was upset?

    (A) Inductive reasoning
    (B) Deductive reasoning
    (C) Process analysis
    (D) Analogy
    (E) Cause-and-effect

3. (Voice) Prince John's view of Lady Rowena and the Saxons can be described as the attitude of one who is

    (A) easily offended
    (B) deeply sentimental
    (C) used to a position of authority
    (D) on the defensive
    (E) willing to accommodate for the needs of others

4. (Tone) De Bracy perceives Prince John's tone when offering him a Saxon bride as

    (A) congenial
    (B) condescending
    (C) facetious
    (D) amusing
    (E) defensive

5. (Character) In the second paragraph, Lady Rowena's character is revealed as

    (A) scared and cowering in her grief
    (B) indecisive in her grief
    (C) having decorum in her grief
    (D) being complacent in her grief
    (E) being immature in her grief

6. (Use of Language) The literary device used to refer to lady Rowena ("the Queen of Love and Beauty," lines 4–5) is called a(n)

    (A) epitaph
    (B) euphemism
    (C) synecdoche
    (D) epithet
    (E) metonymy

7. (Meaning in Context) Based on context, "lists" (line 2) probably refers to

   (A) groups of names
   (B) duty stations
   (C) a registry
   (D) a place of combat
   (E) roll call

Correct Answers and Explanations

1. **(D)** Lines 15–19 summarize the situation.

2. **(A)** He draws the conclusion that Lady Rowena was upset from her suppression of sorrow, "discovered" or revealed by "folded hands and her tearless eyes."

3. **(C)** Both his station in life and that he commands a wedding based on conquest, bloodlines, and wealth attest to his being accustomed to being in a position of authority.

4. **(A)** He considers himself "bound to your Highness for a good deed," a congenial attitude.

5. **(C)** Even Fitzurse labels her reaction as "with such dignity of manner," a very decorous description.

6. **(D)** By definition, an epithet is an adjective, noun, or noun phrase describing (whether in a positive or negative manner) a particular person or thing.

7. **(D)** In the Middle Ages, "lists" referred to the place where often deadly tournaments were held. Today's meaning, not surprisingly, includes actual combat locations.

Selection Two

That the machine has dealt art in the grand old sense a death-blow, none will deny—the evidence is too substantial: art in the grand old sense, meaning art in the sense of structural tradition, whose craft is fashioned upon the handicraft ideal, . . .

Line
(5)   And, invincible, triumphant, the machine goes on, gathering force and knitting the material necessities of mankind ever closer into a universal automatic fabric; the engine, the motor, and the battleship, the works of art of the century!

The machine is intellect mastering the drudgery of earth that the plastic
(10) art may live; that the margin of leisure and strength by which man's life upon
the earth can be made beautiful, may immeasurably widen, its function ultimately to emancipate human expression!

It is a universal educator, surely raising the level of human intelligence, so
carrying within itself the power to destroy, by its own momentum, the greed
(15) which in Morris's time and still in our own time turns it to a deadly engine
of enslavement. The only comfort left the poor artist, sidetracked as he is,
seemingly is a mean one: the thought that the very selfishness which man's
early art idealized, now reduced to its lowest terms, is swiftly and surely
destroying itself through the medium of the machine.

(20) The artist's present plight is a sad one, but may he truthfully say that society is less well off because architecture, or even art, as it was, is dead, and
printing, or the machine, lives? Every age has done its work, produced its art
with the best tools or contrivances it knew, the tools most successful in saving the most precious thing in the world—human effort...

> "The Art and Craft of the Machine:
> Democracy and
> New Forms in Architecture"
> Speech (1901)
> by Frank Lloyd Wright

1. (Meaning) The main idea of the third paragraph implies

   (A) most art is plastic
   (B) computers could master the earth
   (C) life is beautiful
   (D) a prediction that "leisure and strength" will increase
   (E) a relationship between free time and artistic expression

2. (Form) The speech includes elements of

   (A) chronology
   (B) spatial sequence
   (C) definition
   (D) climax
   (E) narration

3. (Voice) The speaker views "the poor artist" (line 16) with an attitude that is

   (A) directly disapproving
   (B) gently satirical
   (C) exaggerated in its criticism
   (D) unconventional in its intensity
   (E) sentimental

4. (Tone) The speaker's use of personification gives the selection a tone that is all of the following EXCEPT

(A) antagonistic
(B) warlike
(C) unrealistic
(D) reasonable
(E) morally just

5. (Character) "Every age" (line 22) is characterized as

(A) complacent
(B) pragmatic
(C) self-indulgent
(D) unwilling to change
(E) nonchalant

6. (Use of Language) Lines 1–4 produce an effect that serves to

(A) exaggerate the speaker's position
(B) amplify "art in the grand old sense" (line 1)
(C) understate the speaker's position
(D) point out paradoxes in art
(E) rhetorically question the "handicraft ideal" (line 4)

7. (Meaning in Context) The "universal educator" in line 13 is

(A) art
(B) human expression
(C) idealized art
(D) greed
(E) the machine

Correct Answers and Explanations

1. **(E)** Answer choice B is tempting; after all, he does state that "the machine is intellect." Sounds like a computer, doesn't it? But look at the date (1901). His main idea is that the machine reduces "drudgery," increasing "leisure and strength" that makes life beautiful. For what purpose (function)? "to emancipate human expression." This idea *implies* that with more free time, mankind can have more freedom in expression (art, music, literature, and so forth).

2. **(C)** Structurally, the speaker defines "art" in the first lines and defines the machine as "intellect" (line 9) and a "universal educator" (line 13) that raises "the level of human intelligence." The speaker does not use elements of plot (climax), spatial sequence, or narration.

3. **(B)** His attitude is projected in his tone toward the artist, describing him as "sidetracked" (line 16) and calling his plight "sad" (line 20).

4. **(B)** The machine killed "art in the grand old sense" in line 1, an act that would be antagonistic and warlike. This tone is continued in the second paragraph, as the personified machine is "invincible, triumphant...gathering force." The rhetorical question in the last paragraph makes the idea that a personified "machine, lives" very reasonable. Finally, as "a universal educator," the machine being instrumental in the destruction of greed in lines 13–15, makes it seem morally just.

5. **(B)** According to the speaker, mankind at "Every age" has been practical in doing what could be done to save "human effort" (labor-saving devices) with the resources available.

6. **(B)** The speaker amplifies art by defining it from different perspectives.

7. **(E)** "It" is a personal pronoun whose antecedent is "The machine" in line 9.

Selection Three

The Parting

Since there's no help, come let us kiss and part—
Nay, I have done, you get no more of me;
And I am glad, yea, glad with all my heart,
Line   That thus so cleanly I myself can free.
(5)   Shake hands for ever, cancel all our vows,
And when we meet at any time again,
Be it not seen in either of our brows
That we one jot of former love retain.
Now at the last gasp of Love's latest breath,
(10)   When, his pulse failing, Passion speechless lies,
When Faith is kneeling by his bed of death,
And Innocence is closing up his eyes,
Now if thou would'st, when all have given him over,
From death to life thou might'st him yet recover.

by Michael Drayton
(ca. 1900)

1. (Meaning) The subject can be stated as

    (A) an angry departure
    (B) dying love
    (C) a reversal of fortunes
    (D) resisting change
    (E) love and hate

2. (Form) What is the role of lines 13–14 to the poem as a whole?

   (A) They summarize that the speaker really no longer is in love.
   (B) They imply that the speaker is still in love.
   (C) They mourn the death of love.
   (D) They establish that death and love are synonymous.
   (E) They reinforce the speaker's determination to end the relationship.

3. (Voice) The context of the poem reveals that the speaker ("I") is

   (A) a social outcast
   (B) an unfaithful lover
   (C) an indifferent friend
   (D) a close, personal friend
   (E) a rejected lover

4. (Tone) The speaker's tone in lines 1–8 can be seen as

   (A) outraged indignation
   (B) incredulous
   (C) fascinated obsession
   (D) courteous
   (E) defensive pride

5. (Character) "…you get no more of me" (line 2) makes the speaker's character seem ruled by

   (A) hurt pride
   (B) hate
   (C) hardness
   (D) an obliging nature
   (E) leniency

6. (Use of Language) With personified Faith kneeling as Love, Passion, and Innocence die (lines 9–12), the effect is to

   (A) render no hope for Love's survival
   (B) emphasize the speaker's anger
   (C) mark a shift in tone
   (D) assert the power of Love
   (E) imply that the speaker still holds hope of reconciliation

7. (Meaning in Context) In the context of the selection, how can "cleanly" (line 4) be defined?

   I. Completely
   II. In a sportsmanlike manner
   III. Morally pure

   (A) I only
   (B) II only
   (C) III only
   (D) I and II only
   (E) I, II, and III

Correct Answers and Explanations

1. **(B)** The speaker's tone seems angry (answer choice A), especially in line 2; however, notice he still holds out hope—but without any supportive evidence on which to base it. He is resisting, but the subject, regardless of the speaker's emotions, is a love relationship that is dying.

2. **(B)** Your knowledge of form is tremendously valuable in these types of questions. This sonnet has an *abab cdcd efef gg* pattern. The rhyme scheme alone is a clue: The poem is divided into four parts. Probably each part will be a progression of thought with the last couplet being perhaps a summary or perhaps a reversal. In lines 1–4 a paraphrase reveals that the speaker has been in a love relationship that is ending. The speaker's attitude? Defiant? Angry? Perhaps resentful? Lines 5–8 indicate that he does not want to let on that they were ever in love. In lines 9–12 he very dramatically personifies love, passion, faith, and innocence as they die. The reader can anticipate in the final couplet a significant point—either confirmation of the attitude he has projected so far or a reversal.

> Now if thou would'st, when all have given him over,
> From death to life thou might'st him yet recover.

Who is "him?" Personified love—the same love that is dying in lines 9–12. The speaker, however, says (in paraphrase), you (the person ending the relationship) can make love "recover." Now look at the answer choices. Obviously, this is a reversal rather than a summary, so answer A is not correct. Answers C, D, and E also do not reflect the meaning of the couplet. But answer B—the lines imply that the speaker is still in love—can be justified, because he has given the object of his love the power to bring love back into being.

How else might the ways form contributes to meaning be questioned in this poem?

- Central contrasts, such as "death" (lines 9–12) and "life" (line 14), "cancel" (line 5) and "recover" (line 14), and so forth.

- Sequence, such as "part" (line 1) to "cancel" (line 5) to "death" (line 11) to "recover" (line 14) emphasize a progression from hopelessness to hope.

3. **(E)** The speaker's love obviously has been rejected because not he, but the listener (silent auditor), is the one who can bring love back to life (lines 13–14).

4. **(E)** Much like the traditional illustration of the rejected child on the playground who, hurt and embarrassed, announces that he or she did not want to play anyway, the speaker's tone in lines 1–8 suggests: OK for you, I don't want your love anyway; who needs it?

5. **(A)** Again, the speaker's pride is so hurt that he will not even kiss his former lover goodbye.

6. **(E)** For Faith to be by their deathbed implies an optimistic trust and sense of hope that is directly stated in the concluding couplet.

7. **(E)** Not only does "cleanly" refer to (I) completely, it also connotatively means in a sportsmanlike manner (II) because line 5 refers to shaking hands—an act of two opponents after a contest. It means "morally pure" (III) because, again in line 5, the speaker cancels vows.

Selection Four

On Time

Fly envious Time, till thou run out thy race,
Call on the lazy leaden-stepping hours,
Whose speed is but the heavy plummet's pace;
Line And glut thy self with what thy womb devours,
(5) Which is no more than what is false and vain,
And merely mortal dross;
So little is our loss,
So little is thy gain.
For when as each thing bad thou hast entombed,
(10) And last of all, thy greedy self consumed,
Then long Eternity shall greet our bliss
With an individual kiss;
And Joy shall overtake us as a flood,
When every thing that is sincerely good
(15) And perfectly divine,
With Truth, and Peace, and Love shall ever shine
About the supreme Throne
Of him, t' whose happy-making sight alone,
When once our heav'nly-guided soul shall climb,
(20) Then all this earthy grossness quit,
Attired with stars, we shall for ever sit,
Triumphing over Death, and Chance, and thee, O Time.

by John Milton
(ca. 1670)

1. (Meaning) Of the ideas listed, which one defines the subject?

(A) Time's destroying power
(B) Eternal happiness
(C) Eternity over Time
(D) Time as a race
(E) Time as a friend

2. (Form) Line 11 contains a change in the poem's

   (A) voice
   (B) tone
   (C) subject
   (D) rhyme scheme
   (E) imagery

3. (Voice) The speaker's attitude toward "the supreme Throne" (line 17) is expressed in terms that are

   (A) worshipful
   (B) unrelenting
   (C) fearful
   (D) defensive
   (E) reluctant

4. (Tone) The speaker's tone in lines 1–2 has a sound that is

   (A) bitter
   (B) lackluster
   (C) futile
   (D) cajoling
   (E) defiant

5. (Character) How does the speaker characterize "Time"?

   (A) As gluttonous
   (B) As hypocritical
   (C) As bluffing
   (D) As mysterious
   (E) As secretive

6. (Use of Language) The direct address in lines 1–10 to personified Time is an example of

   (A) irony
   (B) parody
   (C) apostrophe
   (D) cacophony
   (E) understatement

7. (Meaning in Context) In line 6, "mortal dross" probably is a reference to

   (A) spiritual life
   (B) carnal life
   (C) waste matter
   (D) time itself
   (E) worthless character

Correct Answers and Explanations

1. **(C)** Much of the poem is critical of Time, emphasizing its destructive power (A). However, this description is from a minimalistic perspective ("So little is our loss, / So little is thy gain," lines 7–8), which only serves to emphasize the main subject: the triumph of eternity over Time.

2. **(B)** The speaker's attitude toward Eternity differs greatly from his attitude toward Time and his tone reflects that difference.

3. **(A)** The "supreme Throne" (a biblical allusion to the Throne of God) is surrounded by "every thing that is sincerely good / And perfectly divine" (lines 14–15).

4. **(E)** Using imperative voice to command Time to "Fly" has a tone of defiance.

5. **(A)** Line 4 directly states the answer.

6. **(C)** By definition, apostrophe is direct address to an auditor or listener.

7. **(B)** Context points to elements that are "false and vain" (line 5) and "earthly grossness" (line 20), in other words, carnal life, as contrasted to an eternal, spiritual life.

Selection Five

ACT II. Scene I.

Enter ANGELO, ESCALUS, *a* JUSTICE,
PROVOST, OFFICERS *and other*
ATTENDANTS

ANGELO.   We must not make a scarecrow of the law,
　　　　Setting it up to fear the birds of prey,
　　　　And let it keep one shape till custom make it
Line　　Their perch, and not their terror.
(5)　ESCALUS.   Ay, but yet
　　　　Let us be keen, and rather cut a little
　　　　Than fall and bruise to death. Alas! this gentleman,
　　　　Whom I would save, had a most noble father.
　　　　Let but your honour know,
(10)　　Whom I believe to be most strait in virtue,
　　　　That, in the working of your own affections,
　　　　Had time coher'd with place, or place with wishing,

　　　　Or that the resolute acting of our blood

> Could have attain'd th'effect of your own purpose
> *(15)* Whether you had not sometime in your life
> Err'd in this point which now you censure him,
> And pull'd the law upon you.
> ANGELO.   'Tis one thing to be tempted, Escalus,
> Another thing to fall. I not deny
> *(20)* The jury, passing on the prisoner's life,
> May in the sworn twelve have a thief or two
> Guiltier than him they try. What's open made to justice,
> That justice seizes. What knows the laws
> That thieves do pass on thieves? 'Tis very pregnant,
> *(25)* The jewel that we find, we stoop and take't,
> Because we see it; but what we do not see
> We tread upon, and never think of it.
> You may not so extenuate his offence
> For I have had such faults; but rather tell me,
> *(30)* When I, that censure him, do so offend,
> Let mine own judgment pattern out my death,
> And nothing come in partial. Sir, he must die.
> ESCALUS.   Be it as your wisdom will.

Measure for Measure
by William Shakespeare
(1623)

1. (Meaning) The drama can be summarized as

    (A) two brothers discussing legal theories
    (B) the Deputy defending an accused man
    (C) Escalus defending himself against false charges
    (D) an argument in which a Justice accuses the Deputy of a crime
    (E) a Justice defending an accused man to the Deputy

2. (Form) What happens as a result of the change of rhythm of "Ay, but yet" in line 5?

    (A) It breaks the monotony of the passage.
    (B) It echoes the rhythm of line 9.
    (C) It threatens the unity of the dialogue.
    (D) It emphasizes the speaker's contrasting attitude.
    (E) It reinforces Angelo's point.

3. (Voice) Angelo's attitude has qualities that make him seem

    (A) irresponsible
    (B) unyielding
    (C) ambitious
    (D) contemptuous
    (E) sentimental

4. (Tone) The tone of Angelo's conclusion in line 32 has qualities that are

   (A) bitter and suspicious
   (B) infuriated and retributive
   (C) determined and authoritative
   (D) retaliatory and jaundiced
   (E) jealous and hostile

5. (Character) Escalus's words show him to be someone who

   (A) is given to flights of fancy
   (B) does not understand logical reasoning
   (C) has not fully considered the ramifications of his position
   (D) uses logical reasoning to present his case
   (E) resists authority and defies the law

6. (Use of Language) Angelo makes his point in lines 1–4 by using a(n)

   (A) analogy
   (B) mixed metaphor
   (C) simile
   (D) allusion
   (E) allegory

7. (Meaning in Context) In lines 22–23, justice seizing on someone occurs because of

   (A) opportunity
   (B) vengeance
   (C) the law only
   (D) a sense of fairness
   (E) equal rights

Correct Answers and Explanations

1. **(E)** Escalus, identified as "a Justice," is defending "this gentleman, / Whom I would save…" (lines 7–8).

2. **(D)** Angelo does not want to "make a scarecrow of the law" (line 1). When Escalus begins to speak, the "Ay" agrees, "but yet" introduces contrast of thought—the defense begins.

3. **(B)** Despite Escalus's reasoning, Angelo concludes "he must die" (line 32).

4. **(C)** Escalus attempts to persuade Angelo by bringing in personal elements that would make Angelo put himself in the prisoner's position; however, Angelo does not allow himself to be put in that position. Instead, he makes a simple statement of his view of justice. Notice that he would be willing to apply the same standard to himself.

5. **(D)** Escalus combines logic and elements of persuasion by attempting to make Angelo identify with the prisoner's perspective.

6. **(A)** He compares the law to a scarecrow set up to scare off birds of prey (criminals).

7. **(A)** People who commit crimes are brought to justice only when their crimes become known: "What's open made to justice, / That justice seizes" (lines 22–23).

CHAPTER 8

How Am I Doing Now?

41.25

The following test may seem very difficult. The purpose of this second 60-question diagnostic test, however, is to

1. help you identify which critical reading skills based on the seven major literary elements need additional attention.
2. give you additional practice in working with the structure and format of the test.
3. enable you to understand the rationale behind "correct" versus "incorrect" answer choices.

As with Diagnostic Test One, use the provided answer sheet to record your answers. Allow yourself one hour to complete the test.

Be sure to read all directions carefully, and do not use reference materials of any kind.

After you complete the test, use the Answer Key (see page 263) to check your answers and to determine your raw score. Then use the Analysis: Diagnostic Test Two (see page 265) to help you evaluate your answer choices. Remember: This diagnostic test is intended both as a measurement instrument and as a teaching tool.

Answer Sheet
DIAGNOSTIC TEST TWO

1 Ⓐ Ⓑ Ⓒ Ⓓ Ⓔ	16 Ⓐ Ⓑ Ⓒ Ⓓ Ⓔ	31 Ⓐ Ⓑ Ⓒ Ⓓ Ⓔ	46 Ⓐ Ⓑ Ⓒ Ⓓ Ⓔ
2 Ⓐ Ⓑ Ⓒ Ⓓ Ⓔ	17 Ⓐ Ⓑ Ⓒ Ⓓ Ⓔ	32 Ⓐ Ⓑ Ⓒ Ⓓ Ⓔ	47 Ⓐ Ⓑ Ⓒ Ⓓ Ⓔ
3 Ⓐ Ⓑ Ⓒ Ⓓ Ⓔ	18 Ⓐ Ⓑ Ⓒ Ⓓ Ⓔ	33 Ⓐ Ⓑ Ⓒ Ⓓ Ⓔ	48 Ⓐ Ⓑ Ⓒ Ⓓ Ⓔ
4 Ⓐ Ⓑ Ⓒ Ⓓ Ⓔ	19 Ⓐ Ⓑ Ⓒ Ⓓ Ⓔ	34 Ⓐ Ⓑ Ⓒ Ⓓ Ⓔ	49 Ⓐ Ⓑ Ⓒ Ⓓ Ⓔ
5 Ⓐ Ⓑ Ⓒ Ⓓ Ⓔ	20 Ⓐ Ⓑ Ⓒ Ⓓ Ⓔ	35 Ⓐ Ⓑ Ⓒ Ⓓ Ⓔ	50 Ⓐ Ⓑ Ⓒ Ⓓ Ⓔ
6 Ⓐ Ⓑ Ⓒ Ⓓ Ⓔ	21 Ⓐ Ⓑ Ⓒ Ⓓ Ⓔ	36 Ⓐ Ⓑ Ⓒ Ⓓ Ⓔ	51 Ⓐ Ⓑ Ⓒ Ⓓ Ⓔ
7 Ⓐ Ⓑ Ⓒ Ⓓ Ⓔ	22 Ⓐ Ⓑ Ⓒ Ⓓ Ⓔ	37 Ⓐ Ⓑ Ⓒ Ⓓ Ⓔ	52 Ⓐ Ⓑ Ⓒ Ⓓ Ⓔ
8 Ⓐ Ⓑ Ⓒ Ⓓ Ⓔ	23 Ⓐ Ⓑ Ⓒ Ⓓ Ⓔ	38 Ⓐ Ⓑ Ⓒ Ⓓ Ⓔ	53 Ⓐ Ⓑ Ⓒ Ⓓ Ⓔ
9 Ⓐ Ⓑ Ⓒ Ⓓ Ⓔ	24 Ⓐ Ⓑ Ⓒ Ⓓ Ⓔ	39 Ⓐ Ⓑ Ⓒ Ⓓ Ⓔ	54 Ⓐ Ⓑ Ⓒ Ⓓ Ⓔ
10 Ⓐ Ⓑ Ⓒ Ⓓ Ⓔ	25 Ⓐ Ⓑ Ⓒ Ⓓ Ⓔ	40 Ⓐ Ⓑ Ⓒ Ⓓ Ⓔ	55 Ⓐ Ⓑ Ⓒ Ⓓ Ⓔ
11 Ⓐ Ⓑ Ⓒ Ⓓ Ⓔ	26 Ⓐ Ⓑ Ⓒ Ⓓ Ⓔ	41 Ⓐ Ⓑ Ⓒ Ⓓ Ⓔ	56 Ⓐ Ⓑ Ⓒ Ⓓ Ⓔ
12 Ⓐ Ⓑ Ⓒ Ⓓ Ⓔ	27 Ⓐ Ⓑ Ⓒ Ⓓ Ⓔ	42 Ⓐ Ⓑ Ⓒ Ⓓ Ⓔ	57 Ⓐ Ⓑ Ⓒ Ⓓ Ⓔ
13 Ⓐ Ⓑ Ⓒ Ⓓ Ⓔ	28 Ⓐ Ⓑ Ⓒ Ⓓ Ⓔ	43 Ⓐ Ⓑ Ⓒ Ⓓ Ⓔ	58 Ⓐ Ⓑ Ⓒ Ⓓ Ⓔ
14 Ⓐ Ⓑ Ⓒ Ⓓ Ⓔ	29 Ⓐ Ⓑ Ⓒ Ⓓ Ⓔ	44 Ⓐ Ⓑ Ⓒ Ⓓ Ⓔ	59 Ⓐ Ⓑ Ⓒ Ⓓ Ⓔ
15 Ⓐ Ⓑ Ⓒ Ⓓ Ⓔ	30 Ⓐ Ⓑ Ⓒ Ⓓ Ⓔ	45 Ⓐ Ⓑ Ⓒ Ⓓ Ⓔ	60 Ⓐ Ⓑ Ⓒ Ⓓ Ⓔ

Diagnostic Test Two

Directions: The following questions test your understanding of several literary selections. Read each passage or poem and the questions that follow it. Select the best answer choice for each question by blackening the matching oval on your answer sheet. **Special attention should be given to questions containing the following words: EXCEPT, LEAST, NOT.**

<u>Questions 1–10</u> are based on the following poem.

Art thou poor, yet hast thou golden slumbers?
    O sweet content!
Art thou rich, yet is thy mind perplexed?
Line   O punishment!
(5) Dost thou laugh to see how fools are vexed
To add to golden numbers, golden numbers?
O sweet content! O sweet, O sweet content!
    Work apace, apace, apace, apace;
    Honest labour bears a lovely face;

(10) Then hey nonny nonny, hey nonny nonny!
Canst drink the waters of the crispèd
    spring?
    O sweet content!
Swimm'st thou in wealth, yet sink'st in
    thine own tears?
    O punishment!
(15) Then he that patiently want's burden bears
No burden bears, but is a king, a king!
O sweet content! O sweet, O sweet content!
    Work apace, apace, apace, apace;
    Honest labour bears a lovely face;
(20) Then hey nonny nonny, hey nonny nonny!

               (ca. 1600)

1. The speaker views poverty as

   (A) an unlikely source of happiness
   (B) the only way to find happiness
   (C) not a deterrent to happiness
   (D) an unavoidable condition
   (E) an inspiration to wealth

2. Of the devices listed, the metaphor in line 16 has the effect of

   (A) hyperbole
   (B) meiosis
   (C) fallacy
   (D) oxymoron
   (E) onomatopoeia

3. The repetition of lines 7–10 in lines 17–20 suggests that this poem may be

   (A) a folk ballad
   (B) a hymn
   (C) a nonsense verse
   (D) an aubade
   (E) a song

4. For spring waters to be "crispèd" (line 11), they would be

   (A) very cold
   (B) undulating
   (C) unpolluted
   (D) stagnant
   (E) very calm

5. Line 13 is an example of which of the following?

    I. Antithesis
    II. Paradox
    III. Antonomasia
    (A) I only
    (B) II only
    (C) III only
    (D) I and II only
    (E) I, II, and III

6. Structurally, what change occurs in line 15?

    (A) Line 15 concedes the negative aspects of his premise.
    (B) The speaker departs from the rhetorical question to summarize his point.
    (C) It reverses the poem's theme.
    (D) The speaker provides an answer to the questions posed in the first and second stanzas.
    (E) Line 15 is a restatement of lines 5–6.

7. This poem is best seen as

    (A) a condemnation of wealth
    (B) encouragement to be poor
    (C) an opinion concerning attitudes
    (D) a nonsense verse lacking deep meaning
    (E) a reproach against modern life

8. What is the tone of lines 10 and 20?

    (A) Dynamic
    (B) Endearing
    (C) Frenetic
    (D) Learned
    (E) Derisive

9. Lines 9 and 19 would indicate that the speaker is

    (A) a happy, trustworthy worker
    (B) an anxious person
    (C) naive concerning work
    (D) unrealistic in expectations
    (E) unwilling to take work seriously

10. The contrasts presented in this poem do NOT include

    (A) "poor" (line 1) and "rich" (line 3)
    (B) "slumbers" (line 1) and "perplexed" (line 3)
    (C) "labour" (line 9) and "lovely" (line 9)
    (D) "laugh" (line 5) and "vexed" (line 5)
    (E) "content" (line 2) and "punishment" (line 4)

Questions 11–16 are based on the following passage.

[a letter from an indentured female servant to her father]

Maryland, September 22nd, 1756.

Honored Father:

My being forever banished from your sight will, I hope, pardon the boldness I
Line now take of troubling you with this. My
(5) long silence has been purely owing to my undutifullness to you, and well knowing I had offended in the highest degree, put a tie to my tongue and pen, for fear I should be extinct from your good graces
(10) and add a further trouble to you. But too well knowing your care and tenderness for me, so long as I retained my duty to you, induced me once again to endeavor, if possible, to kindle up that flame again.
(15) O dear father, believe what I am going to relate, the words of truth and sincerity, and balance my former bad conduct [to] my sufferings here, and then I am sure you'll pity your distressed daughter. What
(20) we unfortunate English people suffer here is beyond the probability of you in England to conceive. Let it suffice that I, one of the unhappy number, am toiling almost day and night, and very often in
(25) horse's drudgery, with only this comfort, that "You bitch, you do not half enough!" and then tied up and whipped to that degree that you'd not serve an animal.

Scarce anything but Indian corn and salt
(30) to eat, and that even begrudged…Almost
naked, no shoes nor stockings to wear,
and the comfort after slaving during master's pleasure, what rest we can get is to
wrap ourselves up in a blanket and lie
(35) upon the ground. This is the deplorable
condition your poor Betty endures, and
now I beg, if you have any bowels of com-
passion left, show it by sending me some
relief. Clothing is the principal thing
(40) wanting, which if you should condescend
to, may easily send them to me by any of
the ships bound to Baltimore Town,
Patapsco River, Maryland. Give me leave
to conclude in duty to you and uncles and
(45) aunts, and respect to all friends.

Honored Father,
your undutifull and disobedient child,
Elizabeth Sprigs

11. The speaker's attitude toward her father is
    one of

    (A) evasiveness
    (B) contrition
    (C) contention
    (D) arrogance
    (E) aspiration

12. The speaker's words for her father to
    "believe what I am going to relate" (lines
    15–16) reveal her

    (A) manipulative nature
    (B) complacency toward her father's
        feelings
    (C) resistance to her father's advice
    (D) naturally obedient character
    (E) change in character due to her
        hardships

13. What is the speaker's tone?

    (A) Imposing
    (B) Impartial
    (C) Imploring
    (D) Impregnable
    (E) Impressionable

14. The main topic of the letter is

    (A) a cry for help
    (B) repentance for past sins
    (C) informing family of the situation
    (D) the unwillingness of the girl to come
        home
    (E) possibility of future communication

15. The "flame" (line 14) Elizabeth hopes to
    rekindle is

    (A) her "dutifullness"
    (B) her father's care
    (C) her father's anger
    (D) truth and sincerity
    (E) her own anger

16. Elizabeth "put a tie to my tongue and pen"
    (lines 7–8). What does this phrase mean?

    I. Silence due to lack of writing materials
    II. Silence due to emotion
    III. Silence due to guilt
    IV. Silence due to illiteracy

    (A) I only
    (B) II only
    (C) III only
    (D) II and III only
    (E) III and IV only

Questions 17–26 are based on the following

When I consider how my light is spent[1]
Ere half my days, in this dark world
    and wide,
And that one talent which is death to hide
Lodged with me useless, though my
    soul more bent
(5) To serve therewith my Maker, and present
My true account, lest He returning chide.
"Doth God exact day-labor, light
    denied?"

1 The poet was totally blind at about forty.

I fondly[1] ask. But Patience, to prevent
That murmur, soon replies, "God doth
    not need
(10) Either man's work or his own gifts; who
    best
Bear His mild yoke, they serve Him
    best. His state
Is kingly. Thousands at His bidding speed
And post o'er land and ocean without
    rest;
They also serve who only stand and wait."

---

1. *Imprudently*

(ca. 1652)

17. Line 9 contains a change in which of the elements?

   (A) Meter
   (B) Consonance
   (C) End rhyme
   (D) Mode
   (E) Imagery

18. The content of lines 1–8 contrasts with lines 9–14, but of the following, which is NOT a contrast?

   (A) Question and answer
   (B) Accountability and unaccountability
   (C) Resistance and acceptance
   (D) Self-interest and obedience
   (E) Impatience and patience

19. The phrase "my light is spent" (line 1), as used by the speaker, means which of these concepts?

   I. Lack of understanding
   II. The poet's blindness
   III. Personal tragedy

   (A) I only
   (B) II only
   (C) III only
   (D) I and II only
   (E) I, II, and III

20. The rhythm and number of lines in this poem make it a

   (A) couplet
   (B) ballad
   (C) limerick
   (D) sonnet
   (E) haiku

21. Patience has an attitude toward "I" (line 8) that can be described as

   (A) indifferent
   (B) edifying
   (C) angry
   (D) resentful
   (E) patronizing

22. The central theme of the poem is that

   (A) to serve God is to be obedient in all circumstances
   (B) physical handicaps can limit service to God
   (C) the best service to God is to stand and wait
   (D) blindness has robbed the speaker of being able to serve God
   (E) the speaker is among thousands who serve God

23. What does "that one talent" (line 3) represent?

   I. The natural abilities the speaker would use for God's service if the speaker were sighted
   II. The speaker's sight
   III. Hidden abilities that function despite the speaker's blindness

   (A) I only
   (B) II only
   (C) III only
   (D) I and II only
   (E) I, II, and III

24. "Light" (line 1) is in opposition to "dark" (line 2). This implies all the following opposing concepts EXCEPT

    (A) life and death
    (B) sightedness and blindness
    (C) good and evil
    (D) heaven and earth
    (E) knowledge and ignorance

25. "Day-labor" (line 7) can be paraphrased as

    (A) sighted service
    (B) work during the day
    (C) nine-to-five employment
    (D) physical work
    (E) work-for-hire

26. The indirect reference in line 3 to the "Parable of the Talents" in the Bible, in which the servant who buries his talent is cast into "outer darkness," is an example of

    (A) ambiguity
    (B) archaism
    (C) stock response
    (D) paratactic style
    (E) allusion

Questions 27–34 are based on the following passage.

"You have a tight boat, Mr. Barnstable," he said, "and a gallant-looking
crew. You promise good service, sir, in
Line time of need, and that hour may not be
(5) far distant."

"The sooner the better," returned the
reckless sailor; "I have not had an opportunity of scaling my guns since we quitted
Brest, though we passed several of the
(10) enemy's cutters coming up the Channel,
with whom our bulldogs longed for a
conversation. Mr. Griffith will tell you,
pilot, that my little sixes can speak, on
occasions, with a voice nearly as loud as
(15) the frigate's eighteens."

"But not to as much purpose," ob-
served Griffith; "'vox et præterea nihil,' as
we said at the school."

"I know nothing of your Greek and
(20) Latin, Mr. Griffith," retorted the com-
mander of the Ariel; "but if you mean
that those seven brass playthings won't
throw a round shot as far as any gun of
their size and height above the water, or
(25) won't scatter grape and cannister with
any blunderbuss in your ship, you may
possibly find an opportunity that will
convince you to the contrary before we
part company."

(30) "They promise well," said the pilot,
who was evidently ignorant of the good
understanding that existed between the
two officers, and wished to conciliate all
under his directions; "and I doubt not
(35) they will argue the leading points of a
combat with good discretion. I see that
you have christened them—I suppose for
their respective merits! They are indeed
expressive names!"

(40) "'Tis the freak of an idle moment," said
Barnstable, laughing, as he glanced his
eyes to the cannon, above which were
painted the several quaint names of
"boxer," "plumper," "grinder," "scatterer,"
(45) "exterminator," and "nail-driver."

"Why have you thrown the mid-ship
gun without the pale of your baptism?"
asked the pilot; "or do you know it by the
usual title of the 'old woman'?"

(50) "No, no, I have no such petticoat terms
on board me," cried the other; "but move
more to starboard, and you will see its
style painted on the cheeks of the car-
riage; it's a name that need not cause them
(55) to blush either."

(1823)

27. Within the confines of the excerpt, the narrator is

    (A) intrusive
    (B) limited omniscient
    (C) naive
    (D) unreliable
    (E) a participant

28. What type of language is used by Mr. Barnstable?

    (A) Dialectal response
    (B) A high level of diction
    (C) Subordinating syntax
    (D) Poetic diction
    (E) Professional jargon

29. What is the subject of the conversation?

    (A) An argument between Griffith and Barnstable
    (B) The relative merits of ship armaments
    (C) Strategies for the upcoming battle
    (D) The intricacies of naming guns
    (E) The major components of a war vessel

30. The relationship of Barnstable and Griffith is

    (A) competitive
    (B) antagonistic
    (C) amiable
    (D) discourteous
    (E) ambivalent

31. The names of the cannons (lines 44–45) are

    (A) euphemisms
    (B) personifications
    (C) anthropomorphisms
    (D) epithets
    (E) antonomasias

32. "Our bulldogs longed for a conversation" in the second paragraph is a vehicle in a metaphor describing

    (A) hand-to-hand combat
    (B) a gun battle
    (C) a pit-bulldog fight
    (D) a pre-war conference
    (E) peace negotiations

33. Below are listed several definitions of "freaks." Which defines the use of the word in the phrase "the freak of an idle moment" in line 40?

    I. An abnormal thought
    II. Devoted to the thought
    III. A whim

    (A) I only
    (B) II only
    (C) III only
    (D) II and III only
    (E) I, II, and III

34. Based on his reaction to the exchange of words between Barnstable and Griffith, the pilot's style of leadership is based on

    (A) authoritative control
    (B) laissez-faire
    (C) group dynamics
    (D) chain of command
    (E) constant evaluation

Questions 35–42 are based on the following passage.

The lighthouse keeper said that when the wind blowed strong on to the shore, the waves ate fast into the bank, but when
Line it blowed off they took no sand away; for
(5) in the former case the wind heaped up the surface of the water next to the beach, and to preserve in equilibrium a strong undertow immediately set back again into the sea which carried with it the sand and
(10) whatever else was in the way, and left the beach hard to walk on; but in the latter case the undertow set on, and carried the sand with it, so that it was particularly difficult for shipwrecked men to get to
(15) land when the wind blowed on to the shore, but easier when it blowed off. This undertow, meeting the next surface wave on the bar which itself has made, forms part of the dam over which the latter
(20) breaks, as over an upright wall. The sea

thus plays with the land holding a sand-bar in its mouth awhile before it swallows it, as a cat plays with a mouse; but the fatal gripe is sure to come at last. The sea (25) sends its rapacious east wind to rob the land, but before the former has got far with its prey, the land sends its honest west wind to recover some of its own. But, according to Lieutenant Davis, the (30) forms, extent, and distribution of sand-bars and banks are principally deter-mined, not by winds and waves, but by tides.

. . .

I heard of a party who went off fishing (35) back of Wellfleet some years ago, in two boats, in calm weather, who, when they had laden their boats with fish, and approached the land again, found such a swell breaking on it, though there was no (40) wind, that they were afraid to enter it. At first they thought to pull for Provincetown, but night was coming on, and that was many miles distant. Their case seemed a desperate one. As often as (45) they approached the shore and saw the terrible breakers that intervened, they were deterred; in short, they were thor-oughly frightened. Finally, having thrown their fish overboard, those in one boat (50) chose a favorable opportunity, and suc-ceeded, by skill and good luck, in reach-ing the land, but they were unwilling to take the responsibility of telling the others when to come in and as the other helms-(55) man was inexperienced, their boat was swamped at once, yet all managed to save themselves.

. . .

The annals of this voracious beach! who could write them, unless it were a (60) shipwrecked sailor? How many who have seen it have seen it only in the midst of danger and distress, the last strip of earth which their mortal eyes beheld. Think of the amount of suffering which a single (65) strand has witnessed! The ancients would have represented it as a sea-monster with open jaws, more terrible than Scylla and Charybdis.

(1865)

35. The imagery in the first paragraph makes the sea seem like a playful animal and the east wind like

(A) driven sand
(B) shipwrecked men
(C) a thief
(D) the undertow
(E) a friend to the land

36. The first paragraph, in its entirety,

(A) explains how beaches are formed
(B) hypothesizes the causes of shipwrecks
(C) relates the notion that wind and waves cause sandbars
(D) reinforces the important role of wind to beach formation
(E) describes the cyclical interplay of wind and wave

37. A significant factor presented in the first paragraph is that

(A) the east wind blows onto the shore
(B) the west wind blows onto the shore
(C) sandbar formation is unrelated to winds and waves
(D) winds blowing offshore carry sand away
(E) surface water is heaped up by the west wind

38. Based on context, "Scylla and Charybdis" in the last paragraph probably is a reference to

(A) a special nautical term
(B) sharks
(C) mythology
(D) marine vessels
(E) anthropology

39. What is the purpose of the anecdotal episode in the second paragraph?

    (A) To illustrate the dangers of fishing
    (B) To entertain the reader without a significant point
    (C) To indicate the need for experience when boating
    (D) To illustrate the force of the water when it hits the sandbars
    (E) To sentimentalize the plight of people stranded at sea

40. The personification in the last paragraph indicates the speaker is

    (A) excited about the beautiful beach
    (B) contemplative of suffering
    (C) disgruntled toward the shipwrecked sailors
    (D) contemptuous of change
    (E) high pressured in changing the reader's attitudes

41. What do the words "voracious," "danger," and "terrible" contribute to the tone of the last paragraph?

    (A) Scorn
    (B) Seriousness
    (C) Fear
    (D) Disdain
    (E) Outrage

42. As used in the first paragraph, "rapacious" means

    (A) forceful and greedy
    (B) tearing and destructive
    (C) cold and unrelenting
    (D) hot and gusting
    (E) vile and odious

Questions 43–49 are based on the following passage.

A shrill sound of laughter and of amused voices—voices of men, women, and children—resounded in the street
Line while this wine game lasted. There was lit-
(5) tle roughness in the sport, and much playfulness. There was a special companionship in it, an observable inclination on the part of every one to join some other one, which led, especially among the
(10) luckier or lighter-hearted, to frolicsome embraces, drinking of healths, shaking of hands, and even joining of hands and dancing, a dozen together. When the wine was gone, and the places where it
(15) had been most abundant were raked into a gridiron-pattern by fingers, these demonstrations ceased, as suddenly as they had broken out. The man who had left his saw sticking in the firewood he
(20) was cutting, set it in motion again; the woman who had left on a door-step the little pot of hot ashes, at which she had been trying to soften the pain in her own starved fingers and toes, or in those of her
(25) child, returned to it; men with bare arms, matted locks, and cadaverous faces, who had emerged into the winter light from cellars, moved away, to descend again; and a gloom gathered on the scene that
(30) appeared more natural to it than sun- shine.

The wine was red wine, and had stained the ground of the narrow street in the suburb of Saint Antoine, in Paris,
(35) where it was spilled. It had stained many hands, too, and many faces, and many naked feet, and many wooden shoes. The hands of the man who sawed the wood, left red marks on the billets; and the fore-
(40) head of the woman who nursed her baby, was stained with the stain of the old rag she wound about her head again. Those who had been greedy with the staves of the cask, had acquired a tigerish smear
(45) about the mouth; and one tall joker so besmirched, his head more out of a long squalid bag of a nightcap than in it, scrawled upon a wall with his finger dipped in muddy wine-lees—BLOOD.

(50)   The time was to come, when that wine too would be spilled on the street-stones, and when the stain of it would be red upon many there.

(1859)

43. What does this passage describe?

   (A) A street riot
   (B) An accident
   (C) A political demonstration
   (D) A protest
   (E) A party

44. The last paragraph foreshadows that

   (A) another wine game would occur
   (B) wine will stain
   (C) some people there would kill or be killed
   (D) the people would be stained with wine again
   (E) blood stains more than wine

45. All the following characterizations can be used to describe the people on the street EXCEPT

   (A) destitute
   (B) impulsive
   (C) respited
   (D) harrowed
   (E) predictable

46. As a literary device, the man writing "BLOOD" in wine on the wall is which of the following?

   I. Foreshadowing
   II. A symbolic act
   III. Dramatic understatement

   (A) I only
   (B) II only
   (C) III only
   (D) I and II only
   (E) I, II, and III

47. Why does the speaker use the word "cadaverous" (line 26) when he could have used "pale" or "emaciated"?

   (A) It connotes that these men are like the living dead.
   (B) It identifies that this is science fiction.
   (C) It shows that they needed a break from life's drudgery.
   (D) It exaggerates the extent of the lack of color of their faces.
   (E) It emphasizes a sense of prose rhythm in the line.

48. The genre of this passage can be identified as

   (A) a character study
   (B) descriptive narrative
   (C) prose poetry
   (D) an epic drama
   (E) an epistolary novel

49. Of the list that follows, all can be used to describe the tone of lines 46–49 EXCEPT

   (A) ironic
   (B) comic
   (C) deferential
   (D) ominous
   (E) expectant

Questions 50–55 are based on the following poem.

On This Day I Complete My Thirty-sixth Year

   'Tis time this heart should be
      unmoved,
   Since others it hath ceased to move:
   Yet, though I cannot be beloved,
      Still let me love!

Line
(5)   My days are in the yellow leaf;
   The flowers and fruits of love are gone;
   The worm, the canker, and the grief
      Are mine alone!

   The fire that on my bosom preys
(10)   Is lone as some volcanic isle;

No torch is kindled at its blaze—
   A funeral pile.

The hope, the fear, the jealous care,
   The exalted portion of the pain
(15)   And power of love, I cannot share,
   But wear the chain.

But 'tis not *thus*—and 'tis not *here*—
   Such thoughts should shake my soul,
      nor now,
(20)   Where glory decks the hero's bier,
   Or binds his brow.

                                        (1824)

50. Who is the speaker?

(A) An impassioned lover
(B) An aging paramour
(C) A social outcast
(D) A hermit
(E) An unrequited lover

51. Love is characterized in the third stanza as

(A) hostile to his needs
(B) a fire out of control
(C) an animal
(D) unsatisfying
(E) killing him

52. "The fire that on my bosom preys" is an example of

(A) mixed metaphor
(B) simile
(C) caricature
(D) *carpe diem*
(E) apostrophe

53. The fourth stanza tells the reader that

(A) the speaker is presently in love
(B) love is more pain than pleasure
(C) love is an escaped prisoner
(D) love symbolizes unhappy emotions
(E) the speaker plans to break free of love

54. What is the tone of the first stanza?

(A) Demoralizing
(B) Defiant
(C) Temerarious
(D) Irresolute
(E) Exacerbated

55. Of the definitions listed, all apply to "exalted" (line 14) EXCEPT

(A) spiritually high
(B) magnified
(C) dignified
(D) physically high
(E) extolled

Questions 56–60 are based on the following poem.

What sugared terms, what all-persuading
   art,
What sweet mellifluous words, what
   wounding looks
Love used for his admittance to my heart!
Line Such eloquence was never read in books.
(5)   He promised pleasure, rest, and endless joy,
Fruition of the fairest she alive.
His pleasure, pain; rest, trouble; joy, annoy,
Have I since found, which me of bliss
   deprive.
The Trojan horse thus have I now let in,
(10)   Wherein enclosed these arméd men were
      placed—
Bright eyes, fair cheeks, sweet lips, and
   milk-white skin;
These foes my life have overthrown and
   razed.
Fair outward shows prove inwardly the
   worst:
Love looketh fair, but lovers are accurst.

                                        (1596)

56. What does "she," as used in line 6, symbolize?

    (A) The woman he loves
    (B) Love
    (C) All women
    (D) Joy
    (E) His heart

57. What relationship do lines 13–14 have to the rest of the poem?

    (A) They contain a reversal in thought.
    (B) They introduce a fourth element of love's treachery.
    (C) They summarize the speaker's sense of disillusionment.
    (D) They intensify the promises of love.
    (E) They identify the object of the speaker's love.

58. "The Trojan horse" in the context of line 9 is a

    (A) magnificent animal
    (B) means of deception
    (C) military maneuver
    (D) famous beast
    (E) symbol of true love

59. "Sugared terms" (line 1) can be defined by which of these paraphrases?

    (A) Beguiling enticements
    (B) Beautiful language
    (C) Sweet negotiations
    (D) Coated stipulations
    (E) Kind words

60. Which of the descriptions that follow is the attitude of "I" toward "Love"?

    (A) Hostile antagonism
    (B) Humble contrition
    (C) Resistant pride
    (D) Optimistic anticipation
    (E) Vanquished resignation

Answer Key: Diagnostic Test Two

Step 1. Score Your Test

- Use the following table to score your test.
- *Compare* your answers with the correct answers in the table:
- ✓ Place a check in the "Right" column for those questions you answered correctly.
- ✓ Place a check in the "Wrong" column for those questions you answered incorrectly.
- If you omitted answering a question, leave both columns blank.

Step 2. Analyze Your Test Results

- *Read* the portions of the "Analysis: Diagnostic Test Two" (analysis follows the scoring table) that apply first to those questions you missed.
- *Scan* the rest of the analysis for those questions you answered correctly. This analysis provides the correct answer, identifies the literary element tested by each question, and briefly discusses the answer choice(s).

Step 3. Learn from Your Test Results

- *Circle* the question number on the Answer Key Table for each of the questions you answered incorrectly. Which literary elements were these questions testing?

  Obviously, many of the questions are actually testing more than one literary element. Consequently, these identifications serve only as a guide to pinpoint "problem" areas.
- *Review* the seven literary elements.

For Further Help in Literary Elements:	See Page:
1. MEANING	60
2. FORM	74
3. NARRATIVE VOICE	109
4. TONE	126
5. CHARACTER	145
6. USE OF LANGUAGE	168
7. MEANING(S) IN CONTEXT	202

ANSWER KEY: DIAGNOSTIC TEST TWO

RIGHT	WRONG	ANSWER	1	2	3	4	5	6	7
		1. C			*				
		2. A						*	
		3. E		*					
		4. B							*
		5. D						*	
		6. B		*					
		7. C	*						
		8. E				*			
		9. A					*		
		10. C						*	
		11. B			*				
		12. E					*		
		13. C				*			
		14. A	*						
		15. B						*	
		16. D						*	
		17. C		*					
		18. B		*					
		19. E							*
		20. D		*					
		21. B			*				
		22. A	*						
		23. D						*	
		24. D							*
		25. A							*
		26. E						*	
		27. B			*				
		28. E						*	
		29. B	*						
		30. C					*		

SCORING — *LITERARY ELEMENT TESTED*

SCORING			LITERARY ELEMENT TESTED						
RIGHT	WRONG	ANSWER	1	2	3	4	5	6	7
		31. D						*	
		32. B						*	
		33. C							*
		34. C					*		
		35. C						*	
		36. E	*						
		37. A	*						
		38. C						*	
		39. D		*					
		40. B			*				
		41. B				*			
		42. A							*
		43. B	*						
		44. C							*
		45. E					*		
		46. D						*	
		47. A						*	
		48. B		*					
		49. C				*			
		50. E			*				
		51. E							*
		52. A						*	
		53. A							*
		54. B				*			
		55. D							*
		56. C						*	
		57. C		*					
		58. B							*
		59. A							*
		60. E			*				

TO OBTAIN YOUR RAW SCORE:

_____15_____ divided by 4 = __3.75__   ____45____ minus __3.75__ = __41.25__
Total wrong   Score W   Total right   Score W   Score R

Round Score R to the nearest whole number for the raw score.

How Did You Do?

As with Diagnostic Test One, pinpointing weak areas is more important than a scaled score. Use the following analysis to help you understand any questions you missed. Where do you need more review? How is your timing at this point?

Analysis: Diagnostic Test Two

NOTE: Many of the questions in Diagnostic Test Two test your skills in more than one literary element, and each answer analysis might be viewed from multiple perspectives. Consequently, this analysis should be used as only a part of your study program.

1. **(C)** Element 3 (narrative voice) Upon first reading, the best description of the speaker's view of poverty would seem to be answer B, the only way to find happiness. But does the speaker really assert poverty to be "the only way"—or even "an unlikely source" (A) of happiness? Why are the rich "perplexed" (line 3), "vexed" (line 5), and "in…tears" (line 13) while the poor have "golden slumbers" (line 1)? The state of poverty is not the source of happiness because the speaker admits in line 15 that the poor "want's burden bears." Nevertheless, despite this "burden" placed upon him by want, the poor has contentment (lines 1–2), patience (line 15), and "Honest labour" (line 9) making the burden "No burden." The attitude of the rich who are "vexed / To add to golden numbers" makes wealth a deterrent to happiness, but the contented attitude of those who are poor makes poverty not a deterrent to happiness (C).

2. **(A)** Element 6 (use of language) The speaker compares the poor to a king (a metaphor) in line 16. Although the poor may be in a happier emotional state than the rich, the comparison to a king is exaggerated—hyperbole (A).

3. **(E)** Element 2 (form) The poem cannot be a ballad because it is not narrative; a hymn because it is not religious; a nonsense verse because it has rhythm, logic, and does not have coined words; or an aubade because it is not about early morning. The repetitive lines do, however, suggest a lyric poem meant to be sung (E).

4. **(B)** Element 7 (meanings in context) In the context, "crispèd" is the adjective form of the verb "crisp" that means the twisting movement associated with water that is swirling forth from a spring—undulating (B).

5. **(D)** Element 6 (use of language) Line 13 is a balanced sentence in which the conjunction "yet" establishes a contrast of ideas between two clauses of like grammatical construction (I). This antithesis is paradoxical (II) in that the person is swimming and sinking. Antonomasia is using a proper name for an associated idea—a figure of speech not applicable to line 13.

6. **(B)** Element 2 (form)

Stanza 1
Line 1 Rhetorical question
Line 3 Rhetorical question
Lines 5–6 Rhetorical question

Stanza 2
Line 11 Rhetorical question
Line 13 Rhetorical question
Line 15 "Then he…!"

Line 15 departs from the speaker's established structure of rhetorical questions, each of which is aimed at making the point summarized in line 15: The contented ("patiently want's burden bears") poor worker is without the vexation of the rich ("No burden bears").

7. **(C)** Element 1 (meaning) This poem deals with attitudes. The rich are "vexed / To add to golden numbers, golden numbers" whereas the poor are contented and patient. It is this contrast in attitudes that establishes the meaning of the poem, rather than a condemnation of wealth itself or than an encouragement to be poor. The speaker has implied a generalization, however, that the named attitudes are seen in the states or conditions of wealth and poverty.

8. **(E)** Element 4 (tone) "Nonny" is a dialectal word that is used to call someone a simpleton—producing a derisive tone.

9. **(A)** Element 5 (character) This line has two possible perspectives: (1) the speaker may be personifying "Honest labour" as someone with a "lovely face" and (2) the speaker may feel that someone engaged in "Honest Labour" will have ("bear") a "lovely face"—one that is smiling and happy. Either perspective or attitude is one of a happy, trustworthy worker (A).

10. **(C)** Element 6 (use of language) The poor: characterized as able to slumber, laugh, and be content. This is in contrast to the rich: characterized as being perplexed, vexed, and in punishment. The speaker characterizes "Honest labour" as "lovely."

11. **(B)** Element 3 (narrative voice) The attitude of this poor young woman is sorrow and penitence—one of contrition. She admits the wrongful nature of her actions several times (referring to her "undutifullness" and to her "former bad conduct"). She is by no means evasive either about her situation or about the hardships she must endure. Her letter shows no hint of contention or arrogance, and her only aspiration seems to be that her father will send her some clothing—a small thing in light of her deplorable situation. (Be sure to note the nonstandard spelling in this selection.)

12. **(E)** Element 5 (character) Elizabeth, by her own admission, was undutiful and disobedient, a trouble to her father, and engaged in "bad conduct." Being beaten and starved has changed her character in the sense that she admits the wrongful nature of her former conduct toward the person she is now imploring for help (E). Although some may think she is manipulating the situation (A), the deplorable nature of her current living conditions were too harsh to justify such suspicions; this girl is really in trouble—trouble, perhaps, of her own making—but trouble nonetheless.

13. **(C)** Element 5 (tone) Answers B, D, and E are obviously incorrect; however, answers A and C are an opportunity for you to see how connotation can work in determining an answer choice. The reader can point to several lines in which Elizabeth implores her father for forgiveness, mercy, help; but does she not also impose upon him to send her clothes? In one sense this is true—she does place a burden upon her father to help her; however, the word <u>impose</u> carries with it the connotations of its other meanings, including cheating, taking advantage of others, forcing others to do what one wants—all of which this young woman is in no position to accomplish. As a result, <u>imploring</u> (C) is the <u>better answer choice</u> of the two.

14. **(A)** Element 1 (meaning) Considering her situation, Elizabeth would probably come home in a heartbeat if she could, making answer D improbable (and not supported by the passage). Answers A, B, C, and E are all possible; however, based on context, how can you tell which answer is best? Look at the <u>writer's purpose</u>: why did she write this letter? She wants her family to know that she is in trouble, that she is sorry for what she did, and that they can "easily" communicate with her. She is providing them knowledge, emotional motivation, and the means to do something—she is crying for help.

15. **(B)** Element 6 (use of language) "Flame" is used metaphorically in this context and is identified ("Your care and tenderness for me").

16. **(D)** Element 6 (use of language) The "tie to my tongue and pen" is the result of emotion ("fear") and guilt ("well knowing I had offended in the highest degree").

17. **(C)** Element 2 (form)

    Line 9 marks a change in end-rhyme:

Line 1...spent	a	Line 9...need	c
Line 2...wide	b	Line 10...best	d
Line 3...hide	b	Line 11...state	e
Line 4...bent	a	Line 12...speed	c
Line 5...present	a	Line 13...rest	d
Line 6...chide	b	Line 14...wait	e
Line 7...denied	b		
Line 8...prevent	a		

18. **(B)** Element 2 (form) This two-part structure establishes several contrasts: (A) question ("Doth God exact day-labor, light denied?"—line 7) and answer ("God doth not need / Either man's work or his own gifts"—lines 9–10); (C) resistance ("my soul more bent"—line 4) and acceptance ("They also serve who only stand and wait"—line 14); (D) self-interest ("and present / My true account, lest He returning chide"—lines 5–6) and obedience ("who best / Bear His mild yoke, they serve Him best"—lines 10–11); (E) impatience ("When I consider how my light is spent / Ere half my days"—lines 1–2) and patience ("They also serve who only stand and wait"—line 14).

    Answer B, however, does not establish an accurate contrast. Although the first part includes the concept of accountability, the second part states that "who best / Bear His mild yoke, they serve Him best" (lines 10–11)—another view of being accountable, NOT unaccountable.

19. **(E)** Element 7 (meanings in context) "Spent," as it is used here, can mean something being used up, worn out, tired out, or gone. "Light" can be symbolic of understanding (I), of vision (II), or of happiness (III).

20. **(D)** Element 2 (form) Sonnets are 14-line poems written in iambic pentameter.

21. **(B)** Element 3 (narrative voice) Patience answers Milton's question to instruct him spiritually—edifying (B).

22. **(A)** Element 1 (meaning) The central idea—the theme—of the poem is a statement that summarizes the main point of the poem. What is the main point Milton is making? Whether speeding "O'er land and ocean" (line 13) or standing and waiting (line 14), whether blind or sighted, the best way to serve God is to obey Him in all circumstances (lines 10–11).

23. **(D)** Element 6 (use of language) "And that one talent" (line 3) represents both natural gifts and abilities and sight itself that he would use in service, but both his sight and those abilities he would accomplish with and by means of his sight are "Lodged with me useless" (line 4).

24. **(D)** Element 7 (meanings in context) In the context of this poem, light comes to represent Milton's life ("Ere half my days"—line 2) as contrasted to a "dark world" of death, his sight itself as contrasted to the "dark world" of blindness, good (the means "to serve therewith my Maker"—line 5) as contrasted to a dark work of evil (that does not serve), and knowledge (understanding) as contrasted to the "dark world" of ignorance. Heaven and earth, however, are not suggested in this context.

25. **(A)** Element 7 (meanings in context) "Day-labor" is figurative, representing work or service (labor) that requires sight (day—the time when the sighted can see with the light).

26. **(E)** Element 6 (use of language) This is an allusion—mentioning either directly or indirectly some well-known (literary) work, event, place, or person.

27. **(B)** Element 3 (narrative voice) The passage is obviously taken from a larger work; however, in this excerpt the narrator is seen as limited omniscient because the narrator gives the reader insight into the pilot's mind, but not into the thinking of any of the other characters.

28. **(E)** Element 6 (use of language) Barnstable uses the professional jargon (A) of a seaman: "scaling my guns," "the frigate's eighteens"—expressions indicative of a sailor who is used to high-sea battles.

29. **(B)** Element l (meaning) Barnstable, Griffith, and the man identified as "the pilot" are discussing, in terms of performance, the various types of guns used on warships. Although the pilot does divert the conversation to the names of Barnstable's cannon, the focus is upon the relative merits of ship armaments (B).

30. **(C)** Element 5 (character) Their conversation might support the idea that these two men are competitive (A) or even antagonistic (B), but the narrator reveals that they have a "good understanding" between them, indicating that the banter between them is good-natured and that their relationship is amiable.

31. **(D)** Element 6 (use of language) These "expressive names" that describe "their respective merits" are epithets (D), nouns (in this case) that emphasize the predominant characteristics of something.

32. **(B)** Element 6 (use of language) "Bulldogs" is an epithet-type name for guns. The "conversation" that they long for is the exchange of fire with the guns of the other ship. This metaphor comparing a gun battle (the tenor) with a dog fight (the vehicle) also contains personification of the bulldogs / guns, thus making this also an example of mixed imagery.

33. **(C)** Element 7 (meanings in context) The phrase "the freak of an idle moment" contains the contextual clue to the meaning of freak. Freak can mean all three of the listed definitions. It can refer to the abnormal (I) in a variety of circumstances. It can also be a name used to refer to someone devoted to something (II), especially a hobby or a movie star. In this context, however, the use of "idle moment," i.e., leisure time, indicates that these names are just whims (III).

34. **(C)** Element 5 (character) Although he has misread the implications of the exchange of words between Barnstable and Griffith (he does not recognize their "good understanding"), the pilot does not command the men with authoritative control (A), refrain from interference as one would who subscribes to a laissez-faire philosophy (B), refer them to one higher in command (D), or point out their errors in thinking (E). Instead he attempts to "conciliate" the two men—using human relations within group dynamics (C).

35. **(C)** Element 6 (use of language) The speaker presents the east wind as "rapacious," sent by the sea "to rob the land" like a thief (C).

36. **(E)** Element 1 (meaning) Note that the question specifies "in its entirety":

    Wind blows on shore and waves eat into bank →
    Wind blows off shore and no sand taken away →
    Wind heaps up surface water at beach and undertow carries away sand →
    Undertow meets own surface wave and forms dam →
    Wave breaks over dam → a cyclical interplay of wind and wave (E).

37. **(A)** Element 1 (meaning) Based on the opinion of Lieutenant Davis, the correct answer would be C if it were not for the word "unrelated" in that answer choice. Davis says that sandbar formation is "principally determined, not by winds and waves, but by tides"; he does NOT say it is unrelated. This type of question can be readily answered by using deductive reasoning. Answer A is supported by the following:

    1. "…when the wind blowed strong on to the shore, the waves ate fast into the bank," and
    2. "The sea sends its rapacious east wind to rob the land"; therefore,
    3. the east wind blows on to shore.

38. **(C)** Element 6 (use of language) Context is essential to correctly answering this question: "ancients… sea-monster" (lines 65–66).

    First, establish the context. The writer describes a beach (strand) where many shipwrecked sailors have died. He speculates that ancients would have called it "a sea-monster with open jaws, more terrible than Scylla and Charybdis."

    The context does not support Scylla and Charybdis meaning "a special nautical term" because the comparison to a sea-monster makes them a reference to something supposedly alive. Sharks are alive and have open jaws, but the use of capitalization indicates that these are proper names. "Marine vessels" can immediately be eliminated because they are not alive and generally are not considered monsters. "Anthropology"—the study of mankind—is an obviously incorrect answer choice. The context and process of elimination leaves "mythology" as the correct answer: mythology includes ancient stories about monsters with proper names. FYI: According to mythology, Scylla was a monster off the Italian coast and Charybdis was a monster in a Sicilian whirlpool.

39. **(D)** Element 2 (form) The narrator is using an anecdotal episode to illustrate a point. The short narrative, itself, demonstrates a danger people encounter when fishing (A) and by means of contrast within the story demonstrates the need for experience (C); however, in the context of the entire selection in which he is discussing winds, waves, and sandbars, he uses the short narrative to illustrate just how powerful the water hitting the shore can be—answer D.

40. **(B)** Element 3 (narrative voice) The speaker personifies the beach as both "voracious" and as the witness of suffering—both indicative of someone whose attitude is contemplative concerning the suffering caused by this particular strand.

41. **(B)** Element 4 (tone) In isolation these words are indicative of elements that might cause fear (C) and perhaps outrage (E); however, in context, they project the speaker's contemplative attitude when used within rhetorical questions and figures of speech to intensify the gravity of the subject and to establish a serious tone (B).

42. **(A)** Element 7 (meanings in context) "Rapacious" is an adjective used to describe the act of forceful seizure and the condition of being very greedy (A).

43. **(B)** Element 1 (meaning) That this event is called a "wine game" eliminates answers A and D. Once the wine is gone, the people leave, conflicting with what might have been a demonstration (C). Is it a party (supported by the dancing) or is this event an accident—an unplanned happening because something has happened? The contextual clues support this latter view, especially because "these demonstrations ceased, as suddenly as they had broken out."

44. **(C)** Element 7 (meanings in context) The speaker states in the last paragraph that "that wine"—blood—would stain "many there." How can the stain of blood "be red" upon someone? Either by being wounded oneself or by wounding (killing) someone else. Keeping in mind that for blood to "be spilled" refers to physical conflict/bloodshed/killing: the speaker is implying that some of the very people who had engaged in the "wine game" would eventually kill others or would perhaps be killed themselves.

45. **(E)** Element 5 (character) These poor people are clearly destitute (A), underfed and in rags. That they are impulsive (B) is evidenced by "these demonstrations ceased, as suddenly as they had broken out." In their miserable condition, however, they are respited (C) by this brief episode with the wine somehow spilled in the street. The harrowing (acutely distressing) nature of their situation is readily apparent, but the one thing these people are not is predictable (E).

46. **(D)** Element 6 (use of language) The action of the man writing "BLOOD" in wine on the wall functions as foreshadowing of coming events, as evidenced by the final paragraph of this passage, and functions as a symbolic act on several different levels, such as:

    1. A symbol of the emotional intensity that the spilled wine caused—mirrored in the spilling of blood
    2. A symbol of the impulsiveness with which people can react to spilled wine or to spilled blood
    3. A symbol of underlying bitterness of these poor wretched people, bitterness that could be given temporary respite by a moment of abandon when wine is spilled—or by a moment of abandon when blood is spilled

47. **(A)** Element 6 (use of language) Several of these answer choices are applicable; therefore, you need to evaluate the best answer choice. Where do you look to make this determination? Context. Where do these men with "cadaverous" faces come from and return to? They descend again into cellars—below ground—like corpses. They are alive, but their appearance is as the dead.

48. **(B)** Element 2 (form) The passage consists of a narrative episode (a crowd of people on the street rejoice over wine that has been spilled, then retreat to their previous activities) that uses very descriptive language, with special attention paid to diction.

49. **(C)** Element 4 (tone) A man, slightly drunk with a baggy nightcap almost on his head would be a comic sight (B)—very ironic (A) in its contrast to the ominous (D) nature of the message he wrote—a message that leads the reader to expect (E) that a bloody conflict may well be ahead. The idea of yielding or submitting (C) is not an element of this act.

50. **(E)** Element 3 (narrative voice) The speaker's identity is revealed in the first four lines.

51. **(E)** Element 7 (meanings in context) Because the fire (a vehicle for love) "Is lone" and "No torch is kindled at its blaze" (line 11)—no one is caught by the sparks of his love—the love has become a self-consuming "funeral pile" (line 12)—in other words, love is killing him (E).

52. **(A)** Element 6 (use of language) "Fire" is a vehicle for "love"; "preys" compares fire/love to a predator, hence a mixed metaphor (two or more vehicles for the same tenor).

53. **(A)** Element 7 (meanings in context) The speaker laments that he or she "cannot share" love, "But wear the chain" (line 17). This implies that the speaker does have an object of affection—someone with whom he or she wants to "share" love.

54. **(B)** Element 4 (tone) Despite the conclusion made in the first two lines, the speaker challenges the notion by defiantly proclaiming that although love is not returned, "Still let me love!" (line 4).

55. **(D)** Element 7 (meanings in context) Hope, fear, jealousy, pain, power—these are all emotions, not physical attributes in this context.

56. **(C)** Element 6 (use of language) "She" does indeed refer to the woman the speaker loves on a *literal level*, but the key to the symbolic use is in the <u>syntax</u>: "Fruition of the fairest she alive" (line 6)—"the fairest she alive" acts as the object of the preposition "of" with "the," "fairest," and "alive" modifying "she." In normal syntactical structure, this object would require a noun, not a pronoun. What noun could be the symbolic antecedent of the pronoun in this context? The superlative "fairest...alive" points to all women: the fairest woman alive.

57. **(C)** Element 2 (form) In traditional sonnet form, the rhyme scheme groups this poem's thoughts:

Lines 1–4	Love tricked the speaker.
Lines 5–8	Personified Love broke his promises.
Lines 9–12	The object of his love was a Trojan horse.
Lines 13–14	Love looks fine on the outside, but is not on the inside.

The speaker is disillusioned by love—the deceptive nature of love's appearance (C).

58. **(B)** Element 7 (meanings in context) "Trojan horse" is a literary allusion (a use of language) to the battle over Helen of Troy in which a large wooden horse, filled with soldiers, was left as a "gift" before the enemy's gates. After the enemy brought in the horse, had a party, and fell asleep, the soldiers emerged from the horse and killed them. A "Trojan horse," in the context of this poem then, refers to such deceptions that look fine on the outside but contain an enemy within. Even without being familiar with the story of Helen of Troy, you can determine the meaning in context: The speaker has allowed in armed men (lines 9–11) that were placed in a beautiful body but who have overthrown and razed his life (line l2). The Trojan horse is a means of deception—answer B.

59. **(A)** Element 7 (meanings in context) "To sugar" is a process by which something that is otherwise unpleasant is covered with sugar to make it more pleasant to consume. Love, to gain "admittance to my heart" "sugared," or covered with sweetness, "terms"—referring to conditions of agreement and also referring to words. Such "sugared terms" (line l) are beguiling enticements, answer A.

60. **(E)** Element 3 (narrative voice) The speaker feels betrayed by "Love," but how does he react? You might expect him to be hostile (A), particularly after reading the description of what "Love" did to him, yet nowhere does he convey feelings of hostility. In contrast, he admits defeat (vanquishment) in line 12 and summarizes that "lovers" (among whom he counts himself) "are accurst" in line 14, giving voice to his resignation to the position in which "Love" has placed him.

Selections Used in Diagnostic Test Two

Questions

PART III

PRACTICE

CHAPTER 9

How Do I Get Through the Test in Just One Hour?

Practice Test One

Practice Test Two

Practice Test Three

Practice Test Four

Practice Test Five

Practice Test Six

Practice Test Seven

How Do I Get Through the Test in Just One Hour?

Use the following seven practice tests to sharpen your comprehension skills refine your test strategies, and practice pacing yourself during the test. You may want to develop your own strategy sequence, or you could try the following to see if it works for you.

TEST STRATEGY REMINDERS

For each selection:

1. Skim the questions first.
2. Read the selection, marking key words or ideas. In poems put a slash mark (/) where one sentence ends and another begins.
3. Don't be hasty. Read all the answer choices for each question before selecting an answer.
4. Strike through obviously incorrect answer choices.
5. Compare remaining answer choices, looking for special requirements in the question stem and context clues in the selection.
6. Either write your answer choice next to the question or circle the number of the question (on the test booklet, not the answer sheet) to return to later.
7. Transfer your answer choices for the selection to your answer sheet, making sure you skip those questions you left unanswered, then continue with the next selection. If you decide to answer each question directly on the answer sheet as you go, periodically check to be sure you are answering to the correct space.

Speed Counts!

There is a sixty-minute time limit. Keep focused (think clearly to think quickly) and establish a pace or rhythm that allows you to answer all the questions you feel sure about before returning to questions that you left unanswered. Review the Focus Strategies on page 14.

Practice Test One

Directions: The following questions test your understanding of several literary selections. Read each passage or poem and the questions that follow it. Select the best answer choice for each question by blackening the matching oval on your answer sheet. **Special attention should be given to questions containing the following words: EXCEPT, LEAST, NOT.**

Questions 1–8 are based on the following passage.

    No doubt it was having a strong effect on him as he walked to Lowick. Fred's light hopeful nature had perhaps never
Line had so much of a bruise as from this sug-
(5) gestion that if he had been out of the way Mary might have made a thoroughly good match. Also he was piqued that he had been what he called such a stupid lout as to ask that intervention from Mr
(10) Farebrother. But it was not in a lover's nature—it was not in Fred's—that the new anxiety raised about Mary's feeling should not surmount every other. Notwithstanding his trust in Mr
(15) Farebrother's generosity, notwithstanding what Mary had said to him, Fred could not help feeling he had a rival: it was a new consciousness, and he objected to it extremely, not being in the least ready to
(20) give up Mary for her good, being ready rather to fight for her with any man whatsoever. But the fighting with Mr Farebrother must be of a metaphorical kind, which was much more difficult to
(25) Fred than the muscular. Certainly this experience was a discipline for Fred hardly less sharp than his disappointment about his uncle's will. The iron had not entered his soul, but he had begun to
(30) imagine what the sharp edge would be. It did not once occur to Fred that Mrs

Garth might be mistaken about Mr Farebrother, but he suspected that she might be wrong about Mary. Mary had
(35) been staying at the parsonage lately, and her mother might know very little of what had been passing in her mind.

                              (1871–2)

1. Lines 28–34 imply that

   (A) Fred dislikes Mary
   (B) Fred does not trust Mr. Farebrother
   (C) Fred disliked his late uncle
   (D) Mrs. Garth gossiped about Mary and Mr. Farebrother
   (E) Mary is Mr. Farebrother's sister

2. The narrator's comments in lines 15–22 make Fred seem to be

   (A) unsympathetic and jubilant
   (B) jealous and selfish
   (C) jealous and enraptured
   (D) comfortless and irritating
   (E) indulgent and forbearant

3. The phrase "metaphorical kind" (lines 23–24) conveys the idea that the fight is

   (A) illusionary
   (B) allegorical
   (C) undisciplined
   (D) physical
   (E) mental

4. The statement in lines 25–28 that Fred was disappointed about his uncle's will is intended as

   (A) an observation concerning Fred's character
   (B) an allusion to a large cash settlement
   (C) an implication concerning Fred's financial status
   (D) an inference concerning the value of discipline
   (E) a conclusion concerning his uncle's character

5. The "bruise" in line 4 contextually denotes

   (A) injured flesh
   (B) a beating
   (C) injured feelings
   (D) verbal abuse
   (E) physical abuse

6. Lines 28–30 contain a figure of speech known as

   (A) a simile
   (B) a metaphor
   (C) alliteration
   (D) literary allusion
   (E) personification

7. As the words "light hopeful nature" (line 3), "a stupid lout" (lines 8–9), "a lover's nature" (lines 10–11), and "a new consciousness" (lines 17–18) are used, they

   (A) imply that Fred's character is being challenged
   (B) suggest that Fred is deceitful
   (C) are bitterly ironic in tone
   (D) reinforce the metaphorical aspects of Fred's nature
   (E) indicate that Fred is not really in love

8. An accurate inference from the passage would be that Fred is

   (A) self-sacrificial
   (B) a stupid lout
   (C) a conscientious lover
   (D) a fortune seeker
   (E) somewhat egotistical

Questions 9–21 are based on the following poem.

A Bed of Forget-Me-Nots

Is love so prone to change and rot
We are fain to rear Forget-me-not
By measure in a garden-plot?—
Line   I love its growth at large and free
(5)   By untrod path and unlopped tree,
Or nodding by the unpruned hedge,
Or on the water's dangerous edge
Where flags and meadowsweet blow rank
With rushes on the quaking bank.
(10)   Love is not taught in learning's school,
Love is not parcelled out by rule:
Hath curb or call an answer got?—
So free must be Forget-me-not.
Give me the flame no dampness dulls,
(15)   The passion of the instinctive pulse,
Love steadfast as a fixèd star,
Tender as doves with nestlings are,
More large than time, more strong than death:
   This all creation travails of—
(20)   She groans not for a passing breath—
   This is Forget-me-not and Love.

                         (ca. 1880)

9. The poem's main subject is concerned with the

   (A) brevity of love
   (B) nature of love
   (C) growing of Forget-me-nots
   (D) death of love
   (E) freedom of flower gardens

10. Contextually, "flags" in line 8 are

    (A) weeds
    (B) national symbols
    (C) flowers
    (D) stones
    (E) shaped gardens

     garden

11. "Rank" can have several connotative and denotative meanings. How can it be understood as used in line 8?

    I. Bad taste
    II. Bad smell
    III. Growing vigorously
    IV. In rows

    (A) I only
    (B) II only
    (C) III only
    (D) I and II only
    (E) I, II, and IV only

12. In line 12, "curb" represents which of the following?

    I. Restraint
    II. An edging or border
    III. A market

    (A) I only
    (B) II only
    (C) III only
    (D) I and II only
    (E) I, II, and III

    OK

13. What is the purpose of lines 1–3 as they relate to the rest of the poem?

    (A) They set a mocking tone for the poem.
    (B) They reveal the speaker's sense of insecurity.
    (C) They emphasize the poem's dismal tone.
    (D) They introduce the analogy that is the basis of the poem.
    (E) They reinforce the passionate nature of love.

14. The speaker compares Forget-me-nots and

    (A) flags
    (B) garden-plots
    (C) death
    (D) school
    (E) love

15. In what way do lines 4–9 relate to lines 10–21?

    (A) They are allusional.
    (B) They are metaphorical.
    (C) They reflect extreme pessimism.
    (D) They reinforce a sense of dispassionate sympathy.
    (E) They are allegorical.

16. The speaker's feeling toward love is that

    (A) love is short-lived
    (B) love can be learned
    (C) love should be unrestrained
    (D) love is weak and fragile
    (E) love is disciplined

17. The questions asked in lines 1–3 and line 12 can be considered

    (A) insolent
    (B) hostile
    (C) ambivalent
    (D) indifferent
    (E) rhetorical

18. In the context of the poem, the opposition of "untrod," "unlopped," and "unpruned" (lines 5–6) to "school," "rule," and "curb" (lines 10–12) emphasizes that

    (A) gardens can be unkempt
    (B) love is eternal
    (C) flowers are wild
    (D) love is free
    (E) love can be controlled

GO ON TO THE NEXT PAGE.

19. In line 16, which of these literary devices is used?

    (A) Metaphor
    (B) Simile
    (C) Personification
    (D) Understatement
    (E) Synaesthesia

20. In the first stanza, "garden-plot" (line 3) becomes for the speaker which of the representations listed below?

    (A) A figure for confinement
    (B) A symbol of beauty
    (C) A place to raise Forget-me-nots
    (D) A place of change
    (E) An imaginative place for love to exist

21. The speaker implies in lines 1–3 that we attempt to structure love to

    (A) prevent its destruction
    (B) capture its joy
    (C) measure its impact
    (D) control its effects
    (E) forget its measure

Questions 22–28 are based on the following passage.

"See! Master Coffin," cried the lieutenant, pointing out the object to his cockswain as they glided by it, "the
Line shovel-nosed gentlemen are regaling dain-
(5) tily; you have neglected the Christian's duty of burying your dead."

The old seaman cast a melancholy look at the dead whale, and replied:

"If I had the creature in Boston Bay, or
(10) on the Sandy Point of Munny Moy, 'twould be the making of me! But riches and honor are for the great and the larned, and there's nothing left for poor Tom Coffin to do, but to veer and haul
(15) on his own rolling tackle, that he may ride out the rest of the gale of life without springing any of his old spars."

"How now, Long Tom!" cried the officer; "these rocks and cliffs will shipwreck
(20) you on the shoals of poetry yet; you grow sentimental!"

"Them rocks might wrack any vessel that struck them," said the literal cockswain; "and as for poetry, I wants none
(25) better than the good old song of Captain Kidd; but it's enough to raise solemn thoughts in a Cape Poge Indian, to see an eighty-barrel whale devoured by sharks— 'tis an awful waste of property! I've seen
(30) the death of two hundred of the creaters, though it seems to keep the rations of poor old Tom as short as ever."

The cockswain walked aft, while the vessel was passing the whale, and seating
(35) himself on the taffrail, with his face resting gloomily on his bony hand, he fastened his eyes on the object of his solicitude, and continued to gaze at it with melancholy regret, while it was to be
(40) seen glistening in the sunbeams, as it rolled its glittering side of white into the air, or the rays fell unreflected on the black and rougher coat of the back of the monster. In the meantime, the navigators
(45) diligently pursued their way for the haven we have mentioned, into which they steered with every appearance of the fearlessness of friends, and the exultation of conquerors.

(50)   A few eager and gratified spectators lined the edges of the small bay, and Barnstable concluded his arrangement for deceiving the enemy, by admonishing his crew that they were now about to enter
(55) on a service that would require their utmost intrepidity and sagacity.

(1823)

22. Tom Coffin does not get rich from this whale because

    (A) he is too depressed
    (B) he lacks sufficient line and tackle
    (C) he is not interested in wealth
    (D) he is misled by the lieutenant
    (E) he is too far from a trading center

23. Tom blames his situation in part on

    (A) the shovel-nosed gentleman
    (B) his lack of position and education
    (C) the lieutenant
    (D) the whale
    (E) Captain Kidd

24. Tom compares himself in lines 13–17 to

    (A) fishing tackle
    (B) a ship in a storm
    (C) the whale
    (D) a whaling ship at work
    (E) Boston Bay

25. When the officer refers to "these rocks and cliffs" (line 19), he means that

    (A) dangerous land formations lie ahead
    (B) the ship is about to wreck
    (C) there are setbacks in Tom's life
    (D) they are going to hit a whale
    (E) the ship is sinking

26. The "shovel-nosed gentlemen" in line 4 are

    (A) the ship's crew
    (B) Tom's friends
    (C) sharks
    (D) visiting royalty
    (E) the ship's officers

27. In what tone of voice does the lieutenant say "you have neglected the Christian's duty of burying your dead" (lines 5–6)?

    (A) Patronizing mockery
    (B) Sarcastic teasing
    (C) Accusatory wrath
    (D) Kind insistence
    (E) Aggressive hostility

28. Tom's misunderstanding (lines 22–23) of the officer's remark (lines 18–21) is ironic because

    (A) Tom did not get to salvage the whale
    (B) the boat was already shipwrecked
    (C) Tom was not really sentimental
    (D) the officer lacked insight into Tom's meaning
    (E) Tom, himself, had been speaking metaphorically

Questions 29–37 are based on the following poem.

> "Come down, O maid, from yonder mountain height.
> What pleasure lives in height (the shepherd sang),
> In height and cold, the splendor of the hills?
> But cease to move so near the heavens and

Line   cease
(5) To glide a sunbeam by the blasted pine,
> To sit a star upon the sparkling spire;
> And come, for Love is of the valley, come,
> For Love is of the valley, come thou down
> And find him; by the happy threshold, he,
(10) Or hand in hand with Plenty in the maize,
> Or red with spirted purple of the vats,
> Or foxlike in the vine; nor cares to walk
> With Death and Morning on the Silver Horns,
> Nor wilt thou snare him in the white ravine,
(15) Nor find him dropped upon the firths of ice,
> That huddling slant in furrow-cloven falls
> To roll the torrent out of dusky doors.
> But follow; let the torrent dance thee down
> To find him in the valley; let the wild
(20) Lean-headed eagles yelp alone, and leave
> The monstrous ledges there to slope, and spill
> Their thousand wreaths of dangling water-smoke,

GO ON TO THE NEXT PAGE.

That like a broken purpose waste in air.
So waste not thou, but come; for all the
    vales
(25) Await thee; azure pillars of the hearth
Arise to thee; the children call, and I
Thy shepherd pipe, and sweet is every
    sound,
Sweeter thy voice, but every sound is sweet;
Myriads of rivulets hurrying thro' the lawn,
(30) The moan of doves in immemorial elms,
And murmuring of innumerable bees."

                                    (ca. 1850)

29. The genre of this poem is called

    (A) a pastoral love lyric
    (B) a pastoral love epic
    (C) a didactic narrative
    (D) a dramatic monologue
    (E) a pastoral elegy

30. The poem is written in

    (A) ballad stanza
    (B) blank verse
    (C) couplets
    (D) forced rhyme
    (E) sonnet form

31. The speaker in the poem can be identified
    through context as

    (A) a young girl
    (B) the mountain
    (C) a shepherd
    (D) the hills
    (E) Love

32. Which of the following is NOT personified
    in the poem?

    (A) Love
    (B) Plenty
    (C) Silver Horns
    (D) Death
    (E) Morning

33. The tone of the speaker's question in lines
    2–3 in the context of the poem is

    (A) condemning
    (B) didactic
    (C) impetuous
    (D) explosive
    (E) conciliatory

34. Lines 7–19 refer to love figuratively, making
    it appear as

    (A) a friend of death
    (B) only a visitor to the mountain
    (C) an angry force in the mountain
    (D) someone living happily in the valley
    (E) the victim of the mountain

35. The speaker sees the "mountain height"
    (line 1) and the "valley" (line 7) as symbolic
    of all the following concepts EXCEPT

    (A) lack of love and love
    (B) unhappiness and happiness
    (C) death and life
    (D) day and night
    (E) cold and warmth

36. In this poem, what is the role of the
    mountain?

    I. A symbol of aloofness
    II. A metaphor of snowy climates
    III. The abstract image of the maid

    (A) I only
    (B) II only
    (C) III only
    (D) I and III only
    (E) I, II, and III

37. The poem's meaning is discerned through several elements of opposition; however, which of the following pairs of words does NOT correctly reflect these elements?

(A) "height" (line 1) and "down" (line 8)
(B) "maid" (line 1) and "height" (line 2)
(C) "blasted" (line 5) and "Plenty" (line 10)
(D) "white" (line 14) and "red" (line 11)
(E) "eagles" (line 20) and "children" (line 26)

Questions 38–42 are based on the following passage.

Seven weeks ago tonight I returned from Europe to report on my meeting with Premier Khrushchev and the others.
Line His grim warnings about the future of the
(5) world, his aide-mémoire on Berlin, his subsequent speeches and threats which he and his agents have launched, and the increase in the Soviet military budget that he has announced have all prompted a
(10) series of decisions by the administration and a series of consultations with the members of the NATO organization. In Berlin, as you recall, he intends to bring to an end, through a stroke of the pen,
(15) first our legal rights to be in West Berlin and secondly our ability to make good on our commitment to the two million free people of that city. That we cannot permit...

(20) ... We are there as a result of our victory over Nazi Germany—and our basic rights to be there deriving from that victory include both our presence in West Berlin and the enjoyment of access across
(25) East Germany. These rights have been repeatedly confirmed and recognized in special agreements with the Soviet Union. Berlin is not a part of East Germany but a separate territory under the control of

(30) the allied powers. Thus our rights there are clear and deep-rooted. But in addition to those rights is our commitment to sustain—and defend, if need be—the opportunity for more than two million people
(35) to determine their own future and choose their own way of life.

Thus, our presence in West Berlin, and our access thereto, cannot be ended by any act of the Soviet government. The
(40) NATO shield was long ago extended to cover West Berlin—and we have given our word that an attack in that city will be regarded as an attack upon us all.

For West Berlin—lying exposed 110
(45) miles inside East Germany, surrounded by Soviet troops and close to Soviet supply lines—has many roles. It is more than a showcase of liberty, a symbol, an island of freedom in a Communist sea. It is even
(50) more than a link with the Free World, a beacon of hope behind the Iron Curtain, an escape hatch for refugees.

West Berlin is all of that. But above all it has now become—as never before—the
(55) great testing place of Western courage and will, a focal point where our solemn commitments stretching back over the years since 1945 and Soviet ambitions now meet in basic confrontation.

(1961)

38. Based on the speaker's tone, the listener should consider the Premier's intent to be

(A) amusing and trivial
(B) aggressive and threatening
(C) committed and respectable
(D) uncontrollable and unstoppable
(E) inevitable and ambitious

GO ON TO THE NEXT PAGE.

39. In this passage, the American relationship to West Berlin is figuratively used to

    (A) imply a David and Goliath situation
    (B) provide stimulus for national unity
    (C) represent American integrity
    (D) explain a lost cause
    (E) reveal a new commitment

40. In the fourth paragraph, all the following are metaphors EXCEPT

    (A) "lying exposed"
    (B) "showcase of liberty"
    (C) "island of freedom in a Communist sea"
    (D) "beacon of hope"
    (E) "an escape hatch for refugees"

41. In line 17, "our commitment" implies

    (A) disagreement within the government
    (B) a future committee referral
    (C) a court order concerning the conflict
    (D) a financial responsibility
    (E) an earlier pledge

42. In line 14, "through a stroke of the pen" is a(n)

    (A) simile, comparing the pen to West Berlin
    (B) metaphor, comparing the pen to America
    (C) understatement, emphasizing the gravity of the situation
    (D) overstatement, making the situation seem less grave
    (E) personification, making the pen seem to have a life of its own

Questions 43–53 are based on the following poem.

> Devoid of reason, thrall to foolish ire,
> I walk and chase a savage fairy still,
> Now near the flood, straight on the mounting hill,

Line   Now midst the woods of youth, and vain
desire.
(5)   For leash I bear a cord of careful grief;
For brach I lead an overforward mind;
My hounds are thoughts, and rage despairing blind,
Pain, cruelty, and care without relief.
But they, perceiving that my swift pursuit
(10)   My flying fairy cannot overtake,
With open mouths their prey on me do make,
Like hungry hounds that lately lost their suit,
And full of fury on their master feed,
To hasten on my hapless death with speed.

(1593)

43. Using the more specific word "hounds" (line 7) rather than the more general word "dogs" has which of these effects?

    (A) Emphasizes that they hunt prey
    (B) Illustrates the speaker's sense of drama
    (C) Varies the tone of the poem
    (D) Symbolizes all predators
    (E) Reinforces a sense of grief

44. The hounds in the poem are best set forth as

    (A) a savage fairy
    (B) the speaker's angry thoughts
    (C) the speaker's troubled thoughts
    (D) death
    (E) reason

45. The meaning of "an overforward mind" (line 6) can be seen in the paraphrase

    (A) mentally unstable
    (B) a mind ahead of its time
    (C) precocious
    (D) overactive thoughts
    (E) politically active

46. The phrase "thrall to foolish ire" (line 1), as used in the poem, is mirrored by which of these phrases?

    (A) Seeking fool's gold
    (B) A slave to rash anger
    (C) Desiring vengeance
    (D) Escaped from an asylum
    (E) A man too angry to think clearly

47. The central argument of the poem is that

    (A) the speaker is insane
    (B) the speaker is a sportsman
    (C) an angry enemy is killing the speaker
    (D) anger is self-destructive
    (E) anger is therapeutic

48. By considering the poem in its entirety, the reader should view the speaker's attitude toward the fairy as

    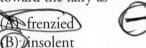

    (A) frenzied
    (B) insolent
    (C) reverential
    (D) derisive
    (E) laudable

49. The role of lines 13–14 in terms of the rest of the poem can be summarized by which of these statements?

    (A) They intensify the speaker's sense of justice.
    (B) They summarize the irony of the speaker's situation.
    (C) They signal a departure from the subject.
    (D) They intensify the falsity of the speaker's words.
    (E) They threaten the position of the fairy established in lines 2 and 10.

50. Lines 13–14 contain which of the following phonic devices?

    (A) Echo rhyme
    (B) Eye rhyme
    (C) Imperfect rhyme
    (D) Onomatopoeia
    (E) Alliteration

51. Lines 9–10 are pivotal to the meaning of the poem because which of the following happens?

    (A) Anger is made more intense.
    (B) The speaker's position changes from attacker to victim.
    (C) The hounds become real.
    (D) The speaker's position changes from fear to anger.
    (E) The fairy is caught.

52. The meaning of the poem is structurally contrasted between lines 1–8 and lines 9–14. This contrast is NOT seen in the words

    (A) "chase" (line 2) and "cannot overtake" (line 10)
    (B) "I lead" (line 6) and "they, perceiving" (line 9)
    (C) "foolish ire" (line 1) and "hapless death" (line 14)
    (D) "savage fairy" (line 2) and "hungry hounds" (line 12)
    (E) "flood" (line 3) and "speed" (line 14)

53. The hounds' attack in lines 9–14 is symbolically ironic because

    (A) the hounds are not really dogs
    (B) dogs do not really chase fairies
    (C) hunting dogs seldom turn on their masters
    (D) the speaker has already confessed to his lack of reason
    (E) the speaker's own angry thoughts are destroying him

Questions 54–60 are based on the following passage.

> *Lusus animo debent aliquando dari,*
> *Ad cogitandum melior ut redeat sibi.*
> —*Phædrus* "Fables," xiv. 5.

Line
(5)   The mind ought sometimes to be diverted, that it may return the better to thinking.

GO ON TO THE NEXT PAGE.

I do not know whether to call the following letter a satire upon coquettes, or a
(10) representation of their several fantastical accomplishments, or what other title to give it; but, as it is, I shall communicate it to the public. It will sufficiently explain its own intentions, so that I shall give it my reader at length, without either pref-
(15) ace or postscript:

"MR. SPECTATOR:

"Women are armed with fans as men with swords, and sometimes do more execution with them. To the end therefore
(20) that ladies may be entire mistresses of the weapons which they bear, I have erected an academy for the training up of young women in the exercise of the fan, according to the most fashionable airs and
(25) motions that are now practised at court. The ladies who carry fans under me are drawn up twice a day in my great hall, where they are instructed in the use of their arms, and exercised by the following
(30) words of command:—Handle your fans, Unfurl your fans, Discharge your fans, Ground your fans, Recover your fans, Flutter your fans. By the right observation of these few plain words of command, a
(35) woman of a tolerable genius, who will apply herself diligently to her exercise for the space of but one half-year, shall be able to give her fan all the graces that can possibly enter into that little modish
(40) machine.

"But to the end that my readers may form to themselves a right notion of this exercise, I beg leave to explain it to them in all its parts. When my female regiment
(45) is drawn up in array, with everyone her weapon in her hand, upon my giving the word to handle their fans, each of them shakes her fan at me with a smile, then gives her right-hand woman a tap upon

(50) the shoulder, then presses her lips with the extremity of her fan, then lets her arms fall in an easy motion, and stands in readiness to receive the next word of command. All this is done with a closed fan,
(55) and is generally learned in the first week...."

(1712)

54. What is the main idea of this selection?

(A) Ladies should never use fans without training.
(B) Fans are deadly weapons in the hands of ladies.
(C) Letters to *The Spectator* are highly edited.
(D) Ladies can be trained to use fans just as men are trained to use swords.
(E) Fans are beautiful when used properly.

55. The effect of the narrator's comments about the letter (lines 7–15) is to

(A) prepare the readers for a shock
(B) reveal the absurdity of the notion of training ladies to use fans
(C) communicate that the letter is self-explanatory
(D) present an alternative view from that of the letter
(E) change the topic in contrast to that of the letter

56. For the letter to be "a satire upon coquettes" (line 8), the writer's attitude toward ladies and their uses of fans would have to be

(A) ironic sadness
(B) a blend of hate and revenge
(C) a blend of humor and censor
(D) inspired sarcasm
(E) a blend of defiance and resistance

Explanations: Practice Test One

> **NOTE:** Most practice tests cannot duplicate the content and conditions of the actual Literature test. Also, the scope and definitions of the literary elements can differ among literary critics; therefore, the rationale behind what constitutes a correct or an incorrect answer choice may vary. Each of these practice tests, however, gives you an opportunity to analyze selections, think critically, and develop your test-taking skills so you can do your personal best on the SAT Subject Test in Literature.

1. **(D)** Although Fred might no longer trust Mr. Farebrother (line 16), lines 30–34 indicate that Mrs. Garth said things about Mary and Mr. Farebrother that may or may not be true, in other words, gossip.

2. **(B)** He felt he had a rival (jealous); he would not give her up for her good (selfish).

3. **(E)** A contrast is made: If the fight is not muscular (physical), it must be mental.

4. **(A)** The context of this entire selection concerns Fred's character or nature, not his money.

5. **(C)** Fred's feelings are the context: They are hurt or injured.

6. **(B)** A knife in the back, a blade in the heart: These are classic metaphors that compare emotional pain caused by others to the pain of a knife blade.

7. **(A)** Context eliminates B, C, and D. Does Fred *really* love Mary? Perhaps not, but he thinks he is "in love" enough to fight for her (E). His "light hopeful nature," however, is being challenged with feelings of jealousy, insecurity, and pain.

8. **(E)** Context contradicts or does not support answer choices A–D. Although not directly stated, the overall tone of the passage indicates that Fred's pride is hurt, implying that he is somewhat egotistical.

9. **(B)** The entire poem is an extended analogy, comparing love and Forget-me-nots (line 21). In this comparison, love's brevity (line 1), death (line 18), and freedom (line 11) are mentioned, but taken together as a whole, the subject is the nature of love.

10. **(C)** You may not know that the iris flower is called a flag; however, context eliminates B, D, and E. In company with Forget-me-nots, meadowsweet, and rushes, flags are flowers, not weeds.

11. **(C)** Again, context provides the answer. A bad taste or smell would ruin the beauty described. To grow "in rows" (IV) contradicts growing free.

12. **(D)** A curb borders a flower bed, restraining growth.

13. **(D)** By eliminating the obviously incorrect answers, D and E remain. Although the speaker is passionate about her subject, this rhetorical question does not address the passion of love. It does, however, establish the comparison of growing love to raising Forget-me-nots.

14. **(E)** Note lines 1–3, 10–14, and 21: "Love is not taught…, not parcelled out by rule:… So free must be Forget-me-not."

15. **(B)** Lines 4–9 describe Forget-me-nots, lines 10–21, love. Line 13 is pivotal to the metaphoric or implied comparison of love to Forget-me-nots.

16. **(C)** Notice lines 10–11: The speaker believes love is not taught and is not subject to rules; both love and Forget-me-nots should grow "free" without restraints.

17. **(E)** These questions are rhetorical by definition. The speaker is making a point, not expecting an answer.

18. **(D)** The central contrast is restraint (lines 10–12) versus unrestraint (lines 5–6) of flowers and love. The emphasis of this contrast supports the speaker's view that love is and should be free of restraints.

19. **(B)** A simile makes a comparison using "like" or "as."

20. **(A)** She loves "its growth at large and free" (line 4), not "By measure" (line 3).

    Note: Technically, the speaker says that Forget-me-nots should be unrestrained like love is unrestrained, making love (an abstract concept) the vehicle and flowers (a concrete thing) the tenor. Usually, the concrete expression is used to describe an abstract idea. This reversal is a way to strengthen her argument, an assumption that love naturally should be unrestrained.

21. **(A)** In line 1, "Change and rot" indicate destruction, so we raise flowers (or figuratively love) in a garden-plot (or restrained environment).

22. **(E)** That if he were in Boston Bay, he would get rich from the whale (lines 8–10) implies that he is too far from a port.

23. **(B)** He claims "riches and honor are for the great and the larned," not for him (lines 11–13).

24. **(B)** A ship has tackle or rigging and spars (to support the sails). The "gale of life" compares his life to a storm.

25. **(C)** The officer continues Tom's analogy, calling his troubles "rocks and cliffs."

26. **(C)** Lines 27–28 identify the "shovel-nosed gentlemen" as sharks.

27. **(B)** Context does not support that the officer is patronizing, wrathful, kind, or hostile. He is teasing Tom in lines 18–21, and personification of the sharks ("shovel-nosed gentlemen") sets a sarcastic tone.

28. **(E)** The officer's teasing is based on Tom's own use of figurative language in lines 13–17. For Tom to suddenly become "literal" is ironic.

29. **(A)** This poem does not tell a story (C), is not an elegy or lament over someone's death (E), and obviously is not part of an epic. You might be tempted with answer choice D, but the shepherd (line 27) and subject (love) make it a pastoral love lyric.

30. **(B)** Blank verse is written in iambic pentameter, with no rhyme scheme.

31. **(C)** Line 2 identifies the speaker as "the shepherd."

32. **(C)** Love (line 8) goes "hand in hand with Plenty" (line 10), but does not walk / with Death and Morning (lines 12–13). Where do they walk? "on the Silver Horns" (line 13).

33. **(E)** The shepherd tries to win over the Maid, echoing "come" in lines 1, 7, and 8.

34. **(D)** Love is "of the valley" (line 8) and "happy" (line 9).

35. **(D)** The "mountain height" symbolizes lack of love, because "Love is of the valley" (line 8). It also represents unhappiness because "What pleasure lives in height?" (line 2), implying that the valley symbolizes pleasure or happiness. Line 13 places Death and Morning (a pun: mourning) on the mountain, which represents cold (lines 3 and 15). The sunbeam does "glide… by the blasted pine" on the mountain; however, the valley does not represent the night (D).

36. **(A)** No comparison (metaphor) is being made, and the mountain is where the maid dwells, not an image of her. The mountain is a traditional symbol representing aloofness: cold.

37. **(B)** Establishing the central contrast will help you: the contrast of mountains (representing cold, aloofness, death) and the valley (warmth, love, and life). In this poem, the maid is currently on the mountain height.

38. **(B)** The Premier's words are called "grim warnings" and "threats."

39. **(C)** The speaker calls West Berlin "the great testing place of Western courage" as it relates to "our solemn commitments" (last paragraph), in other words, elements of integrity (keeping one's word even if conflict results).

40. **(A)** The metaphors in this paragraph compare West Berlin to a showcase, an island, a beacon, and an escape hatch.

41. **(E)** That a pledge had been made previously is confirmed in lines 41–43: "…we have given our word…."

42. **(C)** That two super powers could come to war as the result of "a stroke of the pen" is an understatement of the severity of the action based on its consequences.

43. **(A)** The hounds turn the speaker into prey (line 11). Generally, hounds are hunting dogs.

44. **(B)** Line 7 directly expresses the metaphor. He compares his thoughts to hounds.

45. **(D)** At first glance, "Devoid of reason" (line 1) supports answer choice A. However, a forward mind is bold, eager, moving ahead. To be overforward would be to have thoughts that race ahead. Note: a "brach" is an archaic word for female hound. Context should lead you to the correct answer, however, without knowing the definition of "brach."

46. **(B)** Although E fits the poem's general meaning, B contains the synonyms for each word in the phrase.

47. **(D)** The subject? The speaker's anger. His point? His own angry thoughts, like hounds, are consuming him (line 13).

48. **(A)** He walks and chases the "savage fairy" (line 2). Later, the metaphor shifts to the hound image in lines 6–7, but his attitude remains constant: he is frenzied almost to the point of insanity to overtake the "flying fairy" (line 10), "Devoid of reason."

49. **(B)** The concluding couplet of a sonnet often serves to summarize. The irony? He is "master" of his own angry thoughts, yet they are killing him.

50. **(E)** The repetition of "f" and "h" is alliterative.

51. **(B)** From lines 1 to 6, the speaker chases, bears, and leads. When he admits he cannot overtake his fairy, he becomes the victim of his angry thoughts (hounds).

52. **(E)** Neither "flood" nor "speed" relate to the change from attacker in lines 1–8 to victim in lines 9–14.

53. **(E)** The speaker's condition is an example of situational irony, in which his very own thoughts have become "hungry hounds" that feed on their master.

54. **(D)** The entire selection is based on an extended simile comparing the use of fans to the use of swords.

55. **(C)** The narrator/editor directly states in lines 12–15 that he is presenting the article without editorial comment because "it will sufficiently explain its own intentions...."

56. **(C)** Notice in lines 4–6 the narrator's comment: he views the article as a mental diversion so that "it [the mind] may return the better to thinking." Also, the narrator indulges in a somewhat comical play on words in lines 9–10, calling the "accomplishments" of coquettes "<u>fan</u>tastical." The definition of satire (a work that makes a subject look ridiculous to make a point, often one of censor) points to the correct answer.

57. **(B)** The narrator confesses not to know (line 7) what to call such a letter and purposely removes himself from directly commenting on its contents. Yet, he indirectly expresses his point of view by calling the letter a satire, using a play on words (line 9), and labeling it a mental diversion in lines 4–6. These elements convey a tone with a critical edge.

58. **(E)** The extended simile comparing women's use of fans to men's use of swords is quite imaginative. The description of the exercise drills is especially detailed and colorful.

59. **(D)** The tenor of the simile is women's use of fans. The writer uses men's training and skills with swords as the vehicle, the means to explain his point. He sarcastically views fans in the hands of women as "weapons" (line 21); therefore, the women require training.

60. **(B)** Lines 4–5 directly states the correct answer.

Titles and Authors of Selections in Test One

Answer Sheet
PRACTICE TEST TWO

1 (A) (B) (C) (D) (E)
2 (A) (B) (C) (D) (E)
3 (A) (B) (C) (D) (E)
4 (A) (B) (C) (D) (E)
5 (A) (B) (C) (D) (E)
6 (A) (B) (C) (D) (E)
7 (A) (B) (C) (D) (E)
8 (A) (B) (C) (D) (E)
9 (A) (B) (C) (D) (E)
10 (A) (B) (C) (D) (E)
11 (A) (B) (C) (D) (E)
12 (A) (B) (C) (D) (E)
13 (A) (B) (C) (D) (E)
14 (A) (B) (C) (D) (E)
15 (A) (B) (C) (D) (E)

16 (A) (B) (C) (D) (E)
17 (A) (B) (C) (D) (E)
18 (A) (B) (C) (D) (E)
19 (A) (B) (C) (D) (E)
20 (A) (B) (C) (D) (E)
21 (A) (B) (C) (D) (E)
22 (A) (B) (C) (D) (E)
23 (A) (B) (C) (D) (E)
24 (A) (B) (C) (D) (E)
25 (A) (B) (C) (D) (E)
26 (A) (B) (C) (D) (E)
27 (A) (B) (C) (D) (E)
28 (A) (B) (C) (D) (E)
29 (A) (B) (C) (D) (E)
30 (A) (B) (C) (D) (E)

31 (A) (B) (C) (D) (E)
32 (A) (B) (C) (D) (E)
33 (A) (B) (C) (D) (E)
34 (A) (B) (C) (D) (E)
35 (A) (B) (C) (D) (E)
36 (A) (B) (C) (D) (E)
37 (A) (B) (C) (D) (E)
38 (A) (B) (C) (D) (E)
39 (A) (B) (C) (D) (E)
40 (A) (B) (C) (D) (E)
41 (A) (B) (C) (D) (E)
42 (A) (B) (C) (D) (E)
43 (A) (B) (C) (D) (E)
44 (A) (B) (C) (D) (E)
45 (A) (B) (C) (D) (E)

46 (A) (B) (C) (D) (E)
47 (A) (B) (C) (D) (E)
48 (A) (B) (C) (D) (E)
49 (A) (B) (C) (D) (E)
50 (A) (B) (C) (D) (E)
51 (A) (B) (C) (D) (E)
52 (A) (B) (C) (D) (E)
53 (A) (B) (C) (D) (E)
54 (A) (B) (C) (D) (E)
55 (A) (B) (C) (D) (E)
56 (A) (B) (C) (D) (E)
57 (A) (B) (C) (D) (E)
58 (A) (B) (C) (D) (E)
59 (A) (B) (C) (D) (E)
60 (A) (B) (C) (D) (E)

Practice Test Two

TIME ALLOWED: ONE HOUR

Directions: The following questions test your understanding of several literary selections. Read each passage or poem and the questions that follow it. Select the best answer choice for each question by blackening the matching oval on your answer sheet. **Special attention should be given to questions containing the following words: EXCEPT, LEAST, NOT.**

Questions 1–12 are based on the following poem.

The Spring

Now that the winter's gone, the earth hath lost
Her snow-white robes, and now no more the frost
Candies the grass, or casts an icy cream
Line Upon the silver lake or crystal stream;
(5) But the warm sun thaws the benumbèd earth,
And makes it tender; gives a sacred birth
To the dead swallow; wakes in hollow tree
The drowsy cuckoo and the humble-bee.
Now do a choir of chirping minstrels bring
(10) In triumph to the world the youthful spring.
The valleys, hills, and woods in rich array
Welcome the coming of the longed-for May.
Now all things smile, only my love doth lour;
Nor hath the scalding noonday sun the power
(15) To melt that marble ice, which still doth hold
Her heart congealed, and makes her pity cold.
The ox, which lately did for shelter fly
Into the stall, doth now securely lie
In open fields; and love no more is made
(20) By the fireside, but in the cooler shade
Amyntas now doth with his Chloris sleep

Under a sycamore, and all things keep
Time with the season; only she doth carry
June in her eyes, in her heart January.

(ca. 1620)

1. The relationship between "my love" in line 13 and the "earth" in line 1 can be seen in the relationship of

   (A) "grass" (line 3) and "fields" (line 19)
   (B) "ice" (line 15) and "congealed" (line 16)
   (C) "May" (line 12) and "June" (line 24)
   (D) "hollow tree" (line 7) and "shelter" (line 17)
   (E) "cold" (line 16) and "warm" (line 5)

2. Given the context of the poem, the ox most likely went to shelter in lines 17–19 because it

   (A) was startled by the bee in line 8
   (B) was avoiding the "scalding noonday sun" (line 14)
   (C) was fleeing winter storms
   (D) was seeking "cooler shade" (line 20)
   (E) was afraid of the cold-hearted lover

3. In the final line, the incongruity that "she doth carry June in her eyes, in her heart January" implies that

 (A) her looks are deceptive
 (B) she suffers from poor vision
 (C) she really does enjoy spring
 (D) her actions cover a warm personality
 (E) she dislikes cold weather

4. In its context, "smile" (line 13) makes nature seem

 (A) repugnant and loathsome
 (B) jubilant and responsive
 (C) aesthetic and unrestrained
 (D) wary and deliberate
 (E) impetuous and audacious

5. In the context of the poem as a whole, the speaker has an attitude toward "my love" (line 13) that is projecting

 (A) critical discrimination
 (B) cautious prudence
 (C) undaunted daring
 (D) angry impatience
 (E) apprehensive trepidation

6. In lines 14–16, what literary device is used to describe the coldness of her heart?

 (A) Allegory
 (B) Hyperbole
 (C) Caricature
 (D) Simile
 (E) Interior monologue

7. The synaesthesia of "melt that marble ice" appeals to which of the following senses?

 (A) Thermal, tactile, and visual
 (B) Thermal, aural, and kinesthetic
 (C) Gustatory, thermal, and tactile
 (D) Kinesthetic, olfactory, and visual
 (E) Tactile, visual, and gustatory

8. The poem contains a contrast that can be seen in all the following pairs EXCEPT

 (A) "snow-white robes"…"no more the frost" (line 2)
 (B) "the warm sun"…"the benumbèd earth" (line 5)
 (C) "makes"…"gives" (line 6)
 (D) "dead"…"wakes" (line 7)
 (E) "smile"…"lour" (line 13)

9. The poem can be called

 (A) a pastoral sonnet
 (B) a celebration of spring
 (C) an ode to spring
 (D) a comparison and contrast of the seasons
 (E) an expression of frustration by a daunted lover

10. "Dead" (line 7) contextually means all the following EXCEPT

 (A) barren
 (B) unproductive
 (C) cold
 (D) unfruitful
 (E) unerring

11. As used in this poem, June and January (line 24) figuratively represent all the following EXCEPT

 (A) elements of personality
 (B) months of the year
 (C) warmth and coldness
 (D) change and resistance to change
 (E) new growth and dormancy

12. "Candies" in line 3 means

 (A) to preserve
 (B) to sweeten
 (C) to cover
 (D) to crystallize
 (E) to congeal

Questions 13–23 are based on the following passage.

"Are you mad, old man?" demanded Sir Edmund Andros, in loud and harsh tones. "How dare you stay the march of King
Line James's Governor?"

(5)   "I have stayed the march of a King himself, ere now," replied the gray figure, with stern composure. "I am here, Sir Governor, because the cry of an oppressed people hath disturbed me in my secret place; and
(10) beseeching this favor earnestly of the Lord, it was vouchsafed me to appear once again on earth, in the good old cause of his saints. And what speak ye of James? There is no longer a Popish tyrant on the throne
(15) of England, and by tomorrow noon, his name shall be a byword in this very street, where ye would make it a word of terror. Back, thou that wast a Governor, back! With this night thy power is ended—
(20) to–morrow, the prison!—back, lest I foretell the scaffold!"

The people had been drawing nearer and nearer, and drinking in the words of their champion, who spoke in accents long
(25) disused, like one unaccustomed to converse, except with the dead of many years ago. But his voice stirred their souls. They confronted the soldiers, not wholly without arms, and ready to convert the very
(30) stones of the street into deadly weapons. Sir Edmund Andros looked at the old man; then he cast his hard and cruel eye over the multitude, and beheld them burning that lurid wrath, so difficult to kindle or to
(35) quench; and again he fixed his gaze on the aged form, which stood obscurely in an open space, where neither friend nor foe had thrust himself. What were his thoughts, he uttered no word which might
(40) discover. But whether the oppressor were overawed by the Gray Champion's look, or perceived his peril in the threatening attitude of the people, it is certain that he gave back, and ordered his soldiers to com-
(45) mence a slow and guarded retreat. Before another sunset, the Governor, and all that rode so proudly with him, were prisoners, and long ere it was known that James had abdicated, King William was proclaimed
(50) throughout New England.

(ca. 1825–1842)

13. The tone of "'I have stayed the march of a King himself, ere now'" (lines 5–6) makes the Gray Champion seem

(A) audacious and in rapport
(B) unyielding and conniving
(C) propitious and conducive
(D) challenging and defiant
(E) indulgent and acquiescent

14. Contextually, "stay" in line 3 is a way of saying

(A) to hinder
(B) to wait
(C) to quell
(D) to await
(E) to endure

15. Another way of saying "drinking in" (line 23) is

(A) imbibing liquid
(B) absorbing mentally
(C) swallowing hard
(D) swallowing liquor
(E) toasting

16. Sir Edmund Andros's character in this passage seems as one who is

(A) a cynic
(B) a benefactor
(C) unmercifully cruel
(D) compassionately natured
(E) sympathetic

GO ON TO THE NEXT PAGE.

17. The identity of the Gray Champion can be surmised from this passage to be

    (A) a respected townsman
    (B) well known in the area
    (C) used to public speaking
    (D) too old to fight in the battle
    (E) a mysterious figure

18. Below is a list of statements concerning the passage. All are supported by the context EXCEPT that the

    (A) narrative is at a point of climax
    (B) main character is the Gray Champion
    (C) villain is Sir Edmund Andros
    (D) tone is comical
    (E) tone is patriotic

19. Which of these literary devices is used in lines 14–15?

    (A) Rhetorical question
    (B) Sarcasm
    (C) Foreshadowing
    (D) Satire
    (E) Paradox

20. In lines 13–21, the Gray Champion implies that

    (A) the Governor will escape
    (B) the current king should be respected
    (C) he is afraid
    (D) he can influence future events
    (E) retreat is his only option

21. The Gray Champion's tone in lines 13–21 is

    (A) stolid
    (B) placid
    (C) nonchalant
    (D) indulgent
    (E) threatening

22. Of what significance are the words "ere" (line 6), "ye" (lines 13, 17), "thou" (line 18), and "wast" (line 18)?

    (A) They indicate the time and place of the origin of the speaker.
    (B) They satirize the usual language of the period.
    (C) They imply that the speaker is unbalanced.
    (D) They are the same diction used by the townspeople.
    (E) They suggest that the Gray Champion is German.

23. In line 34, "so difficult to kindle" implies that

    (A) the people do not really care
    (B) the people were incited against their natures
    (C) the people have endured much cruelty
    (D) the people will not continue to be angry
    (E) the people are really on Sir Edmund's side

Questions 24–32 are based on the following poem.

Poems from the Passionate Pilgrim

Fair is my love, but not so fair as fickle;
Mild as a dove, but neither true nor trusty;
Brighter than glass, and yet, as glass is, brittle;
Line   Softer than wax, and yet, as iron, rusty:
(5)   A lily pale, with damask dye to grace her,
      None fairer, nor none falser to deface her.

Her lips to mine how often hath she joined,
Between each kiss her oaths of true love swearing!
How many tales to please me hath she coined,

(10) Dreading my love, the loss thereof still
      fearing!
    Yet in the midst of all her pure
      protestings,
      Her faith, her oaths, her tears, and
        all were jestings.
    She burnt with love, as straw with fire
      flameth,
    She burnt out love, as soon as straw
      out-burneth;
(15) She framed the love, and yet she foiled
      the framing,
    She bade love last, and yet she fell
      a-turning.
    Was this a lover, or a lecher whether?
    Bad in the best, though excellent in
      neither.

                            (ca. 1599)

24. Line 15 is structured as elements

    (A) that understate the case
    (B) in antithesis
    (C) that overstate the case
    (D) of a narrative poem
    (E) of a riddle

25. Which of the following literary devices is
    used in line l?

    (A) Alliteration
    (B) Apostrophe
    (C) Catastrophe
    (D) Forced rhyme
    (E) Metaphor

26. This poem's meaning includes a central con-
    trast that is reinforced by all the following
    pairs EXCEPT

    (A) "Fair"…"fickle" (line 1)
    (B) "fairer"…"falser" (line 6)
    (C) "lips"…"joined" (line 7)
    (D) "burnt with love"…"burnt out love"
        (lines 13–14)
    (E) "lover"…"lecher" (line 17)

27. "She foiled the framing" (line 15) deals with

    (A) the speaker's falsifying of love's
        evidence
    (B) destruction of property
    (C) painted picture frames
    (D) allegorical figures of fine art
    (E) her thwarting of the very love she
        devised

28. The relationship of her dread of the
    speaker's love to her fear of losing it in line
    10 is an example of a(n)

    (A) litote
    (B) paradox
    (C) oxymoron
    (D) malapropism
    (E) induction

29. Which of the following is the best descrip-
    tion of the overall structural development of
    the theme in this poem?

    (A) The poem is a narrative epic.
    (B) The speaker compares, then contrasts,
        and finally praises his lover.
    (C) The speaker develops a series of com-
        pliments and criticisms.
    (D) The poem is a trilogy of love lyrics.
    (E) The speaker and his lover engage in
        dialogue.

30. In line 12, "all were jestings" projects an
    attitude of

    (A) disillusionment
    (B) congeniality
    (C) intimacy
    (D) devotion
    (E) isolation

31. Which of the answers listed identifies the
    literary device used to describe the speaker's
    lover in lines 2–4 and 13?

    (A) Simile
    (B) Metaphor
    (C) Personification
    (D) Synecdoche
    (E) Metonymy

GO ON TO THE NEXT PAGE.

32. The literary device used in lines 10 and 15–16 is

    (A) cacophony
    (B) dissonance
    (C) symbolism
    (D) mock heroism
    (E) irony

Questions 33–42 are based on the following passage.

The rational intercourse kept up by conversation is one of our principal distinctions from brutes. We should therefore
Line endeavor to turn this peculiar talent to
(5) our advantage, and consider the organs of speech as the instruments of understanding: we should be very careful not to use them as the weapons of vice, or tools of folly, and do our utmost to unlearn any
(10) trivial or ridiculous habits, which tend to lessen the value of such an inestimable prerogative. It is, indeed, imagined by some philosophers, that even birds and beasts (though without the power of
(15) articulation) perfectly understand one another by the sounds they utter; and that dogs, cats, etc., have each a particular language to themselves, like different nations. Thus it may be supposed that the
(20) nightingales of Italy have as fine an ear for their own native woodnotes as any signor or signora for an Italian air; that the boars of Westphalia gruntle as expressively through the nose as the inhabitants in
(25) High German: and that the frogs in the dykes of Holland croak as intelligibly as the natives jabber their Low Dutch. However this may be, we may consider those whose tongues hardly seem to be
(30) under the influence of reason, and do not keep up the proper conversation of human creatures, as imitating the language of different animals. Thus, for instance, the affinity between Chatterers

(35) and Monkeys, and Praters and Parrots, is too obvious not to occur at once; Grunters and Growlers may be justly compared to Hogs; Snarlers are Curs that continually show their teeth, but never
(40) bite; and the Spitfire passionate are a sort of wild cats that will not bear stroking, but will purr when they are pleased. Complainers are Screech-Owls; and Story-tellers, always repeating the same
(45) dull note, are Cuckoos. Poets that prick up their ears at their own hideous braying are no better than Asses. Critics in general are venomous Serpents that delight in hissing, and some of them who have got
(50) by heart a few technical terms without knowing their meaning are no other than Magpies. I myself, who have crowed to the whole town for near three years past, may perhaps put my readers in mind of a
(55) Barnyard Cock; but as I must acquaint them that they will hear the last of me on this day fortnight, I hope they will then consider me as a Swan, who is supposed to sing sweetly at his dying moments.

(1780)

33. The main idea in the selection is that

    (A) people who do not use proper conversation are like animals
    (B) animals can talk
    (C) insults can be effective forms of communication
    (D) philosophers believe that animals communicate
    (E) animals have nationalities

34. The selection is structured in part on

    (A) cause and effect
    (B) analogy
    (C) chronological sequence
    (D) spatial sequence
    (E) induction

35. The speaker's attitude concerning those who "do not keep up the proper conversation" (lines 30–31) is revealed as one of

  (A) admiration
  (B) complacency
  (C) intolerance
  (D) amusement
  (E) hypocrisy

36. When the speaker calls critics "Serpents" (line 48), the tone can be seen as

  (A) ironic
  (B) laudatory
  (C) defiant
  (D) concordant
  (E) circumspect

37. The speaker wants his readers to think of him as

  (A) severe
  (B) restrictive
  (C) lenient
  (D) profound
  (E) self-determined

38. The literary device used in lines 57–59 is a

  (A) metonymy
  (B) simile
  (C) punch line
  (D) digression
  (E) metaphor

39. The word "instruments" (line 6) is used to mean all these concepts EXCEPT

  (A) the means to do something
  (B) tools
  (C) sound devices
  (D) formal documents
  (E) implements

40. In line 12, "imagined" suggests that

  (A) the speaker is having a delusion
  (B) philosophers do not really understand animal language
  (C) the speaker does not believe animals understand their own language
  (D) animals never talk under any circumstances
  (E) philosophers consider animals to be mute

41. Structurally, the sentence in lines 28–33 marks

  (A) a shift in tense
  (B) a progression from imagination to reason
  (C) a contrast in thought
  (D) an emphasis on conditional points
  (E) a reversal in thought

42. As used in lines 11–12, "an inestimable prerogative" is best understood as

  (A) an advantage too great to appreciate fully
  (B) a diminishing skill
  (C) a series of questions that cannot be answered
  (D) unbreakable habits of speech
  (E) habits that take priority over others

Questions 43–51 are based on the following poem.

> Somewhere or other there must surely be
>   The face not seen, the voice not heard,
> The heart that not yet—never yet—ah me!
> *Line*   Made answer to my word.
> *(5)* Somewhere or other, may be near or far;
>   Past land and sea, clean out of sight;
> Beyond the wandering moon, beyond the star
>   That tracks her night by night.
> Somewhere or other, may be far or near;
> *(10)*   With just a wall, a hedge, between;
> With just the last leaves of the dying year
>   Fallen on a turf grown green.

(1866)

GO ON TO THE NEXT PAGE.

43. The use of "—never yet—ah me!" in line 3

    (A) renders the speaker's emotion more intense
    (B) illustrates the speaker's lack of communicative skills
    (C) suggests that someone is listening
    (D) implies that no one is really there
    (E) introduces a new thought

44. The speaker's feelings toward "The face" in line 2 project a sense of

    (A) hostility
    (B) longing
    (C) incredulity
    (D) anxiety
    (E) authority

45. As used in this poem, the "heart" (line 3) serves as

    (A) the main point of an argument
    (B) the center of emotions
    (C) an organ that pumps blood
    (D) courage
    (E) memorization

46. Of the following representative pairs of words, which mirrors the contrast between the second and third stanzas?

    (A) reliable …unreliable
    (B) uncertain …certain
    (C) attainable …unattainable
    (D) distant …close
    (E) desolate …inviting

47. In its context, "tracks" (line 8) implies that the star

    (A) marks the sky at night
    (B) is a sportsman
    (C) is hunting
    (D) is seeking the speaker's love
    (E) leads the way

48. What is the result of the use of "grown green" in line 12?

    (A) It contrasts life against the death in line 11.
    (B) It summarizes the meaning of the poem.
    (C) It emphasizes the speaker's hopelessness.
    (D) It suggests that the turf lacks proper care.
    (E) It combines a sense of freedom with care.

49. In the poem, the "face…voice…heart" (lines 2–3) is

    I. a synecdoche representing an unknown person
    II. a metaphor for lost people
    III. a symbol of being alone

    (A) I only
    (B) II only
    (C) III only
    (D) II and III only
    (E) I, II, and III

50. The poem's theme deals with

    (A) roaming to far places
    (B) the importance of a home
    (C) strangers in strange places
    (D) reconciliation with an estranged person
    (E) the existence of a person that the speaker has never met

51. What is the consequence of "near or far" (line 5) and "far or near" (line 9)?

    (A) The reversal interrupts the rhyme scheme.

    (B) The diction places emphasis on the metrical patterns.

    (C) The reversal implies confusion of the speaker.

    (D) The syntactical arrangement places emphasis on "far" in the second stanza and on "near" in the third stanza.

    (E) The syntactical arrangement places emphasis on "near" in the second stanza and on "far" in the third stanza.

Questions 52–60 are based on the following passage.

When my four brothers and I were children, our parents encouraged us to pursue personal projects. My brothers
Line had acquired a skep of honey bees as one
(5) of our wonderful ventures. Honey bees are known as *social* bees and are considered very beneficial because they pollinate vegetable gardens, fruit trees, flowers, and many farm crops, such as clover. Some
(10) amateur beekeepers call their standard wooden hives *bee skeps,* although a "skep" is a special dome-shaped hive made of interwoven straw instead of wood. My brothers were busy with many things, and
(15) I found that I became fascinated with this new project. I was a teenager at the time, and this new interest delighted me. I was very happy that I had made friends with the bees.

(20) One of my projects was bringing ferns and violets from the woods and planting them in the area beneath the front window of the house. The skep of bees had been conveniently located across the
(25) driveway beside my favorite flower bed. By the end of summer, I had removed several delicious combs of honey; and on an

especially beautiful morning, I was about to remove another tempting honeycomb.

(30) The beehive was a square box with a small hole at the lower front edge for the bees to gain entrance. The combs hung down into the box and were removed through the top. My beekeeping downfall
(35) was the result of the covering that prevented rain from entering the hive. This was a single sheet of roofing tin about one foot longer on each side than the size of the box. In the center on the top had been
(40) placed a large rock sufficient in weight to hold the tin in place. I had to remove the rock; the resulting sound was a shot-like blast that must have reverberated through the beehive with such a force that it star-
(45) tled the bees. Before I could realize what had happened, the entire colony of bees attacked me. They settled right on my head, stinging fiercely. When a bee attacks, its muscles force a stinger into
(50) the flesh to pump poison into the victim. Barbs on the stinger hold it tightly in the flesh; the stinger is pulled from the bee's body and the bee soon dies. Of course, I began to scream.

(55) My mother heard my screams and was shocked to see the seething balloon of bees my head had become. My life was saved when God gave her the presence of mind to know what to do in this critical
(60) moment. My mother had been watering flowers nearby and quickly doused my head with a bucket of water. She continued to throw water on me with as much force as possible to dislodge the bees and
(65) managed to pull me into the house. She received a number of stings herself and cried in sympathy as she picked the stingers out of my face, neck, ears, and head. She lost count in the seventies.

GO ON TO THE NEXT PAGE.

(70) I remained in shock for hours, unable to lay my head on a pillow. My eyes, nose, ears, and mouth swelled into a grotesque mask. I looked and felt terrible even weeks later with a blotchy, itchy head, face, and (75) neck and with two black eyes.

Having miraculously survived this ordeal and the following weeks of unbelievable agony, the fact that for a long time I was nervous when I heard a (80) buzzing sound is understandable. For many years even the buzz of an ordinary housefly would make me ill and trembling with fear.

The last of the honey was never (85) removed from that skep of bees. The entire bee hive was hauled away. Many professional beekeepers wear hoods and gloves and, if necessary, use smoke to control angry bees.

(90) Honey bees are essential; we need honey bees for our agricultural crops and honey production. My experience illustrates, however, that we also need to learn how to live in harmony with bees and (95) that care should be taken not to startle or disturb bees, whether domesticated or wild.

(1999)

52. The tone of "conveniently located" in line 24 makes the writer's involvement with the bees seem

   (A) naive
   (B) penitent
   (C) impersonal
   (D) inevitable
   (E) complacent

53. In lines 56–57, the literary device used in "the seething balloon of bees" is a

   (A) metaphor
   (B) simile
   (C) metonymy
   (D) personification
   (E) symbol

54. In lines 42–43, the "sound was a shot-like blast" performs which of these roles?

   I. Descriptive simile
   II. Alliterative illustration
   III. Onomatopoeic description

   (A) I only
   (B) II only
   (C) I and II only
   (D) II and III only
   (E) I, II, and III

55. "I remained in shock for hours" (line 70) is probably the result of all the following EXCEPT

   (A) a concussion from a violent blow
   (B) great surprise
   (C) the effects of the poison
   (D) extreme pain
   (E) the violent nature of the attack

56. "Presence of mind" in lines 58–59 can also be paraphrased as

   (A) daydreaming
   (B) mental dignity
   (C) an anticipatory response
   (D) a flashback
   (E) quick thinking

57. Use of the passive voice in lines 39–41 implies

   (A) the indifference of the speaker
   (B) a sense of urgency
   (C) the rock was too heavy
   (D) a sense of confusion over the events
   (E) the speaker is uncertain who put the rock there

58. The use of italics ("*social*") in line 6 serves to

(A) identify the type of bees involved
(B) emphasize the unusual nature of the bees' friendliness
(C) ironically foreshadow the attack
(D) imply that the bees were very friendly with each other
(E) indicate that bees make good companions

59. All the following pairs mirror the speaker's change in attitude toward the bees EXCEPT

(A) "friends" (line 18)… "care should be taken" (line 95)
(B) "projects" (line 20)… "hauled away" (line 86)
(C) "happy" (line 18)… "trembling with fear" (lines 82–83)
(D) "stinging fiercely" (line 48)… "sympathy" (line 67)
(E) "tempting" (line 29)… "never removed" (lines 84–85)

60. The selection is best described as

(A) biographical
(B) narrative and informative
(C) narrative and persuasive
(D) informative and biographical
(E) argumentative

Answer Key: Practice Test Two

1. **(E)**	7. **(A)**	13. **(D)**	19. **(C)**	25. **(A)**	31. **(A)**	37. **(D)**	43. **(A)**	49. **(A)**	55. **(A)**
2. **(C)**	8. **(C)**	14. **(A)**	20. **(D)**	26. **(C)**	32. **(E)**	38. **(B)**	44. **(B)**	50. **(E)**	56. **(E)**
3. **(A)**	9. **(E)**	15. **(B)**	21. **(E)**	27. **(E)**	33. **(A)**	39. **(D)**	45. **(B)**	51. **(D)**	57. **(E)**
4. **(B)**	10. **(E)**	16. **(C)**	22. **(A)**	28. **(B)**	34. **(B)**	40. **(C)**	46. **(D)**	52. **(D)**	58. **(C)**
5. **(D)**	11. **(B)**	17. **(E)**	23. **(C)**	29. **(C)**	35. **(C)**	41. **(E)**	47. **(C)**	53. **(A)**	59. **(D)**
6. **(B)**	12. **(C)**	18. **(D)**	24. **(B)**	30. **(A)**	36. **(A)**	42. **(A)**	48. **(A)**	54. **(E)**	60. **(B)**

TO OBTAIN YOUR RAW SCORE:

_____ divided by 4 = _____

Total wrong   Score W

_____ minus _____ = _____

Total right   Score W   Score R

Round Score R to the nearest whole number for the raw score.

SCORE CONVERSION TABLE FOR PRACTICE TESTS

(based on estimated values)

Raw Score	Scaled Score	Raw Score	Scaled Score	Raw Score	Scaled Score	Raw Score	Scaled Score
60	800	40	660	20	500	0	330
59	800	38	650	19	490	−1	320
58	800	38	640	18	480	−2	310
57	800	37	640	17	470	−3	300
56	790	36	630	16	470	−4	290
55	790	35	620	15	460	−5	280
54	780	34	610	14	450	−6	270
53	770	33	600	13	440	−7	260
52	760	32	590	12	430	−8	250
51	750	31	590	11	430	−9	240
50	740	30	580	10	420	−10	230
49	730	29	570	9	410	−11	220
48	720	28	560	8	400	−12	210
47	710	27	550	7	390	−13	200
46	710	26	550	6	390	−14	200
45	700	25	540	5	380		
44	690	24	530	4	370		
43	680	23	520	3	360		
42	680	22	510	2	350		
41	670	21	510	1	340		

Explanations: Practice Test Two

NOTE: Most practice tests cannot duplicate the content and conditions of the actual Literature test. Also, the scope and definitions of the literary elements can differ among literary critics; therefore, the rationale behind what constitutes a correct or an incorrect answer choice may vary. Each of these practice tests, however, gives you an opportunity to analyze selections, think critically, and develop your test-taking skills so you can do your personal best on the SAT Subject Test in Literature.

1. **(E)** This relationship is the central contrast of the poem. The earth is now warm, but the speaker's love cannot be melted, even by the sun (lines 14–15).

2. **(C)** A before-and-after relationship is established in line 1: "winter's gone." Before May, the ox would seek shelter from storms. Upon May's arrival, it would "lie / In open fields" (lines 18–19).

3. **(A)** June represents summer warmth. Eyes can represent a wide range of ideas, including "windows to the soul," "flirting eyes," and "giving him the eye" as an expression of invitation. January represents the winter cold. Traditionally, the heart is the seat of emotion or true feelings. She is warm toward him with her eyes, but emotionally she is cold.

4. **(B)** His love frowns ("lours"), but nature smiles, characteristic of someone jubilant and responsive.

5. **(D)** The tone of lines 14–16 is angry and impatient.

6. **(B)** How cold is her heart? It is congealed, as cold as marble ice: exaggerated imagery.

7. **(A)** This phrase appeals to three senses: melt (thermal), marble (visual and tactile), ice (visual and thermal).

8. **(C)** The central contrast is warm, spring-summer, awakening, happy versus cold, winter, sleeping, unhappy. In context of line 6, "makes…gives" are both part of spring.

9. **(E)** The comparison and contrast of the seasons is the vehicle the speaker uses to express his frustration.

10. **(E)** Nature making the transition from a dead, cold winter to warm spring when nature reproduces does not involve the concept of making or not making an error.

11. **(B)** The key to this question is "figuratively." June and January are months of the year *literally*.

12. **(C)** Frost would cover grass.

13. **(D)** Be sure to consider entire answer choices. He does respond in an unyielding manner (B), but he is not conniving. In context with lines 3–4, his response to "How dare you…?" seems *both* challenging and defiant.

14. **(A)** If you are unfamiliar with the word "stay," simply substitute each answer choice in the sentence to see which one fits the context: "How dare you *hinder* the march…?"

15. **(B)** Again, substitute and check the context: "The people had been…absorbing mentally the words of their champion."

16. **(C)** He is "loud and harsh" (line 2) with "hard and cruel" expressions (line 32).

17. **(E)** He came from a "secret place" (lines 3–9) with "accents long disused" (lines 24–25)—mysterious.

18. **(D)** Obviously, there is no comedy in this selection.

19. **(C)** Lines 45–50 confirm the Gray Champion's predictions came true; line 19 foreshadows the future.

20. **(D)** "—back, lest I foretell the scaffold!" (lines 20–21) implies that he believes that if he predicts the Governor's execution, it will happen.

21. **(E)** He threatens his enemy with the scaffold.

22. **(A)** These archaic words would be spoken in a time long ago in a place where English was spoken.

23. **(C)** The people were oppressed and crying (line 8), but it took the words of the Gray Champion to stir their souls (line 27) and bring them to seek stones for weapons (lines 29–30). They obviously have endured much cruelty to reach this degree of "lurid wrath" (line 34).

24. **(B)** The line balances contrasting terms with parallel grammatical structure.

25. **(A)** This line contains repetition of initial "f" sounds.

26. **(C)** The central contrast is expressed in line 1. His love is fair, but also fickle (to a greater degree). Line 7 expounds upon her fair side only.

27. **(E)** To foil is to thwart or stop the success of something. To frame is to devise or make, in this case, love.

28. **(B)** Her emotions are self-contradictory, a paradox.

29. **(C)** Line 1 "Fair,…but…fickle": The same pattern is used in lines 2, 3, 4, 5–6. Lines 7–8 compliment, 9–10 criticize. Versions of this pattern continue to the end of the work.

30. **(A)** The speaker realizes the truth and is no longer under the illusion that her expressions of love are true.

31. **(A)** A comparison using "like" or "as" is a simile.

32. **(E)** Her situation is ironic: She destroys the love she desires or, rather, does not want to lose.

33. **(A)** Although the speaker does elaborate the idea that according to some philosophers animals can talk (lines 12–19) and even speculates on animals common to certain nations in lines 19–27, these ideas only build to his main point in lines 28–33.

34. **(B)** The speaker's premise is based on a simile; in regard to language, he compares people to animals.

35. **(C)** The speaker obviously does not admire those who misuse language, and his opinions are too distinct to be rooted in complacency. Unlike a hypocrite, he at one point casts himself among the guilty by calling himself a "Barnyard Cock" (line 55). His analogy is somewhat comical (D), but notice that none of his companions is flattering. His aim is to focus on misuse and his attitude dictates his purpose: We should not misuse "the organs of speech" (lines 1–12).

36. **(A)** Although the speaker may be referring to professional critics (perhaps critics who have given bad reviews of the speaker's own works?), he seems unaware that he, in this essay, has assumed the role of critic of those who, in his opinion, misuse language. In this position, he is "hissing" by making very unflattering comparisons of people to animals. The tone is made ironic by the speaker not being aware that his attitude is making him a hissing critic of hissing critics.

37. **(D)** He compares himself to a swan (line 58). The speaker is trying to convince readers that because "they will hear the last of me on this day fortnight," he has greater clarity of thought and deeper insight into reality in his "dying moments." He views his insights into the misuse of languages as profound.

38. **(B)** A comparison marked by "like" or "as" is a simile.

39. **(D)** Clearly, the speech organs do not relate to formal documents.

40. **(C)** The speaker sees the idea of animals being able to "understand one another by the sounds they utter" as an idea philosophers have imagined. He obviously does not believe it.

41. **(E)** The speaker shifts from discussing animals sounding like humans to humans sounding like animals.

42. **(A)** By viewing the exchange of ideas through conversation as the dividing line between man and beast, the speaker holds the ability to speak as a great advantage that is beyond measure.

43. **(A)** You do not need to know the literary term "aposiopesis," but you should be able to recognize that when a speaker emotionally stops or hesitates mid-sentence, generally the effect is to make that emotion seem more intense.

44. **(B)** Notice in lines 1–2: "there must surely be / The face…." She has a sense of longing.

45. **(B)** For a heart to make "answer to my word" fits the traditional image of one heart speaking to another: emotions.

46. **(D)** The main contrast is distance: Stanza 2 speaks of a distant place, "Past land and sea"; stanza 3 speaks of a near one, "With just a wall, a hedge, between."

47. **(C)** The star follows the moon like a hunter tracks game.

48. **(A)** Answer choices B, D, and E are obviously unsupported by context. At first glance, lines 11–12 could project hopelessness; however, "just" in line 11 minimizes the importance of the dead leaves.

49. **(A)** No comparison is at work in these lines, and although we might assume the speaker is alone, there is no direct evidence.

50. **(E)** The theme is established in the first stanza: "The face not seen…."

51. **(D)** Go to context to select between answer choices D and E. Lines 6–8 deal with a faraway place; lines 10–13, a near place.

52. **(D)** A type of verbal irony, pointing out the convenience of the location makes the speaker's involvement a natural consequence.

53. **(A)** The metaphor is an implied comparison, in this case comparing the speaker's bee-covered head to a balloon.

54. **(E)** The use of "like" makes the description a simile. The words sound like their meaning (III), and the repetitive initial "s" is alliterative.

55. **(A)** The narrative does not include any mention of the speaker being hit by a "violent blow."

56. **(E)** By definition, "presence of mind" means quick thinking.

57. **(E)** Passive voice emphasizes the rock, rather than the person who placed it there, implying uncertainty. By using the passive, the speaker keeps the focus on the cause of the "shot-like blast."

58. **(C)** The startled bees become extremely unsocial when they attack the speaker.

59. **(D)** The sympathy was the response of the speaker's mother.

60. **(B)** This autobiographical narrative is intended to inform, as evidenced by the use of definition in the text and the conclusions drawn in the last paragraph.

Titles and Authors of Selections in Test Two

Questions

Answer Sheet
PRACTICE TEST THREE

1 Ⓐ Ⓑ Ⓒ Ⓓ Ⓔ
2 Ⓐ Ⓑ Ⓒ Ⓓ Ⓔ
3 Ⓐ Ⓑ Ⓒ Ⓓ Ⓔ
4 Ⓐ Ⓑ Ⓒ Ⓓ Ⓔ
5 Ⓐ Ⓑ Ⓒ Ⓓ Ⓔ
6 Ⓐ Ⓑ Ⓒ Ⓓ Ⓔ
7 Ⓐ Ⓑ Ⓒ Ⓓ Ⓔ
8 Ⓐ Ⓑ Ⓒ Ⓓ Ⓔ
9 Ⓐ Ⓑ Ⓒ Ⓓ Ⓔ
10 Ⓐ Ⓑ Ⓒ Ⓓ Ⓔ
11 Ⓐ Ⓑ Ⓒ Ⓓ Ⓔ
12 Ⓐ Ⓑ Ⓒ Ⓓ Ⓔ
13 Ⓐ Ⓑ Ⓒ Ⓓ Ⓔ
14 Ⓐ Ⓑ Ⓒ Ⓓ Ⓔ
15 Ⓐ Ⓑ Ⓒ Ⓓ Ⓔ

16 Ⓐ Ⓑ Ⓒ Ⓓ Ⓔ
17 Ⓐ Ⓑ Ⓒ Ⓓ Ⓔ
18 Ⓐ Ⓑ Ⓒ Ⓓ Ⓔ
19 Ⓐ Ⓑ Ⓒ Ⓓ Ⓔ
20 Ⓐ Ⓑ Ⓒ Ⓓ Ⓔ
21 Ⓐ Ⓑ Ⓒ Ⓓ Ⓔ
22 Ⓐ Ⓑ Ⓒ Ⓓ Ⓔ
23 Ⓐ Ⓑ Ⓒ Ⓓ Ⓔ
24 Ⓐ Ⓑ Ⓒ Ⓓ Ⓔ
25 Ⓐ Ⓑ Ⓒ Ⓓ Ⓔ
26 Ⓐ Ⓑ Ⓒ Ⓓ Ⓔ
27 Ⓐ Ⓑ Ⓒ Ⓓ Ⓔ
28 Ⓐ Ⓑ Ⓒ Ⓓ Ⓔ
29 Ⓐ Ⓑ Ⓒ Ⓓ Ⓔ
30 Ⓐ Ⓑ Ⓒ Ⓓ Ⓔ

31 Ⓐ Ⓑ Ⓒ Ⓓ Ⓔ
32 Ⓐ Ⓑ Ⓒ Ⓓ Ⓔ
33 Ⓐ Ⓑ Ⓒ Ⓓ Ⓔ
34 Ⓐ Ⓑ Ⓒ Ⓓ Ⓔ
35 Ⓐ Ⓑ Ⓒ Ⓓ Ⓔ
36 Ⓐ Ⓑ Ⓒ Ⓓ Ⓔ
37 Ⓐ Ⓑ Ⓒ Ⓓ Ⓔ
38 Ⓐ Ⓑ Ⓒ Ⓓ Ⓔ
39 Ⓐ Ⓑ Ⓒ Ⓓ Ⓔ
40 Ⓐ Ⓑ Ⓒ Ⓓ Ⓔ
41 Ⓐ Ⓑ Ⓒ Ⓓ Ⓔ
42 Ⓐ Ⓑ Ⓒ Ⓓ Ⓔ
43 Ⓐ Ⓑ Ⓒ Ⓓ Ⓔ
44 Ⓐ Ⓑ Ⓒ Ⓓ Ⓔ
45 Ⓐ Ⓑ Ⓒ Ⓓ Ⓔ

46 Ⓐ Ⓑ Ⓒ Ⓓ Ⓔ
47 Ⓐ Ⓑ Ⓒ Ⓓ Ⓔ
48 Ⓐ Ⓑ Ⓒ Ⓓ Ⓔ
49 Ⓐ Ⓑ Ⓒ Ⓓ Ⓔ
50 Ⓐ Ⓑ Ⓒ Ⓓ Ⓔ
51 Ⓐ Ⓑ Ⓒ Ⓓ Ⓔ
52 Ⓐ Ⓑ Ⓒ Ⓓ Ⓔ
53 Ⓐ Ⓑ Ⓒ Ⓓ Ⓔ
54 Ⓐ Ⓑ Ⓒ Ⓓ Ⓔ
55 Ⓐ Ⓑ Ⓒ Ⓓ Ⓔ
56 Ⓐ Ⓑ Ⓒ Ⓓ Ⓔ
57 Ⓐ Ⓑ Ⓒ Ⓓ Ⓔ
58 Ⓐ Ⓑ Ⓒ Ⓓ Ⓔ
59 Ⓐ Ⓑ Ⓒ Ⓓ Ⓔ
60 Ⓐ Ⓑ Ⓒ Ⓓ Ⓔ

Practice Test Three

TIME ALLOWED: ONE HOUR

Directions: The following questions test your understanding of several literary selections. Read each passage or poem and the questions that follow it. Select the best answer choice for each question by blackening the matching oval on your answer sheet. **Special attention should be given to questions containing the following words: EXCEPT, LEAST, NOT.**

Questions 1–10 are based on the following passage.

Within an hour after the earthquake shock the smoke of San Francisco's burning was a lurid tower visible a hundred
Line miles away. And for three days and nights
(5) this lurid tower swayed in the sky, reddening the sun, darkening the sky, and filling the land with smoke. On Wednesday morning at a quarter past five came the earthquake. A minute later the flames
(10) were leaping upward. In a dozen different quarters south of Market Street, in the working-class ghetto, and in the factories, fires started. There was no opposing the flames. There was no organization, no
(15) communication. All the cunning adjustments of a twentieth-century city had been smashed by the earthquake. The streets were humped into ridge and depressions and piled with debris of fallen
(20) walls. The steel rails were twisted into perpendicular and horizontal angles. The telephone and telegraph systems were disrupted. And the great water mains had burst. All the shrewd contrivances and
(25) safeguards of man had been thrown out of gear by thirty seconds' twitching of the earth's crust.

By Wednesday afternoon, inside of twelve hours, half the heart of the city was
(30) gone. At that time I watched the vast conflagration from out on the bay. It was dead calm. Not a flicker of wind stirred. Yet from every side wind was pouring in upon the city. East, west, north, and
(35) south, strong winds were blowing upon the doomed city. The heated air rising made an enormous suck. Thus did the fire of itself build its own colossal chimney through the atmosphere. Day and night
(40) this dead calm continued, and yet, near to the flames, the wind was often half a gale, so mighty was the suck.

(1906)

1. What was "dead calm" in line 32?

   (A) The city
   (B) The conflagration
   (C) The bay
   (D) The wind
   (E) The heart of the city

2. The use of "cunning" (line 15) and "shrewd" (line 24) is

   (A) ironic
   (A) symbolic
   (A) argumentative
   (A) hyperbole
   (A) stereotypical

Practice Test Three

3. The connotative meanings of "cunning" (line 15) and "shrewd" (line 24) make the speaker's tone sound

   (A) respectful
   (A) belligerent
   (A) comic
   (A) unrestrained
   (A) sarcastic

4. As used in line 3, "lurid" means which of the following?

   I. Glowing through smoke
   II. Startlingly harsh
   III. Violently criminal

   (A) I only
   (B) II only
   (C) III only
   (D) I and II
   (E) I, II, and III

5. The wind was the result of

   (A) the bay
   (B) the fire
   (C) the city
   (D) a colossal cold front
   (E) directional elements

6. The "vast conflagration" is best understood as

   (A) the winds
   (B) the bay
   (C) onshore fighting
   (D) the fire
   (E) heated air

7. Structurally, what is the main purpose of lines 18–24?

   (A) They are a chronological account of the destruction.
   (B) They serve to contrast the account of the fire.
   (C) They illustrate lines 15–17.
   (D) They reinforce a sense of hopelessness.
   (E) They classify the areas that were destroyed.

8. The sequence of the narrative serves to

   (A) chronologically inform the reader
   (B) trivialize the situation
   (C) reflect the mental state of the speaker
   (D) exaggerate the extent of the destruction
   (E) reinforce a sense of man's responsibility for the outcome

9. For winds to be blowing from all directions within a "dead calm" makes the account seem

   (A) unreliable
   (B) paradoxical
   (C) reliable
   (D) naïve
   (E) a tall tale

10. For the fire's heat to "of itself build its own colossal chimney" is

    (A) an example of literary atmosphere
    (B) part of the climate of the account
    (C) a euphemism
    (D) an ironic situation
    (E) a flashback

Questions 11–23 are based on the following poem.

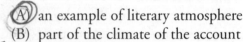

Whoso walks in solitude
And inhabiteth the wood,
Choosing light, wave, rock and bird
Line Before the money-loving herd,
(5) Into that forester shall pass,
From these companions, power and grace.
Clean shall he be, without, within,
From the old adhering sin;
All ill dissolving in the light
(10) Of his triumphant piercing sight:
Not vain, sour, nor frivolous;
Nor mad, athirst, nor garrulous;
Grave chaste, contented tho' retired,
And of all other men desired,
(15) On him the light of star and moon
Shall fall with pure radiance down;
All constellations of the sky
Shall shed their virtue thro' his eye.

Him Nature giveth for defence
(20) His formidable innocence;
The mountain sap, the shells, the sea,
All spheres, all stones, his helpers be;
He shall meet the speeding year
Without wailing, without fear;
(25) He shall be happy in his love,
Like to like shall joyful prove;
He shall be happy while he woos,
Muse-born, a daughter of the Muse.
But if with gold she bind her hair
(30) And deck her breast with diamond,
Take off thine eyes, thy heart forbear,
Tho' thou lie alone on the ground!

(ca. 1867)

11. The subject of the poem deals with

(A) the benefits of living close to nature
(B) wilderness survivals
(C) becoming a hermit
(D) resisting temptations
(E) nature watching

12. Which of the phrases listed below mirrors the paradox seen in the phrase "formidable innocence" (line 20)?

(A) Innovative mistake
(B) Paralyzing fearfulness
(C) Defective fortifications
(D) Legalized permissiveness
(E) Innocuous dreadfulness

13. In lines 9–10, which of the following sound devices is used?

(A) Dissonance
(B) Onomatopoeia
(C) Assonance
(D) Cacophony
(E) Caesura

14. What is the main idea of lines 29–32?

(A) A rejection of wealth
(B) An admonition to reject natural physical beauty
(C) A rejection of the earth's treasure
(D) An admonition to reject a mate who has different values
(E) An admonition to reject all love

15. Based on the context of the rhyme scheme, the writer of this poem probably intends all the following pairs of words to correspond EXCEPT

(A) "solitude" (line 1) and "wood" (line 2)
(B) "bird" (line 3) and "herd" (line 4)
(C) "moon" (line 15) and "down" (line 16)
(D) "innocence" (line 20) and "sea" (line 21)
(E) "love" (line 25) and "prove" (line 26)

16. Line 29 contains a change in

(A) rhythm
(B) rhyme scheme
(C) voice
(D) verse form
(E) dialect

17. "Walks in solitude" in line 1 contrasts with "money-loving herd" in line 4. This contrast

(A) emphasizes the individualism of the forester
(B) emphasizes the loneliness of the forester
(C) echoes the theme of line 22
(D) suggests points of comparison
(E) symbolizes the problems people face with loneliness

18. In the context of the poem, the forester's character is shown to be one of

(A) a malcontent
(B) fearful only of death
(C) higher moral character
(D) unnatural qualities
(E) irresponsible behavior

GO ON TO THE NEXT PAGE.

19. The consequences of shortening words in lines 13, 18, and 32 are

    (A) allusional
    (B) metrical
    (C) symbolic
    (D) rhetorical
    (E) metaphoric

20. The natural elements are portrayed as

    (A) hostile to the forester
    (B) ambivalent to the herd
    (C) compassionate to the daughter of the Muse
    (D) challenges to the forester
    (E) friends to the forester

21. The opposing ideas within the poem are NOT seen in

    (A) individualism…conformity
    (B) courage…fear
    (C) innocence…sinfulness
    (D) justice…injustice
    (E) happiness…unhappiness

22. In the context of the entire poem, the forester (line 5) contrasts to the herd (line 4) and projects which of these ideas?

    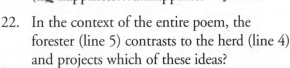

    I. The natural man vs. the artificial man
    II. An indictment against contrived literary forms
    III. A statement of the forester's mistake in judgment
    IV. An indictment against exchanging true values for monetary gain

    (A) I only
    (B) II only
    (C) I, III, and IV only
    (D) I, II, and IV only
    (E) I, II, III, and IV

23. In this poem, the "daughter of the Muse" (line 28) "with gold" in her hair (line 29) is which of these literary uses?

    I. A representative of vanity
    II. A characterization of artificiality
    III. A symbol of contrived literary forms
    (A) I only
    (B) II only
    (C) III only
    (D) I and III only
    (E) I, II, and III

Questions 24–33 are based on the following passage.

> And lest some should persuade ye, Lords and Commons, that these arguments of learned men's discouragement at
> *Line* this your Order are mere flourishes, and
> (5) not real, I could recount what I have seen and heard in other countries where this kind of inquisition tyrannizes; when I have sat among their learned men, for that honor I had, and been counted
> (10) happy to be born in such a place of philosophic freedom as they supposed England was, while themselves did nothing but bemoan the servile condition into which learning amongst them was brought; that
> (15) this was it which had damped the glory of Italian wits; that nothing had been there written now these many years but flattery and fustian. There it was that I found and visited the famous Galileo, grown old, a
> (20) prisoner to the Inquisition for thinking in astronomy otherwise than the Franciscan and Dominican licensers thought. And though I knew that England then was groaning loudest under the prelatical
> (25) yoke, nevertheless I took it as a pledge of future happiness that other nations were so persuaded of her liberty.

                                                           (1644)

24. What is the central topic of the passage?

    (A) Intellectual freedom
    (B) Animosity among countries
    (C) Italy's justice system
    (D) English literature
    (E) Italian licensers

25. The organizational pattern used most by the writer of this passage is best decribed as

    (A) cause and effect
    (B) comparison and contrast
    (C) definition
    (D) process analysis
    (E) analysis and classification

26. What is the speaker's purpose?

    (A) Argumentation
    (B) Information
    (C) Entertainment
    (D) Description
    (E) Persuasion

27. Contextual clues show that "Galileo" (line 19) refers to a(n)

    (A) poet and philosopher of the Order
    (B) rebel against intellectual dictatorship
    (C) English astronomer
    (D) symbol of the Inquisition
    (E) Franciscan licenser

28. The main reason for the irony in the admiration held by other countries for the speaker's country is that

    (A) England truly had more intellectual freedoms
    (B) the other countries did not really know England
    (C) England was less philosophically free than the other countries
    (D) the other countries enjoyed hidden freedoms
    (E) both England and the other countries were partners in the Order

29. According to the speaker, repression of learning in Italy resulted in writing that was

    (A) strong and forthright
    (B) defensive and satirical
    (C) insincere and pretentious
    (D) shocking and cynical
    (E) humble and direct

30. Lines 1–5 put forth the idea that

    (A) supporters of the Order contend that the opposition is just putting on a show
    (B) the Order was not really issued
    (C) there are no supporters for the Order
    (D) there is real general support for the Order
    (E) the opposition to the Order lacks sincerity

31. The "prelatical yoke" (lines 24–25) contributes to meaning as a

    (A) simile for causing a loud noise
    (B) gently satirical view of the Order
    (C) mocking description of ecclesiastical groups
    (D) personification of the Order
    (E) metaphor for ecclesiastical rules governing intellectual matters

32. The final statement of the passage is presented for which of these intents?

    (A) A change in attitude of the speaker
    (B) A statement of the speaker's optimism
    (C) A statement of the speaker's sense of forlornness
    (D) A challenge to other countries
    (E) An example of ungrounded pessimism

GO ON TO THE NEXT PAGE.

33. Use of the word "servile" in line 13 is connotative that

    (A) learning had become submissive to others' dictates
    (B) all philosophic freedoms were gone
    (C) the Order was a slave to philosophy
    (D) England was not a slave-state
    (E) Italy had conquered philosophic freedom

Questions 34–44 are based on the following poem.

The Flower

Once in a golden hour
    I cast to earth a seed.
Up there came a flower,
    The people said, a weed.

Line
(5) To and fro they went
    Thro' my garden-bower,
And muttering discontent
    Cursed me and my flower.

Then it grew so tall
(10)   It wore a crown of light,
But thieves from o'er the wall
    Stole the seed by night.

Sow'd it far and wide
    By every town and tower,
(15) Till all the people cried,
    'Splendid is the flower.'

Read my little fable:
    He that runs may read.
Most can raise the flowers now,
(20)   For all have got the seed.

And some are pretty enough,
    And some are poor indeed;
And now again the people
    Call it but a weed.

                                (ca. 1830)

34. The main theme of the "fable" (line 17) is

    (A) the problems gardeners face with thieves
    (B) a statement concerning dishonesty
    (C) the intense beauty inherent in some plant forms
    (D) how human nature affects perceptions of value
    (E) the probability that something beautiful will be stolen

35. In this poem, the word "runs" (line 18) means which of the definitions listed below?

    I. Moves swiftly or rapidly
    II. Thinks quickly without hindrance
    III. Meditates
    IV. Melts and flows

    (A) I only
    (B) II only
    (C) IV only
    (D) I, II, and III only
    (E) II and III only

36. In its context, "read" (line 18) means which of the definitions listed below?

    I. Utter aloud
    II. Learn true meaning
    III. Foretell
    IV. Record or show

    (A) I only
    (B) II only
    (C) IV only
    (D) I, III, and IV only
    (E) I, II, and IV only

37. In this poem, the progression of "weed" (line 4) to "flower" (line 16) to "weed" (line 24) represents the

    (A) lack of horticultural knowledge of the people
    (B) admiration with which the speaker looks at the flower
    (C) ironic nature of the people's attitude
    (D) despair with which the speaker views the people
    (E) hostility of the people toward the speaker

38. The hour was "golden" in line 1 because

    (A) the sun was shining
    (B) the seed became a splendid flower
    (C) the flower was yellow
    (D) the seed was yellow
    (E) the seed was gold

39. Contextually, "wore a crown of light" (line 10) makes the flower seem

    (A) regal and beautiful
    (B) prolific
    (C) lanky and leggy
    (D) top-heavy and weighted down
    (E) fragile and airy

40. Line 17 contains a change in

    (A) rhyme scheme
    (B) imagery
    (C) tone
    (D) speaker
    (E) voice

41. Of the pairs of words listed below, which mirrors the contrast of the development of "the flower" in this poem?

    (A) Turnips...turnip greens
    (B) Lawn...crabgrass
    (C) Queen Anne's Lace...ragweed
    (D) Roses...thorns
    (E) Grapes...vine

42. The phrase "Cursed me and my flower" (line 8) highlights the people's

    (A) limited vocabularies
    (B) judgmental natures
    (C) acceptance of the situation
    (D) deferential attitude
    (E) diabolical plan

43. The speaker wants the reader to view the fable as

    (A) just a clever story
    (B) an amusing anecdote
    (C) aimed at children
    (D) a tall tale
    (E) an important lesson in life

44. The speaker undergoes a change in attitude toward "my flower" in lines 1–4 and 9–12 in contrast to the description in lines 21–24 because

    (A) the speaker also considers the flower a weed
    (B) the flower will never be a weed to the speaker
    (C) the speaker is no longer emotionally attached to the flower
    (D) the flower really was a weed all along
    (E) the people's perception has not influenced the perception of the speaker

Questions 45–52 are based on the following passage.

    Even if literature were of no other use to the fair sex than to supply them with employment, I should think the
Line time dedicated to the cultivation of their
(5) minds well bestowed: they are surely better occupied when they are reading or writing than when coquetting or gaming, losing their fortunes or their characters. You despise the writings of women—you
(10) think that they might have made a better use of the pen than to write plays, and poetry, and romances. Considering that the pen was to women a new instrument,

GO ON TO THE NEXT PAGE.

(15) I think they have made at least as good a use of it as learned men did of the needle some centuries ago, when they set them-selves to determine how many spirits could stand upon its point, and were ready to tear one another to pieces in the
(20) discussion of this sublime question…You say that the experiments we have made do not encourage us to proceed,…Did you expect that the fruits of good cultiva-tion should appear before the seed was
(25) sown?—You triumphantly enumerate the disadvantages to which women…are liable….and after pointing out all these causes for the inferiority of women in knowledge, you ask for a list of the inven-
(30) tions and discoveries of those who, by your own statement of the question, have not been allowed opportunities for obser-vation. With the insulting injustice of an Egyptian task-master, you demand the
(35) work, and deny the necessary materials.

(1795)

45. The "fair sex" (line 2) is used as a(n)

(A) epithet for women
(B) metonymy for blonds
(C) symbol of equality
(D) amplification to define the subject
(E) rhetorical device for contrast

46. "Egyptian task-master" (line 34) alludes to when the Children of Israel were slaves in Egypt and were required to make brick without straw.

This allusion does NOT serve to

(A) make women appear as victims
(B) emphasize the suffering of women seeking education
(C) convey a sense of indignation
(D) illustrate the irony of the situation
(E) define the parameters of the issue

47. The speaker uses an agricultural metaphor to describe which of the following?

(A) Women's education and writing
(B) Women's employment
(C) Coquetting and gaming
(D) The laws and customs of society
(E) Experiments in women's rights

48. The tone of "This sublime question" (line 20) sounds

(A) affable
(B) altruistic
(C) malevolent
(D) sarcastic
(E) obtuse

49. Which of the following maxims best sum-marizes the central irony in this passage?

(A) What goes around comes around.
(B) A woman cannot win for losing.
(C) You can lead a horse to water, but you cannot make it drink.
(D) Pride goes before a fall.
(E) A woman's work is never done.

50. As used in line 3, "employment" refers to

(A) a job
(B) making a living
(C) keeping busy
(D) business
(E) a referral

51. "This sublime question" (line 20) is an example of

(A) hyperbole
(B) understatement
(C) allegory
(D) verbal irony
(E) personification

52. In context, "opportunities for observation" in lines 32–33 would probably NOT include

(A) gaining an education
(B) participating in research
(C) being watched and admired
(D) exchanging ideas with professionals
(E) engaging in an apprenticeship

Questions 53–60 are based on the following poem.

> My lute, be as thou wast when thou didst grow
> With thy green mother in some shady grove,
> When immelodious winds but made thee move,
> *Line* And birds on thee their ramage did bestow.
> *(5)* Sith that dear voice which did thy sounds approve,
> Which used in such harmonious strains to flow,
> Is reft from earth to tune those spheres above,
> What art thou but a harbinger of woe?
> Thy pleasing notes be pleasing notes no more,
> *(10)* But orphan wailings to the fainting ear;
> Each stop a sigh, each sound draws forth a tear,
> Be therefore silent as in woods before,
> Or if that any hand to touch thee deign,
> Like widowed turtle, still her loss complain.

(ca. 1630)

53. "My lute" in line 1 is an example of the poet's use of

(A) simile
(B) metaphor
(C) personification
(D) apostrophe
(E) litote

54. The poem presents

(A) the speaker's passionate love of music
(B) a contrast of the natural to the unnatural
(C) the speaker mourning the death of a loved one
(D) a youth speaking to his music teacher
(E) an individual addressing music

55. The change in rhyme scheme of lines 5–8 as contrasted to lines 1–4 is echoed in the

(A) change in tone of lines 5–8
(B) change in rhythm
(C) revelation of a reversal in tone in line 9
(D) renewed sense of optimism in line 9
(E) revelation of meaning in lines 5–8

56. The lute's "green mother" (line 2) is a figurative reference to a

(A) tree
(B) grove
(C) wind
(D) bird
(E) singer

57. By using the context of the poem, "widowed turtle" in line 14 can be viewed as

(A) a reptile, known for withdrawing into its hard shell
(B) a turtleback, known in archaeology as a stone implement
(C) a turtledove, known for devotion to its mate
(D) turtlehead herb, known for the shape of its corolla
(E) turtle peg, known for its use in harpooning sea turtles

GO ON TO THE NEXT PAGE.

58. The lute's music seems to represent which of the following for the speaker?

    (A) A musical instrument
    (B) Reflections of the speaker's mood
    (C) A friend and companion
    (D) Light and harmony
    (E) Nature

59. The speaker views the lute with feelings that can be described as

    (A) shocked
    (B) condescending
    (C) dispassionate
    (D) fearless
    (E) antagonistic

60. Of the following, which is the LEAST acccurate statement concerning the poem?

    (A) It is a sonnet.
    (B) Lines 9–10 contain a metaphor.
    (C) Line 2 contains personification.
    (D) The phrase "orphan wailings" (line 10) refers to children of the speaker.
    (E) "Ramage" (line 4) contrasts with "harmonious" (line 6).

STOP

If there is still time remaining, you may review your answers.

Answer Key: Practice Test Three

1. **(D)**	7. **(C)**	13. **(C)**	19. **(B)**	25. **(B)**	31. **(E)**	37. **(C)**	43. **(E)**	49. **(B)**	55. **(E)**
2. **(A)**	8. **(C)**	14. **(D)**	20. **(E)**	26. **(A)**	32. **(B)**	38. **(B)**	44. **(C)**	50. **(C)**	56. **(A)**
3. **(E)**	9. **(B)**	15. **(D)**	21. **(D)**	27. **(B)**	33. **(A)**	39. **(A)**	45. **(A)**	51. **(D)**	57. **(C)**
4. **(D)**	10. **(D)**	16. **(B)**	22. **(D)**	28. **(C)**	34. **(D)**	40. **(A)**	46. **(E)**	52. **(C)**	58. **(B)**
5. **(B)**	11. **(A)**	17. **(A)**	23. **(E)**	29. **(C)**	35. **(E)**	41. **(C)**	47. **(A)**	53. **(D)**	59. **(E)**
6. **(D)**	12. **(E)**	18. **(C)**	24. **(A)**	30. **(A)**	36. **(B)**	42. **(B)**	48. **(D)**	54. **(C)**	60. **(D)**

TO OBTAIN YOUR RAW SCORE:

$\underline{\hspace{3cm}}$ divided by 4 = $\underline{\hspace{2cm}}$
Total wrong $\hspace{3cm}$ Score W

$\underline{\hspace{3cm}}$ minus $\underline{\hspace{2cm}}$ = $\underline{\hspace{2cm}}$
Total right $\hspace{2.5cm}$ Score W $\hspace{1cm}$ Score R

Round Score R to the nearest whole number for the raw score.

SCORE CONVERSION TABLE FOR PRACTICE TESTS

(based on estimated values)

Raw Score	Scaled Score	Raw Score	Scaled Score	Raw Score	Scaled Score	Raw Score	Scaled Score
60	800	40	660	20	500	0	330
59	800	38	650	19	490	−1	320
58	800	38	640	18	480	−2	310
57	800	37	640	17	470	−3	300
56	790	36	630	16	470	−4	290
55	790	35	620	15	460	−5	280
54	780	34	610	14	450	−6	270
53	770	33	600	13	440	−7	260
52	760	32	590	12	430	−8	250
51	750	31	590	11	430	−9	240
50	740	30	580	10	420	−10	230
49	730	29	570	9	410	−11	220
48	720	28	560	8	400	−12	210
47	710	27	550	7	390	−13	200
46	710	26	550	6	390	−14	200
45	700	25	540	5	380		
44	690	24	530	4	370		
43	680	23	520	3	360		
42	680	22	510	2	350		
41	670	21	510	1	340		

Explanations: Practice Test Three

> **NOTE:** Most practice tests cannot duplicate the content and conditions of the actual Literature test. Also, the scope and definitions of the literary elements can differ among literary critics; therefore, the rationale behind what constitutes a correct or an incorrect answer choice may vary. Each of these practice tests, however, gives you an opportunity to analyze selections, think critically, and develop your test-taking skills so you can do your personal best on the SAT Subject Test in Literature.

1. **(D)** "Not a flicker of wind stirred" (line 32).

2. **(A)** These synonyms mean to be extremely clever. Their use is ironic because the "cunning adjustments…and shrewd contrivances and safeguards of men" were destroyed in just "thirty seconds' twitching of the earth's crust."

3. **(E)** Both of these synonyms are negatively connotative of being sly or crafty, thus projecting a sarcastic tone.

4. **(D)** By definition, "lurid" means all three choices. Context, however, supports only the first two choices.

5. **(B)** The "fire of itself" was creating an updraft.

6. **(D)** A "conflagration" is a very destructive fire.

7. **(C)** Streets, steel rails, telephone and telegraph systems, and the water system are all "cunning adjustments" that were destroyed.

8. **(C)** The speaker just witnessed the destruction of a major city. The lack of chronological sequence, the repetition of words and ideas, and the dramatically connotative diction work together to reveal the speaker's state of mind: shocked, somewhat confused, and perhaps even a little angry.

9. **(B)** The idea of winds blowing from all directions and yet the city is surrounded by "dead calm" seems contradictory. The speaker does, however, explain how this seemingly impossible situation is true.

10. **(D)** A fire will die without proper ventilation. How ironic that this fire is so hot that it creates its own chimney and winds to fan the flames and keep it going!

11. **(A)** Notice lines 1 and 5–6: The speaker asserts that living alone in the woods will result in "power and grace."

12. **(E)** For innocence to be formidable, it would elicit dread or fear. For dreadfulness to be innocuous, it would be harmless.

13. **(C)** The vowel "i" is repeated, an example of assonance.

14. **(D)** Whether a figurative mate ("a daughter of the Muse"—line 28) or literal, if she is "Like to like" (line 26) and shares the values described in lines 1–24, fine. If not, the speaker prefers being alone (line 32).

15. **(D)** Here is a quick way to look at rhyme scheme: When the rhymes are in couplets, generally lines 1–2 will rhyme, 3–4 will rhyme, and so forth. Scan the answer choices for the pair that begins with an even line number.

16. **(B)** Lines 29 and 31 rhyme, making a change in rhyme scheme.

17. **(A)** A herd, when referring to people rather than animals, is negatively connotative, showing contempt, making the solitude of the forester more desirable.

18. **(C)** He is not a money-lover (line 4), he has power, grace, is clean from sin (lines 6–7), and so forth.

19. **(B)** Shortening words is generally done to help sustain the established rhythm.

20. **(E)** They give him "power and grace" (line 6) and innocence (line 20).

21. **(D)** First, establish the opposing ideas: a natural life versus one of artificiality. All the answer choices fit these ideas except justice and injustice.

22. **(D)** The first choice is the central contrast of the poem. The muse in line 28 supports II and line 4 supports IV. Answer choice III contradicts the main point.

23. **(E)** The advice by the speaker to reject her means she has not met the "Like to like" test in line 26. Why? Unlike the forester, she is vain and artificial. Also, a Muse is a classic symbol of inspired literature. To be decorated and adorned with gold, in this context, would be contrived.

24. **(A)** Lines 2–4, "arguments of learned men's discouragement at this your Order," in conjunction with his statement concerning England's "prelatical yoke" (lines 24–25) reveal the central topic.

25. **(B)** He compares the lack of intellectual freedom in both England and other countries and contrasts the view other countries hold of England's intellectual freedom.

26. **(A)** We can assume that the speaker does eventually try to persuade his readers to take an action (E). In this small passage, he simply is arguing his point to convince readers that England was suffering under the "prelatical yoke."

27. **(B)** He is a "prisoner…for thinking" (line 20), implying that the Inquisition, an intellectual dictatorship, arrested him as one who rebelled against their ideas.

28. **(C)** Lines 23–24 tells us that "…England then was groaning loudest…."

29. **(C)** In line 17, "flattery" is insincere and "fustian" is pretentious.

30. **(A)** The opposition (supporters of the Order) called arguments against the Order "mere flourishes."

31. **(E)** A yoke is traditionally used metaphorically to refer to difficult rules or oppressive laws placed on people who often have no way to resist.

32. **(B)** The speaker optimistically sees "future happiness."

33. **(A)** Servitude is connotative of submission.

34. **(D)** All five answer choices are correct, but which one best states the theme? Notice the portrayal of the people as they make full circle in their perception of the flower's worth.

35. **(E)** Context does not support I or IV. Lines 17–18 introduce the speaker's conclusion or summary point, which he wants his reader to understand and contemplate.

36. **(B)** Again, "read," and "runs" both relate in meaning to the speaker introducing the point he wants his readers to understand.

37. **(C)** How ironic that people would downgrade as a weed what they do not have, steal it, and call it "Splendid" until everyone has it, then downgrade it again!

38. **(B)** Figuratively, "a golden hour" traditionally refers to a time of happiness or flourishing. Why was it golden? Because the seed became a splendid flower.

39. **(A)** A crown symbolizing royalty and light (as from the sun) is beautiful.

40. **(A)** The *abab* rhyme scheme is broken.

41. **(C)** Those who love its delicate white flowers call this plant in the carrot family "Queen Anne's Lace." Those who hate it growing wild call it "ragweed."

42. **(B)** A character study, this poem reveals how quickly people change in their judgments, depending on how the situation affects them personally.

43. **(E)** According to the speaker, understanding this little lesson of life is important, hence the admonition in lines 17–18.

44. **(C)** Once the flower made the moment golden, but now "some are pretty enough, / and some are poor indeed." His interest no longer centers on the flower, itself, but rather on the lesson taught by the experience.

45. **(A)** The subject of the selection is women and their role in reading and writing literature. The "fair sex" is a traditional reference to women.

46. **(E)** This biblical allusion describes victims of oppression, suffering, and the irony being expected to produce without being given what is necessary for such production. The indignation of such "insulting injustice" is clear, but the allusion does not define the extent to which the injustice goes.

47. **(A)** In lines 4–5, "cultivation of their minds" and in lines 23–25, "fruits of good cultivation should appear before the seed was sown" both refer to the education and writings of women.

48. **(D)** The speaker's tone is sarcastic, pointing out that the pin, an instrument normally associated with women in the eighteenth century, was put to such an unreasonable use by men in earlier times.

49. **(B)** The speaker points out that women are put at a disadvantage, then are expected to excel, and are criticized because they cannot accomplish as much as men.

50. **(C)** The subjective construction ("if literature were of no other use") establishes the attitude that "employment" is simply keeping busy rather than a more serious endeavor.

51. **(D)** The speaker does not believe the question of "how many spirits could stand upon [a pin's] point" is "sublime." The speaker obviously thinks the idea is silly.

52. **(C)** Any means of acquiring knowledge would become an opportunity to invent and discover. In this context, however, women would not be seeking to be watched and admired.

53. **(D)** Apostrophe is direct address to an auditor.

54. **(C)** Addressing his lute is the vehicle the speaker uses to mourn "that dear voice" (line 5) that "Is reft from earth" (line 7).

55. **(E)** The speaker uses lines 5–8 to reveal the death of "that dear voice." The rhyme scheme is *abba baba cdde ff*.

56. **(A)** Lutes of Drummond's day were generally made of wood.

57. **(C)** Traditionally, a turtle in poetry refers to the turtledove. Even if you are unaware of this meaning, context should show that the speaker is explaining devotion for his lost mate. A turtledove is symbolic of such devotion.

58. **(B)** While his love was alive, the lute was "harmonious" (line 6); now it is a "harbinger of woe" (line 8).

59. **(E)** He wants the lute to be silent, as before it was made (lines 1–2, 12).

60. **(D)** A sonnet is fourteen lines in iambic pentameter (A). He compares the music to orphan wailings (B). A tree is personified as a "mother" (C). Birds chirp or warble, implying unstructured sounds; the lute's strains were harmonious, structured, controlled (E). There is no context to support that the speaker has any children (D). The "orphan wailings" are what the "pleasing notes" in line 9 have become.

Titles and Authors of Selections in Test Three

Questions

Answer Sheet
PRACTICE TEST FOUR

1 Ⓐ Ⓑ Ⓒ Ⓓ Ⓔ	16 Ⓐ Ⓑ Ⓒ Ⓓ Ⓔ	31 Ⓐ Ⓑ Ⓒ Ⓓ Ⓔ	46 Ⓐ Ⓑ Ⓒ Ⓓ Ⓔ
2 Ⓐ Ⓑ Ⓒ Ⓓ Ⓔ	17 Ⓐ Ⓑ Ⓒ Ⓓ Ⓔ	32 Ⓐ Ⓑ Ⓒ Ⓓ Ⓔ	47 Ⓐ Ⓑ Ⓒ Ⓓ Ⓔ
3 Ⓐ Ⓑ Ⓒ Ⓓ Ⓔ	18 Ⓐ Ⓑ Ⓒ Ⓓ Ⓔ	33 Ⓐ Ⓑ Ⓒ Ⓓ Ⓔ	48 Ⓐ Ⓑ Ⓒ Ⓓ Ⓔ
4 Ⓐ Ⓑ Ⓒ Ⓓ Ⓔ	19 Ⓐ Ⓑ Ⓒ Ⓓ Ⓔ	34 Ⓐ Ⓑ Ⓒ Ⓓ Ⓔ	49 Ⓐ Ⓑ Ⓒ Ⓓ Ⓔ
5 Ⓐ Ⓑ Ⓒ Ⓓ Ⓔ	20 Ⓐ Ⓑ Ⓒ Ⓓ Ⓔ	35 Ⓐ Ⓑ Ⓒ Ⓓ Ⓔ	50 Ⓐ Ⓑ Ⓒ Ⓓ Ⓔ
6 Ⓐ Ⓑ Ⓒ Ⓓ Ⓔ	21 Ⓐ Ⓑ Ⓒ Ⓓ Ⓔ	36 Ⓐ Ⓑ Ⓒ Ⓓ Ⓔ	51 Ⓐ Ⓑ Ⓒ Ⓓ Ⓔ
7 Ⓐ Ⓑ Ⓒ Ⓓ Ⓔ	22 Ⓐ Ⓑ Ⓒ Ⓓ Ⓔ	37 Ⓐ Ⓑ Ⓒ Ⓓ Ⓔ	52 Ⓐ Ⓑ Ⓒ Ⓓ Ⓔ
8 Ⓐ Ⓑ Ⓒ Ⓓ Ⓔ	23 Ⓐ Ⓑ Ⓒ Ⓓ Ⓔ	38 Ⓐ Ⓑ Ⓒ Ⓓ Ⓔ	53 Ⓐ Ⓑ Ⓒ Ⓓ Ⓔ
9 Ⓐ Ⓑ Ⓒ Ⓓ Ⓔ	24 Ⓐ Ⓑ Ⓒ Ⓓ Ⓔ	39 Ⓐ Ⓑ Ⓒ Ⓓ Ⓔ	54 Ⓐ Ⓑ Ⓒ Ⓓ Ⓔ
10 Ⓐ Ⓑ Ⓒ Ⓓ Ⓔ	25 Ⓐ Ⓑ Ⓒ Ⓓ Ⓔ	40 Ⓐ Ⓑ Ⓒ Ⓓ Ⓔ	55 Ⓐ Ⓑ Ⓒ Ⓓ Ⓔ
11 Ⓐ Ⓑ Ⓒ Ⓓ Ⓔ	26 Ⓐ Ⓑ Ⓒ Ⓓ Ⓔ	41 Ⓐ Ⓑ Ⓒ Ⓓ Ⓔ	56 Ⓐ Ⓑ Ⓒ Ⓓ Ⓔ
12 Ⓐ Ⓑ Ⓒ Ⓓ Ⓔ	27 Ⓐ Ⓑ Ⓒ Ⓓ Ⓔ	42 Ⓐ Ⓑ Ⓒ Ⓓ Ⓔ	57 Ⓐ Ⓑ Ⓒ Ⓓ Ⓔ
13 Ⓐ Ⓑ Ⓒ Ⓓ Ⓔ	28 Ⓐ Ⓑ Ⓒ Ⓓ Ⓔ	43 Ⓐ Ⓑ Ⓒ Ⓓ Ⓔ	58 Ⓐ Ⓑ Ⓒ Ⓓ Ⓔ
14 Ⓐ Ⓑ Ⓒ Ⓓ Ⓔ	29 Ⓐ Ⓑ Ⓒ Ⓓ Ⓔ	44 Ⓐ Ⓑ Ⓒ Ⓓ Ⓔ	59 Ⓐ Ⓑ Ⓒ Ⓓ Ⓔ
15 Ⓐ Ⓑ Ⓒ Ⓓ Ⓔ	30 Ⓐ Ⓑ Ⓒ Ⓓ Ⓔ	45 Ⓐ Ⓑ Ⓒ Ⓓ Ⓔ	60 Ⓐ Ⓑ Ⓒ Ⓓ Ⓔ

Practice Test Four

TIME ALLOWED: ONE HOUR

Directions: The following questions test your understanding of several literary selections. Read each passage or poem and the questions that follow it. Select the best answer choice for each question by blackening the matching oval on your answer sheet. **Special attention should be given to questions containing the following words: EXCEPT, LEAST, NOT.**

Questions 1–7 are based on the following passage.

Mr. And Mrs. Hackit, from the neighbouring farm, are Mrs. Patten's guests this evening; so is Mr. Pilgrim, the doctor
Line from the nearest market-town, who,
(5) though occasionally affecting aristocratic airs, and giving late dinners with enigmatic side-dishes and poisonous port, is never so comfortable as when he is relaxing his professional legs in one of those
(10) excellent farmhouses where the mice are sleek and the mistress sickly. And he is at this moment in clover.

For the flickering of Mrs. Patten's bright fire is reflected in her bright copper
(15) tea-kettle, the home-made muffins glisten with an inviting succulence, and Mrs. Patten's niece, a single lady of fifty, who has refused the most ineligible offers out of devotion to her aged aunt, is pouring
(20) the rich cream into the fragrant tea with a discreet liberality.

Reader! did you ever taste such a cup of tea as Miss Gibbs is this moment handing to Mr. Pilgrim? Do you know the dulcet
(25) strength, the animating blandness of tea sufficiently blended with real farmhouse cream? No—most likely you are a miserable town-bred reader, who think of cream as a thinnish white fluid, delivered
(30) in infinitesimal pennyworths down area

steps; or perhaps, from a presentiment of calves' brains, you refrain from any lacteal addition, and rasp your tongue with unmitigated bohea. You have a vague idea
(35) of a milch cow as probably a white-plaster animal standing in a butterman's window, and you know nothing of the sweet history of genuine cream, such as Miss Gibbs's: how it was this morning in the
(40) udders of the large sleek beasts, as they stood lowing a patient entreaty under the milking-shed; how it fell with a pleasant rhythm into Betty's pail, sending a delicious incense into the cool air; how it was
(45) carried into that temple of moist cleanliness, the dairy, where it quietly separated itself from the meaner elements of milk, and lay in mellowed whiteness, ready for the skimming-dish which trans-
(50) ferred it to Miss Gibbs's glass cream-jug. If I am right in my conjecture, you are unacquainted with the highest possibilities of tea: and Mr. Pilgrim, who is holding that cup in his hands, has an idea
(55) beyond you.

(1858)

1. The narrator of this account can best be described as

   (A) unintrusive and fallible
   (B) intrusive and unconscious
   (C) self-effacing in the first person
   (D) self-effacing in the third person
   (E) intrusive and self-conscious

2. What is the effect of the narrator's condescending attitude toward the reader in the last paragraph?

   (A) It antagonizes the reader.
   (B) It creates hyperbole through descriptive contrast.
   (C) It diminishes the value of the subject.
   (D) It creates an ironic epiphany.
   (E) It makes a paradoxical contrast.

3. That Mr. Pilgrim is "in clover" (line 12) means that he is

   (A) animalistic
   (B) happy
   (C) hedonistic
   (D) a farmer
   (E) affecting airs

4. That Miss Gibbs "refused the most ineligible offers" implies that

   (A) she is a woman of high standards
   (B) her aunt's regard was important to her
   (C) no suitors offered her a better situation
   (D) she prefers being single
   (E) no one ever courted her

5. What is the effect of the narrator addressing the "Reader!" in line 22?

   (A) It draws attention away from Miss Gibbs.
   (B) It makes the narrator seem less credible.
   (C) It establishes a relationship between reader and narrator.
   (D) It diminishes the role of the narrator.
   (E) It introduces the subject.

6. In context, "unmitigated bohea" (line 34) is

   (A) a foreign liquor
   (B) black tea without milk
   (C) tea thinned with milk
   (D) green tea
   (E) black coffee

7. Which of the following pairs of words are used as metaphors in this passage?

   (A) "poisonous port" (line 7)… "mice" (line 10)
   (B) "rich cream" (line 20)… "fragrant tea" (line 20)
   (C) "cream" (line 27)… "brains" (line 32)
   (D) "beasts" (line 40)… "pail" (line 43)
   (E) "incense" (line 44)… "temple" (line 45)

Questions 8–21 are based on the following poem.

The Art of Poetry

A poem, where we all perfections find,
Is not the work of a fantastic mind;
There must be care, and time, and skill, and pains;
Line Not the first heat of inexperienced brains.
(5) Yet sometimes artless poets, when the rage
Of a warm fancy does their minds engage,
Puffed with vain pride, presume they understand,
And boldly take the trumpet in their hand:
Their fustian muse each accident confounds;
(10) Nor can she fly, but rise by leaps and bounds,
Till, their small stock of learning quickly spent,
Their poem dies for want of nourishment.
In vain mankind the hot-brained fool decries,
No branding censures can unveil his eyes;
(15) With impudence the laurel they invade,
Resolved to like the monsters they have made.

Virgil, compared to them, is flat and dry;
And Homer understood not poetry:
Against their merit if this age rebel,
(20) To future times for justice they appeal.
But waiting till mankind shall do them
    right,
And bring their works triumphantly to
    light,
Neglected heaps we in bye-corners lay,
Where they become to worms and moths
    a prey.

(ca. 1680)

8. The topic of this poem is

   (A) writers of artless poetry
   (B) inspired monsters
   (C) writers of artful poetry
   (D) how to compose artful poetry
   (E) the works of Homer and Virgil

9. Concerning "artless poets" (line 5), the speaker conveys an attitude that is

   (A) exultant
   (B) convivial
   (C) beguilingly larkish
   (D) tediously practical
   (E) bitterly disapproving

10. A "fantastic mind" (line 2), in contrast to line 3, is in reference to

    (A) capricious thinking
    (B) wonderfully talented thinking
    (C) genius
    (D) creativity
    (E) imagination

11. "And Homer understood not poetry" (line 18) is an expression that reveals the artless poets'

    (A) submissive humility
    (B) chagrined countenance
    (C) pompous arrogance
    (D) groveling servility
    (E) dignified venerability

12. Which of these statements best conveys a reaction of artless poets to criticism of their poetry?

    (A) They look to Virgil and Homer to prove them correct.
    (B) They accept criticism and use it to improve.
    (C) They refuse any unjustly received rewards.
    (D) They claim that a coming age will prove them correct.
    (E) They discontinue writing and leave their poems in neglected heaps.

13. That the works of artless poets become "neglected" and moth-eaten (lines 23–24) in the future can be seen as

    (A) tragic
    (B) ironic
    (C) surprising
    (D) sentimental
    (E) melodramatic

14. The poem is described in lines 11–12 in terms of a

    (A) bird in flight
    (B) depository of learning
    (C) starving, living thing
    (D) monster to be killed
    (E) proud overseer

15. The speaker's tone in lines 17–18 can be considered

    (A) sarcastic
    (B) uncensorious
    (C) magnanimous
    (D) roguish
    (E) reverential

GO ON TO THE NEXT PAGE.

16. Which of the following phrases identifies the meaning of "laurel" as used in line 15?

   I. Honors and awards for poetry
   II. Fame as artful poets
   III. Plants about which poems are written

   (A) I only
   (B) II only
   (C) III only
   (D) I and II only
   (E) I, II, and III

17. The main contrast of the poem is best reflected by which of these pairs of phrases?

   (A) "the work of a fantastic mind" (line 2) and "a warm fancy" (line 6)
   (B) "Puffed with vain pride" (line 7) and "dies for want" (line 12)
   (C) "care, and time, and skill, and pains" (line 3) and "small stock of learning" (line 11)
   (D) "With impudence" (line 15) and "to worms and moths a prey" (line 24)
   (E) "this age rebel" (line 19) and "to worms and moths a prey" (line 24)

18. The "fustian muse" (line 9), as used in context, represents

   (A) inspired thinking
   (B) beautiful poetry
   (C) a monster
   (D) pompous thoughts
   (E) skill in writing

19. "Nor can she fly, but rise by leaps and bounds" (line 10) serves to emphasize

   (A) that writing requires a muse
   (B) the inconsistent quality of artless poetry
   (C) the experiences gained in writing poetry
   (D) that writing poetry requires time
   (E) that poems lift the reader's thoughts

20. Which of the following statements best reflects the speaker's attitude toward writing poetry?

   (A) Writing poetry takes work.
   (B) Many different styles are necessary.
   (C) Artless poets can learn and grow.
   (D) Poems outlive their writers.
   (E) Even artless poets can contribute to the art of poetry.

21. The speaker implies that artless poets are

   (A) hardworking but untalented
   (B) careful and humble
   (C) disrespectful but talented
   (D) cautious and resolved
   (E) lazy and proud

Questions 22–28 are based on the following passage.

     The sea, vast and wild as it is, bears thus the waste and wrecks of human art to its remotest shore. There is no telling
Line what it may not vomit up. It lets nothing
(5) lie; not even the giant clams which cling to its bottom. It is still heaving up the tow-cloth of the *Franklin*, and perhaps a piece of some old pirate's ship, wrecked more than a hundred years ago, comes
(10) ashore today. Some years since, when a vessel was wrecked here which had nutmegs in her cargo, they were strewn all along the beach, and for a considerable time were not spoiled by the salt water.
(15) Soon afterward, a fisherman caught a cod which was full of them. Why, then, might not the Spice Islanders shake their nutmeg trees into the ocean, and let all nations who stand in need of them pick
(20) them up? However, after a year, I found that the nutmegs from the *Franklin* had become soft.

     You might make a curious list of articles which fishes have swallowed—sailors'

(25) open clasp-knives, and bright tin snuff-
boxes, not knowing what was in them—
and jugs, and jewels, and Jonah. The
other day I came across the following
scrap in a newspaper.

(30)   A RELIGIOUS FISH—A short time
ago, mine host Stewart, of the Denton
Hotel, purchased a rock-fish, weighing
about sixty pounds. On opening it he
found in it a certificate of membership
(35) of the M.E. Church, which we read as
follows:

    Methodist E. Church   Member
    Founded A. D. 1784
    Quarterly Ticket   18
(40)   Minister

    For our light affliction, which is but for
a moment, worketh for us a far more
exceeding *and* eternal weight of glory.
—2 Cor. 4:17.

(45)   O what are all my sufferings here,
    If, Lord, thou count me meet
    With that enraptured host t' appear,
    And worship at thy feet.

    The paper was, of course, in a crum-
(50) pled and wet condition, but on exposing
it to the sun, and ironing the kinks out of
it, it became quite legible.

                        (1865)

22. The *"Franklin"* probably refers to

  (A) a man
  (B) a fish
  (C) a shore
  (D) a cargo
  (E) a boat

23. "Jonah," as used in line 27, is a(n)

  (A) metaphor
  (B) allusion
  (C) simile
  (D) aphorism
  (E) antithesis

24. Of the literary devices listed below, which is
used in line 27 to describe items found in
fishes?

  (A) Slanted rhyme
  (B) Alliteration
  (C) Apostrophe
  (D) Dead metaphor
  (E) Eye rhyme

25. As used in line 23, "curious" can be considered as also meaning

  (A) accurate
  (B) fastidious
  (C) strange
  (D) prying
  (E) desirous to know

26. A possible reason that the certificate of
membership was newsworthy is that

  (A) it was still legible after being eaten by
      a fish
  (B) it was so old
  (C) it was from a shipwreck
  (D) it contained no names or addresses
  (E) it contained a poem in the certificate

27. In line 46, "meet" can NOT be considered
to mean

  (A) encountered
  (B) suitable
  (C) qualified
  (D) adapted
  (E) fit

28. In line 26, "not knowing what was in them"
might lead one to believe that

  (A) fish lack intelligence
  (B) snuff attracts fish
  (C) the fish were attracted by the
      brightness
  (D) snuff is poisonous to fish
  (E) the snuff harmed the fish

GO ON TO THE NEXT PAGE.

Questions 29–42 are based on the following poem.

The Light of Other Days

Oft in the stilly night
    Ere slumber's chain has bound me,
Fond Memory brings the light
Line   Of other days around me:
(5)   The smiles, the tears
            Of boyhood's years,
      The words of love then spoken;
          The eyes that shone,
          Now dimm'd and gone,
(10)   The cheerful hearts now broken!
Thus in the stilly night
    Ere slumber's chain has bound me,
Sad Memory brings the light
    Of other days around me.
(15)   When I remember all
      The friends so link'd together
I've seen around me fall
      Like leaves in wintry weather,
          I feel like one
(20)   Who treads alone
Some banquet-hall deserted,
         Whose lights are fled
         Whose garlands dead,
And all but he departed!
(25)   Thus in the stilly night
    Ere slumber's chain has bound me,
Sad Memory brings the light
    Of other days around me.

                    (ca. 1800)

29. Which of the following is the LEAST applicable definition of "stilly" as it is used in this poem?

    (A) Simple
    (B) Still
    (C) Calm
    (D) Silent
    (E) Quiet

30. "Light" (line 3), in the context of this poem, is connotative of all the following EXCEPT

    (A) a previous time
    (B) understanding
    (C) remembrances
    (D) awareness
    (E) radiation

31. In line 2, sleep is made to appear as a

    (A) weak link
    (B) towing device
    (C) golden necklace
    (D) captor
    (E) thief

32. The speaker uses "Thus" in lines 11 and 25 rather than "Oft" as in line 1. What is the effect?

    (A) It shifts the tense of the stanza.
    (B) "Oft" implies frequence, whereas "Thus" implies infrequency.
    (C) "Thus" establishes a cause-and-effect relationship.
    (D) "Thus" emphasizes the tone.
    (E) "Thus" signals a restatement of the theme.

33. Of the pairs of words listed below, which best reflects the contrast of lines 5–8 to lines 9–10?

    (A) "eyes" (line 8) and "hearts" (line 10)
    (B) "tears" (line 5) and "broken" (line 10)
    (C) "night" (line 1) and "light" (line 13)
    (D) "love" (line 7) and "cheerful" (line 10)
    (E) "Fond Memory" (line 3) and "Sad Memory" (line 13)

34. The speaker in the poem is best described as someone who is feeling

    (A) nostalgic and happy
    (B) lonely and abandoned
    (C) warm and caring
    (D) wistful and peaceful
    (E) angry and bitter

35. The relationship between "friends" in lines 15–18 and "I" in lines 19–24 is also seen in which of the following pairs?

    (A) "fall" (line 17) and "dead" (line 23)
    (B) "wintry" (line 18) and "deserted" (line 21)
    (C) "remember" (line 15) and "feel" (line 19)
    (D) "link'd together" (line 16) and "alone" (line 20)
    (E) "leaves" (line 18) and "lights" (line 22)

36. Of the literary devices listed below, which is used to describe the friends in lines 15–18?

    (A) Simile
    (B) Illusion
    (C) Personification
    (D) Understatement
    (E) Overstatement

37. This poem can best be seen as presenting the thoughts of someone

    (A) who is becoming fearful of death
    (B) whose friends and family are gone
    (C) whose life is just beginning
    (D) who has not adjusted to feelings of guilt
    (E) who is in love

38. Contextually, moving from "boyhood's years" (line 6) to "wintry weather" (line 18) to "departed" (line 24) reflects a change from the

    (A) abstract to the concrete
    (B) sad to the happy
    (C) past to the future
    (D) spoken to the unspoken
    (E) real to the unreal

39. The poem's overall subject is

    (A) youth
    (B) memories
    (C) old age
    (D) death
    (E) sleep

40. Line 19 is notable for introducing which of the following?

    (A) The rhyme scheme changes from that of the first stanza.
    (B) Personification is used to depict the speaker's life.
    (C) Light becomes a symbol for vision.
    (D) The speaker examines his present condition.
    (E) The speaker refuses to be comforted by Memory.

41. What is the effect of the simile as used in lines 19–24?

    (A) It highlights the events missing in the speaker's life.
    (B) It contrasts the role of "Memory" in line 27.
    (C) It introduces the element of fear into the speaker's tone.
    (D) It depicts the speaker's boyhood years.
    (E) It emphasizes the speaker's sense of loneliness.

42. The "banquet-hall" in line 21 is contextually referring to

    (A) a place to eat
    (B) a gathering place
    (C) the speaker's life
    (D) the place where the speaker once met people
    (E) the speaker's old home

Questions 43–47 are based on the following passage.

To the Gas and Electric Lighting Company

　　Gentlemen:

　　　　There are but two places in our whole street where lights could be of any value, by any accident, and you have measured
Line and appointed your intervals so ingen-
(5) iously as to leave each of those places in the centre of a couple of hundred yards of solid darkness. When I noticed that you

GO ON TO THE NEXT PAGE.

were setting one of your lights in such a way that I could almost see how to get
(10) into my gate at night, I suspected that it was a piece of carelessness on the part of the workmen, and would be corrected as soon as you should go around inspecting and find it out. My judgment was right; it
(15) is always right, when you are concerned. For fifteen years, in spite of my prayers and fears, you persistently kept a gas lamp exactly half way between my gates, so that I couldn't find either of them after dark;
(20) and then furnished such execrable gas that I had to hang a danger signal on the lamppost to keep teams from running into it, nights. Now I suppose your present idea is to leave us a little more in the
(25) dark.

Don't mind us—out our way; we possess but one vote apiece, and no rights that you are in any way bound to respect. Please take your electric light and go to—
(30) but never mind, it is not for me to suggest; you will probably find the way, and any way you can reasonably count on divine assistance if you lose your bearings.

S. L. Clemens (ca. 1905)

43. The attitude of the speaker toward the utility company is best described as

(A) amused
(B) irritated
(C) contrite
(D) understanding
(E) responsible

44. The phrase "to leave us a little more in the dark" is intended as a(n)

(A) oxymoron
(B) allusion
(C) play on words
(D) hyperbole
(E) understatement

45. In line 20, "execrable" means which of the following?

I. Poor quality
II. Detestable
III. Hateful
IV. Cursed

(A) I only
(B) II only
(C) III only
(D) I and II
(E) II, III, and IV

46. The overall tone of the letter is created by all the following EXCEPT

(A) irony
(B) banter
(C) ridicule
(D) sarcasm
(E) caustic remarks

47. The reference to "one vote apiece" suggests that

(A) government intervention is necessary
(B) the utility company is privately owned
(C) the utility company is owned by the public
(D) the company has lobbyists
(E) the company plans its stock shares to go public

Questions 48–52 are based on the following poem.

Answer

Sound, sound the clarion, fill the fife!
   To all the sensual world proclaim,
One crowded hour of glorious life
   Is worth an age without a name.

(ca. 1799)

48. The poem exhibits elements that are

    (A) apologetic
    (B) apathetic
    (C) aphoristic
    (D) apocalyptic
    (E) aposiopetic

49. Of the devices listed below, which is used to draw the hearer's attention in line 1?

    (A) Alliteration, echoism, and spondaic foot
    (B) Triple rhyme
    (C) Echoism and pun
    (D) Alliteration, enjambement, and echoism
    (E) Imperfect rhyme

50. Of the following phrases, which best conveys the theme of the poem?

    (A) A glorious life of anonymity
    (B) Quality of life over quantity
    (C) A celebration in the sensual world
    (D) Longevity over reputation
    (E) Responsibilities

51. The contrasting theme of the poem could be expressed as

    I. "Crowded"…"worth"
    II. "Glorious"…"without a name"
    III. "Hour"…"age"
    (A) I only
    (B) II only
    (C) I and II only
    (D) II and III only
    (E) I, II, and III

52. In line 4, the "name" connotes

    (A) a royal title
    (B) a concept or denomination
    (C) a good reputation or honor
    (D) a representative
    (E) an appellation

Questions 53–60 are based on the following passage.

Act I. Scene 1

Narvarre. The King's *park*

Enter the King, Berowne, Longaville, *and* Dumain

KING. Let fame, that all hunt after in their lives,
Live regist'red upon our brazen tombs,
And then grace us in the disgrace of death;
When, spite of cormorant devouring Time,

Line
(5) Th' endeavour of this present breath may buy
That honour which shall bate his scythe's keen edge,
And make us heirs of all eternity.
Therefore, brave conquerors—for so you are
That war against your own affections

(10) And the huge army of the world's desires—
Our late edict shall strongly stand in force:
Navarre shall be the wonder of the world;
Our court shall be a little Academe,
Still and contemplative in living art.

(15) You three, Berowne, Dumain, and Longaville,
Have sworn for three years' term to live with me
My fellow-scholars, and to keep those statutes
That are recorded in this schedule here.
Your oaths are pass'd; and now subscribe your names,

GO ON TO THE NEXT PAGE.

(20) That his own hand may strike his
honour down
That violates the smallest branch
herein.
If you are arm'd to do as sworn to
do,
Subscribe to your deep oaths, and
keep it too.

LONGAVILLE. I am resolv'd; 'tis but a
three years' fast.

(25) The mind shall banquet, though
the body pine.
Fat paunches have lean pates; and
dainty bits
Make rich the ribs, but bankrupt
quite the wits.

(1598)

53. The situation of this drama is that

(A) the king is planning a military battle
(B) three men request the king's help
(C) the king is about to die and plans his final hours
(D) Time has cut into the heart of Navarre
(E) the king enlists three men to three years of study

54. The king's motivation, as described in lines 1–7, is

(A) to establish his reputation beyond his death
(B) to prevent his own death
(C) to reestablish his rule in Navarre
(D) to entrap his three friends
(E) to conquer "the huge army of the world's desires" (line 10)

55. The metaphor in lines 8–10 suggests that the "statutes" in line 17

(A) are laws of Navarre
(B) are part of a peace negotiation
(C) concern physical rules
(D) are part of a military code
(E) resemble a battle plan for soldiers

56. In this scene, there is a symbolic conflict between

(A) youth and age
(B) women and men
(C) peace and war
(D) life and death
(E) learning and ignorance

57. The king's words reveal that he is

(A) a coward
(B) anticipating war
(C) a war hero
(D) new to scholarship
(E) an idealistic man

58. As used in the passage, the contrasts of "banquet…pine" (line 25), "Fat…lean" (line 26), and "rich…bankrupt" (line 27) are designed to

(A) diminish the importance of the statute
(B) mirror the king's search for immortality
(C) emphasize the incompatibility of learning and sumptuous living
(D) impact the grace found in death
(E) imply that Time does not really devour

59. As presented in the drama, the elements in line 27 ("Make rich the ribs, but bankrupt quite the wits") are in

(A) corroboration
(B) trisyllabical form
(C) antithesis
(D) a tragic flaw
(E) a cotangent

60. In the paradoxical relationship of "grace… in the disgrace of death" (line 3), the grace is the result of

(A) posthumous celebrity
(B) the hunt for fame
(C) human greed
(D) death itself
(E) life itself

If there is still time remaining, you may review your answers.

Answer Key: Practice Test Four

1. **(E)**	7. **(E)**	13. **(B)**	19. **(B)**	25. **(C)**	31. **(D)**	37. **(B)**	43. **(B)**	49. **(A)**	55. **(C)**
2. **(B)**	8. **(A)**	14. **(C)**	20. **(A)**	26. **(A)**	32. **(C)**	38. **(C)**	44. **(C)**	50. **(B)**	56. **(D)**
3. **(B)**	9. **(E)**	15. **(A)**	21. **(E)**	27. **(A)**	33. **(E)**	39. **(B)**	45. **(A)**	51. **(D)**	57. **(E)**
4. **(C)**	10. **(A)**	16. **(D)**	22. **(E)**	28. **(C)**	34. **(B)**	40. **(D)**	46. **(B)**	52. **(C)**	58. **(C)**
5. **(C)**	11. **(C)**	17. **(C)**	23. **(B)**	29. **(A)**	35. **(D)**	41. **(E)**	47. **(C)**	53. **(E)**	59. **(C)**
6. **(B)**	12. **(D)**	18. **(D)**	24. **(B)**	30. **(E)**	36. **(A)**	42. **(C)**	48. **(C)**	54. **(A)**	60. **(A)**

TO OBTAIN YOUR RAW SCORE:

_____ divided by 4 = _____
Total wrong   Score W

_____ minus _____ = _____
   Total right   Score W   Score R

Round Score R to the nearest whole number for the raw score.

SCORE CONVERSION TABLE FOR PRACTICE TESTS

(based on estimated values)

Raw Score	Scaled Score	Raw Score	Scaled Score	Raw Score	Scaled Score	Raw Score	Scaled Score
60	800	40	660	20	500	0	330
59	800	38	650	19	490	−1	320
58	800	38	640	18	480	−2	310
57	800	37	640	17	470	−3	300
56	790	36	630	16	470	−4	290
55	790	35	620	15	460	−5	280
54	780	34	610	14	450	−6	270
53	770	33	600	13	440	−7	260
52	760	32	590	12	430	−8	250
51	750	31	590	11	430	−9	240
50	740	30	580	10	420	−10	230
49	730	29	570	9	410	−11	220
48	720	28	560	8	400	−12	210
47	710	27	550	7	390	−13	200
46	710	26	550	6	390	−14	200
45	700	25	540	5	380		
44	690	24	530	4	370		
43	680	23	520	3	360		
42	680	22	510	2	350		
41	670	21	510	1	340		

Explanations: Practice Test Four

NOTE: Most practice tests cannot duplicate the content and conditions of the actual Literature test. Also, the scope and definitions of the literary elements can differ among literary critics; therefore, the rationale behind what constitutes a correct or an incorrect answer choice may vary. Each of these practice tests, however, gives you an opportunity to analyze selections, think critically, and develop your test-taking skills so you can do your personal best on the SAT Subject Test in Literature.

1. **(E)** The speaker's expressed opinions make him intrusive; directly addressing the reader makes him self-conscious.

2. **(B)** Such a superior attitude over tea and milk creates hyperbole disproportionate to the subject. The nature of the subject makes his insulting tone more comical than antagonizing (A). There are no diminishing (C) or paradoxical (E) elements to his descriptions, and although his descriptions hint at an experience of epiphany, his condescending attitude ruins such a moment for the reader.

3. **(B)** To be "in clover" means the fields are producing and you are experiencing prosperous living. Such colloquial phrases vary by region. For example, in Texas a desirable circumstance is "walking in tall cotton."

4. **(C)** The addition of "most ineligible," carries several implications. Publicly, she is devoted to her aunt. She refused most ineligible offers. What made them ineligible? Were there any eligible offers? Would she have refused an eligible offer in favor of her aunt?

5. **(C)** Whether for good or bad, when the narrator directly addresses the reader, a relationship is established.

6. **(B)** Do you know what a "bohea" is? You should know that "unmitigated" means that something has not been lessened or softened. Next, look at context. The subject is cream in tea. If "you refrain from any lacteal addition," then you drink "unmitigated bohea," black tea without milk.

7. **(E)** The narrator explains his metaphor for you in lines 45–46: "that temple of moist cleanliness, the dairy," where, of course, the warm milk sends "incense into the cool air."

8. **(A)** Line 5 reveals the topic: "artless poets" whose poems die (line 12) as "monsters" (line 16).

9. **(E)** He sees such poets as proud (line 7), unlearned (line 11), and impudent (line 15).

10. **(A)** By definition, a "fantastic mind" is capricious. Also, a contrast is established with careful, skillful thinking on one side and fanciful thinking on the other.

11. **(C)** You should be familiar with the names Virgil and Homer, but even if you are not, context tells you that the speaker is holding them in contrast to artless poets. Consequently, they must represent true poets. To criticize their work would be pompous and arrogant.

12. **(D)** Read lines 19–20: They "appeal" to "future times" to "do them right" (line 21).

13. **(B)** Artless poets believe the future will prove them correct, but does this future point ever arrive? Instead, their works are in "Neglected heaps" (line 23), an ironic situation.

14. **(C)** Associating learning and thinking with food (nourishment) is an example of traditional imagery ("food for thought"). For a poem to die "for want of nourishment" relates to such imagery and makes the poem seem like a living, or in this case, starving-to-death thing.

15. **(A)** These artless poets ironically consider themselves better than Virgil and Homer. Such undeserved praise is said with critical intent, sarcasm.

16. **(D)** Context points to honor and fame in the future (lines 20–23). Plants are not involved.

17. **(C)** Define the central contrast: artless poets and their works versus true poets and poetry. Line 3 describes what is necessary for a perfect poem (line 1), in contrast to the quickly exhausted "small stock of learning" (line 11) of the artless poem.

18. **(D)** A fustian work is inflated or pompous.

19. **(B)** Artless poets do not sustain their work at high levels of expression, but inconsistently go up and down in thought and probably form.

20. **(A)** The speaker's position is stated in lines 1–3: Poetry takes "care, and time, and skill, and pains."

21. **(E)** They are unwilling to expend the care, time, skill, and pain necessary (line 3): and they are proud (line 7).

22. **(E)** A ship could have a tow-cloth (line 7) and a cargo (lines 10–12, 21–22), and could be wrecked at sea.

23. **(B)** You should be familiar with the account of Jonah and the whale, a well-known biblical allusion.

24. **(B)** Repetition of the initial "j" sound is an example of alliteration.

25. **(C)** How strange for a fish to swallow an open knife! "Curious" also means "strange" in this context.

26. **(A)** Context shows the speaker's fascination with how long nutmegs were not spoiled by the water. Consistently, he points out that the paper is still legible. Also, note that the paper tells when the church was founded, but not when the words were written.

27. **(A)** Substituting each choice in the line will reveal the correct answer in context with line 46: "encountered" does not make sense used in line 46.

28. **(C)** The fish are not after the contents; therefore, the fact that the boxes were "bright tin" (line 25) implies they are attracted by the brightness.

29. **(A)** Again, substitute each choice in context and you will find that "simple" does not fit the meaning of the line.

30. **(E)** In conjunction with "Fond Memory," radiation is too literal in meaning.

31. **(D)** Of the five answer choices, only a captor would bind another with chains.

32. **(C)** "Thus" can mean "in this or that manner" or "therefore."

33. **(E)** Establish the contrast. (Notice the colon in line 4.) In lines 5–8 the speaker describes "Fond Memory." Lines 9–10 shift to the negative, and line 11 shifts to "thus" as the cause for Memory being labeled "Sad" (line 13).

34. **(B)** Obviously, he is not happy, warm, or peaceful. Is he angry and bitter (E)? Perhaps, however, lines 19–24 clearly describe a lonely, abandoned person.

35. **(D)** Answer choice D reflects the speaker's central point: I had friends (link'd together); now they are gone and I am alone.

36. **(A)** His friends "fall / Like leaves," an example of simile.

37. **(B)** The situation of the speaker is revealed in lines 19–24: He is alone "And all but he departed!"

38. **(C)** Reference to the winter season is traditionally figurative of old age. Line 24 expresses his lonely condition, but also hints at or foreshadows his inevitable future.

39. **(B)** The subject appears in lines 3, 13, and 27: "Fond Memory."

40. **(D)** The speaker deals mostly with his memory to this point. He now reveals how all these memories of the past and his current condition affect him today.

41. **(E)** (A) is a correct answer choice on a literal level. He is missing eating and laughing at banquets with his friends. However, the question asks the effect of the simile. How lonely it sounds to be the last one left when the party is over! Remember: Look for the *best* answer choice.

42. **(C)** Examine the simile: In the banquet-hall of his life, he once dined with friends. Now, his friends are gone and he is alone in life.

43. **(B)** The speaker complains of the locations of the street lights and accuses the utility company of deliberate action against him. He is irritated.

44. **(C)** To leave someone "in the dark" is a traditional expression meaning to keep a secret from the person or to fail to let the person know the reasons behind an action. In this case, the speaker is using the expression as a play on words when he implies that he doesn't know what the electric company officials are thinking of (leaving him in the "dark"), because they are literally leaving him in the "dark."

45. **(A)** All four selections define "execrable." In context, however, the gas was insufficient to keep teams from running into the lamppost, in other words, of poor quality.

46. **(B)** That the workmen would accidently put a street light in a relatively good position, then move it, is an ironic situation. The speaker ridicules the company's attitude toward its customers and uses sarcasm and hyperbole by claiming to be "always right, when you [the company] are concerned." His suggestion about where they can go is definitely caustic (cutting), but nowhere in the letter does he engage in playful teasing (banter).

47. **(C)** In municipally owned utility companies, voters often have a part in deciding major issues.

48. **(C)** Aphorism is a concise statement that makes a point.

49. **(A)** Repetition of initial "s" and "f" is alliteration; repetition of "sound" is echoism; two strong, stressed syllables ("sound, sound") is a spondee.

50. **(B)** The theme is quality ("a glorious life" versus "life without a name") over quantity ("One crowded hour" versus "an age").

51. **(D)** The theme is found in the contrast of line 3 to 4. The speaker prefers a short, glorious life to one that is long, but without glory.

52. **(C)** This name is in contrast "to a glorious life."

53. **(E)** The situation is expressed in lines 16–17: fellow-scholars vow a three-year term.

54. **(A)** "Let fame …Live regist'red upon our brazen tombs…" (lines 1–2). The king wants his headstone to tell future generations of his deeds.

55. **(C)** They are going to "war against …affections / And… the world's desires." Such a battle would require them to agree to rules of conduct. Included is a three-year fast (line 24).

56. **(D)** Time is viewed as one that devours (line 4) in death, but the king seeks to become "heirs of all eternity" or life through fame.

57. **(E)** Ideals are ideas considered goal-worthy, even if impractical. To be idealistic is to live a life based on ideals.

58. **(C)** Again, these contrasts reflect the two sides of the king's figurative war between mind and body.

59. **(C)** A balance of contrasts: you can have food without learning or learning without food.

60. **(A)** "Let fame …Live regist'rd upon our brazen tombs" (lines 1–2). To grace someone is to honor him or her, in this case, after death.

Titles and Authors of Selections in Test Four

Questions

Answer Sheet
PRACTICE TEST FIVE

1 (A) (B) (C) (D) (E)	16 (A) (B) (C) (D) (E)	31 (A) (B) (C) (D) (E)	46 (A) (B) (C) (D) (E)
2 (A) (B) (C) (D) (E)	17 (A) (B) (C) (D) (E)	32 (A) (B) (C) (D) (E)	47 (A) (B) (C) (D) (E)
3 (A) (B) (C) (D) (E)	18 (A) (B) (C) (D) (E)	33 (A) (B) (C) (D) (E)	48 (A) (B) (C) (D) (E)
4 (A) (B) (C) (D) (E)	19 (A) (B) (C) (D) (E)	34 (A) (B) (C) (D) (E)	49 (A) (B) (C) (D) (E)
5 (A) (B) (C) (D) (E)	20 (A) (B) (C) (D) (E)	35 (A) (B) (C) (D) (E)	50 (A) (B) (C) (D) (E)
6 (A) (B) (C) (D) (E)	21 (A) (B) (C) (D) (E)	36 (A) (B) (C) (D) (E)	51 (A) (B) (C) (D) (E)
7 (A) (B) (C) (D) (E)	22 (A) (B) (C) (D) (E)	37 (A) (B) (C) (D) (E)	52 (A) (B) (C) (D) (E)
8 (A) (B) (C) (D) (E)	23 (A) (B) (C) (D) (E)	38 (A) (B) (C) (D) (E)	53 (A) (B) (C) (D) (E)
9 (A) (B) (C) (D) (E)	24 (A) (B) (C) (D) (E)	39 (A) (B) (C) (D) (E)	54 (A) (B) (C) (D) (E)
10 (A) (B) (C) (D) (E)	25 (A) (B) (C) (D) (E)	40 (A) (B) (C) (D) (E)	55 (A) (B) (C) (D) (E)
11 (A) (B) (C) (D) (E)	26 (A) (B) (C) (D) (E)	41 (A) (B) (C) (D) (E)	56 (A) (B) (C) (D) (E)
12 (A) (B) (C) (D) (E)	27 (A) (B) (C) (D) (E)	42 (A) (B) (C) (D) (E)	57 (A) (B) (C) (D) (E)
13 (A) (B) (C) (D) (E)	28 (A) (B) (C) (D) (E)	43 (A) (B) (C) (D) (E)	58 (A) (B) (C) (D) (E)
14 (A) (B) (C) (D) (E)	29 (A) (B) (C) (D) (E)	44 (A) (B) (C) (D) (E)	59 (A) (B) (C) (D) (E)
15 (A) (B) (C) (D) (E)	30 (A) (B) (C) (D) (E)	45 (A) (B) (C) (D) (E)	60 (A) (B) (C) (D) (E)

Practice Test Five

TIME ALLOWED: ONE HOUR

Directions: The following questions test your understanding of several literary selections. Read each passage or poem and the questions that follow it. Select the best answer choice for each question by blackening the matching oval on your answer sheet. **Special attention should be given to questions containing the following words: EXCEPT, LEAST, NOT.**

Questions 1–8 are based on the following passage.

'Could Colonel Forster repeat the particulars of Lydia's note to his wife?'

'He brought it with him for us to see.'

Line
(5) Jane then took it from her pocket-book, and gave it to Elizabeth. There were the contents:

MY DEAR HARRIET,

You will laugh when you know where I am gone, and I cannot help laughing myself
(10) *at your surprise tomorrow morning, as soon as I am missed. I am going to Gretna Green, and if you cannot guess with who, I shall think you a simpleton, for there is but one man in the world I love, so think it no harm*
(15) *to be off. You need not send them word at Longbourn of my going, if you do not like it, for it will make the surprise the greater, when I write to them, and sign my name Lydia Wickham. What a good joke it will*
(20) *be! I can hardly write for laughing. Pray make my excuses to Pratt, for not keeping my engagement, and dancing with him to night. Tell him I hope he will excuse me when he knows all, and tell him I will*
(25) *dance with him at the next ball we meet, with great pleasure. I shall send for my clothes when I get to Longbourn; but I wish you would tell Sally to mend a great slit in my working muslin gown, before they are*
(30) *packed up. Good bye. Give my love to Colonel Forster, I hope you will drink to our good journey.*

Your affectionate friend,
LYDIA BENNET.

(35) 'Oh! thoughtless, thoughtless Lydia!' cried Elizabeth when she had finished it. 'What a letter is this, to be written at such a moment. But at least it shews, that *she* was serious in the object of her journey.
(40) Whatever he might afterwards persuade her to, it was not on her side a *scheme* of infamy. My poor father! how he must have felt it!'

'I never saw any one so shocked. He
(45) could not speak a word for full ten minutes. My mother was taken ill immediately, and the whole house in such confusion!'

'Oh! Jane,' cried Elizabeth, 'was there a
(50) servant belonging to it, who did not know the whole story before the end of the day?'

(1813)

1. Lydia Bennet's letter indicates that she

   (A) is priggish and pedantric in her attitude toward her family
   (B) is going on vacation to Gretna Green
   (C) is eloping with Pratt
   (D) is in love with Pratt
   (E) is eloping with Wickham

2. Of the following, all are correct concerning the letter EXCEPT that

   (A) it reveals that Lydia has planned the trip well in advance
   (B) its tone is giddy and excited
   (C) it reveals that Lydia's plans were not generally known
   (D) its purpose is to announce a surprise
   (E) it was addressed to Mrs. Forster

3. Elizabeth's remarks concerning the letter's contents indicate that

   (A) Lydia is not really in love
   (B) Wickham does love Lydia
   (C) Wickham may not intend to marry Lydia
   (D) the family will take the news well
   (E) Wickham's intentions are sincere

4. Elizabeth's response to the letter shows that she

   (A) disapproves of Lydia's conduct
   (B) is jealous of Lydia's happiness
   (C) does not understand what has happened
   (D) is very happy for Lydia
   (E) wishes that she, too, could elope

5. The expression "a scheme of infamy" (lines 41–42) means

   (A) a respectable idea
   (B) a shameful plan of action
   (C) a well-planned course of action
   (D) an ill-advised idea
   (E) a concise statement of intents and purposes

6. Under the circumstances of the letter, for Lydia to promise Pratt a dance at the next ball reveals that her feelings are

   (A) shy and coy
   (B) embarrassed and resentful
   (C) humble and introspective
   (D) flippant and insolent
   (E) direct and pragmatic

7. The words "simpleton" (line 13), "joke" (line 19), and "laughing" (line 20) show that Lydia

   (A) is a congenial person
   (B) has an inappropriate attitude
   (C) regards her family as emotionally unstable
   (D) has a keen sense of perception
   (E) suspects that the family knew of her plan

8. Elizabeth's question in lines 49–52 reveals that

   (A) she wants to find someone who can tell her more
   (B) such a servant should be dismissed
   (C) she wishes Lydia's action could be kept secret
   (D) the servants are generally unaware of such happenings
   (E) Lydia took care that no servants would learn of her plan

Questions 9–15 are based on the following poem.

May

I feel a newer life in every gale;
    The winds that fan the flowers,
And with their welcome breathings fill the sail,
Line   Tell of serener hours—
(5)   Of hours that glide unfelt away
    Beneath the sky of May.
The spirit of the gentle south-wind calls
    From his blue throne of air,
And where his whispering voice in music falls,
(10)   Beauty is budding there;
    The bright ones of the valley break
    Their slumbers, and awake.
The waving verdure rolls along the plain,
    And the wide forest weaves,
(15) To welcome back its playful mates again,
    A canopy of leaves;
    And from its darkening shadow floats

A gush of trembling notes.
Fairer and brighter spreads the reign of
   May;
(20)   The tresses of the woods
With the light dallying of the west-wind
   play;
      And the full-brimming floods,
   As gladly to their goal they run,
      Hail the returning sun.

                                      (ca. 1850)

9. The "bright ones of the valley" (line 11) probably are

(A) gifted children
(B) sunbeams
(C) flowers
(D) gems
(E) reflective windows

10. The word "verdure" places an emphasis on which of the following?

(A) Movement
(B) Multicolor
(C) Windy conditions
(D) Green color
(E) Flatness

11. "The tresses of the woods" (line 20) is an example of which of these literary devices?

(A) Antithesis
(B) Simile
(C) Metonymy
(D) Synecdoche
(E) Personification

12. The end-rhyme used in lines 20 and 22 is an example of

(A) rime riche
(B) eye rhyme
(C) echo verse
(D) forced rhyme
(E) feminine rhyme

13. The "playful mates" in line 15 are probably

   I. migrating birds
  II. the south (line 7) and west (line 21) winds
 III. children on summer vacation

(A) I only
(B) II only
(C) III only
(D) I and II only
(E) I, II, and III

14. The central imagery of this poem is based on

(A) sound
(B) movement
(C) color
(D) light
(E) darkness

15. In line 8, "his blue throne of air" serves as which of the following?

(A) Hyperbole
(B) Euphemism
(C) Personification
(D) Ambiguity
(E) Plurisignation

Questions 16–24 are based on the following passage.

In the very olden time, there lived a semi-barbaric king, whose ideas, though somewhat polished and sharpened by the
Line progressiveness of distant Latin neigh-
(5) bors, were still large, florid, and untram-melled, as became the half of him which was barbaric. He was a man of exuberant fancy, and, withal, of an authority so irre-sistible that, at his will, he turned his var-
(10) ied fancies into facts. He was greatly given to self-communing, and when he and himself agreed upon anything, the thing was done. When every member of his domestic and political systems moved
(15) smoothly in its appointed course, his nature was bland and genial; but when-

ever there was a little hitch, and some of his orbs got out of their orbits, he was blander and more genial still, for nothing (20) pleased him so much as to make the crooked straight, and crush down uneven places.

Among the borrowed notions by which his barbarism had become semified was (25) that of the public arena, in which, by exhibitions of manly and beastly valor; the minds of his subjects were refined and cultured.

But even here the exuberant and bar-(30) baric fancy asserted itself. The arena of the king was built, not to give the people an opportunity of hearing the rhapsodies of dying gladiators, nor to enable them to view the inevitable conclusion of a con-(35) flict between religious opinions and hungry jaws, but for purposes far better adapted to widen and develop the mental energies of the people. This vast amphitheatre, with its encircling galleries, its (40) mysterious vaults, and its unseen passages, was an agent of poetic justice, in which crime was punished, or virtue rewarded, by the decrees of an impartial and incorruptible chance.

(45) When a subject was accused of a crime of sufficient importance to interest the king, public notice was given that on an appointed day the fate of the accused person would be decided in the king's (50) arena—a structure which well deserved its name; for, although its form and plan were borrowed from afar, its purpose emanated solely from the brain of this man, who, every barleycorn a king, knew (55) no tradition to which he owed more allegiance than pleased his fancy, and who ingrafted on every adopted form of human thought and action the rich growth of his barbaric idealism.

(1882)

16. The words "large, florid, and untrammelled" (lines 5–6) are characteristic of which of the following personality traits?

   I. Unrestrained
   II. Traitorous
   III. Restrained
   IV. Abstruse

   (A) I only
   (B) II only
   (C) III only
   (D) I and IV only
   (E) II and IV only

17. As used in the passage, "self-communing" (line 11) can be recognized as

   (A) schizophrenia
   (B) consulting with counselors
   (C) relying on the thinking of others
   (D) counterintelligence
   (E) introspection

18. Which of the answers below can be considered the vehicle used to describe problems in the king's life?

   (A) Pinballs
   (B) Electrons
   (C) Solar system
   (D) Molecules
   (E) Eyes

19. From where did the king get the idea of the public arena?

   (A) Self-communing
   (B) Distant Latin neighbors
   (C) Nature
   (D) Planetary signs
   (E) Domestic and political systems

20. Within the last paragraph, the king is characterized by the speaker as

   (A) lonely
   (B) dull
   (C) reliable
   (D) morally motivated
   (E) self-confident

21. The words "barbaric idealism" (line 59), as seen as a paradox, compares with which of the following?

    (A) Savage beasts
    (B) Gentle children
    (C) Respectful dignitaries
    (D) Honor among thieves
    (E) Life among enemies

22. Historically, "a conflict between religious opinions and hungry jaws" (lines 35–36) can be exemplified by

    (A) theological debates
    (B) throwing Christians to the lions
    (C) theological criticisms
    (D) the Salem witch trials
    (E) resistance to civil authority

23. As used in line 41, "poetic justice" is used ironically because

    (A) although impartial, chance is in antithesis to true justice
    (B) justice requires no agent
    (C) justice was the subject of the king's poetry
    (D) the amphitheatre is being personified
    (E) crime usually is rewarded and virtue punished

24. As given in line 54, the phrase "every barleycorn a king" can best be thought of as

    (A) a king over an agricultural society
    (B) a king in every respect
    (C) commoners given royal status
    (D) a society that worships grain
    (E) a humorous personification for a drunken king

Questions 25–30 are based on the following poem.

> Ah, sun-flower! weary of time,
> Who countest the steps of the Sun;
> Seeking after that sweet golden clime,
> *Line* Where the traveller's journey is done;
> *(5)* Where the Youth pined away with desire,
> And the pale Virgin shrouded in snow,
> Arise from their graves, and aspire
> Where my sun-flower wishes to go.
>
> (ca. 1783)

25. In the poem, "snow" (line 6) is which of the following?

    I. A symbol of purity
    II. A personified dress
    III. The agent of cold and preservation

    (A) I only
    (B) II only
    (C) III only
    (D) I and III
    (E) I, II, and III

26. Which of the following best expresses the theme developed throughout the poem?

    (A) "Seeking" (line 3) and "arise" (line 7)
    (B) "countest" (line 2) and "pined" (line 5)
    (C) "journey" (line 4) and "sun-flower" (line 8)
    (D) "traveller's" (line 4) and "Youth" (line 5)
    (E) "golden" (line 3) and "pale" (line 6)

27. The word "aspire" (line 7), in context, means which of the following?

    I. Exhale
    II. Desire
    III. Ascend
    IV. Seek

    (A) I only
    (B) II only
    (C) III only
    (D) IV only
    (E) I, II, and III only

GO ON TO THE NEXT PAGE.

28. The sun-flower is described in lines 1–4 in terms of

    (A) a devitalized life form
    (B) ambitious for fame and glory
    (C) able to fulfill its wishes
    (D) bound to the earth
    (E) seeking warmer weather

29. The sun-flower, as defined in the poem, is best seen as

    (A) a symbol of warmth
    (B) a vigorous winter flower
    (C) representing man's journey through life
    (D) a metaphor for beauty
    (E) a weed

30. A conclusion supported by the poem's context is that when the "journey is done"

    (A) the sun-flower's travels will begin
    (B) the sun will find the "sweet golden clime" (line 3)
    (C) counting the sun's steps will cause the sun-flower to die
    (D) wishing will turn to desire
    (E) time will no longer be a factor

Questions 31–40 are based on the following passage.

    Whether heroic verse ought to be admitted into serious plays is not now to be disputed: it is already in possession of
Line the stage; and, I dare confidently affirm
(5) that very few tragedies, in this age, shall be received without it. All the arguments which are formed against it can amount to no more than this—that it is not so near conversation as prose; and therefore
(10) not so natural. But it is very clear to all who understand poetry that serious plays ought not to imitate conversation too nearly. If nothing were to be raised above that level the foundation of poetry would
(15) be destroyed. And if you once admit of a latitude, that thoughts may be exalted, and that images and actions may be raised

above the life, and described in measure without rhyme, that leads you insensibly
(20) from your own principles to mine: you are already so far onward of your way that you have forsaken the imitation of ordinary converse; you are gone beyond it; and to continue where you are is to lodge
(25) in the open field, betwixt two inns. You have lost that which you call natural, and have not acquired the last perfection of art. But it was only custom which cozened us so long: we thought, because
(30) Shakespeare and Fletcher went no farther, that there the pillars of poetry were to be erected; that, because they excellently described passion without rhyme, therefore rhyme was not capable of describing
(35) it. But time has now convinced most men of that error. It is indeed so difficult to write verse that the adversaries of it have a good plea against many who undertake that task without being formed by art or
(40) nature for it.

(1672)

31. Heroic verse is described in lines 1–4 in terms of

    (A) an orphan art form
    (B) a conquering force
    (C) something incapable of sustaining interest
    (D) someone greedy of dramatic presentation
    (E) something resistant to change

32. Lines 4–6 suggest that

    (A) heroic verse is infrequently used
    (B) tragedies do not contain heroic verse
    (C) people do not want heroic verse in tragedy
    (D) audiences and critics expect tragedies to have heroic verse
    (E) most tragedies without heroic verse are received

33. Heroic verse is defined as

    (A) 14-line poems in iambic pentameter
    (B) unrhymed lines in iambic pentameter
    (C) a form of parody
    (D) comic verse
    (E) rhymed couplets in iambic pentameter

34. As revealed in the passage, some argue that prose is

    (A) more natural than heroic verse
    (B) more desirable than heroic verse
    (C) the mainstay of tragedy
    (D) too imitative of conversation
    (E) too exalted

35. The speaker's attitude implies that

    (A) not all tragedies are tragic
    (B) poetry is a higher level of communication than prose
    (C) prose is a higher level of communication than poetry
    (D) unrhymed prose of exalted images is best
    (E) tragedy should imitate natural conversation

36. Lines 32–35 might be called an error in reasoning because the statement is

    (A) based on the false assumption that Shakespeare and Fletcher "excellently described passion without rhyme"
    (B) an overstatement
    (C) a faulty generalization
    (D) an understatement
    (E) describing a construct that is structurally impossible

37. As presented by the speaker, a conclusion might be reached that the tragedies of Shakespeare and Fletcher

    (A) are in heroic verse
    (B) are rhymed
    (C) used no poetic images
    (D) used the exalted language of poetry, but without rhyme
    (E) do not use the exalted language of poetry

38. According to the speaker, "the last perfection of art" (lines 27–28) is acquired through

    (A) rhyme
    (B) rhythm
    (C) prose
    (D) drama
    (E) tragedy

39. The inference of the last sentence is that the speaker

    (A) will entertain no arguments against verse in drama
    (B) views verse as a simple matter to include in drama
    (C) highly respects prose writers
    (D) believes writing verse is a universal skill
    (E) would prefer no verse to poorly written verse

40. Being lodged "in the open field, betwixt two inns" (lines 24–25) metaphorically describes

    (A) conversational prose without rhyme
    (B) conversational prose with rhythm
    (C) images too exalted for conversation, but without the rhyme of poetry
    (D) no rhyme or poetic images
    (E) no poetic images, but rhymed lines

GO ON TO THE NEXT PAGE.

Questions 41–46 are based on the following poem.

> Popular, Popular, Unpopular!
> 'You're no Poet'—the critics cried!
> 'Why?' said the Poet. 'You're unpopular!'
> *Line* Then they cried at the turn of the tide—
> *(5)* 'You're no Poet!' 'Why?'—'You're popular!'
> Pop-gun, Popular and Unpopular!
>
> (ca. 1850)

41. Of the literary devices listed below, which is used to set the tone of the speaker's message in the poem as a whole?

   (A) Simile
   (B) Metaphor
   (C) Personification
   (D) Alliteration
   (E) Apostrophe

42. In the last line, the speaker's meaning is accentuated by the use of

   (A) rhyme
   (B) onomatopoeia
   (C) mixed figures
   (D) genteel comedy
   (E) rhythm

43. Which of the following maxims best summarizes the speaker's meaning?

   (A) What goes around comes around.
   (B) A bird in hand is worth two in the bush.
   (C) A stitch in time saves nine.
   (D) Pride goes before a fall.
   (E) He is between a rock and a hard place.

44. The main situation in the poem can be described as that of

   (A) an unpopular poet
   (B) a popular poet
   (C) a problem of perceptions
   (D) poor poetry
   (E) a problem of talent

45. The label "critics" (line 2) refers to people who

   (A) analyze and review literary works
   (B) hate poetry
   (C) love poetry
   (D) deliberately avoid reading popular poetry
   (E) personally dislike poets

46. The effect of "Pop-gun" in the last line serves to

   (A) imply danger from critics
   (B) emphasize the erratic nature of popularity
   (C) vilify critics
   (D) threaten those who criticize the work
   (E) change the tone of the poem

Questions 47–54 are based on the following passage.

> I need not speak of the voyage home
> but may add a few remarks as to arctic
> work, on points not generally under-
> *Line* stood. The incentive of the earliest north-
> *(5)* ern voyages was commercial, the desire of
> the northern European nations to find a
> navigable northern route to the fabled
> wealth of the East. When the impractica-
> bility of such a route was proven, the
> *(10)* adventurous spirit of Anglo-Saxon and
> Teuton found in the mystery, the danger,
> the excitement, which crystalized under
> the name North Pole, a worthy antagonist
> for their fearless blood. The result of their
> *(15)* efforts has been to add millions to the
> world's wealth, to demonstrate some of
> the most important scientific proposi-
> tions, and to develop some of the most
> splendid examples of manly courage and
> *(20)* heroism that adorn the human record.
>
> Let me call your attention to that flag,
> that tattered and torn and patched flag
> you see hanging over the mantel there.
> That is the flag from which I have taken

(25) pieces for deposit in the cairns I built. You
will notice that three pieces are gone. One
is in the cairn at the "farthest north," 87.6
degrees; a second piece I placed in a cairn
I built on one of the twin peaks of
(30) Columbia, Cape Columbia; and the third
in the cairn on the northern point of
Jesup Land....

In view of the fact that the work has
defined the most northern land in the
(35) world, and has fixed the northern limit of
the world's largest island, was that work a
useless expenditure of time, effort, and
money? Neither the club nor I think so.
The money was theirs, the time and effort
(40) mine.

(1907)

47. The speaker's purpose is best described as

(A) persuasive
(B) argumentative
(C) prescriptive
(D) informative
(E) descriptive

48. As used by the speaker, the LEAST accurate
understanding of "blood" (line 14) is

(A) parental heritage
(B) temperament
(C) life fluid
(D) race
(E) disposition

49. The North Pole is described in lines 11–14
in terms of

(A) a suitable opponent
(B) a villain
(C) a friend to man
(D) the personification of an Anglo-Saxon
or Teuton
(E) a coward

50. By stating "The money was theirs, the
time and effort mine" in the last sentence,
the speaker is

(A) suggesting that he is dissatisfied with
the arrangement
(B) referring to the inequitable aspects of
the journey
(C) indicating that the money was inadequate for the journey
(D) stressing the more romantic elements
of an expedition
(E) suggesting that he views the responsibility for expenditures as an equitable
dichotomy

51. The speaker does NOT credit the
Anglo-Saxon and Teuton explorers with
advances in

(A) bloodline research
(B) economics
(C) science
(D) humanity
(E) exploration

52. A "cairn" (lines 25–27) is

(A) a cavern or cave
(B) an ice cave
(C) a cliff
(D) a landmark
(E) a flag holder

53. Probably, the flag

(A) was desecrated by the explorers
(B) is an antique from the Anglo-Saxons
(C) is worn and torn from the hardships
of the expedition
(D) represents the speaker's family crest
(E) is no longer of any value due to its
condition

GO ON TO THE NEXT PAGE.

54. Of the following definitions, "crystalized" (as it is used in line 12) means

    (A) coated with sugar
    (B) coated with something else to give a false appearance
    (C) caused to form crystals
    (D) was given a definite form
    (E) assumed a crystalline form

Questions 55–60 are based on the following poem.

The Scholar

My days among the Dead are past;
Around me I behold,
Where'er these casual eyes are cast,
Line The mighty minds of old:
(5)   My never-failing friends are they,
With whom I converse day by day.

With them I take delight in weal
And seek relief in woe;
And while I understand and feel
(10) How much to them I owe,
My cheeks have often been bedew'd
With tears of thoughtful gratitude.

My thoughts are with the Dead; with them
I live in long-past years,
(15) Their virtues love, their faults condemn,
Partake their hopes and fears,
And from their lessons seek and find
Instruction with an humble mind.

My hopes are with the Dead; anon
(20) My place with them will be,
And I with them shall travel on
Through all Futurity;
Yet leaving here a name, I trust,
That will not perish in the dust.

                                    (ca. 1795)

55. The subject of this poem is

    (A) dying young
    (B) past scholars
    (C) resisting death
    (D) famous past scholars
    (E) education

56. The speaker can best be labeled as someone who

    (A) is dead
    (B) is a past student
    (C) is a scholar
    (D) is unlearned
    (E) is a future scholar

57. What is the speaker's attitude toward "the Dead" (line 1) as revealed in the central theme of the poem?

    (A) Deferential, but not worshipful
    (B) Ungrateful
    (C) Antagonistic
    (D) Humble, but not responsive
    (E) Shortsighted

58. What effect is produced by the last two lines of the poem?

    (A) They make the speaker seem vain.
    (B) They intensify the pessimistic tone.
    (C) They reinforce the continuous nature of scholarship.
    (D) They indicate that scholarship is rare.
    (E) They stress the sincere nature of scholars.

59. The third and fourth stanzas establish a contrast that is reflected in which of these pairs of words?

    (A) Dead...alive
    (B) Seek...travel
    (C) Humble...hope
    (D) Past and present...future
    (E) Instruction...name

60. Based upon its contextual use, the word
    "live" (line 14) conveys which of these state-
    ments summarizing the speaker's position?

    I. The speaker has forgotten the lives of
       the Dead.
    II. The speaker intellectually feeds on past
        knowledge.
    III. The speaker's mind dwells on the past.

    (A) I only
    (B) II only
    (C) III only
    (D) II and III only
    (E) I, II, and III

STOP

If there is still time remaining, you may review your answers.

Answer Key: Practice Test Five

1. **(E)**	7. **(B)**	13. **(D)**	19. **(B)**	25. **(A)**	31. **(B)**	37. **(D)**	43. **(E)**	49. **(A)**	55. **(B)**
2. **(A)**	8. **(C)**	14. **(B)**	20. **(E)**	26. **(A)**	32. **(D)**	38. **(A)**	44. **(C)**	50. **(E)**	56. **(C)**
3. **(C)**	9. **(C)**	15. **(C)**	21. **(D)**	27. **(C)**	33. **(E)**	39. **(E)**	45. **(A)**	51. **(A)**	57. **(A)**
4. **(A)**	10. **(D)**	16. **(A)**	22. **(B)**	28. **(D)**	34. **(A)**	40. **(C)**	46. **(B)**	52. **(D)**	58. **(C)**
5. **(B)**	11. **(E)**	17. **(E)**	23. **(A)**	29. **(C)**	35. **(B)**	41. **(D)**	47. **(D)**	53. **(C)**	59. **(D)**
6. **(D)**	12. **(B)**	18. **(C)**	24. **(B)**	30. **(E)**	36. **(C)**	42. **(B)**	48. **(C)**	54. **(D)**	60. **(D)**

TO OBTAIN YOUR RAW SCORE:

_____ divided by 4 = _____

Total wrong   Score W

_____ minus _____ = _____

Total right   Score W   Score R

Round Score R to the nearest whole number for the raw score.

SCORE CONVERSION TABLE FOR PRACTICE TESTS

(based on estimated values)

Raw Score	Scaled Score	Raw Score	Scaled Score	Raw Score	Scaled Score	Raw Score	Scaled Score
60	800	40	660	20	500	0	330
59	800	38	650	19	490	−1	320
58	800	38	640	18	480	−2	310
57	800	37	640	17	470	−3	300
56	790	36	630	16	470	−4	290
55	790	35	620	15	460	−5	280
54	780	34	610	14	450	−6	270
53	770	33	600	13	440	−7	260
52	760	32	590	12	430	−8	250
51	750	31	590	11	430	−9	240
50	740	30	580	10	420	−10	230
49	730	29	570	9	410	−11	220
48	720	28	560	8	400	−12	210
47	710	27	550	7	390	−13	200
46	710	26	550	6	390	−14	200
45	700	25	540	5	380		
44	690	24	530	4	370		
43	680	23	520	3	360		
42	680	22	510	2	350		
41	670	21	510	1	340		

Explanations: Practice Test Five

> **NOTE:** Most practice tests cannot duplicate the content and conditions of the actual Literature test. Also, the scope and definitions of the literary elements can differ among literary critics; therefore, the rationale behind what constitutes a correct or an incorrect answer choice may vary. Each of these practice tests, however, gives you an opportunity to analyze selections, think critically, and develop your test-taking skills so you can do your personal best on the SAT Subject Test in Literature.

1. **(E)** Lydia Bennet (lines 18–19) believes she will become Lydia Wickham.

2. **(A)** She did not take any clothes with her and had planned to dance that evening, circumstances that imply a hasty decision.

3. **(C)** Emphasis on "she" in line 38 and her reference to "a scheme of infamy" reveal that Elizabeth questions Wickham's intentions.

4. **(A)** She calls Lydia "thoughtless" (line 35).

5. **(B)** By definition, infamy includes elements of disgrace. Negative connotations of "scheme" reinforce that the plan is shameful.

6. **(D)** She expects to be a married woman in a very structured society. To expect her family to convey such a message shows disregard for others (insolence) and a disrespectful (flippant) attitude.

7. **(B)** By calling Harriet a simpleton and considering her shocking "surprise" a joke, Lydia's diction or choice of words in her letter further communicate her inappropriate attitude.

8. **(C)** The tone reveals her feelings: "Oh! Jane," she cries. To even bring up the subject of servants knowing what happened reveals her distress.

9. **(C)** This line relates to line 10: "Beauty is budding there"; flowers are "The bright ones" that awaken from a winter's sleep.

10. **(D)** "Verdure" refers to the beautiful green colors of growth.

11. **(E)** To have hair forming tresses (curls or braids) generally is a human characteristic, but in this case it is given to the woods, a nonhuman.

12. **(B)** "Woods" and "floods" *look* like a rhyme, regardless of pronunciation.

13. **(D)** Birds play in the leaves (line 16). The south and west winds are normally associated with summer. Children are not mentioned.

14. **(B)** Although elements of all five answer choices can be found in this poem, winds (movement) provide the connecting thread from stanza to stanza. Stanza 1: the gales bring in newer life; 2: the south-wind calls; 3: waving green growth welcomes birds; and 4: the west-wind plays.

15. **(C)** Sitting on a throne is a human characteristic.

16. **(A)** None of these words relates to being a traitor, restrained, and/or abstruse; however, ideas that are "large" or bigger than those of others, "florid" or ornate, and "untrammeled" or unlimited in freedom are unrestrained.

17. **(E)** By definition, self-communion is thinking of or to oneself, involving elements of introspection. Context supports this idea in lines 11–12, "when he and himself agreed upon anything…."

18. **(C)** Lines 17–18 reveals that at times "some of his orbs got out of their orbits…."

19. **(B)** The idea was borrowed (line 23), probably from "distant Latin neighbors" (lines 4–5).

20. **(E)** He was "every barleycorn a king" and had the confidence in his own opinion to insert ("ingraft," a variant spelling of "engraft") his own sense of idealism on the thoughts and actions of others.

21. **(D)** Look for the contradiction: Barbarians are savages, yet have ideals? Thieves steal, yet have honor?

22. **(B)** This historical allusion traditionally can be found in American and British literature and refers to a time when people were thrown into arenas or dens of lions because of their religion.

23. **(A)** True justice requires discernment of guilt or innocence. It cannot be determined by chance.

24. **(B)** Barleycorn is a grain of barley, a cereal grass used to make malt and to thicken soup. Figuratively, the speaker means he is a king in even the smallest areas.

25. **(A)** Context reveals a contrast. The Youth in line 5 "pined away with desire"; the Virgin is "shrouded in snow," a traditional symbol of purity.

26. **(A)** What is the theme? The sun-flower seeks "that golden chime," but is bound to earth. The Youth and Virgin arise and go.

27. **(C)** The word could mean all four definitions; however, context points to "ascend": They ascend where the sun-flower can only wish to go.

28. **(D)** The sun-flower is "weary of time," never leaving its earthbound pattern of following the Sun.

29. **(C)** Until the point of death (line 7), man's journey through life is earth-bound, like the sun-flower.

30. **(E)** The sun-flower is weary of time, implying that those who find the "golden clime" at the end of their journey are no longer concerned with time.

31. **(B)** That heroic verse is "in possession" hints at a time when it was not. Consequently, it has taken possession at some point.

32. **(D)** Without heroic verse, the speaker asserts, few tragedies will "be received" or accepted.

33. **(E)** You should know that heroic verse consists of rhymed couplets in iambic pentameter.

34. **(A)** The speaker says in lines 9–10 that prose is more "near conversation" and "natural."

35. **(B)** His attitude is revealed in lines 13–15: If nothing can go above the imitation of conversation (prose), then "the foundation of poetry would be destroyed."

36. **(C)** Other writers might describe passion well with rhyme.

37. **(D)** The "pillars of poetry" were erected with Shakespeare and Fletcher, but without rhyme.

38. **(A)** Images are raised (line 17), implying use of poetic language beyond "ordinary converse" (lines 22–23), losing the imitation of natural conversation (lines 25–26). What, in context, could be the perfection of poetic language? Rhyme.

39. **(E)** He sees poorly written verse as a "good plea" used by the "adversaries of it."

40. **(C)** Inn #1: You have lost the natural (conversation); Inn #2: You have not acquired perfection (rhyme).

41. **(D)** The irony of the poet's situation causes an explosive tone to his response. This tone is projected by the alliterative repetition of "p."

42. **(B)** "Pop-gun," a word that sounds like its meaning, is a use of onomatopoeia and continues the alliteration of the work.

43. **(E)** A summary of the speaker's point: He is criticized whether he is popular or unpopular.

44. **(C)** What is a "Poet"? How does popularity or the lack of popularity affect the merits of a poet's work? The insights or perception gained from answers to these questions would stop the critics' contradictory judgments.

45. **(A)** By definition in this context, a critic is one who analyzes and reviews literary works.

46. **(B)** A pop-gun is a toy; it would not imply danger (A), vilify (C), or threaten (D) anyone. The poem's tone is consistent; however, a gun that uses air to blow harmless corks or pellets is erratic. Also, it reflects the speaker's opinion of the critics.

47. **(D)** Although the question in the last paragraph hints at argument, the passage is mostly informative.

48. **(C)** The context is the Anglo-Saxon and Teuton explorers. The mention of their "adventurous spirit" would place emphasis on the figurative, not literal. Heritage, temperament, race, and disposition can be "fearless."

49. **(A)** A "worthy antagonist" is somewhat synonymous with "a suitable opponent."

50. **(E)** He aligns himself with the club (lines 36–40) against any who would question the expenditures; a partnership is implied.

51. **(A)** He does credit them with advances in economics (lines 14–16), science (lines 17–18), humanity, and exploration (lines 18–20).

52. **(D)** By definition, a cairn is a pile of stones used as a landmark.

53. **(C)** The flag went with him on his expeditions (lines 24–25).

54. **(D)** Mystery, danger, and excitement are abstracts. The North Pole is a place, symbolically giving these abstracts a definite form.

55. **(B)** Past scholars are the speaker's friends (stanza 1) to whom he is grateful (stanza 2), from whom he learns (stanza 3), and with whom he believes he will spend eternity (stanza 4).

56. **(C)** The speaker is a student of the past, a type of scholar.

57. **(A)** He obviously respects them; however, notice in line 15 that he does not hesitate to condemn their faults.

58. **(C)** Today's scholars learn from yesterday's scholars and become the teachers of tomorrow's scholars.

59. **(D)** "I live in long-past years" (line 14) and "find / Instruction" (line 17–18) in the present, but "I with them shall travel… Futurity" (lines 21–22).

60. **(D)** He "Partake[s] their hopes and fears" (line 16) and studies them "with an humble mind" (line 18).

Titles and Authors of Selections in Test Five

Questions

Answer Sheet
PRACTICE TEST SIX

1 (A) (B) (C) (D) (E)
2 (A) (B) (C) (D) (E)
3 (A) (B) (C) (D) (E)
4 (A) (B) (C) (D) (E)
5 (A) (B) (C) (D) (E)
6 (A) (B) (C) (D) (E)
7 (A) (B) (C) (D) (E)
8 (A) (B) (C) (D) (E)
9 (A) (B) (C) (D) (E)
10 (A) (B) (C) (D) (E)
11 (A) (B) (C) (D) (E)
12 (A) (B) (C) (D) (E)
13 (A) (B) (C) (D) (E)
14 (A) (B) (C) (D) (E)
15 (A) (B) (C) (D) (E)

16 (A) (B) (C) (D) (E)
17 (A) (B) (C) (D) (E)
18 (A) (B) (C) (D) (E)
19 (A) (B) (C) (D) (E)
20 (A) (B) (C) (D) (E)
21 (A) (B) (C) (D) (E)
22 (A) (B) (C) (D) (E)
23 (A) (B) (C) (D) (E)
24 (A) (B) (C) (D) (E)
25 (A) (B) (C) (D) (E)
26 (A) (B) (C) (D) (E)
27 (A) (B) (C) (D) (E)
28 (A) (B) (C) (D) (E)
29 (A) (B) (C) (D) (E)
30 (A) (B) (C) (D) (E)

31 (A) (B) (C) (D) (E)
32 (A) (B) (C) (D) (E)
33 (A) (B) (C) (D) (E)
34 (A) (B) (C) (D) (E)
35 (A) (B) (C) (D) (E)
36 (A) (B) (C) (D) (E)
37 (A) (B) (C) (D) (E)
38 (A) (B) (C) (D) (E)
39 (A) (B) (C) (D) (E)
40 (A) (B) (C) (D) (E)
41 (A) (B) (C) (D) (E)
42 (A) (B) (C) (D) (E)
43 (A) (B) (C) (D) (E)
44 (A) (B) (C) (D) (E)
45 (A) (B) (C) (D) (E)

46 (A) (B) (C) (D) (E)
47 (A) (B) (C) (D) (E)
48 (A) (B) (C) (D) (E)
49 (A) (B) (C) (D) (E)
50 (A) (B) (C) (D) (E)
51 (A) (B) (C) (D) (E)
52 (A) (B) (C) (D) (E)
53 (A) (B) (C) (D) (E)
54 (A) (B) (C) (D) (E)
55 (A) (B) (C) (D) (E)
56 (A) (B) (C) (D) (E)
57 (A) (B) (C) (D) (E)
58 (A) (B) (C) (D) (E)
59 (A) (B) (C) (D) (E)
60 (A) (B) (C) (D) (E)

Practice Test Six

Directions: The following questions test your understanding of several literary selections. Read each passage or poem and the questions that follow it. Select the best answer choice for each question by blackening the matching oval on your answer sheet. **Special attention should be given to questions containing the following words: EXCEPT, LEAST, NOT.**

<u>Questions 1–11</u> are based on the following passage.

'Talking of scandal,' returned Mr Fellowes, 'have you heard the last story about Barton? Nisbett was telling me the other day that he dines alone with the *Line* Countess at six, while Mrs Barton is in
(5) the kitchen acting as cook.'

'Rather an apocryphal authority, Nisbett,' said Mr Ely.

'Ah,' said Mr Cleves, with good-
(10) natured humour twinkling in his eyes, 'depend upon it, that is a corrupt version. The original text is, that they all dined together with six—meaning six children—and that Mrs Barton is an excel-
(15) lent cook.'

'I wish dining alone together may be the worst of that sad business,' said the Rev. Archibald Duke, in a tone implying that his wish was a strong figure of
(20) speech.

'Well,' said Mr Fellowes, filling his glass and looking jocose, 'Barton is certainly either the greatest gull in existence, or he has some cunning secret,—some
(25) philtre or other to make himself charming in the eyes of a fair lady. It isn't all of us that can make conquests when our ugliness is past its bloom.'

'The lady seemed to have made a con-
(30) quest of him at the very outset,' said Mr Ely. 'I was immensely amused one night at Granby's when he was telling us her story about her husband's adventures. He said, "When she told me the tale, I felt I
(35) don't know how,—I felt it from the crown of my head to the sole of my feet".'

Mr Ely gave these words dramatically, imitating the Rev. Amos's fervour and symbolic action, and every one laughed
(40) except Mr Duke, whose after-dinner view of things was not apt to be jovial. He said,—

'I think some of us ought to remonstrate with Mr Barton on the scandal he is
(45) causing. He is not only imperilling his own soul, but the souls of his flock.'

'Depend upon it,' said Mr Cleves, 'there is some simple explanation of the whole affair, if we only happened to know
(50) it. Barton has always impressed me as a right-minded man, who has the knack of doing himself injustice by his manner.'

'Now *I* never liked Barton,' said Mr Fellowes. 'He's not a gentleman....'

(1858)

1. In lines 1–3, Mr. Fellowes's choice of words

   (A) suggests that Barton was the subject of previous scandals
   (B) introduces gossip to their conversation
   (C) marks the beginning of a joke
   (D) renders what he says as unbelievable
   (E) weakens his credibility

2. Mr. Ely characterizes Nisbett as

   (A) a credible witness
   (B) pyschologically unbalanced
   (C) someone not to be believed
   (D) learned and authoritative
   (E) a lawyer

3. Which of the following could be considered synonymous with "corrupt" as used in line 11?

   (A) Rotten
   (B) Evil
   (C) Taking bribes
   (D) Foreign admixtures
   (E) Containing alterations

4. The main difference in meaning between the two versions of the story concerning Barton centers on

   (A) Mrs. Barton's cooking
   (B) whether the Countess was actually there
   (C) greed and corruption
   (D) the prepositions "at" and "with"
   (E) dining in the kitchen

5. "Six," as used in line 5, refers to

   (A) children
   (B) time
   (C) a date
   (D) dinner guests
   (E) age

6. The "figure of speech" (lines 19–20) implied by Duke's tone can be seen as which of these uses?

   (A) Personification of dining
   (B) "Sad business" representing Duke
   (C) "Dining alone together" representing many other bad circumstances
   (D) Apostrophe to Barton
   (E) Rhetorical question for Barton

7. Mr. Fellowes's tone in lines 21–23 can be considered

   (A) humorous
   (B) sad
   (C) angry
   (D) unrelenting
   (E) suspicious

8. Fellowes characterizes Barton in lines 23–24 as either

   (A) guilty or innocent
   (B) naive or clever
   (C) easily deceived or a deviser of a secret plan
   (D) a fraud or possessor of a love charm
   (E) athletic or witty

9. Lines 45–46 contain inferences that Mr. Barton

   (A) is a shepherd
   (B) is a sheep farmer
   (C) does not care about scandal
   (D) resists constructive criticism
   (E) is in a position of leadership

10. The tone of "Now *I* never liked Barton" (line 53) conveys an attitude that is

    (A) overbearing and judgmental
    (B) humorous and charming
    (C) expectant and excited
    (D) respectful and placating
    (E) suspicious and resentful

11. The expression used in lines 35–36 is an example of which of the following?

   (A) Cliché
   (B) Pun
   (C) Satire
   (D) Contradiction
   (E) Witticism

Questions 12–30 are based on the following poem.

The Hurricane

        Happy the man who, safe on shore,
            Now trims, at home, his evening fire;
        Unmov'd he hears the tempests roar,
Line   That on the tufted groves expire:
(5)   Alas! on us they doubly fall,
        Our feeble barque must bear them all.

        Now to their haunts the birds retreat,
            The squirrel seeks his hollow tree,
        Wolves in their shaded caverns meet,
(10)   All, all are blest but wretched we—
        Foredoomed a stranger to repose,
        No rest the unsettled ocean knows

        While o'er the dark abyss we roam,
            Perhaps, with last departing gleam,
(15)   We saw the sun descend in gloom,
            No more to see his morning beam;
        But buried low, by far too deep,
        On coral beds, unpitied, sleep!

        But what a strange, uncoasted strand
(20)   Is that, where fate permits no day—
        No charts have we to mark that land,
            No compass to direct that way—
        What Pilot shall explore that realm,
        What new Columbus take the helm!

                    * * *

(25)   The barque, accustomed to obey,
            No more the trembling pilots guide:
        Alone she gropes her trackless way,
            While mountains burst on either side—
        Thus, skill and science both must fall;
(30)   And ruin is the lot of all.

                            (ca. 1785)

12. The effect of the use of a pause in line 10 is

   (A) to emphasize a sense of contrast
   (B) to imply that animals are of major importance
   (C) to echo the "all" in line 6
   (D) to continue the established meter
   (E) to resume the stress begun in line 5

13. The attitude of the speaker toward the man on shore (line 1) reflects the speaker's

   (A) good humor
   (B) anger
   (C) respect
   (D) sympathy
   (E) fear

14. Why do "Wolves in their shaded caverns meet" (line 9)?

   (A) They are escaping the man on shore.
   (B) They are haunted by the birds and squirrels.
   (C) They are strangers to the land.
   (D) They are seeking shelter from the storm.
   (E) They are being tracked by the barque.

15. The most appropriate descriptive adjective to convey the speaker's tone and meaning concerning the "strange, uncoasted strand" (line 19) is

   (A) exotic
   (B) unfamiliar
   (C) mysterious
   (D) beautiful
   (E) friendly

16. The relationship established in the paradoxical phrase "uncoasted strand" (line 19) is reflected in which of the following phrases?

   (A) Childless mother
   (B) Rainless desert
   (C) Frosted cake
   (D) Mirrored wall
   (E) Uncontrolled anger

GO ON TO THE NEXT PAGE.

17. As used in line 24, "Columbus" represents

    (A) explorers
    (B) weathercasters
    (C) the man on shore
    (D) the dead
    (E) the living

18. Of the following statements, which one best summarizes the effect of "Unmov'd" in line 3?

    (A) It stresses the man on shore's sense of safety.
    (B) It emphasizes the speaker's stubborn attitude.
    (C) It projects the turbulent nature of the storm.
    (D) It echoes the violence of the hurricane.
    (E) It contrasts with the evening fire in line 2.

19. Of the following pairs of words, which pair LEAST effectively illustrates the contrast in content developed within the first two stanzas of the poem?

    (A) "Safe" (line 1)…"Foredoomed" (line 11)
    (B) "hears" (line 3)…"bear" (line 6)
    (C) "barque" (line 6)…"ocean" (line 12)
    (D) "repose" (line 11)…"unsettled" (line 12)
    (E) "happy" (line 1)…"wretched" (line 10)

20. In line 4, the phrase "on the tufted groves expire" reveals the man on shore's

    (A) position of danger
    (B) impending death
    (C) need to escape
    (D) sheltered position
    (E) resistance to escape

21. In line 11, "a stranger" would probably be identified as

    (A) one who is unfamiliar to the speaker
    (B) one who is unaccustomed to rest
    (C) one who is a guest of the speaker
    (D) one who is a visitor on the ship
    (E) one who is a foreigner on the shore

22. An implication of "Foredoomed" (line 11) most likely is that the speaker

    (A) is antagonistic toward strangers
    (B) wants strangers to remain in repose
    (C) believes that repose is only for strangers
    (D) is resistant concerning accepting the outcome of the storm
    (E) believes that his turbulent end is inevitable

23. In line 15, which of the following changes occurs?

    (A) The sun is obscured by fog.
    (B) A shift to personification enlivens the scene.
    (C) A change to past tense of the verb introduces the concept of death.
    (D) Use of first person plural emphasizes the reader's sense of danger.
    (E) Introduction of imperfect rhyme emphasizes danger.

24. What is a "barque" (line 6)?

    (A) A sailor
    (B) A man on shore
    (C) A pilot
    (D) A storm
    (E) A sailing vessel

25. Of the following statements, which one best summarizes the main idea of the concluding couplet (lines 29–30)?

    (A) Skill and science could prevent their loss.
    (B) The ship is a product of science.
    (C) Skill and science caused the ship's destruction.
    (D) Mankind cannot overcome nature.
    (E) Some may escape the ruin of the storm.

26. The "mountains" in line 28 can be thought of as all the following EXCEPT

    (A) the destruction of safety and security as they burst
    (B) symbols of stability in an explosive situation
    (C) part of a metaphor describing the water
    (D) ironic representations of places of safe haven
    (E) part of a simile describing the distant land

27. The word "Perhaps" (line 14) creates an effect that serves to

    (A) suggest that the storm may pass soon
    (B) stress the uncertainty that many will die
    (C) symbolize the hope of the storm's passing
    (D) establish a pattern of alliteration
    (E) suggest some may not have seen the sunset

28. From a contextual perspective, "abyss" (line 13) can mean all the following EXCEPT

    (A) the center of an escutcheon
    (B) a great gulf of water
    (C) immeasurable amounts
    (D) the immensity of depth
    (E) the ocean depths

29. Line 27 refers to the barque figuratively as a

    (A) ship out of control
    (B) vagrant caught in a storm

    (C) social outcast
    (D) pilot lost at sea
    (E) lost, blind woman feeling her way

30. In line 21, "that land" might be seen as which of the concepts listed below?

    I. A distant safe haven
    II. Death
    III. The bottom of the sea

    (A) I only
    (B) II only
    (C) III only
    (D) II and III only
    (E) I, II, and III

Questions 31–38 are based on the following passage.

Hasty Pudding
[corn meal mush] A Poem, in Three Cantos

Omne tulit punctum qui miscuit utile dulci ["He has gained all approval who has mixed the useful with the sweet"—HORACE]

He makes a good breakfast who mixes pudding with molasses.

PREFACE

A simplicity in diet, whether it be considered with reference to the happiness of individuals or the prosperity of a nation, is
Line of more consequence than we are apt to
(5) imagine. In recommending so important an object to the rational part of mankind, I wish it were in my power to do it in such a manner as would be likely to gain their attention. I am sensible that it is one of
(10) those subjects in which example has infinitely more power than the most convincing arguments or the highest charms of poetry. Goldsmith's *Deserted Village*, though possessing these two advantages in
(15) a greater degree than any other work of the kind, has not prevented villages in England

GO ON TO THE NEXT PAGE.

from being deserted. The apparent interest
of the rich individuals, who form the taste
as well as the laws in that country, has been
(20) against him; and with that interest it has
been vain to contend.

The vicious habits which in this little
piece I endeavor to combat, seem to me
not so difficult to cure. No class of people
(25) has any *interest* in supporting them; unless
it be the interest which certain families
may feel in vying with each other in sumptuous entertainments. There may indeed
be some instances of depraved appetites,
(30) which no arguments will conquer; but
these must be rare. There are very few persons but what would always prefer a plain
dish for themselves, and would prefer it
likewise for their guests, if there were no
(35) risk of reputation in the case. This difficulty can only be removed by example; and
the example should proceed from those
whose situation enables them to take the
lead in forming the manners of a nation.
(40) Persons of this description in America, I
should hope, are neither above nor below
the influence of truth and reason, when
conveyed in language suited to the subject.

Whether the manner I have chosen to
(45) address my arguments to them be such as
to promise any success is what I cannot
decide. But I certainly had hopes of doing
some good, or I should not have taken the
pains of putting so many rimes together.
(50) The example of domestic virtues has
doubtless a great effect. I only wish to rank
simplicity of diet among the virtues. In that
case I should hope it will be cherished and
more esteemed by others than it is at
(55) present.

(1793)

31. The speaker probably intends "diet" (line 1)
to convey which of the following meanings?

   I. A regulated manner of living
  II. Eating habits
 III. Daily fare

(A) I only
(B) II only
(C) II and III only
(D) I and III only
(E) I, II, and III

32. The speaker's purpose includes

(A) informing
(B) persuading
(C) hypothesizing
(D) instructing
(E) describing

33. According to the speaker, Goldsmith's
Deserted Village (line 13)

(A) prevented England's villages from
being deserted
(B) is the best poem ever written
(C) is a convincing argument and
charming poetry
(D) overcame English laws
(E) provides a powerful example of his
premise

34. In the context of line 21, "vain" means

(A) having no genuine value
(B) conceited
(C) lacking in sense
(D) trivial
(E) ineffective

35. The second paragraph puts forth that

(A) most people prefer simplicity in diet
(B) the argument will be difficult to
execute
(C) not enough people are willing to take
the lead
(D) truth and reason have been abandoned
(E) the language is not suitable to the
subject

36. The speaker considers simplicity of diet to be

    (A) unattainable
    (B) without interest
    (C) a virtue
    (D) a risk to reputation
    (E) below the influence of truth and reason

37. The speaker's view includes that

    (A) vicious habits cannot be broken
    (B) depraved appetites prevent the general assimilation of virtue
    (C) most people prefer elegant dishes
    (D) leaders should set a good example
    (E) "rimes" (line 49) are of best influence in this case

38. In line 45, "them" should be identified as

    (A) people of depraved appetites
    (B) American social leaders
    (C) families competing in sumptuous entertainments
    (D) English landed gentry
    (E) lawyers

Questions 39–46 are based on the following poem.

> The Muse's fairest light in no dark time,
> The wonder of a learnèd age; the line
> Which none can pass; the most
>   proportioned wit,—
> *Line* To nature, the best judge of what was fit;
> (5) The deepest, plainest, highest, clearest pen;
> The voice most echoed by consenting men;
> The soul which answered best to all well said
>   By others, and which most requital made;
> Tuned to the highest key of ancient Rome,
> (10) Returning all her music with his own;
> In whom, with nature, study claimed a
>   part,
> And yet who to himself owed all his art:

Here lies Ben Jonson! every age will look
With sorrow here, with wonder on his
    book.

(ca. 1637)

39. Based on its subject and form, this poem is best described as a(n)

    (A) literary ballad
    (B) elegiac sonnet
    (C) regular ode
    (D) literary epitaph
    (E) satiric complaint

40. Lines 11–12 address Jonson's

    (A) skill as a painter
    (B) academic career
    (C) nature paintings
    (D) originality
    (E) library or den

41. The hyperbole found in this poem is mostly achieved through the use of

    (A) superfluity
    (B) redundancy
    (C) diminution
    (D) depreciation
    (E) superlatives

42. Line 5, the "pen" figuratively represents which of the following?

    (A) Ben Jonson
    (B) Jonson's literary style
    (C) The quill writing instrument of his day
    (D) A writing instrument that uses ink
    (E) Jonson's style of script

Practice Test Six

GO ON TO THE NEXT PAGE.

43. In line 1, "no dark time" is a litotes (negative affirmation) probably referring to

    (A) a time of mysterious, not easily understood writings
    (B) the Dark Ages
    (C) the speaker's loss of sight
    (D) an age enlightened by inspired knowledge
    (E) the gloomy, disheartening nature of death

44. Which of the following most closely reflects the subject of line 6?

    (A) The lack of acquiescence
    (B) Elocution
    (C) Repeated words and ideas
    (D) Hollow ideas
    (E) Ventriloquism

45. The "line / Which none can pass" in lines 2–3 probably refers to which of the following?

    I. A point of conformity
    II. A succession of great intellectuals
    III. Intellectual achievement

    (A) I only
    (B) II only
    (C) III only
    (D) I and II only
    (E) I, II, and III

46. In lines 9–10, the speaker uses a musical metaphor to

    (A) accentuate the extent of Jonson's originality
    (B) describe Jonson's superb singing voice
    (C) extol the intellectualism of Rome
    (D) praise Jonson's speaking voice
    (E) build on the imagery begun in line 6

Questions 47–53 are based on the following passage.

I went to the place I had seen the collapsible boat on the boat deck, and to my surprise I saw the boat, and the men still
Line trying to push it off. I guess there wasn't a
(5) sailor in the crowd. They couldn't do it. I went up to them and was just lending a hand when a large wave came awash of the deck. The big wave carried the boat off. I had hold of an oarlock and I went
(10) with it. The next I knew I was in the boat. But that was not all. I was in the boat, and the boat was upside-down, and I was under it. And I remember realizing I was wet through and that whatever happened
(15) I must not breathe, for I was under water. I knew I had to fight for it, and I did. How I got out from under the boat I do not know but I felt a breath of air at last. There were men all around me—hun-
(20) dreds of them. The sea was dotted with them, all depending on their lifebelts. I felt I simply had to get away from the ship. She was a beautiful sight then. Smoke and sparks were rushing out of her
(25) funnel. There must have been an explosion, but we heard none. We only saw the big stream of sparks. The ship was turning gradually on her nose—just like a duck that goes for a dive. I had only one thing
(30) on my mind: to get away from the suction. The band was still playing. I guess all of them went down. They were playing "Autumn" then. I swam with all my might. I suppose I was 150 feet away
(35) when the *Titanic*, on her nose, with her afterquarter sticking straight up in the air, began to settle—slowly.

When at last the waves washed over her rudder there wasn't the least bit of suction
(40) I could feel....

47. In contrast to the situation, the simile used to describe the sinking ship makes the *Titanic* seem

    (A) brilliant
    (B) resilient
    (C) morose
    (D) comic
    (D) buoyant

48. The speaker's dramatic use of understatement in lines 13–15

    (A) makes a break in the rhythm of the account
    (B) reinforces his sense of resignation
    (C) contradicts the atmosphere of team work in lines 3–5
    (D) foreshadows the sinking of the ship
    (E) helps to convey his sense of shock

49. Why did the speaker say "…I simply had to get away from the ship"?

    (A) To avoid an explosion
    (B) To get a better view
    (C) To avoid being pulled under
    (D) To help others in the water
    (E) To find a smaller boat

50. "She" in line 23, refers to

    (A) the collapsible boat
    (B) the *Titanic*
    (C) one of the passengers
    (D) the duck
    (E) the speaker

51. Under the circumstances, that the band was playing "Autumn" is

    (A) an example of hyperbole
    (B) melodramatic
    (C) poignantly symbolic
    (D) insignificant to the account
    (E) a trained response

52. The central paradox of the account is reflected in which of the following?

    I. "She was a beautiful sight then."
    II. "The band was still playing."
    III. "The big wave carried the boat off."
    IV. "I simply had to get away from the ship."

    (A) I only
    (B) II only
    (C) III only
    (D) I and II
    (E) I, II, and IV

53. The speaker's attitude toward "the men still trying to push off" seems somewhat

    (A) condescending, yet probably accurate
    (B) angry, with tones of malice
    (C) relieved, but still a little nervous
    (D) afraid and unreasoning
    (E) hopeless, without a sense of direction

Questions 54–60 are based on the following poem.

       My life—to Discontent a prey—
           Is in the sere and yellow leaf.
       'Tis vain for happiness to pray:
Line   No solace brings my heart relief.
(5)   My pulse is weak, my spirit low;
           I cannot think, I cannot write.
       I strive to spin a verse—but lo!
           My rhymes are very rarely right.

       I sit within my lowly cell,
(10)   And strive to court the comic Muse;
       But how can Poesy excel,
           With such a row from yonder mews?
       In accents passionately high
           The carter chides the stubborn horse;
(15) And shouts a 'Gee!' or yells a 'Hi!'
           In tones objectionably hoarse.

GO ON TO THE NEXT PAGE.

In vain for Poesy I wait;
 No comic Muse my call obeys.
My brains are loaded with a weight
(20) That mocks the laurels and the bays.
I wish my brains could only be
 Inspired with industry anew;
And labour like the busy bee,
 In strains no Genius ever knew.

(25) Although I strive with all my might,
 Alas, my efforts all are vain!
I've no *afflatus*—not a mite;
 I cannot work the comic vein.
The Tragic Muse may hear my pleas,
(30) And waft me to a purer clime.
Melpomene! assist me, please,
 To somewhat higher heights to climb.

         (ca. 1880)

54. The rhymes used throughout the poem are remarkable because they are mostly

 (A) synonyms
 (B) homonyms
 (C) similes
 (D) redundant
 (E) transitional

55. Throughout the poem, the speaker characterizes himself as NOT

 (A) moody
 (B) troubled
 (C) conceited
 (D) argumentative
 (E) inspired

56. In the context of the entire poem "the sere and yellow leaf" (line 2) represents

 (A) the poet's preference for tragic poetry
 (B) the condition of the poet's attitude
 (C) the time of year
 (D) the poet's preference for comic poetry
 (E) the end of life

57. The poem emphasizes

 (A) the isolation of the poet
 (B) the poet's genius
 (C) mythology
 (D) the poet's reliance on the Muses for his verse
 (E) the quietness needed for writing poetry

58. In relation to the rest of the poem, the last four lines include

 (A) a change of rhythm
 (B) the speaker's discontent replaced by tragedy
 (C) a mood shift from futile to hopeful
 (D) change of rhyme scheme
 (E) a mood shift from despairing to self-reliant

59. Personified "Discontent" in line 1

 (A) shows the speaker's anger
 (B) serves as a friend
 (C) emphasizes a desire to change
 (D) serves to victimize the speaker
 (E) comforts the speaker

60. The speaker can be described as all the following EXCEPT

 (A) discouraged
 (B) self-reliant
 (C) wanting to write comic poetry
 (D) dependent
 (E) wanting the Muses to get to work

If there is still time remaining, you may review your answers.

Answer Key: Practice Test Six

1. **(A)**	7. **(A)**	13. **(E)**	19. **(C)**	25. **(D)**	31. **(E)**	37. **(D)**	43. **(D)**	49. **(C)**	55. **(E)**
2. **(C)**	8. **(D)**	14. **(D)**	20. **(D)**	26. **(E)**	32. **(B)**	38. **(B)**	44. **(C)**	50. **(B)**	56. **(B)**
3. **(E)**	9. **(E)**	15. **(B)**	21. **(B)**	27. **(E)**	33. **(C)**	39. **(B)**	45. **(C)**	51. **(C)**	57. **(D)**
4. **(D)**	10. **(A)**	16. **(A)**	22. **(E)**	28. **(A)**	34. **(E)**	40. **(D)**	46. **(A)**	52. **(D)**	58. **(C)**
5. **(B)**	11. **(A)**	17. **(A)**	23. **(C)**	29. **(E)**	35. **(A)**	41. **(E)**	47. **(B)**	53. **(A)**	59. **(D)**
6. **(C)**	12. **(A)**	18. **(A)**	24. **(E)**	30. **(D)**	36. **(C)**	42. **(B)**	48. **(E)**	54. **(B)**	60. **(B)**

TO OBTAIN YOUR RAW SCORE:

_____ divided by 4 = _____
Total wrong   Score W

_____ minus _____ = _____
   Total right   Score W   Score R

Round Score R to the nearest whole number for the raw score.

SCORE CONVERSION TABLE FOR PRACTICE TESTS

(based on estimated values)

Raw Score	Scaled Score	Raw Score	Scaled Score	Raw Score	Scaled Score	Raw Score	Scaled Score
60	800	40	660	20	500	0	330
59	800	38	650	19	490	−1	320
58	800	38	640	18	480	−2	310
57	800	37	640	17	470	−3	300
56	790	36	630	16	470	−4	290
55	790	35	620	15	460	−5	280
54	780	34	610	14	450	−6	270
53	770	33	600	13	440	−7	260
52	760	32	590	12	430	−8	250
51	750	31	590	11	430	−9	240
50	740	30	580	10	420	−10	230
49	730	29	570	9	410	−11	220
48	720	28	560	8	400	−12	210
47	710	27	550	7	390	−13	200
46	710	26	550	6	390	−14	200
45	700	25	540	5	380		
44	690	24	530	4	370		
43	680	23	520	3	360		
42	680	22	510	2	350		
41	670	21	510	1	340		

Explanations: Practice Test Six

> **NOTE:** Most practice tests cannot duplicate the content and conditions of the actual Literature test. Also, the scope and definitions of the literary elements can differ among literary critics; therefore, the rationale behind what constitutes a correct or an incorrect answer choice may vary. Each of these practice tests, however, gives you an opportunity to analyze selections, think critically, and develop your test-taking skills so you can do your personal best on the SAT Subject Test in Literature.

1. **(A)** Line 2: "the last story" implies previous stories.

2. **(C)** Line 7: "an apocryphal authority" would be false by definition.

3. **(E)** The corrupt version of a story would not be accurate.

4. **(D)** "At" six would refer to the hour; "with" six refers to the number of children there. The other answer choices are not central to the contrast.

5. **(B)** See the explanation above.

6. **(C)** An oxymoron, this expression represents the confused story about dining as part of a larger scandal.

7. **(A)** To be jocose is to be joking.

8. **(D)** His amplification in lines 24–26 explains his meaning. A gull is a cheat or trickster, and a philter is a love potion or charm.

9. **(E)** "Flock" is a traditional, biblical symbol for the members of the church. Figuratively, the leader is the pastor or shepherd.

10. **(A)** Mr. Fellowes begins the gossip about Barton in the first paragraph and does not accept the kinder sentiments toward Barton that Cleves expresses in lines 47–49. The emphasis on "I" also makes him seem overbearing and judgmental.

11. **(A)** This cliché is still in use: from the top of my head to the bottom of my feet.

12. **(A)** Birds, squirrels, and wolves have places to go for shelter ("All, all"), but the speaker does not.

13. **(E)** The description of the happy, safe man on shore further emphasizes the fear felt by the man on the ship.

14. **(D)** The tempests are roaring (line 3); a hurricane is coming.

15. **(B)** At first, this description may seem mysterious, but context reveals the place to be the bottom of the sea, where there are no charts. It is unfamiliar.

16. **(A)** A strand is a shoreline; a coast is the land next to the sea. How can a shoreline not have a coast? How can a mother not have a child?

17. **(A)** Sometimes, a proper name represents an idea. In this case, Columbus represents explorers.

18. **(A)** "Unmov'd" refers to his lack of need to move to a place of safety and to his calm state of mind.

19. **(C)** Lines 1–4 describe man in safety; lines 5–12 describe man and animal in danger. Answer choices A, B, D, and E reflect this contrast.

20. **(D)** The dangerous storm expires, ceases, or terminates on shore.

21. **(B)** To be a "stranger to repose" would be not to know rest.

22. **(E)** To be "Foredoomed" is a reference to predestination; in this case to be doomed to destruction is inevitable.

23. **(C)** The use of past tense for their last sunset foreshadows death, further emphasizing his sense of hopelessness.

24. **(E)** By definition, a barque is a ship or sailing vessel.

25. **(D)** Despite the skill of the sailors or the scientific principle used to design a seaworthy vessel, nature is stronger.

26. **(E)** No simile (a comparison using "like" or "as") appears in the last stanza.

27. **(E)** "Perhaps" can mean "by chance" or "possibly" and modifies the verb.

28. **(A)** An escutcheon is a shield with a family's coat of arms on it.

29. **(E)** To grope is to feel your way blindly; trackless is to be without a path or rail.

30. **(D)** In this land, there is "no day" (line 20), nor are there charts or compass directions. In other words, this refers to death at the bottom of the sea.

31. **(E)** Lines 1–5 reveal the context to be greater than just eating habits; he connects diet with individual happiness and national prosperity.

32. **(B)** Lines 44–55 reveal that the speaker wishes to change his readers' minds and, by implication, their habits.

33. **(C)** Goldsmith's poem possesses "these two advantages" (line 14) listed in lines 9–13.

34. **(E)** Goldsmith's poem could not overcome those against him: to be "vain to contend" is to be useless to fight against.

35. **(A)** Notice lines 31–33: only a "few persons but what would always prefer a plain dish."

36. **(C)** His point is directly expressed in lines 51–52: "I…rank *simplicity of diet* among the virtues."

37. **(D)** Lines 35–39 deal with leadership; some people should set an example.

38. **(B)** The pronoun's antecedent is found in line 40: "Persons of this description." What description? "those whose situation enables them to take the lead" (lines 37–39).

39. **(B)** "Here lies Ben Jonson!" (line 13) makes this an elegy. It is fourteen lines written in iambic pentameter (sonnet form).

40. **(D)** As defined by context, art can include creativity (original thinking and production). This idea is supported by the idea that study (of other's work) claimed part of him "And yet…," a qualifying conjunction meaning "nevertheless."

41. **(E)** The superlatives include "fairest" (line 1), "most proportioned" (line 3), "best" (line 4), four superlatives in line 5, "best" (line 7).

42. **(B)** Jonson, not his writing instruments or penmanship, is the subject, eliminating C, D, and E. Does this line praise Jonson or his style? The choice of adjectives points to his literary style.

43. **(D)** Notice the appositive in line 2: "the wonder of a learnéd age."

44. **(C)** Lines 4–10 deal with Jonson's interaction with others. He could judge what was fit (line 4), could answer well (line 7), and could improve upon the ancients (line 10). In this context, others would echo or repeat his ideas and expressions.

45. **(C)** The "line" in this context obviously is a point of excellence set by Jonson that no one else can go beyond. His, according to the speaker, is the best wit, literary style, intellect, and character.

46. **(A)** The implied tenor of the metaphor is the literary achievement of Rome. Jonson returned Rome's music and added his own.

47. **(B)** For a sinking ship to be compared to "a duck that goes for a dive" is comic until viewed against the severity of the situation.

48. **(E)** The speaker is plunged under water with a boat over him. The understatement concerning being "wet through" and realizing "I must not breathe" serves to convey to readers his sense of shock at the suddenness of his situation.

49. **(C)** Lines 29–31: "I had only one thing on my mind: to get away from the suction."

50. **(B)** Traditionally, ships (including the *Titanic*) are referenced by feminine pronouns.

51. **(C)** Seasons are often used symbolically to represent stages of life. In this case, a band playing "Autumn" as the ship sinks is a very emotional image.

52. **(D)** The explosive destruction of the ship and all who remained on board being called "beautiful" and the band playing as the ship was destroyed are both contradictory images.

53. **(A)** The speaker condescendingly assumes that "there wasn't a sailor in the crowd," yet the fact remains "They couldn't do it."

54. **(B)** Homonyms are words that sound the same, but have different meanings and often different spellings.

55. **(E)** He seeks the comic Muse (line 10), but "In vain" (line 17).

56. **(B)** He wants to write comic Posey, but cannot. He is so discontented that "My life…," he says, "Is in the sere [dried up] and yellow leaf." On a deeper level, note that he considers writing tragic poems (lines 29–30). In that case, the leaf could represent the serious elements in his life as a basis for tragic poems.

57. **(D)** Note lines 10, 18, and 29–32 in which he courts, waits on, and makes pleas to muses.

58. **(C)** The speaker has become hopeful because "The Tragic Muse *may* hear my pleas…" (emphasis added).

59. **(D)** He does not want his life to be like dried leaves, but rather he wants to be happy (line 3). Notice, however, that he sees himself as Discontent's "prey," in other words, a victim.

60. **(B)** He is discouraged (line 6) because he wants to write "Poesy" (lines 9–10), but he is dependent on muses of mythology, calling on them to help him (lines 29–32). He is not self-reliant.

Titles and Authors of Selections in Test Six

1–11	*Amos Barton* by George Eliot
12–30	"The Hurricane" by Philip Freneau
31–38	"The Hasty Pudding" by Joel Barlow
39–46	"To the Memory of Ben Jonson" by John Cleveland
47–53	"The Sinking of the *Titanic*" by Harold Bride
54–60	"My Life—to Discontent a Prey" by Henry S. Leigh

Answer Sheet
PRACTICE TEST SEVEN

1 Ⓐ Ⓑ Ⓒ Ⓓ Ⓔ	16 Ⓐ Ⓑ Ⓒ Ⓓ Ⓔ	31 Ⓐ Ⓑ Ⓒ Ⓓ Ⓔ	46 Ⓐ Ⓑ Ⓒ Ⓓ Ⓔ
2 Ⓐ Ⓑ Ⓒ Ⓓ Ⓔ	17 Ⓐ Ⓑ Ⓒ Ⓓ Ⓔ	32 Ⓐ Ⓑ Ⓒ Ⓓ Ⓔ	47 Ⓐ Ⓑ Ⓒ Ⓓ Ⓔ
3 Ⓐ Ⓑ Ⓒ Ⓓ Ⓔ	18 Ⓐ Ⓑ Ⓒ Ⓓ Ⓔ	33 Ⓐ Ⓑ Ⓒ Ⓓ Ⓔ	48 Ⓐ Ⓑ Ⓒ Ⓓ Ⓔ
4 Ⓐ Ⓑ Ⓒ Ⓓ Ⓔ	19 Ⓐ Ⓑ Ⓒ Ⓓ Ⓔ	34 Ⓐ Ⓑ Ⓒ Ⓓ Ⓔ	49 Ⓐ Ⓑ Ⓒ Ⓓ Ⓔ
5 Ⓐ Ⓑ Ⓒ Ⓓ Ⓔ	20 Ⓐ Ⓑ Ⓒ Ⓓ Ⓔ	35 Ⓐ Ⓑ Ⓒ Ⓓ Ⓔ	50 Ⓐ Ⓑ Ⓒ Ⓓ Ⓔ
6 Ⓐ Ⓑ Ⓒ Ⓓ Ⓔ	21 Ⓐ Ⓑ Ⓒ Ⓓ Ⓔ	36 Ⓐ Ⓑ Ⓒ Ⓓ Ⓔ	51 Ⓐ Ⓑ Ⓒ Ⓓ Ⓔ
7 Ⓐ Ⓑ Ⓒ Ⓓ Ⓔ	22 Ⓐ Ⓑ Ⓒ Ⓓ Ⓔ	37 Ⓐ Ⓑ Ⓒ Ⓓ Ⓔ	52 Ⓐ Ⓑ Ⓒ Ⓓ Ⓔ
8 Ⓐ Ⓑ Ⓒ Ⓓ Ⓔ	23 Ⓐ Ⓑ Ⓒ Ⓓ Ⓔ	38 Ⓐ Ⓑ Ⓒ Ⓓ Ⓔ	53 Ⓐ Ⓑ Ⓒ Ⓓ Ⓔ
9 Ⓐ Ⓑ Ⓒ Ⓓ Ⓔ	24 Ⓐ Ⓑ Ⓒ Ⓓ Ⓔ	39 Ⓐ Ⓑ Ⓒ Ⓓ Ⓔ	54 Ⓐ Ⓑ Ⓒ Ⓓ Ⓔ
10 Ⓐ Ⓑ Ⓒ Ⓓ Ⓔ	25 Ⓐ Ⓑ Ⓒ Ⓓ Ⓔ	40 Ⓐ Ⓑ Ⓒ Ⓓ Ⓔ	55 Ⓐ Ⓑ Ⓒ Ⓓ Ⓔ
11 Ⓐ Ⓑ Ⓒ Ⓓ Ⓔ	26 Ⓐ Ⓑ Ⓒ Ⓓ Ⓔ	41 Ⓐ Ⓑ Ⓒ Ⓓ Ⓔ	56 Ⓐ Ⓑ Ⓒ Ⓓ Ⓔ
12 Ⓐ Ⓑ Ⓒ Ⓓ Ⓔ	27 Ⓐ Ⓑ Ⓒ Ⓓ Ⓔ	42 Ⓐ Ⓑ Ⓒ Ⓓ Ⓔ	57 Ⓐ Ⓑ Ⓒ Ⓓ Ⓔ
13 Ⓐ Ⓑ Ⓒ Ⓓ Ⓔ	28 Ⓐ Ⓑ Ⓒ Ⓓ Ⓔ	43 Ⓐ Ⓑ Ⓒ Ⓓ Ⓔ	58 Ⓐ Ⓑ Ⓒ Ⓓ Ⓔ
14 Ⓐ Ⓑ Ⓒ Ⓓ Ⓔ	29 Ⓐ Ⓑ Ⓒ Ⓓ Ⓔ	44 Ⓐ Ⓑ Ⓒ Ⓓ Ⓔ	59 Ⓐ Ⓑ Ⓒ Ⓓ Ⓔ
15 Ⓐ Ⓑ Ⓒ Ⓓ Ⓔ	30 Ⓐ Ⓑ Ⓒ Ⓓ Ⓔ	45 Ⓐ Ⓑ Ⓒ Ⓓ Ⓔ	60 Ⓐ Ⓑ Ⓒ Ⓓ Ⓔ

Practice Test Seven

TIME ALLOWED: ONE HOUR

Directions: The following questions test your understanding of several literary selections. Read each passage or poem and the questions that follow it. Select the best answer choice for each question by blackening the matching oval on your answer sheet. **Special attention should be given to questions containing the following words: EXCEPT, LEAST, NOT.**

Questions 1–6 are based on the following passage.

I do not think that we ever knew his real name. Our ignorance of it certainly never gave us any social inconvenience,
Line for at Sandy Bar in 1854 most men
(5) were christened anew. Sometimes these appellatives were derived from some distinctiveness of dress, as in the case of "Dungaree Jack"; or from some peculiarity of habit, as shown in "Saleratus Bill,"
(10) so called from an undue proportion of that chemical in his daily bread; or from some unlucky slip, as exhibited in "The Iron Pirate," a mild, inoffensive man, who earned that baleful title by his unfor-
(15) tunate mispronunciation of the term "iron pyrites." Perhaps this may have been the beginning of a rude heraldry; but I am constrained to think that it was because a man's real name in that day
(20) rested solely upon his own unsupported statement. "Call yourself Clifford, do you?" said Boston, addressing a timid new-comer with infinite scorn; "hell is full of such Cliffords!" He then intro-
(25) duced the unfortunate man, whose name happened to be really Clifford, as "Jaybird Charley,"—an unhallowed inspiration of the moment, that clung to him ever after.

(ca. 1870)

1. The narrator's comments concerning "Saleratus Bill" reveal that he

   (A) especially enjoyed bread
   (B) used large amounts of cornmeal
   (C) earned a high salary
   (D) made bread that was sour
   (E) used large amounts of baking soda

2. Lines 5–11 contain elements of all the following EXCEPT

   (A) cause and effect
   (B) amplification
   (C) example
   (D) metonymy
   (E) personification

3. The LEAST accurate description of "a rude heraldry," as used in line 17, is

   (A) a barbarous devising of family lineage
   (B) a discourteous announcement
   (C) a robust harbinger of official status
   (D) a vulgar granting of nomenclature
   (E) an inaccurate genealogical lineage

4. That "The Iron Pirate" was named mispronouncing "iron pyrites" might indicate that

   (A) Sandy Bar was a shipping port
   (B) Sandy Bar was a mining town
   (C) the man really was a pirate
   (D) the man was known as a thief
   (E) the man was born in Sandy Bar

397

5. In line 23, "with infinite scorn" emphasizes Boston's

   (A) sense of indignation
   (B) anger at injustice
   (C) insolence
   (D) resistance of authority
   (E) quiescence

6. The statement made in lines 1–5 can be described as

   (A) a statement of reality regarding the situation
   (B) an opinion held by the narrator only
   (C) a controversial premise to an argument
   (D) a contention in a debate
   (E) a feeble excuse for inexcusable conduct

Questions 7–16 are based on the following poem.

The Sonnet
II

Scorn not the sonnet; Critic, you have frown'd,
Mindless of its just honours; with this key
    Shakespeare unlock'd his heart; the melody
Of this small lute gave ease to Petrarch's wound;
Line
(5)   A thousand times this pipe did Tasso sound;
        With it Camöens sooth'd an exile's grief;
        The Sonnet glitter'd a gay myrtle leaf
Amid the cypress with which Dante crown'd
His visionary brow: a glow-worm lamp,
(10)   It cheer'd mild Spenser, call'd from Faery-land
To struggle through dark ways; and, when a damp
    Fell round the path of Milton, in his hand
The Thing became a trumpet; whence he blew
Soul-animating strains—alas, too few!

(ca. 1790)

7. In the poem in its entirety, the speaker reveals an attitude toward "Critic" (line 1) that can be considered

   (A) angry and belligerent
   (B) reproachful and retaliatory
   (C) censorious and didactic
   (D) provocative and probing
   (E) class-conscious and authoritative

8. From the context, "Camöens" (line 6) probably refers to a

   (A) political prisoner
   (B) poet
   (C) revolutionary
   (D) critic
   (E) sonnet

9. The speaker's use of "alas, too few!" in the last line produces which of the effects listed below?

   (A) It summarizes that not enough poets write sonnets.
   (B) It contends that more critics should appreciate the sonnet.
   (C) It sets forth an element of quantity over quality.
   (D) It heightens the sense of nostalgia and melancholy of the sonnet.
   (E) It shifts emphasis to a yearning for Milton to have written more sonnets.

10. The phrase "a gay myrtle leaf / Amid the cypress" (lines 7–8) figuratively means that

   (A) Dante wrote sonnets about nature
   (B) myrtle leaves are pretty in cypress arrangements
   (C) the sonnet provided a contrast among Dante's works about death
   (D) myrtle leaves and cypress were used to foretell the future
   (E) Dante favored sonnets over more serious poetic forms

11. In this poem, the vehicles "key" (line 2), "lute" (line 4), and "trumpet" (line 13) emphasize

    (A) the weaknesses of Shakespeare, Petrarch, and Milton
    (B) the means by which poets achieve their ends
    (C) the ways sonnets can be used musically
    (D) the emotional release, solace, and stimulus that the sonnet provides
    (E) the contrast to Tasso, Camöens, and Dante

12. That Tasso wrote a thousand sonnets (line 5) may be a(n)

    (A) simile
    (B) hyperbole
    (C) irony
    (D) allusion
    (E) metonymy

13. The effect of the syntactical placement of "in his hand" in line 12 is to

    (A) emphasize Milton's skill
    (B) make "The Thing" (line 13) of greater importance
    (C) put aside the theme of the poem
    (D) recognize the balance of subject and execution
    (E) attract greater attention to the poem over the poet

14. In the last line, "alas, too few!" is said in a tone that is

    (A) nonchalant
    (B) zealous
    (C) wistful
    (D) ambitious
    (E) incendiary

15. In line 9, "a glow-worm lamp" is a metaphoric reference to

    (A) a critic
    (B) Spenser
    (C) a sonnet
    (D) Faery-land
    (E) Dante

16. In line 14, the speaker uses the word "Soul-animating" for the purpose of

    (A) making the sonnet into a higher literary form
    (B) varying the rhythm
    (C) suggesting that Milton had died
    (D) establishing an alliterative relationship with "strains"
    (E) symbolizing death

Questions 17–26 are based on the following passage.

So much for Industry, my Friends, and Attention to one's own Business; but to these we must add *Frugality*, if we would
Line make our *Industry* more certainly success-
(5) ful. A Man may, if he knows not how to save as he gets, *keep his Nose all his life to the Grindstone*, and die not worth a *Groat* at last. A *fat Kitchen makes a lean Will*, as Poor Richard says; and,

(10)   Many Estates are spent in the Getting,
        Since Women for Tea forsook Spinning
            and Knitting,
        And Men for Punch forsook Hewing and
            Splitting.

If you would be wealthy, says he, in another Almanack, *think of Saving as well
(15) as of Getting: The Indies have not make Spain rich, because her* Outgoes *are greater than her* Incomes. Away then with your expensive Follies, and you will not have so much Cause to complain of hard Times,
(20) heavy Taxes, and chargeable Families; for, as Poor Dick says,

GO ON TO THE NEXT PAGE.

Women and Wine, Game and Deceit,
Make the Wealth small, and Wants
great.

And farther, *What maintains one Vice,*
(25 *would bring up two Children.* You may
think perhaps, That a *little* Tea, or a *little*
Punch now and then, Diet a *little* more
costly, Clothes a *little* finer, and a *little*
Entertainment now and then, can be no
(30) *great* Matter; but remember what Poor
Richard says, *Many* a Little *makes a Mickle*;
and farther, *Beware of* little *Expences; a*
small Leak will sink a great Ship; and again,
Who Dainties love, shall Beggars prove; and
(35) moreover, *Fools make Feasts,* and *wise Men*
eat them.

(1758)

17. The speaker is most concerned with which
    of the following topics?

    (A) Economy and temperance
    (B) Occupation and commerce
    (C) Socials and hospitality
    (D) Taxes and wages
    (E) Food and drink

18. Which of the following pieces of advice
    can be best understood literally but not
    figuratively?

    (A) "A fat Kitchen makes a lean Will."
        (line 8)
    (B) "If you would be wealthy…think of
        Saving as well as of Getting." (lines
        13–15)
    (C) "What maintains one Vice, would
        bring up two Children." (lines 24–25)
    (D) "A small Leak will sink a great Ship."
        (lines 32–33)
    (E) "Who Dainties love, shall Beggars
        prove." (line 34)

19. A "Groat" (line 7) can be thought of as

    (A) a small farm animal
    (B) a portion of fabric
    (C) a portion of rum cut with water
    (D) a trivial amount
    (E) a painful cry

20. Which of the following adjectives can be
    used to describe Poor Richard's advice?

    (A) Dialectal
    (B) Episodic
    (C) Aphoristic
    (D) Epistolary
    (E) Satiric

21. Use of the term "Poor Dick" (line 21) con-
    tributes to the sense that

    (A) the speaker feels sorry for Dick
    (B) Dick is actually not wealthy
    (C) Dick did not follow his own advice
    (D) the speaker is being sarcastic
    (E) the speaker feels comfortable in quot-
        ing him

22. In the selection, "Nose…to the Grindstone"
    (lines 6–7) is a saying that expresses which of
    the following ideas?

    I. Working at close range to a millstone
    II. Staying at hard, steady labor
    III. Unremitting self-requirement in work
        and duty
    (A) I only
    (B) III only
    (C) I and II only
    (D) II and III only
    (E) I and III only

23. The "fat Kitchen" (line 8) is actually

    (A) a heavyset cook
    (B) an oversized kitchen
    (C) extravagance in the food budget
    (D) a diet too rich in animal fat
    (E) a greasy kitchen

24. As supported by the context of the passage, "lean Will" (line 8) alludes to

    (A) undernourishment
    (B) poor diet
    (C) a dwindling estate to inherit
    (D) a life-threatening illness
    (E) hard labor

25. "Many a Little makes a Mickle" (line 31) might be restated as which of the following expressions?

    (A) Gain a little, lose a little
    (B) Sew on the bottom what you took off the top
    (C) It all adds up to trouble
    (D) One step forward and two steps back
    (E) Pennies add up to dollars

26. "Away then" in line 17 has a tone that is

    (A) bombastic
    (B) desiderative
    (C) obsequious
    (D) authoritative
    (E) disparaging

Questions 27–32 are based on the following passage.

    I used to see packs of half-wild dogs haunting the lonely beach on the south shore of Staten Island, in New York Bay,
Line for the sake of the carrion there cast up;
(5) and I remember that once, when for a long time I had heard a furious barking in the tall grass of the marsh, a pack of half a dozen large dogs burst forth on to the beach, pursuing a little one which ran
(10) straight to me for protection, and I afforded it with some stones, though at some risk to myself; but the next day the little one was the first to bark at me. Under these circumstances I could not
(15) but remember the words of the poet:

Blow, blow, thou winter wind
Thou art not so unkind
    As *his* ingratitude;
Thy tooth is not so keen,
(20) Because thou art not seen,
    Although thy breath be rude.
Freeze, freeze, thou bitter sky,
Thou dost not bite so nigh
    As benefits forgot;
(25) Though thou the waters warp,
Thy sting is not so sharp
    As friend remembered not.

(1865)

27. The overall theme of this passage is

    (A) a defense for an unwise action
    (B) a musing upon an ironic situation
    (C) an angry accusation against disloyalty
    (D) a revelation of poor judgment
    (E) an attempt at appearing confident

28. In the passage, what is the literary role of the little dog?

    I. A vehicle in an analogy
    II. A symbol of ingratitude
    III. A character representing a type of person

    (A) I only
    (B) II only
    (C) I and III only
    (D) II and III only
    (E) I, II, and III

29. Because of the events and circumstances of the episode, the speaker's attitude toward the little dog becomes

    (A) betrayed and hurt
    (B) hostile and angry
    (C) confused and ambivalent
    (D) sympathetic and concerned
    (E) determined and aggressive

GO ON TO THE NEXT PAGE.

30. The incident at New York Bay brings the poem to the speaker's mind because

    (A) the speaker is feeling sentimental and lonely
    (B) the poem describes the weather at the bay
    (C) the speaker is reminiscing about a former friend
    (D) the poem describes the cruelty of an unrequited friendship
    (E) the speaker was stimulated intellectually by the fear of the event

31. In the poem, the speaker seems to view the natural elements as

    (A) dangerous threats
    (B) symbols of deception
    (C) understandable harshness
    (D) unexplainable phenomena
    (E) unrelenting challengers

32. In the second stanza of the poem, the "bitter sky" is an example of

    (A) alliteration
    (B) paradox
    (C) irony
    (D) synaesthesia
    (E) digression

Questions 33–38 are based on the following passage.

> She heeded nothing of what I said; but when she had tasted the water and drawn breath, she went on thus—

Line
(5)
> 'I tell you I could not forget it; and I took my revenge: for you to be adopted by your uncle, and placed in a state of ease and comfort, was what I could not endure. I wrote to him; I said I was sorry for his disappointment, but Jane Eyre was dead: she had died of typhus fever at Lowood. Now act as you please: write and contradict my assertion—expose my falsehood as soon as you like. You were born, I think, to

(10)

be my torment: my last hour is racked by
(15) the recollection of a deed which, but for you, I should never have been tempted to commit.'

> 'If you could be persuaded to think no more of it, aunt, and to regard me with
(20) kindness and forgiveness—'

> 'You have a very bad disposition,' said she, 'and one to this day I feel it impossible to understand: how for nine years you could be patient and quiescent under any
(25) treatment, and in the tenth break out all fire and violence, I can never comprehend.'

> 'My disposition is not so bad as you think. I am passionate, but not vindictive. Many a time, as a little child, I should have
(30) been glad to love you if you would have let me: and I long earnestly to be reconciled to you now: kiss me, aunt.'

> I approached my cheek to her lips: she would not touch it. She said I oppressed
(35) her by leaning over the bed, and again demanded water. As I laid her down—for I raised her and supported her on my arm while she drank—I covered her ice-cold and clammy hand with mine: the feeble
(40) fingers shrank from my touch—the glazing eyes shunned my gaze.

> 'Love me, then, or hate me, as you will,' I said at last, 'you have my full and free forgiveness: ask now for God's and be at
(45) peace.'

(1847)

33. The element of conflict in this passage revolves around

    (A) two women angry over past wrongs
    (B) a woman struggling against death
    (C) two people both wanting child custody
    (D) a woman and her conscience
    (E) a mother and her daughter

34. The woman probably complained that Jane "oppressed her by leaning over the bed" (lines 34–35) because she

    (A) really felt ill
    (B) was communicating her continued hatred
    (C) was protecting Jane from contagion
    (D) needed fresh air and space
    (E) wanted to intensify Jane's sense of guilt

35. After the woman's admission concerning the adoption, why would Jane behave as she does?

    (A) She never really wanted to be adopted.
    (B) She is anticipating developing a new relationship.
    (C) She is building on the bond of their old relationship.
    (D) The woman is very ill and Jane truly forgives her.
    (E) Jane is pretending forgiveness to achieve family status.

36. The tone of lines 11–13 can be considered

    (A) reconcilable
    (B) propitious
    (C) audacious
    (D) collaborative
    (E) synergetic

37. As evidenced in the second paragraph, the woman's attitude is best summarized by which of these statements?

    (A) She blames the uncle for abandoning Jane.
    (B) She blames Jane for the wrong she did to Jane.
    (C) She is truly sorry and accepts full responsibility.
    (D) She is released from her tormented guilt.
    (E) She assumes that Jane will forgive her.

38. Of the following list of literary devices, which one is used in lines 25–26 to describe Jane's personality?

    (A) Simile
    (B) Personification
    (C) Synecdoche
    (D) Metonymy
    (E) Metaphor

Questions 39–45 are based on the following poem.

A Winter Piece

From frozen climes, and endless tracts of
    snow,
From streams which northern winds forbid
    to flow,
What present shall the muse to *Dorset*
    bring,
Line Or how, so near the pole, attempt to sing.
(5)   The hoary winter here conceals from sight
All pleasing objects which to verse invite.
The hills and dales, and the delightful
    woods,
The flow'ry plains, and silver-streaming
    floods,
By snow disguis'd, in bright confusion ly,
(10) And with one dazzling waste fatigue the
    eye.

     No gentle breathing breez prepares the
      spring,
No birds within the desert region sing,
The ships, unmov'd, the boist'rous winds
    defy,
While rattling chariots o'er the ocean fly.
(15) The vast *Leviathan* wants room to play,
And spout his waters in the face of day.
The starving wolves along the main sea
    prowl,
And to the moon in icy valleys howl.
O'er many a shining league the level main
(20) Here spreads itself into a glassy plain:
There solid billows of enormous size,
Alps of green ice, in wild disorder rise.

(1709)

GO ON TO THE NEXT PAGE.

39. The speaker alludes to which of the following as the occasion for this poem?

    (A) A letter home from a boy to Dorset
    (B) A poet speaking to "the muse" (line 3)
    (C) A poet examining the winter landscape for inspiration
    (D) Dorset inviting a writer to describe a blizzard
    (E) An individual learning to sing about nature

40. The readers can presume in lines 3–7 that

    (A) the speaker is inspired by the "frozen climes" (line 1)
    (B) Copenhagen is a center for poetic activity
    (C) the speaker is expecting a gift to be sent
    (D) ideas for writing poetry are influenced by geographic location
    (E) the speaker is seeking a gift to purchase

41. All the pairs listed below reflect the main contrast developed in the poem EXCEPT

    (A) "frozen" (line 1)…"flow" (line 2)
    (B) "winds" (line 2)…"sing" (line 4)
    (C) "conceals"…"sight" (line 5)
    (D) "forbid" (line 2)…"invite" (line 6)
    (E) "confusion" (line 9)…"delightful" (line 7)

42. As used in line 10, the literary role of "waste" is as a(n)

    (A) allusion to well-lit areas
    (B) ironic allusion
    (C) symbol of man's problems
    (D) hyperbole
    (E) play on words

43. Why is there a lack of "room to play" (line 15)?

    (A) Frozen water
    (B) Severe wind
    (C) Encroaching civilization
    (D) Severe drought
    (E) Snowdrifts

44. The "glassy plain" (line 20) is an example of which of these literary devices?

    (A) Antithesis
    (B) Personification
    (C) Metaphor
    (D) Synecdoche
    (E) Metonymy

45. The use of "rattling" in line 14 is a phonic device known as

    (A) oxymoron
    (B) onomatopoeia
    (C) alliteration
    (D) euphony
    (E) low style

Questions 46–52 are based on the following poem.

To His Son

Three things there be that prosper all apace
And flourish, while they are asunder far;
But on a day they meet all in a place,
And when they meet, they one another
Line mar.
(5) And they be these: the wood, the weed, the wag.
The wood is that that makes the gallows tree;
The weed is that that strings the hangman's bag;
The wag, my pretty knave, betokens thee.
Now mark, dear boy: while these assemble not,
(10) Green springs the tree, hemp grows, the wag is wild;

But when they meet, it makes the timber
    rot,
It frets the halter, and it chokes the child.
    God bless the child!

              (ca. 1600)

46. The speaker's message is primarily a

   (A) description
   (B) warning
   (C) reminder
   (D) play on words
   (E) statement on nature

47. There are three parts of the poem (lines 1–5, lines 6–8, and lines 9–13). Which of these sets of words most clearly reflect those parts?

   (A) Generalization; application; threat
   (B) Definition; application; warning
   (C) Generalization; explanation; warning
   (D) Warning; explanation; threat
   (E) Application; warning; threat

48. The change in line 8 from the third person "they" (line 5) to the first person "my" and second person "thee" indicates that the speaker's attitude in the poem is

   (A) didactic
   (B) hostile
   (C) impersonal
   (D) mocking
   (E) cruel

49. The speaker's tone might lead the hearer to regard the boy as

   (A) gallant
   (B) a thief
   (C) mischievous
   (D) supine
   (E) incorrigible

50. The literary use of apostrophe (a figure of speech) can be found in

   (A) Line 1
   (B) Line 5
   (C) Line 7
   (D) Line 8
   (E) Line 9

51. The "wood, the weed, the wag" (line 5) perform which of these roles?

   I. Symbols of warning
   II. An alliterative device
   III. Dead metaphors

   (A) I only
   (B) II only
   (C) I and II only
   (D) I and III only
   (E) I, II, and III

52. "Frets the halter" in line 12 can be paraphrased as

   (A) worries the timid
   (B) wears the noose
   (C) ruffles the garment
   (D) irritates the hesitant
   (E) gnaws the animal

Questions 53–60 are based on the following passage.

Act I
Scene, an Apartment at Charlotte's
CHARLOTTE *and* LETITIA *discovered*

LETITIA.   And so, Charlotte, you really think the pocket-hoop unbecoming.

CHARLOTTE.   No, I don't say so. It
Line may be very becoming to saunter round
(5) the house of a rainy day; to visit my grand-mamma, or to go to Quakers' meeting: but to swim in a minuet, with the eyes of fifty well-dressed beaux upon me, to trip it in the Mall, or walk on
(10) the battery, give me the luxurious, jaunty, flowing, bell-hoop. It would have delighted you to have seen me the last evening, my charming girl! I was dangling o'er the battery with Billy
(15) Dimple; a knot of young fellows were upon the platform; as I passed them I faltered with one of the most bewitching false steps you ever saw, and then

GO ON TO THE NEXT PAGE.

(20) recovered myself with such a pretty confusion, flirting my hoop to discover a jet
black shoe and brilliant buckle...how
my little heart thrilled to hear the confused raptures of—"Demme, Jack, what
a delicate foot!" "Ha! General, what a
(25) well-turned—"

LETITIA. Fie! fie! Charlotte [stopping her
mouth], I protest you are quite a libertine.

CHARLOTTE.   Why, my dear little
(30) prude, are we not all such libertines?
Do you think, when I sat tortured two
hours under the hands of my friseur,
and an hour more at my toilet, that I
had any thoughts of my Aunt Susan, or
(35) my cousin Betsey? though they are both
allowed to be critical judges of dress.

LETITIA.   Why, who should we dress to
please, but those who are judges of its
merit?

(40) CHARLOTTE.   Why, a creature who
does not know Buffon from Soufflé—
Man!—my Letitia—Man! for whom we
dress, walk, dance, talk, lisp, languish,
and smile. Does not the grave Spectator
(45) assure us that even our much bepraised
diffidence, modesty, and blushes are all
directed to make ourselves good wives
and mothers as fast as we can? Why, I'll
undertake with one flirt of this hoop to
(50) bring more beaux to my feet in one
week than the grave Maria, and her sentimental circle, can do, by sighing senti-
ment till their hairs are grey.

LETITIA.   Well, I won't argue with you;
(55) you always out-talk me: let us change
the subject. I hear that Mr. Dimple and
Maria are soon to be married.

CHARLOTTE.   You hear true. I was
consulted in the choice of the wedding

(60) clothes. She is to be married in a delicate white satin, and has a monstrous
pretty brocaded lutestring for the
second day....

(1790)

53. The girls' conversation consists of

(A) a didactic tone
(B) metaphoric constructions
(C) casual language
(D) poetic diction
(E) highly structured syntax

54. In lines 61–62, "monstrous pretty" is an
example of which of the following literary
devices?

(A) Hyperbole
(B) Apostrophe
(C) Simile
(D) Oxymoron
(E) Alliteration

55. The context reveals that seemingly the
"Spectator" (line 44) refers to a(n)

(A) bodyguard
(B) accepted authority on conduct
(C) nanny
(D) religious leader
(E) overseer

56. Charlotte (lines 14–18) probably

(A) accidentally fell
(B) was at a wild, drunken party
(C) was surprised by the boys' admiration
(D) is defensive of her conduct
(E) deliberately tripped

57. The word "swim" (line 7) connotatively
suggests

(A) too large clothing
(B) moving through water
(C) to be in a flood
(D) smooth motions
(E) covered with liquid

58. A "libertine" (lines 27–28), as used in this context, is someone who is

    (A) morally unrestrained
    (B) a freedman
    (C) a skeptic
    (D) politically involved
    (E) a member of a sect

59. Maria is characterized by Charlotte as

    (A) headstrong
    (B) lacking in social skills
    (C) emotional
    (D) older
    (E) argumentative

60. From her comments, Charlotte indicates that she

    (A) has a fiance
    (B) is as sentimental as Maria
    (C) resents Letitia's attitude
    (D) concurs with the "Spectator"
    (E) was insulted by Letitia's protest

If there is still time remaining, you may review your answers.

Answer Key: Practice Test Seven

1. (E)	7. (C)	13. (A)	19. (D)	25. (E)	31. (C)	37. (B)	43. (A)	49. (C)	55. (B)
2. (E)	8. (B)	14. (C)	20. (C)	26. (D)	32. (D)	38. (E)	44. (C)	50. (D)	56. (E)
3. (E)	9. (E)	15. (C)	21. (E)	27. (B)	33. (D)	39. (C)	45. (B)	51. (C)	57. (D)
4. (B)	10. (C)	16. (D)	22. (D)	28. (E)	34. (B)	40. (D)	46. (B)	52. (B)	58. (A)
5. (C)	11. (D)	17. (A)	23. (C)	29. (A)	35. (D)	41. (B)	47. (C)	53. (C)	59. (C)
6. (A)	12. (B)	18. (B)	24. (C)	30. (D)	36. (C)	42. (E)	48. (A)	54. (D)	60. (D)

TO OBTAIN YOUR RAW SCORE:

_____ divided by 4 = _____

Total wrong   Score W

_____ minus _____ = _____

  Total right   Score W   Score R

Round Score R to the nearest whole number for the raw score.

SCORE CONVERSION TABLE FOR PRACTICE TESTS

(based on estimated values)

Raw Score	Scaled Score	Raw Score	Scaled Score	Raw Score	Scaled Score	Raw Score	Scaled Score
60	800	40	660	20	500	0	330
59	800	38	650	19	490	−1	320
58	800	38	640	18	480	−2	310
57	800	37	640	17	470	−3	300
56	790	36	630	16	470	−4	290
55	790	35	620	15	460	−5	280
54	780	34	610	14	450	−6	270
53	770	33	600	13	440	−7	260
52	760	32	590	12	430	−8	250
51	750	31	590	11	430	−9	240
50	740	30	580	10	420	−10	230
49	730	29	570	9	410	−11	220
48	720	28	560	8	400	−12	210
47	710	27	550	7	390	−13	200
46	710	26	550	6	390	−14	200
45	700	25	540	5	380		
44	690	24	530	4	370		
43	680	23	520	3	360		
42	680	22	510	2	350		
41	670	21	510	1	340		

Explanations: Practice Test Seven

NOTE: Most practice tests cannot duplicate the content and conditions of the actual Literature test. Also, the scope and definitions of the literary elements can differ among literary critics; therefore, the rationale behind what constitutes a correct or an incorrect answer choice may vary. Each of these practice tests, however, gives you an opportunity to analyze selections, think critically, and develop your test-taking skills so you can do your personal best on the SAT Subject Test in Literature.

1. **(E)** Saleratus is baking soda, an ingredient used in biscuits.

2. **(E)** Human qualities are not given to any nonhuman in this passage.

3. **(E)** To be rude is not necessarily to be inaccurate.

4. **(B)** Iron pyrite is a mineral found in mines.

5. **(C)** Clifford was timid and a newcomer. Lines 16–21 indicate that the men did not trust one another, even to believe their names. The bullylike behavior toward the newcomer, combined with distrust, projects an insolent attitude.

6. **(A)** The speaker is simply explaining the situation as it existed in 1854 in Sandy Bar.

7. **(C)** First, he reproves the Critic in line 1; then he teaches him his error through citing many examples of famous poets who wrote sonnets. The sonnet was a key to Shakespeare, a lute to Petrarch, a pipe to Tasso, soothing to Camöens, a leaf to Dante, a lamp to Spenser, and a trumpet to Milton.

8. **(B)** Context tells you that all the men's names in this poem refer to poets.

9. **(E)** The "damp" around Milton alludes to his blindness, a sadly emotional allusion that, in combination with describing his sonnets as "soul-animating," projects a tone of yearning.

10. **(C)** Even if you are unfamiliar with Dante's work, you can look at context to answer this question. The sonnet is compared to a "gay myrtle leaf." The figurative language used eliminates the literal nature of answer choices A and B. There are no hints in context that Dante foretold the future (D) or favored sonnets (E). However, the gay myrtle leaf (sonnet) "glitter'd …amid the cypress"—a contrast.

11. **(D)** The sonnet provides emotional release (an opened heart), musical solace to a wounded nature, and stimulus for soul-animating poems.

12. **(B)** This line could be an exaggeration, although some poets are very prolific.

13. **(A)** Would the sonnet become a trumpet in anyone else's hand? The implication is that it would not, emphasizing Milton's skill.

14. **(C)** A wistful tone includes vague yearnings. The speaker wishes Milton had written more sonnets.

15. **(C)** The poem's movement depends on a series of vehicles explaining the sonnet. The sonnet is a key, lute, pipe, gay myrtle leaf, glow-worm lamp, and trumpet.

16. **(D)** The "s" is repeated, creating alliteration.

17. **(A)** Economy or frugality (line 3); temperance (lines 26–36): Notice that what normally is viewed as showing self-restraint or temperance ("a little tea"), Poor Richard views as too much, using verbal irony to be sarcastic.

18. **(B)** This advice is best taken literally. In contrast, a "fat Kitchen" represents high expenses, "two Children" represent any obligation or necessity that requires money to maintain, the Leak in the Ship represents when money is lost and lives are ruined as a result, and Dainties represent anything overpriced and/or unneeded.

19. **(D)** A groat is a small amount.

20. **(C)** He uses a series of concise statements intended to make his point. FYI: [Poor] Richard Saunders was Benjamin Franklin's pseudonym.

21. **(E)** Using a nickname projects a sense of familiarity in this context.

22. **(D)** This line is a traditional saying relating to perseverance in work.

23. **(C)** The speaker's point in line 8 is that buying costly ingredients and foods will drain the food budget until there is not enough money to buy food at all.

24. **(C)** Also, a "lean Will" is a play on words (pun) referring to an inheritance wasted by extravagance.

25. **(E)** "Mickle" means "much." Add up many small amounts and you will have a comparatively large amount.

26. **(D)** The entire selection has the tone of one who has authority based on confidence that he is right. Also, "Away then…" is a command such as used by people in positions of authority.

27. **(B)** He perhaps used poor judgment in confronting a pack of dogs (A and D) and he seems to feel the dog was disloyal, but he projects no anger (C). The situation, however, is ironic, and quoting a poem that reflects that irony reveals the speaker's contemplative mood.

28. **(E)** The poem serves to pull what would have otherwise been just an anecdote into what is now an analogy in which the dog, a symbol of ingratitude, represents friends "remembered not."

29. **(A)** Context eliminates B, C, and E. When defending the dog, the speaker probably felt concern for its safety and sympathetic to its situation, but those feelings changed when the dog barked at him.

30. **(D)** The concept of ingratitude and the feelings of hurt it elicits are found in both the incident and the poem.

31. **(C)** The speaker understands harshness in nature (lines 17, 24, 26), but not in friends.

32. **(D)** Bitter is gustatory (taste); the sky is visual: a blend of senses.

33. **(D)** Context eliminates answer choices B, C, and E. Are both women angry? No (lines 42–45). The dying woman is struggling with her conscience (lines 13–17).

34. **(B)** She also shrank from Jane's touch (lines 37–40).

35. **(D)** The last paragraph reveals Jane's response; she forgives her.

36. **(C)** Daring Jane to reveal her "falsehood" is audacious.

37. **(B)** Her attitude reflects a classic abuser who blames the victim for his or her own wrongdoing.

38. **(E)** She describes Jane's personality in the tenth year as "fire and violence," an implied comparison.

39. **(C)** Lines 3–6 reveal his intent to write a poem, but the winter snow is concealing the usual objects of poetry (lines 7–10).

40. **(D)** The speaker is "so near the pole"—a factor in nature and his poetry.

41. **(B)** What is the contrast? Winter (line 5) versus spring (line 11). In winter, things are frozen, concealed, forbidding, and confused. In spring, they flow, are in sight, are inviting, and are delightful.

42. **(E)** "Waste" can refer to the "dazzling" all-white snow blanketing the scene and to the loss of the inspiring scene beneath it.

43. **(A)** *Leviathan* is a biblical allusion to a sea creature mentioned in the book of Job and commonly used in literature to represent a large size and/or such a large animal as a whale. Even without being familiar with this allusion, the context of line 16 places the *Leviathan* playing in water.

44. **(C)** The "main" (line 19) can refer to the sea or be short for "mainland." Context supports the sea. Regardless, "glassy plain" compares the main to glass, a metaphor.

45. **(B)** The word "rattling" sounds like its meaning (onomatopoeia).

46. **(B)** The simple phrase, "Now mark, dear boy:" in line 9 is a clear warning.

47. **(C)** A quick analysis of this poem reveals lines 1–5 generalize that things go well when wood, weed, and wag are apart; however, when together, trouble follows. Lines 6–8 explain that the wood and weed make the means to hang a wag (in this case, the speaker's son). Lines 9–12 contain the obvious warning: Do not put yourself in a situation in which you could be hanged.

48. **(A)** The didactic or instructive attitude of the speaker is evident in his detailed explanation and dramatic warning. However, the shifts from the plural third-person pronoun (that connotes a universal principle affecting all) to the inclusionary first person in "my pretty knave" (that establishes the speaker-hearer relationship), in conjunction with the shift to direct address of "thee" as the "dear boy" is a classic teaching pattern: (a) point out a principle, (b) establish teacher-student relationship, and (c) make the principle relevant (personal) for the student.

49. **(C)** Is the boy incorrigible or simply mischievous? Threatening a boy with a hangman's noose sounds like a very serious and extreme situation. You need to look at the tone of this threat, however. The father is calling his son "my pretty knave," "dear boy," and a wild "wag" (line 10). By definition, a wag is a joker. Notice also his prayer in the final line. Based on the overall tone, his son is a mischievous boy who needs to be warned not to go too far.

50. **(D)** The use of apostrophe is when he directly addresses his "dear boy" in line 9.

51. **(C)** They represent a practical joker going too far and being hanged. Each word begins with "w," an example of alliteration. These are not, however, dead metaphors.

52. **(B)** In this context, a halter is a hangman's noose. To fret it would be to wear by friction.

53. **(C)** The girls, particularly Charlotte, are speaking as friends in a revealing, casual tone.

54. **(D)** The two words ("monstrous pretty") are self-contradictory, in other words, an oxymoron.

55. **(B)** This literary allusion is clearly a reference to a respected authority on the need for women to become good wives and mothers. FYI: *The Spectator* was a daily periodical written by Richard Steele and Joseph Addison in the early 1700s.

56. **(E)** Her accident was a "bewitching false step," implying her intent.

57. **(D)** One can swim in a dance, connotative of smooth movements.

58. **(A)** The language and references used reveal that this play is depicting a period of formal society and conservative moral judgments. As such, for Charlotte to flirt openly, exposing her ankle to view, would be a morally unrestrained act.

59. **(C)** She calls Maria "grave" (line 51) and contrasts Maria's sentimental attitudes to her own flirting.

60. **(D)** She attempts to use *The Spectator* to prove her point in lines 44–48.

Titles and Authors of Selections in Test Seven

Questions

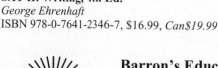

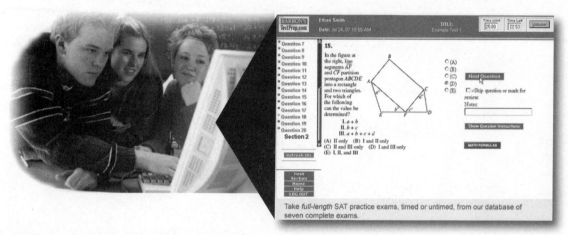

NOTES

How to Use the CD-ROM

The software is not installed on your computer; it runs directly from the CD-ROM. Barron's CD-ROM includes an "autorun" feature that automatically launches the application when the CD is inserted into the CD-ROM drive. In the unlikely event that the autorun feature is disabled, follow the manual launching instructions below.

Windows®

Insert the CD-ROM and the program should launch automatically. If the software does not launch automatically, follow the steps below.
1. Click on the Start button and choose "My Computer."
2. Double-click on the CD-ROM drive, which will be named **SAT Lit**.
3. Double-click **BarronsSAT.exe** application to launch the program.

Macintosh®

1. Insert the CD-ROM.
2. Double-click the CD-ROM icon.
3. Double-click the **SAT Lit** icon to start the program.

SYSTEM REQUIREMENTS

The program will run on a PC with:
Windows® Intel® Pentium II 450 MHz
or faster, 128MB of RAM
1024 X 768 display resolution
Windows 2000, XP, Vista
CD-ROM Player

The program will run on a Macintosh® with:
PowerPC® G3 500 MHz
or faster, 128MB of RAM
1024 X 768 display resolution
Mac OS X v.10.1 through 10.4
CD-ROM Player